991 92082   72868
619   V. 3

DATE DUB			
GAYLORD M-2			PRINTED IN U.S.A.

STUDIES IN
MEDIEVAL AND RENAISSANCE HISTORY

Volume III

STUDIES IN
Medieval and Renaissance
History

Volume III

Edited by
WILLIAM M. BOWSKY
University of Nebraska

UNIVERSITY OF NEBRASKA PRESS · LINCOLN
1966

Publishers on the Plains

UNP

901.92082
St 9
72868
Jan., 1971

MANUFACTURED IN THE UNITED STATES OF AMERICA

CONTENTS

INTRODUCTION

Studies in Medieval and Renaissance History is a series of annual volumes designed for original major articles and short monographs in all fields of medieval and renaissance history.

The first impetus for the creation of this series came from a belief that there is a need for a scholarly publication to accommodate the longer study whose compass is too large for it to be included regularly in existing media but too small for it to appear in book form. The editors will consider articles in all areas of history from approximately the fourth through the sixteenth centuries—economic, social and demographic, political, intellectual and cultural, and studies that do not fit neatly into a single traditional category of historical investigation.

The editorial board hopes that the *Studies* will create another link between the work of medieval and renaissance scholarship; for many articles pertinent to both disciplines appear in publications consulted almost exclusively by either medieval or renaissance scholars.

Although this series is devoted primarily to the publication of major studies, it will contain occasional bibliographic essays and briefer articles dealing with unpublished archival or manuscript resources. The *Studies* will also make available in translation original articles by scholars who do not write in English.

Studies in Medieval and Renaissance History is not the official organ of any association or institution. Publication in the series is open to all historians whose research falls within its scope and fields of interest.

ON THE EDGE OF TWO WORLDS IN THE HEART OF THE NEW EMPIRE: THE ROMANCE REGIONS OF NORTHERN GAUL DURING THE MEROVINGIAN PERIOD

André Joris

University of Liége

ON THE EDGE OF TWO WORLDS IN THE HEART OF THE NEW EMPIRE: THE ROMANCE REGIONS OF NORTHERN GAUL DURING THE MEROVINGIAN PERIOD[1]

I. THE COLLAPSE

1. *The Invasions in Northern Gaul*[2]

In our history books Merovingian times begin at the sound of a thunderstroke. On December 31, 406, Vandals, Alans and Suevi crossed the Rhine, which had been left unguarded by its "Roman" defenders. The cities of Mainz and Treves were captured immediately. At the rear, Amiens, Rheims, Thérouanne and Tournai were sacked and burned. *Uno fumavit Gallia tota rogo.* "All Gaul flamed like a torch"! An auspicious

1. This new synthesis of our knowledge of a well-determined region where particular problems are found is inspired from more extensive works, the reading of which is indispensable for factual information and for knowledge of major trends. Let us mention here F. Lot, C. Pfister, and F. L. Ganshof, *Les destinées de l'Empire en Occident de 395 à 888* (*Histoire générale*, ed. G. Glotz, *Moyen Age*, I [2d ed.; Paris, 1940–41]), and F. Lot, *La fin du monde antique et le début du moyen âge*, Coll. l'Évolution de l'Humanité (2d ed.; Paris, 1951, XXXI). General views on the history of regions are studied in H. Pirenne, *Histoire de Belgique* (5th ed.; Brussels, 1929), I; F. Rousseau, "La Meuse et le pays mosan. Leur importance historique avant le XIIIᵉ siècle," *Annales de la Société Archéologique de Namur*, XXXIV (1930); and F. L. Ganshof, "Het tijdperk van de Merowingen," Ch. VII of H. van Werveke, J. A. van Houtte, J. F. Niermeyer, J. Presser, and J. Romein, *Algemene Geschiedenis der Nederlanden* (Utrecht-Ghent-Brussels-Antwerp-Louvain, 1949), I, a fundamental work. G. Faider-Feytmans, *La Belgique à l'époque mérovingienne* (Brussels, 1964), offers a good outline of recent archaeological acquisitions. L. Génicot's article, "Aux origines de la civilisation occidentale. Nord et Sud de la Gaule," *Miscellanea historica in honorem L. Van der Essen* (Brussels, 1947), opens original perspectives on the general evolution of the period studied.

2. General works: E. Stein, *Histoire du Bas-Empire romain*, French ed. by J. R. Palanque (2 vols.; Brussels, 1949–59); F. Lot, *Les invasions germaniques* (Paris, 1945); M. Bloch, "Observations sur la conquête de la Gaule romaine par les rois francs," *Revue historique*, LIV (1927); *idem*, "Une mise au point: les invasions," *Annales d'Histoire Sociale*, I–II (1945); *idem*, "Sur les grandes invasions: quelques positions de problèmes," *Revue de Synthèse*, LX (1945). These three studies were republished in the *Mélanges historiques*, ed. M. Bloch (Paris, 1963), I; R. Latouche, *Les grandes invasions et la crise de l'Occident au Vᵉ siècle* (Paris, 1947); J. B. Bury, *History of the Later Roman Empire from the Death of Theodosius I to the Death of Justinian* (London, 1923), I; and *idem*, *The Invasion of Europe by the Barbarians* (London, 1928).

image from the pen of the mediocre poet Orientius, which in fact pictures the profound confusion of his contemporaries better than it reflects the raw reality of facts.[3]

It is true that, from the fifth century on, the rhythm of penetration into the Roman Empire by Germanic tribes was suddenly accelerated: the push, still as incoherent as before, then became uninterrupted and brutal, a repercussion of the devastating raids led by the Huns at the limits of eastern and central Europe. However, the danger was not new, and, except for its spectacular aspect and its intensity, the great invasion of 406 was but an episode in the constant fight which had opposed Rome to the peoples who bordered its frontiers, namely the Germans. In 102–101 B.C., Teutons and Cimbri, whom Marius finally crushed at Aix-en-Provence and at Vercelli in northern Italy, had already made the Romans conscious of a threat which could be fatal. The campaigns of Julius Caesar in Gaul, then those of Augustus and Tiberius in Germany, aimed largely at the prevention of any new breakout of that kind. Their successors exerted themselves waging war for that purpose, as much on the Rhine as on the Danube. From the time of Marcus Aurelius the Roman attitude was entirely changed: conquering up to then, the empire now fell back on itself. It chose to limit itself to an exhausting and permanent defense system. Even more seriously, it occurred more and more frequently that armies abandoned the protection of the frontiers to support with arms one of the competitors for the empire in Italy.

Serious alarm: in the middle of the third century Alamanni and Franks crowded into Gaul and advanced as far as Milan. Destructive raids occurred repeatedly between 275 and 291, while, on the North Sea, Saxon and Frankish pirates ransomed the coasts of the island of Britain and northern Gaul.[4] First taken up by the Gauls themselves, as by the

3. Orientius, *Commonitorium*, II, vs. 181, ed. Ellis, *Corpus Scriptorum Ecclesiasticorum Latinorum*, XVI, 234. This individual is identified as Orens, bishop of Auch (d. 439). On the very controversial bearing of these often literary developments, see P. Courcelle, *Histoire littéraire des grandes invasions germaniques* (Paris, 1948), especially pp. 76–78, as well as the pertinent reservations expressed by F. Vercauteren, "Note sur les ruines de la Gaule d'après quelques auteurs contemporains des invasions germaniques," *Mélanges J. Bidez, Annuaire de l'Institut de philologie et d'histoire orientales*, II (1933–34).

4. H. Nesselhauf, *Die spätromische Verwaltung der gallisch-germanischen Ländern*, Abhandlungen der Preuss. Akad. der Wissenschaften (Berlin, 1938); H. Koethe, "Zur Geschichte Galliens im dritten Viertel des 3. Jahrhunderts," *32. Bericht der römisch-germanischen Kommission* (1942); P. Van Gansbeke, "La mise en état de défense de la Gaule au milieu du IIIe siècle," *Latomus*, XIV (1955), 404–25. On the invasions of Saxon pirates, see the recent works of A. R. Lewis, *The Northern Seas: Shipping and Commerce in Northern Europe (A.D. 300–1100)* (Princeton, 1958), pp. 57 ff.; J. Mertens, "Oudenburg et le litus

emperor Posthumus or the Menapian Carausius,[5] the counter-offensive continued with unequal fortune under the leadership of Aurelian and Probus. Under Diocletian the situation had deteriorated so much that one of the caesars, Maximian, had to establish himself in Treves and set up his headquarters there (286); and his successors made it the hub of the entire defense of Roman Gaul. It was there, from that time on, that the army chief, the *magister equitum per Gallias*, resided. Directly threatened towns and *vici* tightened their inhabited areas and surrounded themselves with strong enclosures: a significant reaction that was resorted to at Tongres, at Tournai, at Arlon, and at Bavai.[6] In spite of this, respite was brief. Soon after, in 350, Alamanni again penetrated up to Autun, while Franks were crossing the lower Rhine.[7] If Julian succeeded in crushing the former in Strasbourg (357), he had to be satisfied with driving back part of the latter beyond the Rhine, tolerating, however, that some of them would settle in a region called *Toxandria*[8] as "subjugated people"

saxonicum en Belgique," *Helinium*, II (1962), 51–62; D. A. White, *Litus Saxonicum* (Madison, 1961); and E. Demougeot, "Les invasions germaniques et la rupture des relations entre la Bretagne et la Gaule," *Le Moyen Age*, LXVIII (1962), 1–50.

5. P. Van Gansbeke, "Les invasions germaniques en Gaule sous le règne de Postume," *Revue Belge de Numismatique*, XCVIII (1952), 5–30; E. Janssens, "Carausius, premier souverain national de Grande-Bretagne," *Latomus*, I (1937), 269–77.

6. J. Breuer, *La Belgique romaine* (2d ed.; Brussels, 1946), pp. 66 ff. On Tongres: *idem*, "Roman Ramparts of Tongres," *Archaeologica Belgica*, LI (1960). On Tournai: F. Vercauteren, *Étude sur les Civitates de la Belgique seconde* (Brussels, 1934), pp. 234–36; M. Amand and I. Eykens-Dierickx, *Tournai romain*, Dissertationes Archeologicae Gandenses (Bruges, 1960), V, 159 ff. On Arlon: J. Vannerus, "Trois villes d'origine romaine dans l'ancien pays de Luxembourg-Chiny: Arlon, Bitbourg et Yvois," *Bull. Acad. Royale de Belgique, Classe des Lettres*, Ser. 5, XXI (1935), 150–75. On Bavai: E. Will, "Les enceintes du Bas-Empire à Bavai," *Revue du Nord*, XLIV (1962), 391–401.

7. L. Schmidt, "Aus den Anfängen des salfränkischen Königtums," *Clio*, XXXIV (1942); C. Verlinden, "Frankish Colonization: A New Approach," *Transactions of the Royal Historical Society*, Ser. 3, III (1954), 1–17; *idem, Les origines de la frontière linguistique en Belgique et la colonisation franque* (Brussels, 1955); W. J. De Boone, *De Franken van hun eerste optreden tot de dood van Childerik* (Amsterdam, 1954); B. H. Stolte, "De gegevens der antieke schrijvers over de Franken en hun interpretatie," *Mededelingen van de Vereniging voor Naamkunde te Leuven*, XXXVII (1961), 1–30.

8. The location of ancient Toxandria cannot be determined with sufficient accuracy. J. Vannerus, "Tessenderloo et la Toxandrie," *Feestbundel H. J. Van de Wijer* (Louvain, 1944), I, 395 ff., would locate it in the north of present-day Campine, on the strength of later texts. B. H. Stolte, "Apud Toxiandriam locum," *Tijdschrift voor Geschiedenis*, LXVI (1953), 131, proves that it is a matter of a locality, not of a region. P. Roosens, "Toxandria in de romeinse en merovingise tijden," *Toxandria*, XXX (1958), 33–131, and XXXI–XXXII (1959–60), 1–78, has gathered and commented on clues related to the question. However, J. F. Niermeyer, "Het midden-nederlands rivierengebied in de frankische tijd

(*dediticii*), or, in other words, as autonomous auxiliaries at the service of the empire. Fighting continued under Valentinian I until 375.

These sudden and strictly military changes should not conceal the real progress of the peaceful penetration of the Germanic peoples.[9] The recruiting crises induced the Roman leaders to call more frequently on barbarian auxiliaries: *leti*, or Letes, those who "established themselves in the countryside on 'letic' lands of which they would have hereditary fruition, on the condition that the children would be subjected to military service like their parents."[10] Dependents of twelve *praefecti laetorum*, they were placed under the authority of the *magister militum praesentalis*. The *Notitia Dignitatum* allows us to localize, as far as *Germania Secunda* is concerned, a group near Tongres (*praefectus laetorum lagensium prope Tungros Germaniae Secundae*), and, as far as *Belgica Prima* is concerned, a group at Yvois-Carignan, in the French Ardennes (*praefectus laetorum Actorum Epuso Belgicae primae*). Others had been quartered in northern France, and at Tongres itself, and around Tournai.[11]

Under these circumstances it can be admitted that the cemeteries of Condroz around Namur (Haillot-Samson, Pry, Eprave, Furfooz), some of which date back to the second half of the fourth century, attested their presence in this area.[12] This also could explain how a region of northern

---

op grond van de Ewa quae se ad Amorem habet," *Tijdschrift voor Geschiedenis*, LXVI (1963), 145–69, based on the *Lex Francorum Chamavorum* (eighth century), draws the conclusion of an absence of Frankish influence in this area. See also the criticism expressed by J. Stengers, *La formation de la frontière linguistique en Belgique ou de la légitimité de l'hypothèse historique* (Brussels, 1959), pp. 16–22, on the subject of an exact localization of this place, which, according to him, is to be found "somewhere between Tongres and the frontier of the empire."

9. J. Dhondt, S. J. De Laet, and P. Hombert, "Quelques considérations sur la fin de la domination romaine et les débuts de la colonisation franque en Belgique," *L'Antiquité classique*, XVII (1948), 133–56; *idem*, "La fin de la domination romaine et les débuts de la colonisation franque en Belgique," *Handelingen der Maatschappij voor Geschiedenis en Oudheidkunde te Gent*, III (1948), 116–21.

10. F. Lot, *La fin du monde antique* (above, n. 1), p. 122. The problem of the *leti* has been renewed by J. Werner, "Zur Entstehung der Reihengräberzivilisation," *Archaeologica Geographica*, I (1950), 23 ff.; *idem*, "Kriegergräber aus der ersten Hälfte des 5. Jahrhunderts zwischen Schelde und Weser," *Bonner Jahrbücher*, CLVIII (1958), 372 ff. But these views have been questioned by some Belgian scholars (see n. 12).

11. *Notitia dignitatum*, Pars Occidentis (XLII, 38–43), ed. O. Seeck (Berlin, 1876), p. 217. On the source which describes the military situation in the empire between 375 and 428, see F. Lot, "La Notitia dignitatum utriusque imperii, ses tares, sa date-de composition, sa valeur," *Revue des Études anciennes*, XXXVIII (1936), 285–338. For Tournai, see M. Amand and I. Eykens-Dierickx, *Tournai romain* (above, n. 6), p. 89.

12. S. J. de Laet, J. Dhondt, and J. Nenquin, "Les laeti du Namurois et l'origine de la civilisation mérovingienne," *Études d'histoire et d'archéologie namuroises dédiées à F.*

Gaul, populated by armed people—the Letes—established within a marked breakwater—within the Ardennes and its environs—may have remained outside the area ravaged by the Great Invasion.[13] On the other hand, those Germanic peoples who had been incorporated in the Roman forces showed loyalty to the empire. Therefore, osmosis was more marked than is often thought. Characteristic of the era is the fact that great military leaders of the time are either Romanized barbarians, as were the Franks Richomer and Arbogast or the Vandal Stilicho, or barbarized Romans, as was Aetius, Attila's vanquisher.

At the beginning of the fourth century the disintegration of the empire was accentuated and the cadence of the Germanic raids accelerated. The transfer of the imperial residence at Treves, on the Moselle river, to Arles, on the Rhone, perfectly illustrates the falling back of Rome. Although they had remained faithful until then, the Rhine Franks ended up by following the move. Cologne was seized; Treves fell into their hands three times between 413 and 428; and Aetius, general of Valentinian III, had to come in person to talk sense with them. Collapse was general. In northern Gaul other Frankish troops—perhaps those organized by the emperor Julian—had started out.[14] Their principal effort was carried out in the western regions.

One of their "kings," Chlodion, seized Tournai and Cambrai, and his troops infiltrated as far as the Somme river. The threat of an invasion by the Huns made them "allies" of the Roman people, who moreover participated enthusiastically, under the leadership of Aetius, in defeating Attila at *Campus Mauriacus* near Troyes (451). A few years later the Frankish king, Childeric, who had been helping Aegidius subdue Visigoths and Saxons on the banks of the Loire, took Tournai as his capital. It was there that he was buried: his tomb, found in 1653, contained his arms, his jewelry, and Roman coins.[15]

Courtoy (Namur, 1952), pp. 149–72, and J. Nenquin, *La nécropole de Furfooz*, Dissertationes archéol. Gandenses (Bruges, 1953), I, feel that the tombs studied cannot be attributed with certainty to a population of Letes, whereas J. Breuer and H. Roosens, "Le cimetière franc de Haillot," *Annales de la Soc. Archéol. Namur*, XLVIII (1956), 171–376, share the views of J. Werner. On the implanting of new Germanic elements among the earlier-established Letes, see the penetrating article of A. Dasnoy, "La trouvaille de Suarlée et la grande invasion de 406–407," *ibid.*, L (1960–61), 123–35.

13. A. Dasnoy, *op. cit.* (n. 12), pp. 132–33. The Ardennes' role was perfectly clarified from the point of view of geography by P. Vidal de La Blache, *Tableau de la géographie de la France* (Paris, 1911), p. 70.

14. See above, n. 8.

15. E. Babelon, *Le tombeau de Childéric et les origines de l'orfèvrerie cloisonnée* (Paris, 1924); H. Arbmann, "Les épées du tombeau de Childéric," *Bulletin de la Société Royale de Lund*,

Clovis, in fact, was originally an unimportant Frankish king whose actual power scarcely extended to the city and its immediate environs.[16] At the same time, other leaders ruled other clans: Ragnacher at Cambrai, his brothers Richard and Rignomer at Le Mans, Siegebert at Cologne, and Chararic perhaps at Tongres. Clovis' later success, however, was overwhelming. In less than thirty years he eliminated Syagrius, the "last of the Romans," who had settled at Soissons. Then, after causing his rivals and relatives to perish, and after assuring Salic unity for his own benefit, he subjugated the Alamanni, crushed the Visigoths and threw them back beyond the Pyrenees, and extended his authority to Cologne's Ripuarians and to the other small Frankish groups. His baptism at Rheims by St. Remigius (506) won for him the support of the clergy of all Gaul, who were less-well disposed toward other Germans of Arian persuasion.[17] After his death (511), his successors, without stopping, seized Burgundy, Thuringia, Provence, the Alamannic Alps, and Bavaria.

Thus, about 550, the Franks were exercising a real hegemony over Gaul and Germany. It was, however, in those countries which extend from the Loire to the Rhine that their power was most solidly fixed. Most of the royal residences, including Paris, were situated in this region: Rheims, Soissons, and later Metz replaced Tournai and Cambrai. "Because of the success of a king from Tournai, Gaul was to be called France." Felix Rousseau's formula makes a happy synthesis of an exceptional fate.[18]

III (1947–48), 97–131. These objects are reproduced in F. Lot, *La fin du monde antique*, Pl. III, p. 233.

16. F. Vercauteren, *Étude sur les civitates*, pp. 237 ff.

17. Since G. Kurth's *Clovis* (3d ed., 2 vols.; Brussels, 1923), the traditional chronology of this king's reign has been considerably modified by several studies of A. Van de Vyver: "La victoire contre les Alamans et la conversion de Clovis," *Rev. Belge de Philol. et d'Histoire*, XV (1936), 859–914, and XVI (1937), 35–94; *idem*, "L'unique victoire contre les Alamans et la conversion de Clovis en 506," *ibid.*, XVII (1938), 793–813; *idem*, "Clovis et la politique méditerranéenne," *Études d'Hist. dédiées à la mémoire d'H. Pirenne* (Brussels, 1937), pp. 367–87. The change of the generally admitted date of Clovis' victory over the Alamanni and that of his conversion, from 496–506, has not been accepted by F. Lot, "La victoire sur les Alamans et la conversion de Clovis," *Rev. Belge de Philol. et d'Histoire*, XVII (1939), 63–69, nor by J. Calmette, "Observations sur la chronologie de Clovis," *Comptes-rendus de l'Acad. des Inscriptions et Belles-Lettres* (Paris, 1946), pp. 193–202. A. Van de Vyver has vigorously replied to these objections in "La chronologie du règne de Clovis d'après la légende et d'après l'histoire," *Le Moyen Age*, LII (1947), 177–96. On these problems see now G. Tessier, *Le baptême de Clovis* (Paris, 1964).

18. F. Rousseau, "Les Wallons et l'Histoire," *Actes du 2e Congrès Culturel Wallon* (Liége, 1957), p. 7.

Although it is only an outline, the preceding account remains approximate on a number of points and subject to controversy. The documentation is irritating because of its paucity, and its sources and value are very diversified. Moreover, a critical interpretation is difficult. The often-guessed conclusions, produced by auxiliary sciences, indeed prevent our arriving at a clear-cut and precise rectification.[19] Why hide it? We must admit that history is a discipline which progresses daily: every day it is enriched by another discovery.

2. *The Linguistic Border and Frankish Colonization*

Such a commotion and such a stirring of populations did not happen without provoking profound disturbances in the structures of Roman Gaul as well as in the living conditions of its inhabitants. In the area of modern Belgium, one fact has especially retained the attention of historians: the coexistence of two populations speaking different languages. Germanic was spoken by the invaders, vulgar Latin by the Belgo-Romans.

Actually, the phenomenon was not limited to northern and eastern Gaul; it happened wherever foreign nations settled in the Roman Empire and created new kingdoms. The mark that they left in their country of adoption, however, was far from being the same everywhere. While Latin culture completely disappeared in North Africa under the Arab expansion, Ostrogoths and Visigoths were completely assimilated in Italy and in Spain. On the other hand, the linguistic situation created in northern Roman Gaul would not be of the slightest influence, before the nineteenth century, on the economical, political, or religious evolutions of the countries which were part of it.

All the medieval principalities of present-day Belgium, except Namur, were bilingual, just as were the large dioceses of Liége and Cambrai, which divided most of these territories along a north-south axis. We had to wait for the nineteenth century—and, more precisely, for its last twenty years—for this to become a problem of present-day interest, under the influence of the cultural development of the Flemish and Walloon communities, and also, but to a lesser extent, because of the spread of pan-Germanism. In its own way, the linguistic border is thus a product of the

19. On the innumerable methodological problems posed by the study of the sources used in this paragraph, see J. Stengers, *La formation de la frontière linguistique* (above, n. 8), and R. Wenskus, *Stammesbildung und Verfassung. Das Werden der frühmittelalterlichen gentes* (Cologne-Graz, 1961).

well-known principle of nationalities which dominates contemporary politics. We must remember that the terms *Flanders* and *Wallonia* were not used before 1850 with the geographical significance that we must give them today.[20]

The layout of this line, with its clear-cut crests, which separates the Germanic domain from the Romance in the north and in the east, seems rather strange.[21] Starting in the region of Dunkirk, it runs in an easterly direction, from Mouseron to Landen and Glons, then, after passing a little south of Maastricht, it reaches Aubel. Next it pivots and goes from north to south towards Malmédy, Martelange, and Arlon. It follows, on its entire run, no political border whatever, old or modern. Neither does it correspond to a natural geographical limit.

The enigma is too tempting not to have fascinated historians, and some saw it as an opportunity for testing the interpretive power of their discipline. In Belgium, at least, it was the northern section which most attracted the searchers' attention, perhaps because the eastern part, entirely by chance, coincided at the time *grosso modo* with a political frontier—with the exception of the Romance enclave of Malmédy in Prussia and the Germanic enclaves of Beho and Arlon in Belgian territory.[22]

How can the capricious drawing of a so-well-marked borderline be explained? To which historical circumstances can its birth be attributed? To answer these questions, texts and ordinary research materials have proved to be of little help. Aid from auxiliary sciences was called for.

20. "Flanders" originally designated only the country situated west of the Scheldt. After Belgium's independence (1830), the designation was extended to the northern part of the country in general, that area which was occupied by the "Flemish," or in other words by Belgians who spoke Flemish dialects and Dutch. Made up shortly before 1850, the term "Wallonia" applies to the southern part of the country, where Romance dialects (Walloon, Picard, Lorrain) and French are spoken. On the influence of these movements on Belgian historiography, see F. Vercauteren, *Cent ans d'histoire nationale en Belgique* (Brussels, 1959), I, 185–204. Also see E. Legros, "Littérature wallonne et sentiment wallon au 19ᵉ siècle," *La Vie Wallonne*, XXXI (1957), 194–205, and H. J. Elias, *Geschiedenis van de Vlaamse Gedachte* (3 vols.; Antwerp, 1963–64), Vol. I: *De Grondslagen van de nieuwe tijd (1780–1830)*, Ch. III, pp. 397 ff.

21. See Map 1. Notice that Brussels, capital of the country, although situated in the Flemish half, is a city where the use of French is dominant. For more detail, see *Atlas linguistique de la Wallonie. Tableau géographique des parlers de la Belgique romane*, I and III (Liége, 1953 and 1955).

22. On the eastern border of Belgium, set up by the Congress of Vienna (1815) and by the treaties of 1839, they remained this way until 1919. See F. L. Ganshof, *Atlas historique de la Belgique* (Brussels-Paris, 1920), Maps XII (1814–30) and XIII (1830–39), and his comments.

Archaeology, with A. Wauters; toponymy, with G. Kurth; and later geography, history of law, and agrarian systems with G. Des Marez— with as many investigative methods as these scholars and their successors believed could be applied to the problem—were brought to bear. And not without reason, for these sciences allowed them to bring forth and expand many important facts—although, at the same time, they caused more than one researcher who manipulated their delicate mechanisms with insufficient critical precaution to get lost.

Without hesitation, G. Kurth, in his important book, *La Frontière Linguistique en Belgique et dans le Nord de la France*, attributed "the germanization of the northern part of our country"—and, more precisely, because of their great invasion of 406—to the Franks.[23] It was at that time, according to him, "that the deluge was passing by and the Franks were spreading into northern Belgium." An ingenious and attractive hypothesis; but one had to explain why this Germanization had not extended to other regions, and why it had stopped on the line we have been discussing.

In the absence of a firm documentary base, it is on that point that the "combining imagination" of scholars was to be given free course, not without several times undergoing the influence of military conceptions and, sometimes, the political debates of their time.[24] A. Wauters (1885) perceived an artificial military hindrance of a "camp-line (*castra*) scaled on the almost straight line going from the sea to Maastricht."[25] G. Kurth's opinion was slightly different, and the Liége scholar called for an artificial and natural barrier as well: on the one hand, the big Roman road from Bavay to Cologne, "whose strategic importance cannot be contested," protected it in addition to "defense works strong and numerous enough to put it out of danger of unexpected attack." On the other hand, beyond Bavai the Charbonnière forest [*Silva Carbonaria*] "went from east to west, from the confluence of the Sambre with the Meuse to the banks of the

23. *Mémoires de l'Académie Royale de Belgique* (2 vols.; Brussels, 1896–98).

24. This is the case for A. Wauters, who wrote at the time (1885) that the question of the "forts" on the Meuse, destined to prevent an eventual German invasion, excited Belgian public opinion. See H. Pirenne, *Histoire de Belgique* (Brussels, 1932), VII, 309, and F. Van Kalken, *La Belgique contemporaine (1780–1949)* (2d ed.; Paris, 1950), pp. 141–45. Also, H. Van Houtte admits having been influenced forty years later, for example, by the "front" of 1914–18. There is an excellent report of these opinions in the introduction of J. Vannerus, *Le limes et les fortifications gallo-romaines de Belgique. Enquête toponymique*, Mémoires Acad. Roy. de Belgique, Cl. des Lettres (4to; Brussels, 1943), pp. 9–48.

25. A. Wauters, "Les origines de la population flamande de la Belgique," *Bull. de l'Acad. Royale de Belgique*, Ser. 3, X (1885), esp. pp. 112–14.

Scheldt, masking with its vast leafy curtain all Hainaut, and stopping, if not conquest, at least colonization of peoples who came from the north." In Kurth's eyes, indeed: "the forest was the desert, it was the end of culture and fertility."[26] Was it not this forest which, in the form of the Ardennes, was responsible for the eastern section of the linguistic border? A surprising affirmation to be applied to a people such as the Franks, who lived in a semi-nomadic condition.

During a thirty-year period these views, which enjoyed the advantage of being simple and coherent, were accepted, and they inspired most of the historians. Naturally, Henri Pirenne took them up in the first edition of his *Histoire de Belgique* (1902).[27] Criticism began to appear, however, after 1920. The Charbonnière forest was the first object of criticism. Its impervious or repulsing nature was first questioned by G. Cumont,[28] while H. Vanderlinden established, with texts in hand, the soundness of an old opinion of Duvivier, and one that had been rejected by Kurth: far from extending transversely across Belgium, the forest was oriented according to a north-south axis and had therefore "never constituted an obstacle to the ethnic or linguistic expansion coming from the north."[29]

These arguments rapidly won the agreement of specialists, and consequently the forest-barrier concept of the Ardennes was struck with the same discredit. One was now restricted to stating that the forests could not have played a role in the fixation of the linguistic border other than "locally and on limited expanses." Considered "childish," the hypothesis of the Charbonnière forest as the origin of the Belgian linguistic border was thus "put aside from the path of historical and philological research."[30]

Specialists now favored a *limes* that had been built at the end of the Roman occupation. As early as 1923, H. Van Houtte, combining geography and strategy, conceived it as being "a strategic line established on the highlands of central Belgium, comparable to what the Yser river had been during World War One, and which had been held by the Romans during long years at the time of the German invasions (259-

---

26. G. Kurth, *op. cit.* (above, n. 23), I, 545.

27. H. Pirenne, *Geschichte Belgiens* (Gotha, 1899), I, 10–11; French ed. (Brussels, 1902), p. 13. This opinion was also shared by F. Cumont, *Comment la Belgique fut romanisée* (2d ed.; Brussels, 1919), pp. 106–8.

28. *L'ancienne frontière du flamand en Belgique* (Brussels, 1920).

29. "La Forêt Charbonnière," *Rev. Belge de Philol. et d'Histoire*, II (1923), 203–14. The forest actually extends from the Sambre to the Dyle and is oriented S.W.–N.E. (see Map 1).

30. The expression comes from H. Van Houtte in the article cited in n. 31.

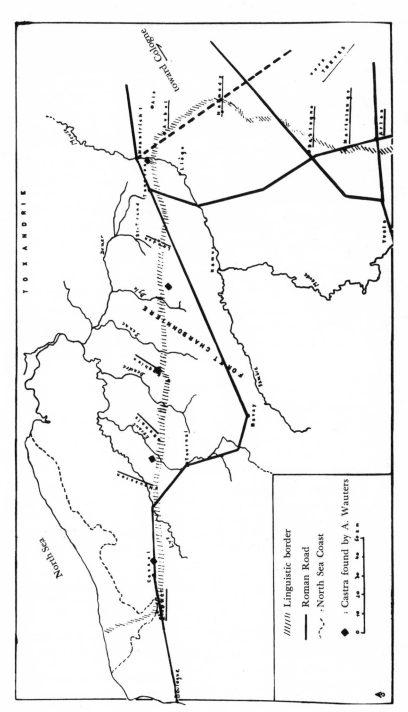

I. The Actual Linguistic Frontier and the Locations of the Principal Obstacles Noted for Locating It

406)." [31] The hypothesis of a Roman system of fortifications was as fragile as that of the Charbonnière; and an archaeologist as well-informed as J. Breuer did not fail to express his reservations, underlining the difficulty of "making archaeological discoveries coincide with hypotheses brought up on the subject of the linguistic border." [32]

This did not prevent G. Des Marez, in his *Le problème de la colonisation franque et du régime agraire en Belgique* (1926),[33] from holding the views proposed by Wauters and Kurth, then modified by Van Houtte, on the role played by a vast, fortified Roman complex—based on the great roads —in the formation of the linguistic border. Besides, after Des Marez, the great French archaeologist A. Grenier (1930), then H. Nesselhauf (1938), J. Vannérus (1943), and more recently Mrs. G. Faider-Feytmans (1948) continued to adopt roughly this same point of view—although making corrections, and some important, which did not improve its fundamental optics. [34]

On the other hand, C. Dubois continued to explain the eastern separation line between the Germanic and the Romance languages in the same way; that is, by the influence of the Roman road Arlon–Mande–St.-Étienne–Amblève, extended across the Fagnes highlands by the *Via Mansuerisca* (1930).[35]

In spite of all this, J. Breuer's doubts concerning the existence of the *limes* and its defensive efficiency, based on some carefully selected cases,[36]

31. "L'origine de la frontière linguistique en Belgique," *Rev. Belge de Philol. et d'Histoire*, III (1924), 116–19.

32. "La frontière linguistique et l'hypothèse d'un *limes* en Belgique au IVe siècle," *Annales de la Fédération Archéologique et Historique de Belgique* (Bruges, 1925), pp. 99–101. J. Breuer's reservations were caused, in major part, by an examination of the dates of occupation of the military posts studied. See J. Stengers, *La formation de la frontière linguistique*, p. 39.

33. *Mémoires de l'Académie Royale de Belgique*, Cl. des Lettres (4to; Brussels, 1926).

34. A. Grenier, "La *Notitia Dignitatum* et les frontières de l'est et du nord de la Gaule," *Mélanges Paul Thomas* (Bruges, 1930), pp. 387–93; H. Nesselhauf (above, n. 4); J. Vannérus (above, n. 24), who bases archeological research on preliminary toponymic investigation; G. Faider-Feytmans, "La frontière du Nord de la Gaule sous le Bas-Empire," *Mélanges J. Marouzeau* (Paris, 1948), imagines an organized withdrawal of the population to the south of the *limes*. This is a concept which owed much to the contemporary military practices of the Siegfried and Maginot lines. The author, moreover, abandoned this point in his last work (n. 1).

35. "L'influence des chaussées romaines sur la frontière linguistique de l'est," *Rev. Belge de Philol. et d'Histoire*, IX (1930), 454–94. See the more developed theory of J. Meyers, *Studien zur Siedlungsgeschichte Luxemburgs* (Luxemburg, 1932).

36. J. Breuer, "Le *Burgus* de Morlanwelz et la frontière de l'Empire au IVe siècle," *Ier Congrès International de Géographie historique, Communications* (Brussels, 1931), I, 56. There

have been shared by several Belgian specialists, namely H. Draye, J. Gilissen (1938) and C. Verlinden (1955), as well as by foreign specialists such as F. Steinbach and F. Petri.[37] These scholars, in general backing their argument with extensive toponymic and archaeological material, declared themselves very sceptical about the influence that the large Roman roads—which were ways of penetration as well as fortified lines— could have had on fixing the linguistic border.

Gradually, as debates and controversies followed one another, the exchange of views had the indirect result of projecting a stronger light on the actual conditions under which Frankish colonization had taken place. More and more, theses of a catastrophic Frankish invasion and of the setting up "all at once" of a linguistic border appeared unable to account satisfactorily for facts brought up by opponents. Also, from 1930 on, one became exposed to explanations that were less bound to the history of events. Two of these explanations did not take long to impose themselves: first, the differences in population density, at the time of the Romans, north and south of the line which was going to become the linguistic border; secondly, the hypothesis of a Frankish colonization effected in stages.

Kurth perspicaciously focused on the first point, and Pirenne also favored it in the last edition of the first volume of his *Histoire de Belgique*.[38] It then received new impetus as a consequence of the editing of the archaeological map of the *villae* by R. De Maeyer in 1937.[39] The examination of this document threw into clear relief the fact that the Roman *villae* were extremely rare in the northern part of present-day Belgium but

---

is a recent revision by S. J. De Laet, "La Gaule septentrionale à l'époque romaine à la lumière des fouilles, des recherches et des publications les plus récentes (1935–50)," *Bull. Institut Historique Belge de Rome*, XXVI (1950–51), 187–250. Once and for all, it is a matter of half a dozen small forts, meant to assure safety on the roads.

37. H. Draye, "De frankische Kolonisatie en het Kolenwoud," *Mededelingen uitgegeven door de Vlaamsche Toponymie Vereniging*, XIV (1938), 21–51; J. Gilissen, "Note sur la colonisation germanique en Brabant," *Rev. Belge Philol. et Hist.*, XVII (1938); C. Verlinden, *Les origines de la frontière linguistique en Belgique et la colonisation franque* (Brussels, 1955); F. Steinbach, *Studien zur westdeutschen Stammes- und Volksgeschichte* (Bonn, 1926); F. Petri, *Germanisches Volkserbe in Wallonien und Nordfrankreich. Die fränkische Landnahme in Frankreich und den Niederlanden und die Bildung der westlichen Sprachgrenze* (2 vols.; Bonn, 1937).

38. H. Pirenne, in *Histoire de Belgique* (5th ed.; Brussels, 1929), I, 18, n. 1, explicitly rejects the theory proposed by H. Van Houtte.

39. *De romeinse villa's in België. Een archeologische studie* (Ghent, 1937), and *De overblijfselen der Romeinse villa's in België* (Antwerp–The Hague, 1940).

that they crowded in tight rows throughout the southern part. The conclusion was a real demographic contrast between these two regions of the country. Not having been numerous, Frankish invaders would have been absorbed in the south, while in the north they had easily assimilated the few Gallo-Roman elements which had survived their invasion. H. Draye, J. Dhondt and E. Legros granted their preference to this attractive explanation.[40]

Pertinent objections have been raised, however, against this concept. The most serious objection concerns the utilizing of De Maeyer's map: conditions on this document reflect the second-century situation but do not correspond to that of the fourth and fifth centuries (from four hundred and fifty-five the number of *villae* fell to twenty-two, then to seven at the end of the fifth century). Moreover, the explanation does not coincide with what the abstracts of archaeological findings of all kinds show: the subsoil of zones that apparently had no *villae* nevertheless yields many objects and money treasures.[41] Hence one wonders whether De Maeyer's map does not reflect rather the area of extension of large domains, or even, very simply, whether it brings out only the zone of predominance of stone construction. Nevertheless, we get the impression from all of these observations that the south was effectively inhabited by a population which, if not more numerous, at any rate enjoyed a more developed way of life. But, in the absence of any numerical clue, it would be at least very adventurous to take the risk of making an evaluation at present.

Prudence is also called for, and for the same reason, in conjecturing upon the Frankish invaders. Of course the example of the other Germanic tribes which were assimilated in Gaul and Italy, pleads—at least at the time of the fifth-century invasions—in favor of the hypothesis of the *Herrensiedlung*; or, in other words, for an occupation by a small group of Franks who acted as lords. This would explain the important traces they have left in the toponymy of the southern regions, where they were too few to have imposed their language on the population residing there. But one should immediately concede that this is a matter of deduction, very plausible deduction, of course, but one not drawn from scientifically

40. H. Draye, "De invloed van de bevolkingsdichtheid op het onstaan van de Vlaams-Waalse taalgrens," *Miscellanea historica L. Van der Essen* (Brussels, 1947); J. Dhondt, "Essai sur l'origine de la frontière linguistique," *L'Antiquité classique*, XV (1948); E. Legros, "Note sur l'origine de la frontière linguistique," *ibid.*, XXI (1952).

41. This pertinent objection was brought forth by J. Stengers, *La formation . . .*, pp. 39–42. On the reduction of the number of *villae*, see J. Breuer, *La Belgique romaine*, p. 107. On the findings of coins and the tombs, see J. Stengers, *op. cit.*, p. 40, n. 2.

established facts. Also, it tends to negate any active role-for the Franks in the colonization of the northern part of the country.[42]

In addition to the benefit it represented insofar as method is concerned, G. Des Marez' study contained a suggestion which was to prove fruitful in other ways. We already know that the author thought that Frankish colonization had been a relatively slow process, that it had taken place step by step, according to a very strict geographical determinism. Although giving up several ideas defended by Des Marez, several historians adopted the idea of mobility, which was at their base. At the same time (1933), F. L. Ganshof stated precisely that it was the Loire—not the Lys, as Kurth and Des Marez had claimed—which the oldest writing of the Salic law had assigned as the frontier of the Frankish kingdom, as well as the Charbonnière.[43]

The most spectacular of all these attempts, in our opinion, is that of F. Petri.[44] Starting from material which had not been sufficiently tested, and only from a critical point of view, he came to the conclusion that there had been a profound ethnic and linguistic Germanization in Belgium and northern France. The present frontier between the Romance and Germanic languages would then have arisen from a Germanic recess, about the eighth century, and from a slow reconquest of this territory by the Romance languages. Not exempt from ulterior political motives, these views provoked justified criticism.

Very recently, C. Verlinden conjectured that the fifth-century Franks

42. J. Dhondt, in "Essai sur l'origine de la frontière linguistique" (above, n. 40), gives the figure of 60,000 Frankish invaders. This assumption has weak support, as B. H. Stolte has shown in "De getalsterkte der Salischen Franken," *Wetenschappelijke Tijdingen*, XVII (1957), and J. Stengers in *op. cit.*, pp. 43–45.

43. F. L. Ganshof, "Note sur le sens de 'Ligeris' au titre XLVII de la Loi Salique et dans le 'Querolus'," *Historical Essays in Honor of James Tait* (Manchester, 1933), pp. 111–20. This article greatly influenced later theories.

44. F. Petri, *op. cit.* (above, n. 37). For the misleading aspect of the large-scale toponymic maps which were set up by E. Gamillscheg and F. Petri, see the critical remarks of F. Lot, *Les invasions germaniques*, pp. 332–34, as well as the revisions of E. Legros, "Le Nord de la Gaule romane, linguistique et toponymie," *Bull. Commission Royale de Toponymie et Dialectologie*, XVI (1942), and J. Warland, "Bild und Bildung der germanisch-romanischen Sprachgrenze in Belgien," *Album R. Verdeyen* (Liége, 1943). F. Petri has since shown greater moderation of his former opinions, "Zum Stand der Diskussion über die fränkische Landnahme und die Entstehung der germanisch-romanischen Sprachgrenze," *Rheinische Vierteljahrsblätter*, XV–XVI (1950–51). Recent *status quaestionis* of high quality, from the linguistic point of view, by R. Schützeichel, "Das Westfränkisches Problem," *Deutsche Wortforschung in europäischen Bezügen*, ed. L. E. Schmitt (Giessen, 1963), II, pp. 469–523.

had not advanced step by step across present-day Belgium.[45] Leaving Toxandria, where emperor Julian had placed them, they had simply bounded across the country to settle immediately in northern France, and, because of their limited number, they had been absorbed by the Gallo-Roman population. Consequently, one should not persist "in seeing in the linguistic border a phenomenon dating from the era of the invasions." It is, in reality, the result of centuries of evolution, started during the Roman epoch and finished, roughly, by the sixth century.

While the theory of the "bound" was reproached as being based mainly on a gap in textual sources,[46] M. Gysseling tried hard to reconstitute, at the end of a painstaking and patient toponymic investigation, the variations in the outline of the linguistic border between the Roman epoch and the eleventh and twelfth centuries.[47] According to him, all populations living on present-day Belgian territory would have been Germanized, and to a great extent, at about 50 B.C.—a concept which had been favored by scholars before G. Kurth. Four centuries of Romanization would then have left their mark on present-day Belgium (except the Campine region) as well as on the southern part of the Rhine province, without having entirely supplanted the Germanic influence. On the other hand, the Low Countries and the northern half of the Rhine province would have undergone a less profound influence. In the sixth century, all northern Gaul would have formed a linguistically mixed territory, where a "frontier" of languages existed only in the west, the present-day Pas-de-Calais, and in the southeast or Rhine province (except for the Moselle valley, which had remained Romance).

If one reduces to its essentials the fluctuations recorded between the sixth and the twelfth centuries, one notes that, in the section from the

45. C. Verlinden, "De Franken en Aëtius," *Bijdragen tot de geschiedenis der Nederlanden* (1946); *idem*, "Frankish Colonisation, A New Approach," *Transactions of the Royal Historical Society*, Ser. V, IV (1954); and his book, *Les origines de la frontière linguistique*, Ch. II. The essentials of his arguments rest on the dating and locating of a passage from Sidonius Appolinarius on the subject of a fight between Aetius and Clodion's Franks, which was believed to have taken place at *Vicus Helena*. Verlinden adopts, following Schmidt, the year 446—against F. Lot, who favors 428—and also the village of Helesmes (France, Nord Dept.) against A. Loyen, who chooses Vitry or Vis-en-Artois (France, Pas-de-Calais) in his article "A la recherche de Vicus Helena," *Rev. des Études Anciennes*, XLVI (1944).

46. J. Stengers, *op. cit.*, pp. 45–48.

47. The balance sheet of such an enquiry is contained in M. Gysseling, *Toponymisch Woordenboek van België, Nederland, Luxemburg, Noord-Frankrijk en West-Duitsland (voor 1226)* (2 vols.; Brussels, 1960), a fundamental work from which he has shown the conclusions from the point of view that we are occupied with, in "La genèse de la frontière linguistique dans le Nord de la Gaule," *Revue du Nord*, XLIV (1962), 5–38.

North Sea to Brabant, the Romance languages progressed according to a rhythm which varies with the region—at the expense of the Germanic languages—reaching, finally, the present separation line. The role played by bishoprics like Tournai and Arras in this wave of degermanization would have been predominant. In the east, on the contrary, the situation remains relatively stable, the Romance domain losing, between the tenth and eleventh century, the small "islands" which would have survived around Aix-la-Chapelle—a zone which had remained mixed for a long time—and around St.-Trond, and, more toward the south, the Moselle valley with Treves.[48] On the Meuse, the *cité* of Liége would have constituted a center of radiation for the Romance languages, and one can even wonder if the surrender of Maastricht by St. Hubert at the beginning of the eighth century had not caused unexpected repercussions in the matter of language.[49] The Germanic populations responsible for the colonization of the northern coastal regions (Boulonnais and Flemish Belgium) would then have been Thuringians, Chatti, Hessians, Gauti, or Suevi; or, in earlier times, Tongri and Toxandri.[50] The Salians, then, would have settled down between the Charbonnière forest and the Loire—according to the hypothesis defended by C. Verlinden.

Attractive and ingenious no doubt, yet obviously too radical on certain points; for example, in attempting to draw the conclusion of a long-surviving Germanism in the region of the town of Thuin on the Sambre,[51] and this from the analysis of three toponyms. But the investigation of M. Gysseling had the great merit of limiting itself to the linguistic domain, and thus he avoided binding his results to well-determined historical facts. It does insist, however—but with much prudence—on the Romance influence exercised by cultural centers (bishoprics and great abbeys)

48. The existence of these Romance "islands" is confirmed by recent research. For the regions of St.-Trond and Maastricht, see P. Tummers, "Tweetaligheid in Zuid-Limburg," *Koninklijke Nederlandse Akademie van Wetenschappen, Akademiedagen* (Amsterdam, 1957), X, 49–71; *idem, Romaans in Limburgse Aardrijkskundige Namen,* Studia Theodisca (Assen, 1962), II. For Treves and the Moselle valley, see E. Ewig, *Trier im Merowinger-reich. Civitas. Stadt. Bistum* (Trier, 1954), pp. 61–77; W. Jungandreas, *Historisches Lexikon der Siedlungs- und Flurnamen des Mosellandes* (Trier, 1962–63); K. Böhner, *Die fränkischen Altertümer des Trieren Landes* (Trier, 1958); and M. Gysseling, "La genèse de la frontière . . . ," pp. 32–34.

49. F. Rousseau, *La Meuse et le pays mosan,* pp. 55–57.

50. For the Suevi's contribution, see R. L. Reynolds, "Reconsideration of the History of the Suevi," *Rev. Belge de Philol. et Hist.,* XXXV (1957), 19–47. For the others', see M. Gysseling, "La genèse de la frontière linguistique," pp. 28, 37.

51. M. Gysseling, "Le Namurois, région bilingue jusqu'au VII⁰ siècle," *Bull. Commission Roy. de Toponymie et Dialectologie,* XXI (1947).

while also emphasizing the extent of the Germanic penetration at the North Sea edge, and these together could explain the border-warping in this region. In the present state of research, however, it appears to furnish only a working hypothesis of rather limited range because only the language question has been examined. But the explanation is nevertheless acceptable if it should be enriched and substantiated, or corrected, by means of elements which other disciplines would be able to gather.

Such are the principal themes around which explanations of the origin of a linguistic border in Belgium have been centered. Is the result as completely insufficient as has often been claimed? Can it end up only by "avowing incapacity" [52] in a lack-luster report? It would be wrong to deny that any progress has been realized; certainly the progress is slight, and, everything considered, not proportionate to the enormous high-quality effort brought to bear on the subject, but it is nevertheless valuable. To disassociate two notions as different as "invasion" and "colonization," to set aside the myth of a frontier with a linear tracing set up "all at once" as a consequence of the eruption of Franks, [53] to clarify the extremely important consequences of the settlement of the Letes in certain regions at the end of the Late Empire, to emphasize the part of other Germanic tribes disembarked in the coastal zone of the North Sea, all this is probably advancing our knowledge.

We can note that, despite the objections, Verlinden's and Gysseling's suggestions still awaken a broader vision of the problem, which allows placing it on its real terrain and discovering that "other reason, deriving, for example, from the different way of cultivation applied to one or another kind of soil: a geographical and economic phenomenon at the same time," which J. Breuer's lucidity made him perceive as early as 1925. [54] One cannot now deny that the definitive placing of linguistic blocks, Romance and Germanic, took several hundred years, and that it was accompanied by local fluctuations of variable size.

What should be studied with unremitting care and accuracy are phases and aspects of this settlement—first of all from the point of view of disposable soil. There was a landscape much different from the one we know today: a coastal fringe cut into by coves, and scattered islands,

---

52. J. Stengers, *La formation de la frontière linguistique*, p. 51. This contains too radical an opinion of what the author considers a "work of combat" (p. 6, n. 1); however, it is enriched with new insights and justified criticism.

53. "Thus it is not from its origin that the linguistic border took the linear aspect which we know it has now," P. Bonenfant noted in "Le pagus de Brabant," *Bull. de la Société Belge d'Etudes géographiques*, V (1935), 25–76. (Passage cited, p. 35.)

54. J. Breuer (above, n. 32), p. 99.

forests more numerous and thicker, and fewer cultivated areas.[55] Besides, the Germanic techniques and agrarian usages were different from Gallo-Roman techniques and usages, and consequently the selections of types of soils were also different.[56]

This dependence on the point of view of men and the variations of their habitats and customs—as far as they can be detected now—should be considered next. Because of the insecurity set loose by the third-century invasions, the population concentrated, in a defensive reflex, in small nuclei of group habitats which offered a better or a more violent resistance to penetration by newcomers, but which also tended to favor assimilation in a comparatively short period.[57] It is from these small hearths that, later on, the reorganization of society and the evangelization which followed the troubled period of the invasions would radiate. The consequences of the extension of lands for cultivation during the Carolingian era and the consequences of the various confusions caused by the Norman invasion should be measured in the same perspective.[58]

There is no doubt that the flow of farmers to the cities (in full flood since the eleventh century) and the displacement of rural labor (which we can assume from the resumption of the cultivation of new lands and the progress of diking) strongly contributed to the modification of the linguistic division in many sectors.[59] Finally, from the point of view of

55. On this point we recommend the penetrating research of A. E. Verhulst, "Historische geografie van de Vlaamse Kustvlakte tot omstreeks 1200," *Bijdragen voor de geschiedenis der Nederlanden*, XIV (1959), 1–37, and his "L'évolution géographique de la plaine maritime flamande au moyen âge," *Rev. de l'Université de Bruxelles*, new series, XV (1962–63), 90–106.

56. This aspect has not yet been the object of intensive study. Interesting observations have however been made in Touraine by J. Boussard, "Essai sur le peuplement de la Touraine du Ier au VIIIe siècle," *Le Moyen Age*, LX (1954), 261–91.

57. A. Van Doorselaer, "De gallo-romeinse begraafplaatsen in België. Verspreiding en algemene beschouwingen," *Annales du 36e Congrès de la Fédération Archéologique et Historique de Belgique* (Ghent, 1956), pp. 35–44, and G. Faider-Feytmans, "Les vici du Nord de la Gaule à l'époque romaine," *Annales du 35e Congrès* (Courtrai, 1955), pp. 11–16.

58. G. Duby, *L'économie rurale et la vie des campagnes dans l'Occident médiéval* (2 vols.; Paris, 1962), I, 53–130 (with bibliography); F. Vercauteren, "Comment s'est-on défendu au 9e siècle dans l'Empire franc contre les invasions normandes," *Annales du 30e Congrès de la Féd. Archéol. et Hist. de Belgique* (Brussels, 1936), pp. 117–32.

59. See M. Gysseling, "La genèse . . . ," p. 27, for St.-Omer. For Flanders, see A. E. Verhulst, "Die Binnenkolonisation und die Anfänge der Landgemeinde in Seeflandern," *Vorträge und Forschungen* (Constance-Stuttgart, 1964), VII, 447–60. For a general outlook, see L. Génicot, "Sur les témoignages d'accroissement de la population en Occident, du XIe au XIIIe siècle," *Cahiers d'histoire mondiale*, I (1953), and J. C. Russell, *Late Ancient and Medieval Population*, Transactions of the American Philosophical Society, new series, XXXXVIII (Philadelphia, 1958).

men and their mentality, one should not disregard the powerful influence of cultural factors which were often bound to religious movements, both secular and regular.[60] More than a work of the centuries, the linguistic border is a work of men. The solution of this difficult problem, which has been haunting Belgian historiography for more than eighty years, undoubtedly lies in the most flexible, the most varied, and the most cosmic approaches to the manifold aspects of the phenomenon of population.

II. Toward a New Equilibrium

1. *Material Living Conditions* [61]

After the reign of Clovis, the Frankish kingdom recovered a measure of stability. Certainly the conqueror's descendants, regarding the state as a private heritage, indulged in continuous partitions by dint of the different successions which offered the opportunity for many brutal assassinations and internal wars. Small, often ephemeral kingdoms were created, which did not always survive the violent deaths of their rulers.[62] Through

60. For a recent example, see N. Kyll, "Siedlung, Christianisierung und Kirchliche Organisation der Westeifel," *Rheinische Vierteljahrsblätter*, XXVI (1961), 159–242; also, M. Roblin, *Le terroir de Paris aux époques gallo-romaine et franque* (Paris, 1951).

61. Inspired by concepts which were predominant in their time, historians have made diversified judgments on the place occupied by the Merovingian period in the political, economic, and social evolution of Europe. One fact, however, is beyond doubt: all structures of society underwent a profound change at that time. This was negative in certain points (literary culture and urban life *à l'antique*, for example), but the end result in other aspects was less negative (metalworking for example). At the same time, the nuances were obvious among the different regions of Gaul. From the point of view of economics, specialists' opinions differ because of the scarcity of sources and because of the difficulties of interpreting them. Views in favor of a cultural continuity, defended by A. Dopsch, *Wirtschaftliche und soziale Grundlagen der europäischen Kulturentwicklung aus der Zeit von Caesar bis auf Karl dem Grossen* (2d ed., 2 vols.; Vienna, 1923–24), and by H. Pirenne, *Mahomet et Charlemagne* (Brussels-Paris, 1937), seem to open more fruitful perspectives on the basis of establishing various connections and adaptations by the use of a more extensive documentation (coins, archaeology, etc.). On this point we would be inclined, along with A. R. Lewis (*The Northern Seas*, p. 110), to see in the period under study a time of "new beginnings" rather than an "economy adrift," as defined by R. Latouche (*Les origines de l'économie occidentale*, p. 164). For the rest, greatly inspired by the bright picture which F. L. Ganshof made, we have limited ourselves to regional manifestations of diverse forms of human activity, without, however, masking their complexity. The reader may refer to Map 2 to locate the places that have been cited.

62. E. Ewig, "Die fränkischen Teilungen und Teilreiche (511–613)," *Abhandl. der Mainzer Akademie der Wissenschaften*, Geistes- und Sozialwiss. Klasse, No. 9 (1952)

constant territorial modifications, the old Roman administrative divisions of the former provinces rapidly lost their significance. Only the Church, heiress of antique tradition, preserved the provincial borders for her dioceses, and thus perpetuated their memory.[63] It was also through her that most of the old Roman cities kept a remnant of fame and continued to play a certain role. The Merovingian kings made their favorite residences in some of these cities, Soissons and Rheims—and later in Metz, in northern Gaul.[64]

Political unity, although recreated several times and for brief periods, remained artificial. Antagonistic forces were soon opposed across two huge territorial compounds, of ill-defined outlines but separated by a north-south axis. In the east was Austrasia, where a turbulent aristocracy ruled the country under Pepin the Old and Arnulf (who became the bishop of Metz), two leaders of two great families whose union would assure the ascension of the Carolingians. The territory extended westward to the Vosges and the Ardennes, and would soon reach Champagne. But in Belgium, the Charbonnière forest and the Scheldt formed the western borders of this territory, although the real center of gravity lay between the lower Rhine and the middle course of the Meuse. However the town of Metz, on the Moselle, was chosen by personal preference as the sovereigns' residence.

The regions west of the Scheldt—that is, the territory of the old *civitates* of Tournai and Cambrai, as well as Boulogne and Thérouanne, Arras and Noyon—were part, at least between 600 and 650, of a duchy, the *Ducatus Dentelini*, established to face invasions coming from the sea; but they were later incorporated into the kingdom of Neustria. Thus the Scheldt already acted as a border between the Merovingian kingdoms, one of the main functions it would serve until the sixteenth century.

From its origin, Austrasia manifested a very definite tendency toward autonomy, and its rulers had found it necessary to placate the spirit of

pp. 65–175; *idem*, "Die fränkischen Teilreiche von 7. Jahrhundert" (613–714), *Trierer Zeitschrift*, XXII (1954), 85–144.

63. E. De Moreau, *Histoire de l'Eglise en Belgique* (Brussels, 1945), I, and map in IV (1950); J. Lestocquoy, "L'origine des évêchés de la Belgique seconde," *Rev. de l'hist. de l'Église de France*, XXXII (1946), 43–52; H. Van Werveke, *Het bisdom Terwaan* (Ghent-Paris, 1924); J. Warichez, *Les origines de l'église de Tournai* (Louvain, 1902); A. Verbeek, "Spuren der frühen Bischofskirche in Tongern und Maastricht," *Bonner Jahrbücher*, CLVIII (1958), 346–71.

64. E. Ewig, "Résidence et capitale pendant le haut moyen âge," *Rev. historique*, CCXXX (1963), 25–72.

independence of the local aristocracy with numerous concessions.[65] From the middle of the seventh century, under Pepin II's pressure, this tendency was constantly reinforced. The victory of Tertry over Neustria (687) consecrated its success once and for all. From then on, as the only mayor of the palace for both kingdoms, Pepin exercised real hegemony over the whole Frankish kingdom, to the benefit of Austrasia. Strongly entrenched in the region of the Ardennes and of the Meuse, and in the Rhine and the Moselle valleys, which were also developing, the Carolingian family did not delay taking the decisive step of superseding the Merovingian kings, who had no longer any claim to the throne other than that of heredity.[66]

Inside these two large "countries," more limited administrative units appeared in the seventh and eighth centuries: the *pagi*, over which a king's representative exercised authority. Belgium was divided into the following parts: around Thérouanne, in the West, was the *pagus Taruanensis*; in the upper Scheldt valley the *pagus Cameracensis* extended around Cambrai, facing the Ostrevant on the left bank; and the Tournai region was part of the *pagus Turnacensis*. Between the Scheldt and the Dyle was the *pagus Brabantensis* and, down the Meuse, were the *pagus Condrustensis* and the *pagus Mosariorum*, the latter situated downstream from Liége.[67]

The administration of these lands was in no way different from that of other parts of the kingdom. It is known that the Merovingian was an absolute monarchy, totally centered on the royal institution. As a true despot, the king ruled all of his subjects with limitless power, whether they were Franks, Gallo-Romans, or Burgundians. But it was nevertheless a weak monarchy, for it did not have a reliable or perfect organ for carrying out its decisions.

In fact, its administration was confounded with the private service of the prince. The palace (*palatium*) united his faithful friends and favorites around him, and the most important had charge of aulic functions: the mayor of the palace, the superintendent of the royal treasury, the seneschal, and the constable or even the count of the palace, to whom the

65. F. Steinbach, "Austrien und Neustrien. Die Anfänge der deutschen Volkswerdung und des deutsch-französischen Gegensatzes," *Rheinische Vierteljahrsblätter*, X (1940), 217–28.

66. L. Dupraz, *Le Royaume des Francs et l'ascension politique des maires du palais au déclin du VIIe siècle* (Fribourg, 1948).

67. Here we follow F. L. Ganshof, "Het tijdperk der Merowingen." For certain *pagi*, in addition to the outdated work of C. Piot's *Les pagi de la Belgique* (Mémoires de l'Académie Royale de Belgique [Brussels, 1869], 4to), see P. Bonenfant's studies (above, n. 53) and C. Roland, "Les pagi de Lomme et de Condroz et leurs subdivisions," *Annales de la Soc. Archéol. de Namur*, XXXIV (1920), 1–126.

supervision of justice was entrusted. In the offices, directed by clerks and provided with lay personnel, royal diplomas confirming donations and privileges were produced on papyrus. The principal local executive was the count, who was also a favorite of the king. Frankish or Gallo-Roman native, his duty was to supervise and maintain public peace, to assure the functioning of justice, and to hold military command. Subalterns (*centenarii, domestici*) cooperated with him in the performance of his diverse duties. Obviously, this was a rudimentary system, certainly incapable of guaranteeing a coherent governing of the state.[68]

It would be very interesting to have more precise information on population figures for the era, and on its repartition, in order to study more closely the repercussions of the fifth-century turmoil. If on the first point we may have to settle for a complete and perhaps final ignorance, we can at least glean some information on the second point from an examination of the maps of 450 Merovingian cemeteries which we now possess. Manipulating these delicate clues[69] with the proper prudence, we can ascertain that Hainaut, Namur, and Liége are the three modern provinces whose subsoil up to now has yielded the greatest number of Merovingian tombs and the most complete graveyards. Indeed, a wide belt appears on the map: from southern Hainaut it stretches towards the east, beyond the Sambre, and then covers Condroz, Famenne, and Hesbaye. The localities of Amay, Ciney, Han-sur-Lesse, and Thuillies are places of particular density. There are also other important concentrations in the area north of the Sambre-Meuse axis in Hainaut, in the region around Namur, and in the north and south Luxemburg provinces.

This picture, as far as inhabited area is concerned, is only slightly different from the one delivered by the examination of Roman graveyards and this allows the supposition of an identical implantation of

68. Besides F. Lot's *La fin du monde antique*, pp. 399 ff., see the recent studies by R. Büchner in "Die Römischen und die germanischen Wesenzüge in der neuen politischen Ordnung des Abendlandes," *Caratteri del secolo VII in Occidente*, I, pp. 223–69 (Settimane de Studio del Centro Italiano di Studi sull'alto medioevo [Spoleto, 1958], V). Büchner believes that the royal power was less absolute than F. L. Ganshof's assessment of it in (the latter's) "Les traits généraux du système d'institutions de la monarchie franque," *Il passagio dall'antichità al medioevo in Occidente*, pp. 91–127 (Settimane . . . [Spoleto, 1962], IX). Also see the recent bibliography by F. L. Ganshof and R. C. van Caenegem, *La Monarchie franque*, Introduction bibliographique à l'histoire du droit et à l'ethnologie juridique (Brussels, 1964), Vol. B, No. 6.

69. H. E. Roosens, *De Merovingische Begraafplaatsen in België. Repertorium—Algemene Beschouwingen* (Ghent, 1948); G. Faider-Feytmans, "L'aire de dispersion des cimetières mérovingiens en Belgique," *Études Mérovingiennes (Actes des Journées de Poitiers)* (Paris, 1953), pp. 103–9.

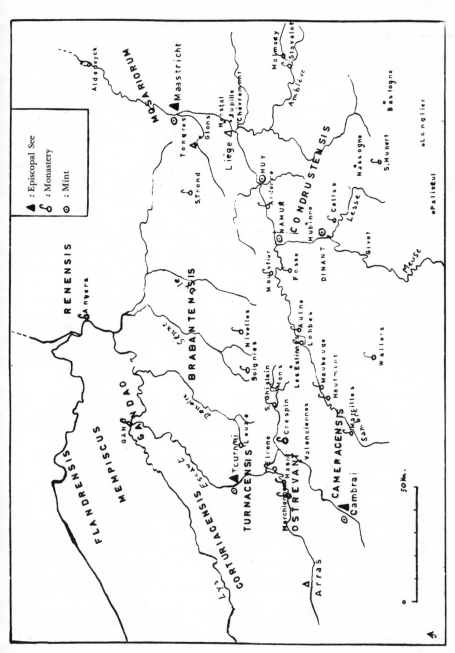

II. The Romance Regions of Northern Gaul in the Sixth and Seventh Centuries

habitations. However, on the local level, one perceives that Merovingian habitations had been differently placed, established along watercourses. Was this attraction to the hydrographic network felt because this was the only way to assure a regular water supply after the destruction of the diversion and waterline works that had been built by the Romans? Was it because of an attraction to certain soils, or to certain landscapes that were more conformable to the agricultural economy practiced by the invaders? The questions remain unanswered.[70]

From the social point of view, the population presents a repartition identical to the one known elsewhere, and which the rates charged for compositions (*Wergeld*) contained in texts of customs or laws (Šalic law, for example) clarify to a degree. One first notices the category of freemen. The most powerful Frankish leaders, as well as great Gallo-Roman landlords, constitute a real aristocracy, rich in very numerous and very large landholdings.[71] We are reminded of the numerous donations of the Pepin family which permitted the establishment of the monasteries of Nivelles, Fosse and Andenne, or of the respectable heritage of a certain deacon Adalgisele-Grimon, whose testament (634) allows us to locate diverse elements scattered across the bishoprics of Metz, Verdun, and Tongres. There were also, among others, parts of a *villa* at Flémalle on the Meuse, at Grand-Han on the Ourthe, at Bastogne, and vineyards in the Moselle valley.[72] Furthermore, this aristocracy was constantly enriched with an important part of the royal domains, which the Merovingian rulers disposed of for their own profit. Also free, but of an inferior rank, the *coloni* (farmers) were attached to the great landlords' domains. The Letes,

70. G. Faider-Feytmans, *La Belgique à l'époque mérovingienne*, pp. 56–63. In the explanation of this situation one should avoid appealing to the naturally-fertile-soils notion. In this approach everything is related to the way of life of the inhabitants, to agricultural technique, and to the agrarian structure existing at a determined epoch. Such vineyards, for example, have been cultivated intensively in Belgium since the early middle ages up to the nineteenth century; that is to say, in a climate and on a soil which are not "naturally" favorable. See J. Halkin, "Étude historique sur la culture de la vigne en Belgique," *Bull. Soc. Art et Histoire du diocèse de Liége*, IX (1895), 1–146.

71. See the works of K. F. Stroheker, *Der Senatorische Adel im spätantiken Gallien* (Tübingen, 1948); A. Bergengrün, *Adel und Grundherrschaft im Merowingerreich* (*Vierteljahrschrift für Sozial- und Wirtschaftsgeschichte* [Wiesbaden, 1958], Supplement 41); R. Sprandel, *Der merowingische Adel und die Gebiete östlich des Rheins* (Freiburg im B., 1957). A revision has recently been made by L. Génicot, "La noblesse au moyen âge dans l'ancienne *Francie*," *Annales. ESC*, XVII (1962), 1–22.

72. W. Levison, "Das Testament des Diakons Adalgisel-Grimo," *Trierer Zeitschrift*, VII (1932), 69–85 (reprinted in *Aus fränkischer und rheinischer Frühzeit* [*s.l.*, 1948], pp. 118–38).

whose number seems to have been particularly high in the northern part of Belgium, were in the same straits. Finally, slavery had not disappeared. There appear to have been many slaves at the beginning of the Merovingian era, and the existence of an important slavetrade can be seen in an episode of the life of St. Géry, in which the bishop of Cambrai tried very hard to obtain the liberation of several slaves whom a merchant was taking across his diocese.[73]

A movement which is striking for the whole period is that the apathy of the state encouraged the multiplication of personal protective ties, which arose from former Germanic customs. In this way a network of bonds of private dependency developed in which one may recognize one of the origins of the feudal system.[74]

Thus, except for judicial matters, no segregation seems to have existed between newcomers and former occupants.[75] The conquest had not brought about any systematic expropriation. All the subjects of the Merovingian kings, whatever their ethnic origin, were placed on the same footing. A common faith brought both groups together and was favorable, in a large measure, to the creation of mixed marriages. Court service and military service, done in common, accelerated the fusion even more. Arms, clothing, and even people's names were more and more inspired from Germanic patterns—eloquent testimony of the considerable prestige that the Franks enjoyed.

Certain obstacles still existed, however, that were capable of slowing down the assimilation. First of all, there was the doubtlessly predominately barbarian character of the Frankish people. We have noted that Salic and Ripuarian laws are, of all Germanic customs, those which least present traces of the influence of Roman law. The Franks nevertheless remained fiercely attached to them and vigorously maintained the autonomy of their own customs in the face of Roman law, as the long survival of the principle of the "personality" of the law attests. In justice, due process of

---

73. C. Verlinden, *L'esclavage dans l'Europe médiévale*, Vol. I: *Péninsule ibérique. France* (Ghent, 1955), pp. 700–702; *idem*, "Traite et esclavage dans la vallée de la Meuse," *Études sur l'histoire du pays mosan au moyen âge (Mélanges F. Rousseau)* (Brussels, 1958), pp. 673–86; *idem*, "Problèmes d'histoire économique franque. Le franc Samo," *Rev. Belge de Philol. et d'Histoire*, XII (1933), 1090 ff. On the episode of St. Géry, see *Vita Gaugerici*, ed. B. Krusch, *MGH, SS. rer. merov.*, III, 656.

74. F. L. Ganshof, "Note sur les origines de l'union du bénéfice avec la vassalité," *Études d'histoire dédiées à la mémoire de H. Pirenne* (Brussels, 1937), pp. 173–89; *idem*, "L'origine des rapports féodo-vassaliques," *I problemi della civilta carolingia*, pp. 27–69 (Settimane . . . [Spoleto, 1954], I); *idem*, *Qu'est-ce que la féodalité* (3d ed.; Brussels, 1957).

75. F. Lot, *Invasions germaniques*, p. 191 ff.

law was carried out and sentence was delivered according to either barbarian or Roman law, whichever the accused or the guilty preferred.
For some time Salic and Roman law coexisted in all of the region north
of the Loire. From the seventh century on, Frankish law, with its oral
and formalistic procedure and its primitive methods of proof (oath,
ordeal) definitely prevailed, finally imposing itself upon the entire
territory. A new border area, which would separate the customary
law (totally affected by Germanic influence) from the written law
inspired from Roman codes, was established on the Loire, where it
survived for centuries. Despite these obstacles, assimilation was carried
out rapidly.[76]

If one enquires into the occupations of this population, one notices at
first sight that the "agricultural predominance of Merovingian life is its
most unquestionable characteristic."[77] Nevertheless, though very essential then, this activity remains very much unknown to us; a lack of
documentation hinders an accurate and sufficient study of the problem.[78]
It is certain that there was a number of large and even huge domains or
villae whose functioning was closely copied from the Roman model. They
are the ones, naturally, that we know more thoroughly because of donations made by rulers or members of the aristocracy, who handed them over
to the patrimony of churches and abbeys. Thus the *villa* of Nivelles—à
property of the Pepin family which covered an area of 7,800 hectares—
and most of the domains of Lobbes and Stavelot-Malmédy included a
large number of *villae*.[79] In addition, despite the fact that they also
included cultivated fields and large areas of forest, swamp and meadow,
their effective output remained very small because of the very elementary
methods of agriculture which were practiced. It also appears that this type
of exploitation found its full growth in the silt zone in Hesbaye, but that

76. H. Brunner and C. von Schwerin, *Deutsche Rechtsgeschichte* (2d ed.; Munich-
Leipzig, 1928), II; P. Vinogradoff, *Roman Law in Medieval Europe* (3d ed.; Oxford, 1929).

77. Latouche, *Origines de l'économie occidentale*, p. 106.

78. There are two fundamental and overall views in F. L. Ganshof, "Manorial
Organization in the Low Countries in the Seventh, Eighth and Ninth Centuries,"
Transactions of the Royal Historical Society, Ser. 4, XXXI (1949), and "Quelques aspects
principaux de la vie économique dans la monarchie franque au VIIe siècle," *Caratteri del
secolo VII in Occidente*, I, 73–101 (Settimane . . . [Spoleto, 1958], V). We borrow the main
lines of this résumé from the above, and we note that they provide a very complete list
of the works related to the problem.

79. See, for example, J. J. Hoebanx, *L'abbaye de Nivelles des origines au XIVe siècle*
(Brussels, 1952), pp. 89–90. H. Platelle, *L'évolution du temporel de l'abbaye de Saint-Amand
des origines à 1340* (Paris, 1962), Ch. I, sets off a primitive block of 12,000 hectares (see
below, n. 83).

elsewhere it could continue only with difficulties.[80] Another characteristic is that in these agrarian cells, where a division into two very distinct elements is already visible, it was the *reserve* which constituted the real point of exploitation while the *tenures*, being very few at that time, played only an auxiliary role. Everything considered, the number of those very large domains, properties of the royal fisc or of powerful people or ecclesiastical institutions, does not seem to have been particularly high during the centuries in which we are interested.

There were many other properties of smaller size, which were called *locellum*, *mansionile*, and *villare*. Indeed, there has recently been an emphasis on the extreme mobility of real estate in the seventh and at the beginning of the eighth century: inheritances, exchanges, and selling and buying constantly modified the extent of private real estate, often involving the breaking up of large domains into smaller units (*portiones*),[81] and often autonomously exploited. On the other hand, there is good reason to admit the existence in the north and east of Gaul of small agricultural holdings which the occupant improved exclusively for his own account, calling sometimes for servile labor or labor of equal rank.[82]

It is more difficult to specify, from what we know, the extent to which common holdings of the German type were able to multiply in certain areas. On the whole, arable space increased very little, making much less progress than has at times been believed. Land was cleared in the immediate surroundings of abbeys, but most of the *villae*, objects of gifts from important persons, consisted of domains ready to be exchanged.[83] Forests held a first rank in this economy. They were, in the eyes of the king and of his favorites, hunting reserves full of game; and for the small farmers, still faithful to a semi-itinerant culture, forests were a providence, a source of timber and firewood and a pasture for cattle.[84] The cultivation

80. A. E. Verhulst, "En Basse et Moyenne Belgique pendant le haut moyen âge. Différents types de structure domaniale et agraire," *Annales. ESC*, XI (1956), 61–70.

81. F. L. Ganshof, in "Aspects," p. 90, n. 1, remarks that Adalgisèle-Grimo's heritage was composed of six complete *villae* and ten *portions* (see above, n. 72).

82. *Ibid.*, p. 74, according to a passage of the Salic law (*Pactus Legis Salicae*, tit. XLV, ed. K. A. Eckhardt, *MGH, LL* [Hanover, 1962], IV, 1, 173). For the general problem of small, individual exploitations, see *ibid.*, p. 75, n. 3, and R. Latouche, *Origines de l'économie occidentale*, pp. 75–83.

83. L. Génicot, "Donations de villae ou défrichements. Les origines du temporel de l'abbaye de Lobbes," *Miscellanea historica in honorem A. de Meyer* (Louvain, 1946), I, 288–96. We repeat that our sketch is limited to the Romance regions of northern Gaul; the situation in the untilled zone of the area of present-day Flanders presents itself under rather different aspects.

84. Ganshof, *op. cit.*, p. 88 and notes. For forested domains of the Ardennes that were

of grain crops remained predominant, but one should notice the rapid extension of viticulture, already widely practiced in the Moselle valley and in other less-well exposed spots in the north.[85] It is possible that liturgical necessities, imposed by the Christian Church, encouraged this progress.

It may seem risky to devote space to the activities of artisans in the Merovingian era since here, again, our information is limited largely to objects exhumed from burial grounds, and only very recently have they been studied and carefully examined with scientific methods.[86] A very definite conclusion evolves from this effort: specialists in metallurgy had maintained their activity in the central valley of the Meuse without interruption between the fifth and eighth centuries.[87]

Medals to be attached to sword sheaths still illustrate the perfect artisanry in the smelting of iron. The smelting of bronze was practiced with skill by smelters trained in the Gallo-Roman tradition but also capable of assimilating new techniques—like that of partition—and also capable of renewing the motifs of their inspiration, based on Germanic or (sometimes) Nordic symbolism. The even more complicated smelting of brass utilized second-hand materials in periods of crisis, before the

---

used for hunting (Longlier) or breeding (Bastogne), see E. Ewig, "Les Ardennes au haut moyen âge," *Anciens Pays et Assemblées d'États*, XXVIII (1963), 3–38, and especially F. Rousseau, "Les Carolingiens et l'Ardenne," *Bull. de la Classe des Lettres de l'Acad. Royale de Belgique*, Ser. 5, XLVIII (1962), 187–221.

85. For the Belgian region, see the study by J. Halkin (n. 70), and a more general treatment by R. Dion, *Histoire de la vigne et du vin en France des origines au 19ᵉ siècle* (Paris, 1959).

86. For tombs in Belgium, see the recent, well-documented pages by G. Faider-Feytmans, *La Belgique à l'époque mérovingienne*, Ch. VI, pp. 117 ff., and J. Werner, *Munz-datierte austrasische Grabfünde* (Berlin, 1935).

87. For the techniques used, see E. Salin, *La civilisation mérovingienne d'après les sépultures, les textes et le laboratoire* (4 vols.; Paris, 1949–59), esp. Vol. III (1957); R. J. Forbes, *Man the Maker: A History of Technology and Engineering* (New York, 1950); C. Singer, E. J. Holmyard, A. R. Hall, and T. I. Williams, *A History of Technology* (Oxford, 1954–56), I–II; E. Salin and A. France-Lanord, *Le fer à l'époque mérovingienne* (Paris, 1943); A. France-Lanord, "La fabrication des épées damassées aux époques mérovingienne et carolingienne," *Le Pays Gaumais*, X (1949), 19–45; idem, "Les techniques métallurgiques appliquées à l'archéologie," *Revue de Métallurgie*, XLIX (1952), 411–22. For the regions studied, see especially S. Collon-Gevaert, *Histoire des arts du métal en Belgique* (Brussels, 1951), pp. 69–105; G. Faider-Feytmans, "Les arts du métal dans la vallée de la Meuse du Iᵉʳ au Xᵉ siècle," *L'Art mosan* (Paris, 1953), pp. 29–37; J. Werner, "Zu fränkischen Schwertern des 5. Jhts.," *Germania*, XXXI (1953), 38–44, and XXXIV (1956), 156–58. See also A. Dasnoy and J. Werner's appendixes to J. Breuer's and H. Roosens' study, "Le cimetière franc de Haillot" (above, n. 12).

stocking of raw materials from the distant sources of Cornwall or Harz. Their production, which also comprised objects of rough manufacture, such as knives with straight backs and scales, enjoyed a great success. It spread to very distant places, traces of its usage having been found in the Rhine delta, in the British Isles, at the mouth of the Elbe, and in Bohemia.

Their craftmanship in working precious metals explains the presence of numerous minters striking coins in the workshops of the Meuse valley, mainly in the sixth century.[88] Getting their inspiration from Mediterranean models, they created a style of striking which allows recognition of their works at first glance. Blacksmiths, engravers, goldsmiths, and minters gave a remarkable splendor to the art of metalworking, a vocation particular to the Meuse valley. It may be due to a contact with those handicrafts that the art of stone-working experienced a surprising renewal. In Tournai, quarries furnished a first-choice limestone to many sculptors. In the Meuse region, the enigmatic sculptures of the Glons arch and the Hubinne columns, carved in the rock of Barrois, attest the scope of a school which little by little replaced the famous marble-workers of Aquitaine. They are the only vestiges of monuments built by these architects and masons, whose fame spread to England.[89] Let us also mention the glassblowers: beginning in the fifth century, in the region of Namur, their cups and bowls, decorated with Christian symbols, perpetuated the methods and traditions honored during the Late Empire;[90]

88. P. Le Gentilhomme, "Le monnayage et la circulation monétaire dans les royaumes barbares en Occident (Vᵉ au VIIIᵉ siècle)," *Revue Numismatique*, Ser. 5, VIII (1945), 26–27; F. Rousseau, "La Meuse et le pays mosan," p. 41; P. C. Boeles, *Friesland tot in de elfde eeuw. Zijn voor- en vroege geschiedenis* (2d ed.; The Hague, 1951), pp. 258–316. For the minters, see R. S. Lopez, "An Aristocracy of Money in the Early Middle Ages," *Speculum*, XXVII (1953), 1–43.

89. P. Rolland, "L'expansion tournaisienne aux XIᵉ et XIIᵉ siècles. Art et commerce de la pierre," *Annales de l'Académie Royale d'Archéologie de Belgique*, LXXI (1924), 175–219; L. Tollenaere, *La sculpture sur pierre de l'ancien diocèse de Liége à l'époque romane* (Louvain, 1957). See, especially, the fundamental works of A. Dasnoy, "Symbolisme et décor des piliers de Hubinne," *Annales de la Société Archéologique de Namur*, XLV (1949–50), 165–81, and "Les sculptures mérovingiennes de Glons," *Rev. Belge d'Archéologie et d'Histoire de l'Art*, XXII (1953), 137–52.

90. J. Werner, "Les écuelles de verre soufflé en moule," and A. Dasnoy, "Coupes en verre ornées de symboles chrétiens du Namurois," appendixes II and VII of the article by Breuer and Roosens cited above (n. 12). See also R. Chambon, *Histoire de la verrerie en Belgique du IIᵉ siècle à nos jours* (Brussels, 1955), pp. 34–40; D. B. Harden, "Glass-making Centres and the Spread of Glass-making from the First to the Fourth Century A.D.," *Annales Iᵉʳ Congrès International d'Histoire du Verre* (Liége, 1959), 47–62; G. Faider-Feytmans, "Les verreries des époques romaine et mérovingienne au Musée de Mariemont," *Rev. Belge d'archéologie et d'histoire de l'art*, X (1940), 211–19; R. Chambon

and there were potters as well, whose productions were abundantly represented in the Merovingian cemeteries of Hainaut and the region of Namur.[91]

All this constitutes a positive and definitive balance sheet, but one significant detail merits special attention.[92] Many of these specialists, minters, bronze-workers, stone-carvers and glassblowers, were itinerant craftsmen. They therefore represented an industrial type which was not bound to an urban economy, and which, in many places, suffered less from the invasion than has been said. Roman and Oriental influences, transmitted through Christianity, and motifs borrowed from Germanic or Nordic art were blended into a harmonious mixture which gave the Merovingian era its original character.

For two centuries, trade more or less preserved its traditional structure, oriented first of all toward the Mediterranean.[93] However, the network of strategic roads set up by the Romans do not seem to have had great significance. Rivers and waterways became the favorite arteries, and were used by pilgrims, travelers, and merchandise with striking regularity.[94] At the end of the fourth century, towns on the Roman roads, like Tongres, Cassel and Bavay, began to fade away in favor of Maastricht, Tournai and Cambrai, which were situated on the Meuse and the Scheldt. The movement increased during the Merovingian era, as two celebrated verses of Fortunatus (d. about 600) attest: *aut Mosa dulce sonans, quo grus, granta, anser olorque est | Triplice merce ferax: alite, pisce, rate.*[95]

The examination of coins allows a further determination of the existence of a real commercial current in the seventh century, a current which started on the coast of the Mediterranean and flowed toward

---

and H. Arbman, "Deux fours à verre d'époque mérovingienne à Macquenoise (Belgique)," *Meddelanden Frän Lunds Universitets Historiska Museum*, VII (1952), 199 ff.

91. M. E. Mariën, *La céramique en Belgique de la préhistoire au moyen âge* (Brussels, 1961), pp. 67–72.

92. F. Petri, "Merowingerzeitliche Voraussetzungen für die Entwicklung des Städtewesens zwischen Maas und Nordsee," *Bonner Jahrbücher*, CLVIII (1958), 233–45 (esp. 239–40).

93. F. L. Ganshof, "Quelques aspects principaux . . . de la vie économique," pp. 91 ff.; A. R. Lewis, *The Northern Seas*, pp. 117 ff.

94. Roman roads continued to be used by official couriers; see F. L. Ganshof, "La Tractoria. Contribution à l'étude des origines du droit de gîte," *Tijdschrift voor Rechtsgeschiedenis*, VIII (1928), 69–91. For the role played by rivers, see F. Rousseau, "La Meuse et le pays mosan," p. 41, and A. Joris, "Der Handel der Maasstädte im Mittelalter," *Hansische Geschichtsblätter*, LXXIX (1961), 15–33 (esp. 22–23); A. R. Lewis, *loc. cit.* (above, n. 93).

95. Venantius Fortunatus, *Carmina*, VII, 4, 11–12, *MGH, AA*, IV, 155.

England and Scandinavia along the Meuse valley. The city of Verdun, already famous at the time of Gregory of Tours for the spirit of enterprise of its merchants, was a true pivot.[96] Several mints—at Mouzon, Dinant, Namur, Huy, and Maastricht—marked out at regular distances the course of the river, a sign of accord. The number of minters who were occupied in these places was very high (twelve in Maastricht, twelve in Huy, seven in Dinant, five in Namur), attesting, in its own way, the incontestable growth in the importance of the entire Meuse region.[97] This animation continued to increase downstream on the Meuse, culminating with the bonded warehouse of Dorestad (near Utrecht). The coinage which was struck there was inspired by the Verdun type, which had been imported by a minter from Maastricht.[98] This is proof of a very real cohesion in the entire Meuse valley, at least at the level of inter-regional trade.

As for the Scheldt valley, its development occurred somewhat later, as its numismatic indigence indicates.[99] While texts that tell of commercial trading in Tournai and Cambrai must be cautiously interpreted for the Merovingian period,[100] it is nevertheless true that the *Vie de Saint Géry*

96. H. Jankuhn, "Die frühmittelalterlichen Seehandelsplätze im Nord- und Ostseeraum," *Studien zu den Anfängen des europäischen Städtewesens*, 451–98 (esp. 455–56) (Vorträge und Forschungen [Lindau-Constance, 1958], IV); H. L. Adelson, "Early Medieval Trade Routes," *American Hist. Review*, LXV (1960), 271–87; A. R. Lewis, *The Northern Seas*, pp. 115–18, 157–58. For the role of Verdun, see Y. Dollinger-Leonard, "De la cité romaine à la ville médiévale dans la région de la Moselle et la Haute Meuse," *Studien zu den Anfängen*, pp. 195–226. The role of this city in the slave traffic does not antedate the end of the eighth century; see C. Verlinden, "Traite et esclavage dans la vallée de la Meuse" (above, n. 73), p. 686.

97. F. Rousseau, *La Meuse et le pays mosan*, p. 41; idem, *Namur, ville mosane* (2d ed.; Brussels, 1958), pp. 37–45; J. Vannerus, "Où chercher dans nos contrées les ateliers monétaires mérovingiens," *Rev. Belge Numismatique*, XCIII (1947), 40–56; C. Meert, "Les monnaies mérovingiennes de l'atelier de Dinant," *Rev. belge de Numismatique*, CVI (1960), 19–50; A. Joris, *La ville de Huy au moyen âge* (Paris, 1959), pp. 81–88; H. U. Bauer, "Der Triens des Rauchomaros," *Schweizer Münzblätter. Gazette numismatique suisse*, II (1951), 96–102; P. C. Boeles, *Friesland tot in de XI. eeuw* (2d ed.; The Hague, 1951), pp. 296–300. F. Petri notes that ("Merowingerzeitliche Voraussetzungen . . . ," p. 238, n. 22) the pieces from these workshops that have been found are fewer than have been found from the Marseilles or Paris workshops. It is dangerous, however, to draw a statistical argument from these numbers because the actual findings may be unrepresentative (see Jankuhn, *op. cit.*, p. 468).

98. P. C. Boeles, *op. cit.*, pp. 300–304; J. F. Niermeyer, "La Meuse et l'expansion franque vers le Nord," *Études sur l'histoire du pays mosan au moyen âge* (*Mélanges F. Rousseau*) (Brussels, 1958), pp. 455–63.

99. J. Dhondt, "Essor urbain entre Meuse et Mer du Nord à l'époque mérovingienne," *Studi in onore di A. Sapori* (Milan, 1957), I, 55–78.

100. P. Rolland, *Deux tarifs du tonlieu de Tournai des XIIe et XIIIe siècles* (Lille, 1935),

mentions the passage (in Famars, near Valenciennes) of a group of slaves led by a merchant. A minter, called Madelinus, known especially for his Meuse-issues of the end of the seventh century, also struck coins in Famars,[101] so there was perhaps a closer relationship between the two basins and the cities of northern Gaul (Soissons) than has been thought. Finally, far to the west, on the coast of the channel, Quentovic (near Étaples), the jumping-off point for trade with England, took over the trade function of old Boulogne. Its development during the seventh century is easily perceptible. A group of Roman roads connected this city with the Scheldt valley, with the Meuse, and even with the Rhine, but it was first of all a necessary halting place on the *Via Rectissima*, which led the pilgrims to Rome.[102]

Traditional bonds weakened, however, at the beginning of the eighth century: Egyptian papyrus was replaced by parchment, and oil by wax for the lighting of sanctuaries.[103] Under the impetus of the Anglo-Saxons, whose role would be taken up and continued after 750 by the famous Frisian merchants,[104] our regions would henceforth be attracted to the North Sea orbit.

---

pp. 17, 27–28 (contains mention of gold commerce and of slaves that go back, according to the author, to the Merovingian era), and H. Pirenne, "Le commerce du papyrus dans la Gaule mérovingienne," *Compte-rendus de l'acad. des Inscriptions et Belles-Lettres* (1928) (reprinted in *Histoire de l'Occident médiéval* [Bruges, 1951], pp. 90–100 [spices and papyrus at Cambrai, pp. 96–97]). F. L. Ganshof does not admit that these references date back to the Merovingian era; see "A propos du tonlieu sous les Mérovingiens," *Studi in onore di A. Fanfani* (Milan, 1962), I, 303, n. 44, and *La Belgique carolingienne* (Brussels, 1958), p. 123.

101. For the episode of St. Géry, see n. 73. For Madelinus, see F. Petri, "Merowinger-zeitliche Voraussetzungen," p. 244.

102. A. R. Lewis, *The Northern Seas*, pp. 125–26; J. Dhondt, "Les problèmes de Quentovic," *Studi in onore di A. Fanfani* (Milan, 1962); I, 183–248; E. Sabbe, "Les relations économiques entre l'Angleterre et le continent au Haut Moyen Age," *Le Moyen Age*, LVI (1950), 169–94.

103. H. Pirenne, "Le commerce du papyrus dans la Gaule mérovingienne," *loc. cit.* Nevertheless, papyrus was used after 700, namely, by the pontifical chancery; see R. S. Lopez, "Mohammed and Charlemagne: A Revision," *Speculum*, XVIII (1943), 15 ff., and E. Sabbe, "Papyrus et parchemin au haut moyen âge," *Miscellanea L. Van der Essen* (Brussels-Paris-Louvain, 1947), I, 95–103.

104. The problem of the Frisian trade has been the subject of an abundant literature. We cite only some of the most recent works. B. Rohwer, *Der friesische Handel im frühen Mittelalter* (Kiel, 1937), and D. Jellema, "Frisian Trade in the Dark Ages," *Speculum*, XXX (1955), 15–36. P. C. Boeles, *Friesland tot in de XI. eeuw*, pp. 369–81, insists that nothing is definitely known of this subject before 753; see also his "De handel van Groter-Friesland met Frankrijk in de Merowingische tijd," *Bijdragen voor de geschiedenis der Neder-landen*, VIII (1954), 237–50, and A. R. Lewis, *op. cit.*, pp. 145–46.

The superiority of connections by waterways, as opposed to connections by land routes, and the early development of small centers on the Meuse are two characteristics of the picture of urban life.[105] Indeed, the ancient Roman cities, administrative and strategic creations situated on the main roads, sank to obscurity in the upheaval. Such was the fate of Cassel, Tongres, and Bavai. Only those which were favored by luck, which placed them, like Tournai and Cambrai, on the banks of a river, survived— because of their location.[106] In other cases, did an eclipse of urban living occur? The answer must be notably differentiated.[107]

In the Meuse area there were no longer any Roman "cities." On the other hand, *castra*, fortified boroughs that dated back to the Late Empire, settled their populations within their walls.[108] Mouzon, Dinant, Namur, Huy, and Maastricht form a line and dot the valley every thirty kilometers. Halting places of inland water transport, but also issue points of former roads which penetrated the backlands, such well-protected localities were numerous, active, and animated markets—if one considers the quantity of currency issued in their names and its extraordinary diffusion, and if one also considers the increase of productive tolls, or *tonlieux*, in Givet, Huy, and Dinant (743–747).[109] Besides, the only Mero-

105. J. Dhondt, in "Essor urbain," called attention to this fact. There are some general views in F. Petri "Die Anfänge des mittelalterlichen Städtewesens in den Niederlanden und dem angrenzenden Frankreich," *Studien zu den Anfängen des europäischen Städtewesens*, pp. 227–96.

106. F. Vercauteren, *Étude sur les civitates de la Belgique seconde. Contribution à l'histoire urbaine du Nord de la France de la fin du IIIe à la fin du XIe siècle*, Mémoires Acad. Royale Belgique, Cl. des Lettres (Brussels, 1934), pp. 353–64; P. Rolland, "Le problème de la continuité à Tournai et dans la Gaule du Nord," *Annales. ESC*, VII (1935), 245–84.

107. R. Latouche, *Les origines de l'économie occidentale*, pp. 114 ff. F. Lot, who has a similar opinion (*La fin du monde antique*, pp. 425–26), observes the matter strictly from the point of view of ancient urbanism, and he minimizes the role of *castra* and *vici*. We adopt a more differentiated position, similar to that defended by J. Hubert in his "Recherches sur la topographie religieuse des cités de la Gaule du IVe au IXe siècle," *Comptes-rendus de l'Acad. des Inscriptions et Belles-Lettres* (Paris, 1945), pp. 314–17.

108. F. Rousseau, *La Meuse et le pays mosan*, p. 37 ff.; F. Vercauteren, "De wordingsgeschiedenis der Maasteden in de hoge Middeleeuwen," *Bijdragen en Mededelingen van het historisch Genootschap te Utrecht*, LXXXI (1957), 12–28; idem, "La vie urbaine entre Meuse et Loire du VIe au IXe siècle," *Città nell'alto medioevo*, pp. 453–84 (Settimane . . . [Spoleto, 1959], VI); A. Joris, "Der Handel der Maasstädte," pp. 16–24; E. Ennen, "Das Städtewesen Nordwestdeutschlands von der fränkischen bis zur salischen Zeit," *Das Erste Jahrtausend* (Düsseldorf, 1965), II, 785–820.

109. For the *tonlieux*, we refer to the reports of F. L. Ganshof, "A propos du tonlieu sous les Mérovingiens" (above, n. 100), pp. 302, 307, and "Het tolwezen in het frankisch Rijk onder de Merovinger," *Mededelingen van de Koninklijke Vlaamsche Akademie voor Wetenschapen, Letteren en Schone Kunsten van België*, Klasse der Letteren, XX, No. 4 (1958). Givet is called *vicus Gabelium* in the *Vita Hugberti*, c. 743, *MGH, SS. rer. merov.*, VI, 485.

vingian golden coin of the area that has been found was struck in Huy, a fact which merits emphasis because of the growing scarcity of currency made with this metal.[110] These small but important boroughs (*petites bourgades*), the temporary residences of bishops in which churches with Merovingian patronyms (St.-Hilaire, St.-Pierre, St.-Étienne) are numerous, form many religious centers which will later serve as bases for conversion. They were *cités*, according to "Anonymous of Ravenna," a geographer who lacked accuracy in his vocabulary and who was at work about the year 700.[111] This is an undeniable misuse of language but it reveals quite well the importance of these refuges of urban living during two centuries—a life very much different from the one known in the Roman era because it fulfilled other needs. Additional proof of this fact is that several Merovingian rulers consented repeatedly to hold pleas and solemn meetings in these towns (Maastricht 594 and 670, and Namur 692).[112]

The Scheldt valley offers a rather different picture. There the old cities of Cambrai and Tournai survived, but they lived such a sluggish existence that some do hesitate to compare them to the important *castra* on the Meuse. Yet they preserved their walls, and King Chilperic I sought refuge in Tournai in 584; however, their inhabited space had shrunk and Tournai was no larger than fourteen hectares.[113] The number of these cities' inhabitants was also greatly reduced. They remained the

110. A Joris, *La ville de Huy*, p. 81. The problem of gold, which related to its rarefaction and the cessation of its use for the striking of coins, roused great controversies in which M. Bloch, M. Lombard, S. Bolin, F. Himly, P. Grierson, and others participated. For the region studied, there is a recent revision that is due to F. Vercauteren, "Monnaie et circulation monétaire en Belgique et dans le Nord de la France du VIe au XIe siècle," *Moneta e Scambi nell'alto medioevo*, pp. 279–311 (Settimane . . . [Spoleto, 1961], VIII).

111. *Ravennatis Anonymi Cosmographia et Guidonis Geographica*, eds. M. Pinder and G. Parthey (Berlin, 1860), p. 233; ed. J. Schnetz, pp. 59, 62 (Itineraria Romana [Leipzig, 1940], II). Written in the first quarter of the eighth century, this source describes, for the region studied here, a situation existing around 700. See J. Schnetz, *Untersuchungen über die Quellen der Kosmographie des anonymen Geographen von Ravenna*, Sitzungsberichte der Bayerischen Akademie, Phil. Hist. Klasse (Munich, 1942); B. H. Stolte, *De Cosmographie van den Anonymus Ravennas. Een studie over de bronnen van boek II–V* (Amsterdam, 1949); idem, "De datering van de Anonymus Ravennas," *Tijdschrift v. h. Koninklijk Nederlands Aardrijkskundig Genootschap*, LXXIII (1956), 260–61; A. Vincent, "Les localités belges chez l'Anonyme de Ravenne," *Latomus*, V (1946), 373–79.

112. F. Rousseau, *La Meuse et le pays mosan*, pp. 40, 53, following *MGH, LL*, I, 15 (Childebert II, 594); Halkin and Roland, *Recueil des chartes de Stavelot-Malmedy* (Brussels, 1909), I, 18–23, 35–38 (Childeric II, 670; Clovis III, 692). Let us also add that about 550 Maastricht became the principal residence of the bishop of Tongres; see E. de Moreau, "Le transfert de la résidence des évêques de Tongres à Maestricht," *Rev. Histoire Ecclésiastique*, XX (1924), 457–64.

113. F. Vercauteren, *Étude sur les Civitates*, p. 209.

seats of a mint and the centers of active religious life, but their decline, although not irremediable, was nevertheless perceptible as the years passed. Neither was used as a royal residence, and Tournai finally lost its diocesan standing to Noyon.[114] The chronological shift, as compared with that of the Meuse valley, was very obvious, and it was only from the middle of the ninth century that the new Scheldt *portus*, Valenciennes and Ghent, began their real growth. Here too, in order to survive,[115] urban living would adapt forms similar to those we have previously observed.

Trying to determine the true position of greatest influence, at the end of this brief sketch, one is certainly impressed by the importance attained in the material domain by the eastern regions centered in the Meuse valley. Whether it was a matter of industrial, monetary, or commercial activity, or of urban growth proportional to the scale of the time, the eastern regions give the impression of having formed an active, coherent, solid whole. In this perspective, the conquest of hegemony by Austrasia and the parallel ascendancy of the Carolingians really seem like the natural political consequences of such a situation.

2. *The Church and Evangelization*

"In the fifth and sixth centuries the Church became the real *patria* of the Gallo-Roman population." Ferdinand Lot's formula has kept all its pertinence. It explains how unity managed to survive Frankish partitions. It enlightens, at the same time, the predominant action of dioceses in every field, and mainly the part they assumed in maintaining Roman culture, debased as it was, and sometimes even causing this culture to progress in these regions.[116] It is significant in this respect that Arras, Tournai, and even Treves constituted true bastions from which, advancing hand in hand, were spread Christianity and the Romance language.[117]

114. J. Warichez, *Les origines de l'église de Tournai* (Louvain-Paris, 1902), pp. 58 ff. It was accomplished under the bishop St. Achaire (626–637), and the two dioceses remained united until 1146.

115. F. Deisser-Nagels, "Valenciennes, ville carolingienne," *Le Moyen Age*, LXVIII (1962), 51–90. There is a *palatium* mentioned since 693. See H. Van Werveke, *Kritische Studiën betreffende de oudste geschiedenis van de stad Gent* (Ghent, 1933), pp. 41–44; F. Blockmans, "Les 2 portus successifs de Gand," *Rev. Nord*, XXVI (1943), 5–20.

116. The basic work is E. de Moreau's *Histoire de l'Église en Belgique* (2d ed.; Brussels, 1947), I; also see W. Neuss, *Die Anfänge des Christentums im Rheinlande* (2d ed.; Bonn, 1933).

117. M. Gysseling, "La genèse de la frontière linguistique," pp. 29–30.

They did this to such an extent that one may wonder, as does Felix Rousseau, whether the transfer of the diocesan center from Maastricht to Liége (725) did not indirectly seal the withdrawal of Romance and the loss, after a comparatively short period, of the small "island" of Aix-la-Chapelle, which had survived up to that time. From a more general point of view, it is necessary to acknowledge that when Gaul's dioceses fully supported the cause of Clovis, a barbarian converted to Roman Christianity, the Frankish kings, in return, did not cease to sustain the bishops' actions encouraging the reconstruction of their bishoprics and their fight against paganism.

Here also, the eastern and western parts of our regions were opposed on more than one issue. In the province of *Germania Inferior*, Christianity seemed to be strongly rooted from the end of the Roman era on. Established by St. Maternus, bishop of Cologne (314), it radiated rapidly from the Rhine metropolis and from Treves. St. Servais was bishop of the *civitas Tungrorum* in the middle of the fourth century (343–351). Several small Christian communities were born in the Meuse valley in Namur, in Maastricht, and perhaps in Huy, just as in Arlon and Yvois, belonging to the bishopric of Treves. In what measure did the fifth-century invasions threaten their existence?[118] The question cannot be answered, but it is very curious to observe that, in St. Remi's time, Bishop Falco (d. before 532) had already resumed normal activity in the diocese of Tongres. We even see him, carried away by his zeal, ordaining new priests at Mouzon, a locality of the upper Meuse subject to the diocese of Rheims.

From this epoch on, indeed, the Meuse had visibly become the backbone of the diocese. Settled in Maastricht, the bishops oriented their efforts of evangelization and organization according to its course.[119] They had temporary residences in these important fortified boroughs (*castra*): Huy, Namur, Dinant and Givet, whose vitality we have already underlined. The most ancient churches were uniformly dedicated to Our Lady; also, many episcopal sepulchres—or graves reputed to be such—were found there: in Maastricht the St. Servatius tomb, in Huy the tombs of the bishops St. Domitian (about 535) and John the Lamb (about 632–647), in Dinant that of St. Perpetius.[120] Such continuity of action soon

118. B. H. M. Vlekke, *S. Servatius. De eerste nederlandse Bisschop in Historie en Legende* (Maastricht, 1935); A. Verbeek, "Spuren der frühen Bischofskirchen in Tongeren und Maastricht," *Bonner Jahrbücher*, CLVIII (1958), 346–71.

119. This movement will continue until the middle of the eighth century; see J. F. Niermeyer, "La Meuse et l'expansion franque vers le Nord," (above, n. 98).

120. F. Rousseau, *La Meuse et le pays mosan*, pp. 38–42.

bore fruit. The number of small Christian centers[121] grew continuously from 600 on, and one can say that the Meuse valley was at that time forever won over to Christianity.

A single glance at the episcopal list confirms this situation: the recruitments became largely native from the end of the sixth century on. The bishop Monulph (d. about 500), John the Lamb (d. about 647), and Lambert (d. 705) came, respectively, from Dinant, Huy, and Maastricht. Also, the effort of evangelization, mainly carried on in the solitudes of the Ardennes and later on in Toxandria, was supported by the valley. It is known that St. Amand, the "Apostle of Belgium," could not keep his episcopal function at Maastricht (647–649), but the recriminations—visibly excessive—which he addressed to Pope Martin (649), deploring the carelessness of the local clergy, reflected first of all the profound deception of this born missionary: "a burning nature, but one quickly discouraged, full of wonderful zeal which often precipitates him too hastily in new enterprises"—according to his most recent biographer.[122] The fact was that the administration of the diocese, which had already become routine, could not satisfy the enthusiasm of an animator of this kind.

Strongly rooted in the major part of the Meuse country, Christianity had passed the stage of missionary expansion which was still its lot in the west. There is no doubt that the ever-growing favor that the prelates enjoyed with the rulers and mayors of the palace finally harmed certain members of the higher aristocracy. Théodard (d. 670) and Lambert (d. 705) both died by the hands of assassins, the latter in an obscure *villa publica*, Liége, to which he occasionally liked to retire. The devotion of the public, which attracted ever-growing crowds to the grave where the corpse of the martyr had been transferred (717–718), assured the wealth of the place. By establishing their residence there (725), St. Hubert and his successors raised it to the rank of *cité* which it was to keep throughout the centuries.[123]

In contrast with this situation was the very different one that existed in the former *Belgica Secunda*, whose area extended to the west of the Charbonnière forest, and which answered to the metropolitan church of

121. For example, Amay, between Huy and Liége, is cited in the testament of Adalgisèle-Grimon (634); see *Vita Sanctae Odae Viduae*, ed. M. Coens, *Analecta Bollandiana*, XLV (1947), 196–244.

122. E. de Moreau, *Saint Amand, apôtre de la Belgique et du Nord de la Gaule* (Louvain, 1927); M. Coens, "S. Amand," *Biographie Nationale de Belgique*, Supplement III (Brussels, 1961), I, cols. 17–24. The only known response of the pope was published in *MGH, SS. rer. merov.*, V, 452–56.

123. F. Rousseau, *La Meuse et le pays mosan*, p. 56.

Rheims.[124] It is true, however, that the mark of Christianity in the Roman epoch had been generally less profound there and that the Frankish conquest had caused very serious upheavals. That is why an unevenness can be perceived in the work of episcopal reorganization. That is also why the fight against paganism would be conducted with particular vigor. The reorganization was achieved along the lines of the old Roman plan of administration.

Yet changes had occurred that necessitated adaptations. In Rheims, St. Remi was active at the dawn of the sixth century and the predominant role he played in Clovis' conversion is well-known. A little later, St. Vaast (d. about 540), a native of Toul, was bishop of the diocese of Arras, which would fuse a bit later with that of Cambrai, made famous by St. Géry, who was born at Yvois in the Ardennes (d. 625). Before the middle of the seventh century Tournai yielded the primacy to Noyon, where Acharius (d. 626) and then the famous St. Eloi (641–660) had settled.[125] The founding of the diocese of Thérouanne, which also comprised the territory of the ancient city of Boulogne, was not earlier than this date (626–639), and St. Omer was probably its first prelate.[126] One fact which even more underlines the contrast between the western and eastern parts of our regions should be repeated: in the West, episcopal recruiting was marked by a definite predominance of elements alien to the country. The first wave of clerics (sixth century) came from the east, like St. Vaast and St. Géry; the second wave (seventh century), often trained in the "Irish" monastery of Luxeuil, were natives of more southern countries—from Aquitaine, like St. Acharius and St. Eloi, or from Brittany, like St. Omer and his Breton auxiliaries.[127]

The major preoccupations of the bishopric were of course the evangelization of the population and the fight against paganism. Here again the same contrast reappears between the diocese of Tongres and its counterparts in *Belgica Secunda*. On both sides, however, the role played by rivers in this diffusion of Christianity should be emphasized. As far as religion is concerned, they were the major axes of penetration during the Merovingian period, and nothing better illustrates their "victory" over

124. J. Lestocquoy, "L'origine des évêchés de la Belgique seconde," *Revue d'Histoire de l'Église de France*, XXXII (1946), 43–52; D. A. Stracke, "Over de eerste Kerstening van Nord-West Gallië," *Bijdragen over de geschiedenis v. h. oud. Hertogdom Brabant*, XLIV (1961), 5–30.

125. J. Warichez, *Les origines de l'église de Tournai*, pp. 56 ff.

126. H. Van Werveke, *Het bisdom Terwaan* (Ghent-Paris, 1924), pp. 14–28.

127. H. Wieruszowski, "Die Zusammensetzung des gallischen und fränkischen Episkopats bis 843," *Bonner Jahrbücher*, CXXVII (1922), 25 ff.

the old highways. In both parts, also, the vigorous action of missionaries from Aquitaine and Ireland is noticeable after 630, even if it did not manifest itself with as much strength in the diocese of Tongres as it did elsewhere.

It is in this region, less ravaged by the invasions, that the actions of the bishops seem to have had a more coherent and more efficient aspect than they had anywhere else. The legend of St. Domitian destroying dragons and purifying the water of Huy, as late as it might have been, still reminds us of the prelate's efforts in the boroughs of the valley, just as the life of St. Monon, a protégé of the bishop John the Lamb and founder of a hermitage at Nassogne, contains the faint echo of the episcopal projects of the conversion of the Ardennes peoples (about 650).[128] In this vast, isolated, and sparsely inhabited forest two missionaries "of Aquitaine" settled slightly later: St. Remaclius, founder of the monasteries of Stavelot and Malmédy (d. 670/676), and his disciple St. Hadelin, founder of Celles on the Lesse river. Parallel with the conversion efforts of later bishops, St. Lambert and St. Hubert carried out their tasks principally in that part of Toxandria—the present Campine—which was in their jurisdiction.[129]

The missionaries' role, on the other hand, was much more active in the west. In the sixth century, an early phase of evangelization is noticed in the apostolates directed by the bishops St. Vaast, St. Eleutherus, and St. Géry, whose *vitae* show them very busy destroying idols. But the decisive impulse came either from those missionaries called "Aquitainians," who came in fact from the center and from the south of Gaul,[130] or from Anglo-Saxons disembarked from Ireland and England and

---

128. *Vita Domitiani episcopi Traiectensis, AASS,* May, II (3d ed.; 1865), 146–52; *Vita Mononis, AASS,* October, VIII (3d. ed.; 1869), 367–69 and *Analectes pour servir á l'histoire ecclésiastique de la Belgique,* V (1868), 410–14. For what is known of the lives of these two saints through later writings (eleventh and twelfth centuries) see L. Van der Essen, *Étude critique et littéraire sur les "vitae" des saints mérovingiens de l'ancienne Belgique* (Paris-Louvain, 1907), pp. 168–72, 144–49; I. Snieders, "L'influence de l'hagiographie irlandaise sur les "vitae" des saints irlandais de Belgique," *Rev. Hist. Ecclésiastique,* XXIV (1928), 596–627, 827–68.

129. Only St. Hubert has been the subject of a valuable critical study, the elements of which are unfortunately scattered in several reviews and publications. We refer to the latest review: F. Baix, "Saint Hubert. Sa mort, sa canonisation, ses reliques," *Mélanges F. Rousseau* (Brussels, 1958), pp. 71–80.

130. W. Levison, "Metz und Südfrankreich im frühen Mittelalter," *Elsass. Lothringisches Jahrbuch,* XI (1938); E. Ewig, "L'Aquitaine et les pays rhénans au haut moyen âge," *Cahiers de civilisation médiévale,* I (1958), 37–54; P. Riché, *Éducation et culture dans l'Occident barbare (VIe au VIIIe siècle)* (Paris, 1962), pp. 257–59.

designated *Scotti*.[131] Both groups further combined in the formation of "Irish" monasteries, like Luxeuil in the Vosges and Solignac on the upper Loire, real "nurseries" for evangelizers destined to go to regions which were still pagan.[132] Whether they had been natives of Romance-language regions or only the heirs of a Latin literary and cultural background, when one considers the period, these foreigners, in their daily contact with the population, played the role of agents for Romanization, the progress of which was identified, on a number of points, with the progress made by religion.

To avoid going too deeply into detail, it will suffice if we only indicate the major orientation they gave to their movement. St. Amand's activities for the most part developed—with the exception of the Meuse interlude—in the Scheldt and Scarpe valleys. After founding Elnone (now St.-Amand) and converting the whole region, he moved up the Scheldt, by stages, as far as Antwerp. He was helped in his efforts by the influential St. Eloi, known as a goldsmith and minter, counselor of Dagobert I, who was at the same time bishop of Noyon-Tournai, and, as such, heedful of the need for the annihilation of paganism in the Scheldt and Lys valleys. At about the same time, St. Omer, the new bishop of Thérouanne, pursued identical work in the region between the Canche and the Yser with the help of disciples who were natives of his country, such as St. Bertin, and Bretons such as Judocus, and even an Alaman, Bertulfus. In his diocese, St. Omer's effort was limited to one important foundation: Sithiu, on the Aa river, which later on—as was frequently the case—took the name of its founder, St. Bertin. In the diocese of Cambrai, which was already strongly Christianized, the apostolate of the Irishman St. Feuillian, in the lower Sambre valley (about 650), and the achievements of SS. Landelin and Ursmer should be mentioned. With the support of Bishop Aubert they greatly increased the number of monasteries in this region.

Between 625 and 730 we see a real flourishing of monasticism in our regions.[133] Bishops were often the first to encourage this movement, but it also fulfilled the wishes of missionaries who wanted to consolidate the progress realized in evangelization; and it enjoyed the support of great

131. Dom L. Gougaud, *Christianity in Celtic Lands* (London, 1932); P. Riché, *op. cit.*, pp. 371–83; F. Masai, *Essai sur les origines de la miniature dite irlandaise* (Brussels, 1947).

132. F. Baix, "S. Remacle et les abbayes de Solignac et de Stavelot-Malmédy," *Rev. Bénédictine*, LXI (1951), 167–207.

133. E. de Moreau, *Les abbayes de Belgique (VIIe au XIIe siècle)* (Brussels, 1952); Dom Ph. Schmitz, *Histoire de l'ordre de Saint Benoît* (2d ed.; Maredsous, 1948), I–II.

landlords who had been won over to the new religion. This explains the very great number of monasteries: there were no fewer than forty-six in just the four dioceses of Thérouanne, Tournai, Cambrai, and Tongres-Maastricht.

From the very beginning the geographical repartition of these Merovingian foundations showed two striking characteristics. First, there was an exceptional concentration in the Romance part of present-day Belgium, where nearly forty monasteries can be counted. Second, and here we again find a characteristic mentioned often in this study, there was a disposition that strongly coincided with the main fluvial axes. Where can we find the cause of this state of things? The nature of the soil and the geographical features certainly exercised an influence in some places, determining without doubt what choices would be made on the local level, for in this domain it was necessary to consider not only the location of land offered as a donation but also the particular aspirations of every community. Should one presume that a larger population, more Christianized and more Romanized, would allow more recruiting of monks? Or can it be explained by the fact that *villae* fit to be used as objects of donations were more numerous and more strongly implanted in the Romance part of our regions?

If one sets aside the original, fruitless attempt of St. Walfrey (of Lombard origin), who lived near Yvois in the time of the historian Gregory of Tours (538–594) and is known as the only stylite of the Occident,[134] it was the arrival of St. Columban in Gaul (590) which started the spread of monasticism. Besides, most of these monasteries adopted the very strict rule imposed by Columban; however, they moderated its rigor by means of St. Benedict's precepts.[135] Several institutions were double abbeys. Monasticism and the apostolate remained tightly associated, provoking, among other things, an ardent emulation among the large landlords who had been converted. Thus we first see St. Amand founding Elnone (now St.-Amand) about 639, probably Marchiennes on the Scarpe, then St.-Peter's in Ghent, an abbey in Antwerp, and similar institutions in Leuze and in Renaix.[136] As bishop of Liége he pursued his activity at the western

134. Gregory of Tours, *Historia Francorum*, VIII, Ch. 15, ed. B. Krusch, *MGH, SS rer. merov.*, I, 333–36.

135. For the era of the *regula mixta*, see S. G. Luff, "A Survey of Primitive Monasticism in Central Gaul," *Downside Review*, LXX (1952), 180–203. For the era in general, see T. P. MacLaughlin, *Le très ancien droit monastique de l'Occident*, Archives de la France monastique (Paris, 1935), XXXVIII.

136. E. de Moreau, "La Vita Amandi prima et les fondations monastiques de S. Amand," *Analecta Bollandiana*, LXVII (1949), 447–64.

borders of his diocese, encouraging the creation of Nivelles and establishing a monastery in Moustier-sur-Sambre.[137] On both sides of his domain his example inspired more than one rich landlord. In a similar way St. Landelin and his disciple St. Ursmer, both trained in Cambrai, covered the Sambre valley with a vast new network of abbeys: Lobbes, Aulne, Wallers-en-Fagne, and Crespin, immediately causing the foundation of similar institutions by members of the local aristocracy.[138] The whole family of St. Aldegond, who herself was foundress of Maubeuge, endowed St.-Ghislain, St.-Vincent in Soignies, and St.-Waudru in Mons, Hautmont, and Maroilles.

Was this the result of a stronger ecclesiastical organization? This is not known. But in the diocese of Tongres the action of the missionaries was much less spectacular and they more often played only the part of instigator or counselor. The influence of laymen seems predominant, especially that which was exercised by the Carolingians, who at that time were in full ascent. The widow of Pepin the Old, Itta, and her two daughters, Gertrude and Begga, helped in the foundation of the abbeys of Nivelles (before 652) and Andenne (692), and the Irish monastery of Fosse (649), which St. Feuillian has rendered famous. Andage (today St.-Hubert), in the heart of the Ardennes, owes its birth to Pepin the Young, mayor of the palace (about 700).[139] In Hesbaye a rich landlord named Trudo founded, in Sarchinium (modern St.-Trond), on land which was still half Romance at the time, a flourishing abbey which would be united to the church in Metz, whose diocese was soon to be run by Chrodegang, a native of Hesbaye (742–762).[140]

The founders of Aldeneyck, close to the Meuse, were also people of the highest class. Irish influence and the intervention of the mayor of the palace, Pepin II, are definitely perceptible at Susteren and in Odilienberg.[141] The list is truly impressive. Among the missionaries' activities are

137. G. Despy, "Moustier-sur-Sambre, abbaye mérovingienne," *Annales de la Soc. Archéol. de Namur*, XLV (1949–50), 147–61.

138. J. Warichez, *L'abbaye de Lobbes depuis les origines jusqu'à 1200* (Tournai, 1909).

139. J. Hoebanx, *L'abbaye de Nivelles* (Brussels, 1952); F. Baix, "Begge," *Dictionnaire d'Histoire et de Géographie ecclésiastique*, VII (1934), cols. 441–48; J. Crepin, "Le monastère des Scots à Fosses," *Terre Wallonne*, VIII (1923), and P. Grosjean, "Notes d'hagiographie celtique, S. Feuillien," *Analecta Bollandiana*, LXXVIII (1957), 373–420; G. Kurth, "Les premiers siècles de l'abbaye de Saint Hubert," *Bull. Commission Royale d'Histoire*, Ser. 5, VIII (1898), 7–112.

140. H. Kesters, "De abdij van Sint-Truiden," *Limburg*, XXX (1951), 61–74, 81–91; F. Rousseau, *La Meuse et le pays mosan*, p. 51 (following *MGH, SS*, II, 267).

141. J. F. Niermeyer, "La Meuse et l'expansion franque vers le Nord," pp. 459–60.

the establishment of the monastic colonies of Stavelot and Malmédy, instituted by St. Remaclius on lands which had been given to him by King Sigebert III, and the monastery of Celles on the Lesse, thanks to the initiative of Remaclius' disciple, St. Hadelin.[142]

If one considers all this, this brief outline will reveal an evident disparity between the western part of our regions, including the Scheldt and Sambre valleys, which had remained a terrain of missionary work where evangelization reached its highest intensity, and the diocese of Tongres, which, like the Cambrai region, had the aspect of an already-stabilized Christianity, except in its distant borderland. No doubt the joint efforts of the bishopric and the monks from Aquitaine and Ireland, very much marked by Romance influence either because of their origin or their training, finally contributed to the counter-balancing, on the cultural level, of the consequences of a rather strong Germanization. This would explain what is called the "reconquest of Romance" in the west, as well as the relative stability of the separation line between Romance and Germanic in the east.

In the eighth century paganism was in full retreat. Yet, despite the efforts and sacrifices, customs remained in many respects close to barbarism: assassinations and brutalities were common occurrences; and the coarsest superstitions continued to be practiced. In a letter to Gerbald, bishop of Liége, Charlemagne was amazed that, about 802–805, a number of common people were still ignorant of the most elementary prayers.[143]

3. Intellectual and Artistic Culture

To appraise with ever-so-little precision the level of intellectual culture in our regions is a delicate and complex enterprise.[144] On this point, as on many others for the era we are dealing with, documentation remains poor

142. J. Yernaux, "Les premiers siècles de l'abbaye de Stavelot-Malmédy (648–1020)," *Bulletin de la Société d'art et d'Histoire du diocèse de Liége,* XIX (1910), 261–436; F. Baix, *Étude sur l'abbaye et la principauté de Stavelot-Malmédy* (Paris, 1924), I.

143. W. A. Eckhardt, *Die Kapitulariensammlung Bischof Ghaerbalds von Lüttich,* pp. 112–14 (Germanenrechte, Neue Folge. Deutschrechtliches Archiv [Göttingen, 1955], V).

144. M. L. W. Laistner, *Thought and Letters in Western Europe: A.D. 500–900* (2d ed.; London, 1957); idem, *The Intellectual Heritage of the Early Middle Ages: Selected Essays* (Ithaca, 1957); P. Lehmann, "Panorama der literarischen Kultur des Abenlandes im 7. Jahrhundert," pp. 845–71, *Caratteri del secolo VII in Occidente* (Settimane . . . [Spoleto, 1958], V, 2) (republished in *Erforschung des Mittelalters,* V, [Stuttgart, 1962], pp. 258–74); P. Riché, *Éducation et Culture dans l'Occident barbare. VIᵉ au VIIIᵉ siècle* (Paris, 1962), from which we borrow the thread of the following report.

and it is necessary to call on rather ill-matched clues in trying to be clear-sighted in the matter.

It is certain, however, that educational concern had not entirely disappeared and that it was even conveyed to the invaders, at least to those who belonged to a somewhat higher social class. But classical education, honored during the last centuries of antiquity, had, if not disappeared in the turmoil of invasions, progressively weakened. Two factors explain this decline: first, it no longer answered either to the structure or to the aspirations of a society fundamentally different from that of the Late Empire; second, having been until that time narrowly integrated only with classical urban living, it shared in the decline of urban living.[145]

Of course it is known that most Frankish princes received at least an elementary education. Even though all of them did not reach the rather limited mastery of King Chilperic I, they knew how to write and they had a basic religious training, which required a certain amount of education. The same was true for the mayors of the palace, who were often in charge of the young sovereigns' education and the education of members of the high aristocracy (like Arnulf of Metz, an ancestor of the Carolingians, or Grimwald and Gertrude, Pepin the Old's children), as well as that of important government officials (counts, etc.). This seemed to have been essentially professional training, in which, however, religious preoccupations and initiation to "sacred" literature were emphasized.[146]

The movement was even more accentuated by the development of educational centers put up and operated by the clergy: the episcopal and monastic schools whose number increased from the seventh century on. In one of these, established in the former Roman *castrum* of Yvois, St. Géry, future bishop of Cambrai, received the first elements of his religious training.[147] For reasons which are easy to understand, the needs of the Church oriented the activities of these centers. This tendency affirmed itself more and more in monasteries, where the influence of the *Scotti* was manifesting itself. Henceforth the literary and oratorical aspect of classical literature was consigned to the background, to the advantage of Bible study and the celebration of the liturgy. This explains how St.

145. P. Riché, "La survivance des écoles publiques en Gaule au Ve siècle," *Le Moyen Age*, LXIII (1957), 421–36.

146. H. Pirenne, "De l'état de l'instruction des laïcs à l'époque mérovingienne," *Rev. Bénédictine*, XLVI (1934), 165–77 (republished in *Histoire économique de l'Occident Médiéval* [Bruges, 1951], pp. 137–50); P. Riché, "L'instruction des laïcs en Gaule mérovingienne au VIIe siècle," *Caratteri del secolo VII in Occidente*, pp. 873–88.

147. *Vita Gaugerici*, ed. Krusch, *MGH, SS. rer. merov.*, III, 652.

Gertrude, abbess of Nivelles, procured some *saints ouvrages* in Rome to enrich her convent's library.[148] In this way, then, Anglo-Saxon missionaries were the true initiators of the new concept of culture which reached full growth during the middle ages. After 680, an almost absolute monopoly of teaching passed into the hands of clergymen, practically the sole possessors or depositories of practical knowledge.

After all allowances have been made, it can be said that much was written in Gaul during the Merovingian epoch: on wax tablets, on papyrus, and on parchment—which replaced papyrus about 700, after the shutting off of the Mediterranean Sea by the Arabs.[149] Written material thus remained rather significant in administrative affairs, at least to the middle of the seventh century. After this its use was limited, on the private level, "to furnish proof or help furnish proof of individual rights." In many cases, however (as has been shown for certain foreign countries, like Bavaria), its true value was largely symbolic, even superstitious, rather than judicial.[150] Written language became more and more incorrect, and this decline was as marked in public or private acts as it was in narrative texts or in the rare inscriptions which have been preserved[151]— the inscription found at Glons, which dates from the time of Sigebert III (633–656), is not an exception.[152]

Curiously, one cannot single out, as far as literature is concerned, one personality of importance north of the Loire who could be compared with Fortunatus or Gregory of Tours. The most remarkable productions were the *vitae*: hagiographies destined first of all for the edification of their auditors and readers.[153] On a background of truth that is difficult to isolate, these authors shamelessly embellished their stories, borrowing

---

148. *Vita Geretrudis, MGH, SS. rer. merov.,* II, 458.

149. See above, n. 103.

150. F. L. Ganshof, "Charlemagne et l'usage de l'écrit en matière administrative," *Le Moyen Age,* LVII (1952), 1–25 (esp. pp. 1–2); P. Riché, *Éducation et culture,* p. 262. For Bavaria: H. Fichtenau, "Carta et notitia en Bavière du VIIIe au Xe siècle," *Le Moyen Age,* LXIX (1963), 105–20 (esp. pp. 114–15).

151. J. Vielliard, *Le latin des diplômes royaux et des chartes privées de l'époque mérovingienne* (Paris, 1927); R. M. Bonnet, *Le latin de Grégoire de Tours* (Paris, 1890).

152. G. Monchamp, "Une inscription mérovingienne inédite à Glons," *Bull. Acad. Roy. de Belgique,* Cl. des Lettres (1901), p. 646: "*Fitaeri tempore Segoberto regi Crodoaldus Fecit,*" or: "*Fieri (?) tempore Sigeberti regis Crodoaldus fecit.*"

153. L. Van der Essen, *Étude critique et littéraire sur les vitae des saints mérovingiens de l'ancienne Belgique* (Paris-Louvain, 1907); W. Wattenbach–W. Levison, *Deutschlands Geschichtsquellen im Mittelalter. Vorzeit und Karolinger,* No. I: *Die Vorzeit von den Anfängen bis zur Herrschaft der Karolinger* (Weimar, 1952); No. 2: *Die Karolinger vom Anfang des 8. Jahrhunderts bis zum Tode Karls des Grossen* (Weimar, 1953).

whole passages from similar works and increasing style-clichés and edifying anecdotes for the purpose of magnifying their heroes' virtues.

The life of St. Géry (*Vita Gaugerici*), composed in Cambrai by a local cleric after 627, belonged to this literary style. The life of St. Vaast (*Vita Vedasti*), written at Elnone about 642 by Jonas de Bobbio, who was also the author of a life of St. Columban, is another example of this style. It was a cleric of northern Gaul (perhaps Baudemond, a monk of Elnone, who later became abbot of St. Peter's in Ghent) who wrote the life of St. Amand (about 690), while in Nivelles, where Irish influence was vigorous, the lives of St. Gertrude (about 670) and St. Aldegonde (about 684) were composed. Two lives of bishops originated in the diocese of Tongres-Maastricht: that of St. Lambert (*Vita Lamberti*, between 718–743) and that of his successor St. Hubert (*Vita Hugberti*, about 743), both written by members of the local clergy.[154] The monastery of Lobbes, however, seems to have had a meritorious literary activity under the leadership of the abbot Ermin (d. 737).[155]

All this forms a rapid survey, whose shady spots it would be vain to try to dissimulate. All these works are known to us, furthermore, only in copies that were transcribed after the dates of their composition. Indeed, only very rare original fragments of the era have survived: a leaf of a monastic rule, the form of which betrays an Irish influence and which came forth from Nivelles, Andenne, or Aldeneyck (600–800); some fragments of a manuscript of Paulus Orosius (about 700), of which nothing is known except that it was in the library of Stavelot monastery during the middle ages; and some excerpts from bookbinders' sides (of which they constituted the support). These bits of written debris are almost the only remaining witnesses of the beginnings of medieval culture in these regions.[156]

154. These different *vitae* were reedited by Krusch and Levison in Vols. II–VII of the *MGH, SS. rer. merov.* See H. Pirenne, *Bibliographie de l'histoire de Belgique* (Brussels, 1931), Nos. 2523–35. For the *Vita Amandi*, which E. de Moreau (above, n. 136) finally attributed to a cleric native to northern Gaul writing at the start of the eighth century, see D. A. Stracke, "Over de Vita Sancti Amandi," *Handelingen van het Geschied-en Oudheidkundige Kring van Kortrijk*, new series, XXVI (1953), 99–179, which supports attributing it to Baudemond and the date 690.

155. E. de Moreau, *Histoire de l'Église*, 2d ed., I, 326–27.

156. F. Masai, "Le manuscrit à miniatures: l'âge pré-roman," *Art mosan et arts anciens au pays de Liége* (Liége, 1951), pp. 63–64. For the first of these manuscripts, preserved in the middle ages in the abbey of St.-Jacques at Liége, see a note by F. Masai in *Scriptorium*, II (1948), 215–20. Remnants of the second manuscript are dispersed between the libraries of Brussels, London, and Paris.

In the artistic field the documentation is more varied, although there are few surviving structures or handicrafts. Most of the funeral *basilicae* whose existence we know of—in Amay, Huy, Namur, and Dinant—were constructed of mud and wood, and so they were unable to resist the forces of time for very long. Even the stone churches that had been built principally in episcopal cities—as in Cambrai on St. Médard's tomb (sixth century), in Maastricht on the tomb of St. Servais (built by Bishop Monulf [about 600]), and in Liége, finally, on the tomb of the martyr St. Lambert (seventh century) [157]—all these, unfortunately, have disappeared. But there are a few vestiges of great value that allow us to appreciate the mastery of certain Merovingian sculptors and builders: the remnants of the arch of Glons, which, on the basis of an inscription, dates back to the reign of Sigebert III (633–656), and the columns of the small church of Hubinne, doubtlessly erected in the first years of the eighth century.[158]

Probably sculpted on the spot by traveling craftsmen, these stones came from quarries in the Ornain valley, southeast of Bar-le-Duc. While they do not have the quality of the almost contemporary reliefs of Jouarre, their extraordinary sense of decorum deserves attention on several counts. Besides the traditional motifs of the Christian East (palmtrees, interwoven foliage, *croix pattée*). transmitted by the marble-workers of Aquitaine, whose decline had already begun (precisely at the end of the seventh century), there are, mainly at Glons, elements of adornment whose success was admired in the eighth and ninth centuries: stalks ending in a spiral, and rosettes surrounded by stylized foliage and scroll patterns stuccoed directly into the rock.[159] According to A. Dasnoy, the arches of Glons and of Hubinne

" bring the proof that a sculpture in stone worthy of interest has manifested itself in the former diocese of Tongres since the Early Middle Ages. This sculpture, decorative and symbolic at the same time, entirely impregnated with Eastern traditions, was not an isolated occurrence, neither was it a servile imitation of some object brought back from the East. It was engraved in the art of an era. . . . Its birth coincided with a true renewal which manifested itself in fields as diverse as economy, letters, and political and religious life."

157. E. de Moreau, *Histoire de l'Église*, 2d ed., II, 336, 370; G. Faider-Feytmans, *La Belgique à l'époque mérovingienne*, p. 107. See also J. Mertens, "Recherches archéologiques dans l'abbaye mérovingienne de Nivelles," *Miscellanea in honorem J. Breuer, Archaeologia Belgica*, LXI (1962), 89–113, which describes the recently unearthed foundations of several Merovingian oratories of the seventh century.

158. See the remarkable works of A. Dasnoy (above, n. 89).

159. In general, see the important works of J. Hubert, *L'art préroman* (Paris, 1938), and *L'architecture religieuse du Haut Moyen Âge en France* (Paris, 1952).

Let us compare this precious evidence with the Merovingian snake of Nivelles, whose style recalls that of certain bronze buckles in Burgundian sculptures: they are perhaps one of the very first autochthonous sculptures cut into rock, as is the sarcophagus with the lid ornamented with stylized leaves that was discovered some time ago in Lobbes.[160] One must be more reserved about the two ivory reliefs representing St. Peter and St. Paul. Made at the end of the sixth or at the beginning of the seventh century, in a workshop of northern Gaul, they probably belong to the Moselle valley rather than to the Meuse.[161]

There are other riches; and the most brilliant contributions of the Germanic invasion in the field of art were in the metallic crafts.[162] The Merovingian tombs, including that of Childeric (d. 480), uncovered in Tournai, and those in the numerous graveyards of the Namur region (Pry, Samson, Eprave, Haillot) and of Hainaut (Trivières) have yielded an impressive amount of jewelry presumably worn with pride by men of the time: necklaces, bracelets, earrings, rings, buttons, belt-plates, and fibulas. And there are decorated arms, axes, hatchets, swords, and even shields.[163]

According to the era, diverse styles influenced the shapes of these objects, but, beyond the multiple varieties, some common traits are recognizable. The range of decorative motifs is very large. They were borrowed from the most diverse civilizations; simple geometric patterns which primitive peoples cherished (squares, lozenges, circles, crosses) go side by side with the interweavings, carved flowers, and scroll ornaments inspired by the East. The taste for stylized ornaments—foliage, animals, or even human effigies—overcame all other considerations.[164] It is a "blacksmith's art," but of sufficient skill to work precious metals with the same competence as iron, bronze, or brass. The most intricate procedures

160. L. Tollenaere, *La sculpture de l'ancien diocèse de Liége à l'époque romane*, pp. 83–84, 286, and Pl. 12C.

161. W. F. Volbach, "Ivoires mosans du haut moyen âge originaires de la région de la Meuse," *L'Art mosan*, ed. P. Francastel (Paris, 1953), pp. 39–46; M. Laurent, "Les ivoires pré-gothiques conservés en Belgique," *Annales de la Société d'Archéologie de Bruxelles*, XXV (1912), 5–25; E. de Moreau, *op. cit.*, 2d ed., II, 358.

162. E. Salin, *La civilisation mérovingienne d'après les sépultures, les textes et le laboratoire*, Vol. III: *Les techniques* (Paris, 1957); G. Faider-Feytmans, *La Belgique à l'époque mérovingienne*, pp. 77–117 (has detailed bibliography).

163. J. Werner, *Münzdatierte austrasische Grabfunde* (Berlin, 1935).

164. There are many general works on the artistic aspect: B. Salin, *Die altgermanische Tierornamentik* (2d ed.; Stockholm, 1935); N. Aberg, *The Occident and the Orient in the Art of the Seventh Century*, Vol. III: *The Merovingian Empire* (Stockholm, 1947); W. Holmqvist, *Germanic Art during the First Millennium A.D.* (Stockholm, 1955); J. Hubert, *Les origines de l'art français* (Paris, 1947).

withheld no secret from these men: neither damascening, the casting of gold and silver in furrows previously carved into the iron, nor partitioning, by which a design is put on a metal plate by means of a golden thread or brazed copper—empty spaces being encrusted with precious stones or colored glass. The brightness of the colors and the clear-cut designs are as surprising as is the manual skill they imply of their craftsmen.[165]

It would be wrong to consider these people "barbarians." They were the heirs of an already-old tradition, and the Gallo-Roman goldsmiths rapidly adapted themselves to their patrons' taste. This fact is certain, at least as far as the Namur region is concerned in the fifth century, and it is admissible with no difficulty at all later on when local artists are seen to have assimilated the style of Irish miniatures with the same success, as is proven by the Merovingian shrine of Andenne.[166] Nor should we forget that the Limousin, Eloi, bishop of Noyon-Tournai and Dagobert's adviser, has also left us the glowing memory of a goldsmith of exceptional talent. Far from declining, this artistic growth constantly increased in the course of the centuries under study, and, at the start of the eighth century, the perfection of this art, as of many others, had definitely moved to northern Gaul.

III. CONCLUSION: THE ASCENT OF AUSTRASIA AND THE CAROLINGIANS

It is undeniable that northern Gaul suffered more during the fifth century, under Germanic invasions and after these incursions, than did the southern regions. Under the impulse of Frankish kings—and monks and bishops, of course—but also under the impulse of artists and anonymous artisans "it makes up for its delay"; and it can be said that this was finally done in the eighth century.[167] Everything had changed, however, from what it had been in the Roman era: state structures, religious beliefs, forms of

165. E. Salin, *op. cit.*, pp. 166–210; *idem*, "Les origines de la damasquinure mérovingienne," *Hommage à W. Deonna* (Paris, 1957), pp. 435–41; W. Holmqvist, *Tauschierte Metallarbeiten des Nordens aus Römerzeit und Völkerwanderung* (Stockholm, 1951) (for the importance of the Meuse basin, pp. 53–54); A. Dasnoy, "Les premières damasquinures mérovingiennes de la région namuroise," *Annales de la Soc. Archéologique de Namur*, XLVII (1954), 267–85; *idem*, "Les trouvailles mérovingiennes de Dinant," *Mélanges F. Rousseau* (Brussels, 1958), pp. 191–200.

166. A. Dasnoy, "Le reliquaire mérovingien d'Andenne," *Annales de la Soc. Archéologique de Namur*, XLIX (1958), 41–60.

167. L. Génicot, "Aux origines de la civilisation occidentale," pp. 90–91. See also L. Dupraz (above, n. 66).

economy, and the arts; rivers had taken over the role formerly played by roads and small boroughs had taken the place of the *civitates*.

Within this whole, moreover, local differences were also perceptible. In the end, areas grouped in the territory of the former diocese of Tongres seem to have suffered less than those farther west, which sheds light on the fact that a more rapid renewal obtained in the Tongres area in both religious affairs and in the most ordinary aspects of material living. The survival of metallurgy and the early awakening of trade in the Meuse valley created centers where an embryonic urban life came into being. In the west, on the contrary, upheavals had been more serious and the Germanic imprint was more deeply engraved. The reconstruction of ecclesiastical organization was slower, the fight against paganism was more vigorous, and the revival of trade in the Scheldt valley was more protracted.

Already visible in the sixth century, the disparity became more evident in the seventh. This explains the increasingly important influence exercised by Austrasia within the Frankish kingdom, and the ravages undergone by the southern regions underline the disequilibrium even more. Through many political vicissitudes, Austrasia's power and cohesion was strengthened. Consequently, the role of its aristocracy, under the leadership of the descendants of Arnulf of Metz and Pepin the Old, whose family heritage was concentrated between the Rhine, the Meuse and the Moselle, acquired a more and more distinct outline.

First being more or less autonomous, Austrasia later dominated the entire Frankish realm. This success was the work of Pepin II (d. 714), but it would be exploited and extended by Charles Martel, his prestige bolstered and ensured by his energetic fight against the Arabs. As a sign of the times, it was in Estinnes that the council in charge of the reform of the Frankish church gathered in 743; and henceforth the residences of Jupille, Herstal, and Chèvremont were to welcome the mayors of the palace during important assemblies and important religious holidays.[168]

168. C. de Clercq, *La législation religieuse franque de Clovis à la fin du 9ᵉ siècle. Étude sur les actes des conciles et des capitulaires, les statuts diocésains et les règles monastiques* (2 vols.; Louvain-Paris, 1936–58). For the presence of Carolingians at Jupille: F. L. Ganshof, "Note sur une charte privée carolingienne datée de Jupille," *Mélanges F. Rousseau* (Brussels, 1958), pp. 309–19; and at Herstal: *idem, La Belgique carolingienne* (Brussels, 1958), pp. 22–23, 47; F. Rousseau, "Les Carolingiens et l'Ardenne" (above, n. 84) and E. Ewig, "Résidence et capitale" (above, n. 64), pp. 54, 57–58. One will find a provisory list of Carolingian domains in F. Rousseau, *La Meuse et le pays mosan*, pp. 221–43; J. W. Thompson, *The Dissolution of the Carolingian Fisc in the Ninth Century* (Berkeley-London, 1935); G. Rotthoff, *Studien zur Geschichte des Reichsgutes in Niederlothringen und Friesland während der sächsisch-salischen Kaiserzeit*, Rheinisches Archiv (Bonn, 1953), LXIV.

Placed by fate at the borders of an expanding Germanic world, our Romance regions—mainly those that were centered in the Meuse valley, and by paying the price of an adaptive effort which did not exclude sacrifice or renouncement—succeeded in recreating a new equilibrium. At the same time they set free unsuspected forces whose impetus Pepin the Short and Charlemagne were to master and control, and with which they would build a new empire.

KHAN BORIS AND THE CONVERSION OF BULGARIA: A CASE STUDY OF THE IMPACT OF CHRISTIANITY ON A BARBARIAN SOCIETY

Richard E. Sullivan

Michigan State University

KHAN BORIS AND THE CONVERSION OF BULGARIA:
A CASE STUDY OF THE IMPACT OF CHRISTIANITY ON A BARBARIAN SOCIETY

In 601 Pope Gregory the Great sent the following exhortation to King Ethelbert of Kent:

> Therefore, glorious son, take care with a solicitous mind of the grace you have divinely received. Hasten to extend the Christian faith among the people subjected to you. Multiply the zeal of your righteousness for their conversion. Suppress the worship of idols. Overthrow the temples. Edify the manners of your subjects by great cleanness of life, by exhorting, terrifying, soothing, correcting, and illustrating with the example of good works, so that you will find in heaven your rewarder whose name and reputation you have spread on earth.[1]

This passage tempts the historian of Christian expansion in the early middle ages to think that he has within his grasp important clues relating to a vital issue in missionary history, namely, the nature of the impact of Christianity on a pagan society. Pope Gregory unmistakably implies that the introduction of the new faith into a pagan land would work profound changes on the entire culture of that land. He indicates that traditional institutions, manners, ethical standards, ideas, and values would be transformed under the weight of a completely new order. He broadly hints that this transformation would eventuate in so striking an improvement in the condition of the converts that God Almighty would be pleased and the fame of the reborn people would rise in the view of the entire world. Gregory further suggests that the ruler of a people in the process of conversion holds the key to this great transformation. Upon the ruler's assiduousness, devotion, and skill in the execution of his heavy responsibilities would hinge not only the success of the conversion of a whole nation but also the nature of the impact of the new religion on an entire cultural pattern.

However, sober reflection on this passage—seemingly so rich in terms of assessing the impact of conversion—suggests caution. Gregory was not

1. *Gregorii I papae Registrum Epistolarum*, XI, 9, eds. Paulus Ewald and Ludowicus M. Hartmann, *MGH, Epistolae*, II, 308–9.

reporting what had actually happened in Kent as a consequence of the acceptance of Christianity by the people living there, nor was he recording what Ethelbert had done to assure the successful conversion of his people and to effect a change in their customary pattern of culture; the pope was expressing only a pious expectation which suggests the possibilities of the revolutionary impact of Christianity without revealing what actually happened.

Most of the sources that deal with Christian expansion in the early middle ages suffer from this basic limitation. Although they broadly hint that Christianity exerted a powerful transformational influence on pagan cultures and that the role of princes was decisive in the conversion process, they provide exceedingly scant information about the exact way the new religion worked to change pagan societies and about the issues posed for newly converted rulers as they undertook to introduce Christianity into their realms. Ranging over the whole era, from the conversion of Clovis at the end of the fifth century to the conversion of Scandinavia in the twelfth century, one finds little evidence upon which to construct an adequate picture of what conversion implied for newly converted kings and the societies under their command. This lacuna in the sources, attributable chiefly to the fact that most material dealing with missionary history was written to glorify the deeds of missionaries and to laud the support given them by their lay and ecclesiastical sponsors dwelling behind the religious frontier, has long made any attempt to discuss early medieval Christian expansion somewhat one-sided and incomplete. More significantly, it has made any firm grasp of the impact of the conversion process on primitive societies virtually impossible. Although the conversion experience was decisive in the history of these societies, the modern historian has been unable to adequately discuss this critical aspect in the making of medieval civilization.

However, at least one case appears to offer a good opportunity for penetrating the darkness that surrounds the impact of conversion on the policies and actions of a newly converted ruler and on the culture of the society over which he ruled. This case is the conversion of the Bulgars during the reign of Khan Boris (c. 852–889). Because this event became involved in the larger issues of the so-called Photian schism, a relatively greater amount of information pertaining to Boris' activities has survived than is usual for the early middle ages, and this study will analyze this information primarily with the view of reconstructing the situation in Bulgaria during the conversion period. A correlative attempt has been to extract from this information as precise a description as possible of the manner in which the coming of the new religion affected Bulgar institutions and ideas. Moreover, the scrutiny of this material, primarily from the Bulgar point of view, seems to suggest valuable new insights into the tasks facing a newly converted ruler bent on completing the conversion of his people, and it also seems to throw considerable light on the impact of the new religion on a primitive, undeveloped culture.

The impact of Christianity on Bulgaria is much more easily discernible than in most other cases involving the conversion of entire nations during the early middle ages because of the unique nature of the sources pertaining to the conversion process in Bulgaria. These sources, in turn, derive their special quality primarily from the historical situations that produced them. Therefore a brief description of the major documents and an explanation of the circumstances surrounding their creation is a necessary preliminary step for a study of the impact of Christianity on Bulgar society.

The conversion process commenced in Bulgaria long before the reign of Boris. As early as the seventh century, when the Bulgars made their first assaults on Byzantine territory south of the Danube, these invaders began to feel the impact of Byzantine civilization, including its religion. In the incessant wars between these two states, Christian prisoners who were captured by the Bulgars continued to practice their religion among the pagans. On the other hand, Bulgar captives were carried off to Constantinople, converted to Christianity, and later returned to their native land, where they remained Christian. Byzantine merchants and ambassadors circulated in Bulgaria and Bulgars traveled in the Byzantine Empire. Bulgar rulers also established diplomatic relationships with the Frankish kings and consequently learned something of the religion and culture of the western European world. However, despite these important penetrations of the Bulgar state by Christian influences during the seventh, eighth, and early ninth centuries, the Bulgars remained, officially, a pagan people until 864.

In that year, however, a dramatic turn of events occurred. Byzantine forces, provoked by Boris' efforts to form an alliance with the kingdom of the East Franks against Moravia, suddenly attacked and defeated the Bulgars. As a part of the peace settlement that followed the Greek victory, Boris agreed to accept baptism and to convert his people under Greek auspices. This decision, as we shall see, caused a considerable stir not only in Bulgaria but throughout the Christian world. The interest of outsiders in Bulgar affairs was intensified in 866 when Boris turned his back on Constantinople to seek help from Rome. And it reached a crisis when, in 870, the Bulgars returned to Byzantium for religious guidance. Thus, as the Christianization of Bulgaria proceeded under the leadership of Boris, a vigorous competition arose between Rome and Constantinople for jurisdiction over the Bulgars. That dispute raged throughout the reign of Boris. Out of the combination of circumstances connected with the original conversion, the transfer of allegiance, and the jurisdictional battle, several documents emerged which permit us to see with unusual clarity how Boris and his kingdom were affected by the ruler's acceptance of Christianity and by his decision to impose the new religion on his subjects.[2]

By far the most important piece of evidence relating to this problem is a long pastoral letter written to Boris by Pope Nicholas I in 866.[3] Nicholas' letter was prompted by the appearance in Rome, in 866, of a delegation sent by the khan, who had become displeased with the Greek clergymen who entered his realm in 864 to help in the task of converting his people. Through his legates, Boris made known his willingness to

---

2. For a treatment of the early history of the Bulgars, their relationships with the Byzantine Empire and the Franks, and the penetration of Byzantine-Christian influences into Bulgaria, see Francis Dvornik, *Les Slaves, Byzance, et Rome au IXe siècle* (Paris, 1926), pp. 99–103, 184–86; Matthew Spinka, *A History of Christianity in the Balkans: A Study in the Spread of Byzantine Culture among the Slavs, Studies in Church History*, Vol. I (Chicago, 1933), pp. 25–36; Steven Runciman, *A History of the First Bulgarian Empire* (London, 1930), pp. 22–98; W. N. Slatarski, *Geschichte der Bulgaren*, Pt. I: *Von der Gründung des Bulgarischen Reiches bis zur Türkenzeit (679–1396)* (*Bulgarische Bibliothek*, ed. Gustav Weigand, No. 5) (Leipzig, 1918), pp. 1–41; Christian Gérard, *Les Bulgares de la Volga et les Slaves du Danube. Le problème des races et les barbares* (Paris, 1939), pp. 6–182. These accounts deal adequately with the major Greek literary sources concerning Byzantine-Bulgar relations prior to the conversion; however, some interesting new insights may be gained from a study of inscriptions from the pre-conversion period; see V. Beševliev and H. Grégoire, "Les inscriptions protobulgares," *Byzantion*, XXV–XXVI–XXVII (1955–56–57), 853–80; XXVIII (1958), 253–323; XXIX–XXX (1959–60), 477–500, for the texts of some of these inscriptions, a translation into French, and extensive commentary (this work has not yet been completed). An extensive bibliography concerning Bulgaria is provided by Gyula Moravcsik, *Byzantinoturcica*, Vol. I: *Die byzantinischen Quellen der Geschichte der Türkvolker* (2d ed.; Berlin, 1958), pp. 112–19.

3. *Nicolai I. Papae Epistolae*, No. 99, ed. Ernestus Perels, *MGH, Ep.*, VI, 568–600. Hereafter this letter will be cited as Nicholas, *Ep.*, No. 99, with appropriate chapter and page number. This letter has also been published with a Bulgarian translation in *Fontes Latini Historicae Bulgaricae*, eds. Ivan Dujčev, Mihail Vojnov, Strašimir Lišev, and Borislav Primov (Academia Litterarum Bulgarica. Institutum Historicum. *Fontes Historiae Bulgaricae*, VII) (2 vols.; Sofia, n.d.), II, 65–125.

accept Roman spiritual overlordship and to place the missionary undertaking in Roman hands. The Bulgar legates brought with them a series
of topics upon which the khan desired information. Nicholas framed his
responses with care and dispatched them to Bulgaria, along with books
and a law code, in the hands of two bishops, Paul of Populonia and
Formosus of Porto.[4]

An analysis of Nicholas' responses provides several clues which
demonstrate the crucial importance of his document in reconstructing
the situation in Bulgaria at this critical moment in the conversion process.
Nicholas indicates that Boris had directed a list of specific questions to
the papal curia. At the very beginning of his letter the pope speaks of
vestra consulta and apologizes for not being able to answer at length *per
singula*.[5] In another place he refers to Boris' *questiones*.[6] Nicholas repeatedly
reveals the manner in which the khan had addressed him in search of
guidance. In many places he indicates that Boris had made a positive
statement to him on some matter about which a papal opinion was
desired, and in these cases the pope began his response with expressions
like *dicitis, asseritis, enarratis,* and *indicatis*.[7] In other places the pope
indicates that the khan had asked a question, and in these cases he
employed such expressions as *consulitis, nosse cupitis, scire cupitis, inquiritis,
interrogatis, exquiritis, investigatis, scire velle significatis, sciscitamini, requisites,
requiritis, postulatis,* and *desideratis nosse*.[8] These terms, followed in each
case by a dependent clause introduced by "that...," leave little doubt
that Nicholas repeatedly paraphrased Boris' statements or questions in
framing the opening sentence of each response, and it is sometimes obvious
that he simply restated Boris' words exactly as they had been received.[9]
Furthermore, there is evidence that in composing his letter Nicholas

---

4. The chief sources discussing the appearance of the Bulgar delegation in Rome are
the following: the biography of Nicholas I in *Le Liber Pontificalis*, text, introduction, and
commentary by Abbé L. Duchesne (*Bibliothèque des écoles françaises d'Athènes et de Rome*)
(2d ed., 3 vols.; Paris, 1955–57), II, 164; the biography of Pope Hadrian II, *ibid.*, p. 185;
Annales Bertiniani, annus 866, ed. G. Waitz, *MGH, Scriptores rerum Germanicarum in usum
scholarum* (Hanover, 1883), pp. 85–86; *Iohannis VIII. papae Epistolae*, No. 192, ed. Ericus
Caspar, *MGH, Ep.*, VII, 154; and *Anastasii Bibliothecarii Epistolae sive Praefationes*, No. 5,
eds. E. Perels and G. Laehr, *MGH*, VII, 412.

5. Nicholas, *Ep.*, No. 99, p. 568.

6. *Ibid.*, Chs. 1, 13, pp. 568, 575, also in the concluding statement, p. 600.

7. *Ibid.*, Chs. 3, 6, 14, 25, 33, 35, 38, 40, 42, 54, 55, 57, 62, 66, 67, 77, 78, 79, 86, 94,
103, 104, pp. 569, 572, 575, 579–83, 587–91, 593–95, 597, 599.

8. *Ibid.*, Chs. 7–13, 15–18, 34, 37, 39, 45, 47–49, 51–53, 56, 59–61, 63, 68–75, 80, 81,
83–85, 87, 88, 90, 92, 93, 95, 98, 99, 101, 103–5, pp. 572–75, 576, 577, 581, 582, 585–99.

9. *Ibid.*, Chs. 4, 20, pp. 570–71, 579.

followed an order dictated by the listing he had received from Boris. He began his first response by writing *in prima questionum vestrorum*, and he occasionally used such words as *praeterea* and *porro* for introducing a new topic. He opened his last response with *postremo*.[10]

This internal evidence convincingly demonstrates that Nicholas' letter provides a direct link with Bulgar affairs. Boris had, through his legates, placed a list of specific questions before Nicholas, and had, it seems evident, compiled these questions on the basis of problems that had arisen in Bulgaria between his conversion in 864 and the dispatch of his legation to Rome in 866. Nicholas I, ignorant except for the most general knowledge of affairs in Bulgaria prior to the appearance of the legates bringing these questions, was content to organize his pastoral responses around Boris' questions, and in almost every answer he restated, in some form, the statement or question with which the Bulgar khan had confronted him. The papal letter is therefore filled with reflections on genuine Bulgar problems that had been formulated by the Bulgar ruler. It is not, in other words, a document which the pope composed by bringing together a variety of ideas and admonitions which he thought ought properly be called to the attention of any newly converted prince. The letter—when looked at in terms of what Boris asked—supplies precious details about the problems and situations which confronted a ruler and a society during the early stages of the conversion process; but it has not received adequate attention from this point of view. In the pages that follow, this document will constitute not only the fundamental source of information about the impact of Christianity on Bulgaria but also the major control for the evaluation of several other sources.

Less revealing, but still important, is another pastoral letter dispatched to Boris, this one written by Photius, patriarch of Constantinople.[11] This lengthy document was composed after the baptism of Boris, which probably occurred in the summer of 865, and before the replacement of

---

10. *Ibid.*, Ch. 1, p. 568, Chs. 6, 7, 14, 15, 34, 49, 63, pp. 572–73, 575–76, 581, 586, 590, Ch. 106, p. 599.

11. Φώτιου . . . Πατριάρχου Κωνσταντινουπόλεως 'Επιστολαί (No. 6) ὑπο Ιωαννου Ν. Βαλεττα (London, 1864), pp. 200–248. This work will be cited hereafter as Photius, *Ep.*, ed. Valetta, with appropriate letter and page numbers. The letter is also printed in Migne, *PG*, CII, cols. 628–96. Basil Laourdas, "A New Letter of Photius to Boris," 'Ελληνικα, XIII (1954), 263–65, provides a pertinent letter missing from the Valetta edition. In this letter Photius announced to Boris the death of the Emperor Michael; but it does not throw any specific light on the situation in Bulgaria.

Greek missionaries in Bulgaria by those sent from Rome in 867.[12] Photius' letter was not, like Nicholas', prompted by any specific request for information. The patriarch gratuitously conceived it to be his duty to instruct his spiritual son, Boris, at a vital moment in the prince's career.

> I place these few out of many tokens of friendship and filiation from God, these original notes of virtue before you, O my true and genuine spiritual son, so that when you turn your eyes to them and conform and compare yourself to them, you will not have difficulty in observing and understanding what sort are the actions which will make beauty flourish in your mind.[13]

To this end, Photius drew together a series of remarks touching on two major issues. First he set forth the orthodox tenets of the faith, basing his discussion on the decisions of the seven ecumenical councils and highlighting the heretical ideas disposed of by these councils; then he turned to a discourse on the moral qualities befitting a Christian and especially a Christian prince. His concerns ranged over a great variety of matters, indicating that he intended his letter to serve as a handbook for the moral education of an audience unfamiliar with Christian ethical concepts. All of these matters are treated with considerable grandiloquence, which gives the tract a sophisticated tone.

At first glance Photius' letter seems to have little bearing on the situation in Bulgaria. Its tone and manner appear too stilted to answer to the needs of a newly converted prince wrestling with the problems of Christianizing his primitive subjects, and the theological issues are treated on a level that seems beyond the grasp of the neophyte Bulgars—including the khan. These features of the letter have led some authorities to suggest that Photius was simply displaying his vast learning to impress an untutored barbarian recently brought under the sway of Byzantium,[14] but such a judgment is unwarranted and unjustified. An analysis of this letter in the light of other sources—especially Pope Nicholas' responses—

12. V. Grumel, *Les regestes des actes du patriarchat de Constantinople* (Istanbul, 1932), I, Pt. 2, No. 478, 87, thinks that the letter dates from May, 866. Moravcsik, *Byzantinoturcica*, I, 475, says the letter was sent "um das Jahr 866."

13. Photius, *Ep.*, No. 6, Ch. 114, ed. Valetta, pp. 247–48. For an interesting discussion of the intent of Photius' letter, see I. Dujcev, "Au lendemain de la conversion du peuple bulgare. L'Épitre de Photius," *Mélanges de science religieuse*, VIII (1951), 211–16. Dujcev concludes, somewhat surprisingly, that the tone of Photius' letter played a significant role in forcing Boris to turn to Rome.

14. J. Hergenröther, *Photius, Patriarch von Constantinopel. Sein Leben, seine Schriften und das griechische Schisma* (3 vols.; Regensburg, 1867–69), I, 604.

reveals that Photius' discussion was pointed toward the very issues that Boris found difficult to handle in his efforts to convert his subjects: the problem of orthodoxy; the question of moral reform (especially as the prince should exemplify Christian conduct for his people); the problem of adding Christian principles to the administration of justice, to the choice of the royal advisers, and to other political processes; and the means of offsetting resistance to these new policies.

Photius was in an excellent position to possess considerable knowledge of Bulgar problems by virtue of his relationship with Greek clergymen who worked there as missionaries and with Greek and Bulgar diplomatic agents who passed back and forth between Byzantium and Bulgaria during the period of the letter's composition. The crucial importance of Bulgaria to imperial policy must certainly have prompted high Greek officials to seek information on Bulgar affairs, information which Photius shared by virtue of his high office. On other occasions Photius had demonstrated a keen interest in Byzantine missionary expansion, the prime case being the dispatch of Cyril and Methodius to Moravia just prior to the opening of the Bulgar mission. This experience also armed the patriarch with some knowledge of what was significant to a newly converted prince.

In analyzing his letter in detail it would appear that it takes its tone of sophistication not so much from the issues dealt with as from the exalted role its author assigns to a prince in a Christian society. One would hardly expect less from an ardent admirer of the Byzantine imperial court and of the refinements of the Byzantine court circle. The patriarch's exaltation of the Christian prince in a Christian society need not preclude the possibility that he can also direct his spiritual son's attention to those practical issues which the patriarch knew were vital to the advance of Christianity in Bulgaria. Nor did Photius' grandiose style necessarily preclude Boris' understanding the letter's ideas upon the essential features of the conversion process.

What the patriarch seemed determined to achieve by sending his letter to Boris was to place in the hands of his spiritual son a set of principles and a list of practical suggestions which would be useful in facing the problems likely to confront the newly converted ruler. As a promoter of Byzantine missionary expansion, and as an astute political figure well informed in imperial relationships with foreign powers, Photius was in all likelihood fully aware of some of the actual problems in Bulgaria and fully capable of anticipating problems that might arise to face a newly converted prince struggling to Christianize his subjects.

Thus there appear to be many justifications for using Photius' letter as a source that indirectly reflects conditions and problems existing in Bulgaria shortly after the official introduction of Christianity. On the basis of our knowledge of Photius' interests and inclinations, it also appears that his letter mirrors with some accuracy those problems relating to the role of the prince in the conversion process, to the political impact of the new religion on a primitive regime, to dogmatic and disciplinary issues, and to the intellectual life in a newly converted realm. Although not as directly derived from a specific Bulgar source as was Nicholas' letter, the patriarch's letter to Boris warrants respect as an indirect reflection of the Bulgar situation as seen by a sagacious ecclesiastical statesman; it is worthy of respect because of Photius' knowledge of a wide range of issues.

These two pastoral letters are supplemented by other letters that throw light on the situation in Bulgaria during the years between Boris' conversion and his retirement to a monastery. All of these documents originated either in the papal curia or at the Byzantine court, and all in some way bore on the bitterly debated issue of ecclesiastical jurisdiction over Bulgaria.[15] Some were addressed by Popes Hadrian II and John VIII to the Byzantine court and the patriarch, threatening the use of strong measures if the Greeks did not leave Bulgaria to Roman juris-diction.[16] Others went from Rome to Bulgaria, pleading with Boris and his advisers to return to Roman jurisdiction after the Bulgar defection from Rome in 870.[17] Internal evidence offers excellent grounds for believing that the popes based these letters, in part, on a knowledge of

15. The quarrel over Bulgaria is traced in detail by Hergenröther, *ibid.*, *passim*; by Dvornik, *The Photian Schism, History and Legend* (Cambridge, 1948); by Émile Amann, *L'époque carolingiennne* (*Histoire de l'église depuis les origines jusqu'à nos jours*, publiée sous la direction de Augustin Fliche et Victor Martin, T. VI) (Paris, 1947), pp. 465–501; and by A. Lapôtre, *L'Europe et le Saint-Siège à l'époque carolingienne*, Pt. 1: *Le pape Jean VIII* (Paris, 1895), *passim*.

16. *Hadriani II. Papae Epistolae*, Nos. 41, 42, ed. Ernestus Perels, *MGH, Ep.*, VI, 759–62; *Iohannis VIII. Papae Epistolae*, Nos., 68, 69, 207–9, 259, ed. Caspar, *MGH, Ep.*, VII, 62–65, 173–74, 179–80, 185–86, 229; *Fragmenta Registri Iohannis VIII. Papae*, No. 40, ed. Ericus Caspar, *MGH, Ep.*, VII, 296. See also Jaffé-Wattenbach, *Regesta Pontificum Romanorum*, No. 2915 (Leipzig, 1885), I, 371.

17. *Iohannis VIII. Papae Epistolae*, Nos. 66, 67, 70, 71, 182, 183, 192, 198, 298, 308, ed. Caspar, *MGH, Ep.*, VII, 58–62, 65–67, 146–47, 153–54, 158–59, 260, 266–67; *Fragmenta Registri Iohannis VIII. Papae*, Nos. 7, 37, ed. Caspar, *MGH, Ep.*, VII, 277, 294–95. The parts of these papal letters pertaining to Bulgar affairs, as well as those cited in the preceding note, are printed with a Bulgarian translation in *FLHB*, eds. Dujčev *et al.*, II, 129–31 (Hadrian's letters), 137–81 (John VIII's letters).

affairs in Bulgaria derived from their agents who had journeyed there or from Bulgar legations to Rome.

One letter of Photius to the patriarchs of the eastern churches sought to enlist their aid in attaching Bulgaria to Constantinople.[18] This letter reflects the patriarch's extensive knowledge of the activities of Roman missionaries in Bulgaria; it also suggests not only that Photius was interested in Bulgar affairs but that he had means of keeping informed of developments there even when the Romans were in command of the missionary operation. Pope Nicholas I wrote Archbishops Hincmar of Rheims and Luitbertus of Mainz, informing them at some length on Bulgar affairs, and attempting in this fashion to involve them, their kings, and their suffragans in the struggle over Bulgaria.[19]

The Bulgar issue was dealt with by the papal secretary, Anastasius Bibliothecarius, in a prefatory letter to his Latin version of the decrees of the general council held in Constantinople in 869–870.[20] Anastasius was in Constantinople at the time of this council, before which a Bulgar legation appeared to request a decision on the question of whether Bulgaria was subject to Roman or Greek jurisdiction. Thus he was in a position to garner some first-hand information about Bulgar affairs. (However, he was not present at the sessions of the council when the Bulgar issue was debated; his account of that event is derived from other papal legates who were in attendance.)

As might be expected, all these documents are strongly partisan and given to distortion in the hope of gaining advantage in the struggle for Bulgaria. Most of the authors felt the need to explain what had happened in Bulgaria, but most of the recipients were also aware of the course of events in Bulgaria, which made it pointless to misrepresent the truth too badly. As a result, these letters rather accurately reflect the progress made in the Christianization of Bulgaria. From them emerges additional and definite information on the problems encountered by Boris in converting his people.

Finally, there are some miscellaneous sources that touch upon the situation in Bulgaria. The biographies of Popes Nicholas I and Hadrian II

18. Photius, *Ep.*, No. 4, ed. Valetta, pp. 165–81.

19. See *Nicolai I. Papae Epistolae*, No. 100, ed. Perels, *MGH, Ep.*, VI, 600–609, for the letter to Hincmar of Rheims. *Annales Fuldenses*, a. 868, ed. Fridericus Kurze, *MGH, SS. rer. Germ.* (Hanover, 1891), pp. 66–67, signifies that the same letter was sent to the bishops of the East Frankish kingdom.

20. *Anastasii Bibliothecarii Ep. sive Praef.*, No. 5, eds. Perels and Laehr, *MGH, Ep.*, VII, 411–15. That portion of this document appropriate to Bulgar affairs is printed with a Bulgarian translation in *FLHB*, II, 196–203.

made careful record of the conversion of Bulgaria, especially in view of Boris' submission to Rome in 866 and his ultimate return to Constantinople.[21] Both Byzantine and Latin chroniclers were impressed enough by the baptism of Boris and the events connected with it to supply some information, although, unfortunately, they did not remain sufficiently interested in Bulgar affairs to complete the story of the Christianization of the land.[22] There is also a biography of St. Clement of Ochrida, a disciple of the famous Moravian missionary, Methodius. Clement entered Bulgaria about 885, after being driven from Moravia, and he spent the rest of his life working as a missionary in various part of Bulgaria.[23] A fragmentary life of St. Nahum, another refugee from Moravia who labored in Bulgaria, also survives.[24] From these sources one catches an occasional glimpse of Boris' actions and problems, although this information hardly permits a full reconstruction of the progress of Christianity in Bulgaria.

21. *Liber pontificalis*, ed. Duchesne, II, 164–65, 182–85. The portions of these papal lives relevant to Bulgar affairs are printed with a Bulgarian translation in *FLHB*, II, 184–95; however, the Latin version supplied here has been taken from the inferior edition in Migne, *PL*, CXXVIII, cols. 1379–96.

22. *Annales Bertiniani, a.* 864, 866, ed. Waitz, *MGH, SS. rer. Germ.*, pp. 72, 85–86; *Annales Fuldenses, a.* 863, 866, 867, ed. Kurze, *MGH, SS. rer. Germ.*, pp. 56, 65–66; Regino of Prum, *Chronicon, a.* 868, ed. F. Kurze, *MGH, SS. rer. Germ.* (Hanover, 1890), pp. 95–96; Georgius Monachus (Continuatus), *Vitae imperatorum recentiorum: De Michaele et Theodora*, Ch. 16, ed. I. Bekker, *Corpus Scriptorum Historiae Byzantinae* (Bonn, 1838), p. 824; Georgius Cedrenus, *Compendium Historiarum*, ed. I. Bekker, *CSHB* (2 vols.; Bonn, 1838–39), II, 151–53; Josephus Genesius, *Regum Liber IV de Michaele Theophili Filio*, ed. C. Lachmann, *CSHB* (Bonn, 1834), p. 97; Theophanes Continuatus, *Chronographia*, IV, Chs. 13–15, ed. I. Bekker, *CSHB* (Bonn, 1838), pp. 162–65; Symeon Magister ac Logotheta, *Annales: De Michaele et Theodora*, Chs. 21–22, 25, ed. I. Bekker, *CSHB* (Bonn, 1838), pp. 664–66; Ioannas Zonaras, *Epitomae Historiarum libri XIII–XVIII*, XVI, Ch. 2, ed. T. Büttner-Wobst, *CSHB* (Bonn, 1897), pp. 387–89; Theophylactus Bulgariae Archiepiscopus, *Historia Martyrii XV Martyrum*, Chs. 28–55, Migne, *PG*, CXXVI, cols. 189–221. The portions of the Latin chronicles relevant to Bulgarian history are printed with a Bulgarian translation in *FLHB*, II, 43–45 (*Annales Fuldenses*), 287–88 (*Annales Bertiniani*), 306–7 (Regino).

23. Theophylactus Bulgariae Archiepiscopus, *Vita s. Clementis*, Migne, *PG*, CXXVI, cols. 1193–239. A better edition of this work, A. Milev, *Teofilakt Ohridski, Žitie na Kliment Ohridski. Prevod ot grŭckija original, uvod i beležki* (Sofia, 1955), was not available for this study. For the authorship of this life, see Methodie Kusseff, "St. Clement of Ochrida," *Slavonic (and East European) Review*, XXVII(1948–49), 193–215, and especially I. Snegarov, "Les sources sur la vie et l'activité de Clément d'Ochrida," *Byzantinobulgarica*, I (1962), 79–119.

24. The old Slavonic text and an English translation of this life are provided by Methodie Kusseff, "St. Nahum," *Slavonic and East European Review*, XXIX (1950–51), 142–44.

Viewed collectively, these several sources leave much to be desired when one contemplates the task of assessing the impact of Christianity on Bulgar society and the role of the prince in promoting the conversion of Bulgaria. None of them emanated directly from Bulgaria, a fact which obviously precludes certainty in their treatment of affairs in Bulgaria. The historian is forced to proceed by inference in using these sources, never an ideal—or even adequate—mode of argument. Many of the documents are surcharged with partisan issues, which very likely caused their authors to disregard more significant factors existing in Bulgaria simply because these matters had no direct relevance to the issue under dispute. Moreover, all were written by men who, at best, had limited contact with the Bulgars and who had never been in Bulgaria as eye-witnesses to the events they treated. Such reporters were bound to suffer serious limitations in their grasp of realities in Bulgaria and conclusions derived from such evidence must be tentative. Nevertheless, these documents abound in quick glimpses and veiled allusions to conditions in Bulgaria. This is so primarily because their authors had a vital interest in conditions in Bulgaria. The winning or losing of jurisdiction over that important realm depended, to some degree, upon a grasp of the situation there. Unlike so many other cases in missionary history, these documents were not composed to recount the heroic deeds of missionaries and to record the victories won for the faith. A careful, systematic exploitation of these documents, governed by a firm effort to see the conversion process from the Bulgar position, yields a considerable body of information bearing on the problems raised for a prince by his decision to convert his people and on the influences exerted on the culture of a nation by the new religion. At least the harvest is richer than in most other cases involving the conversion of entire nations in the early middle ages.

The sources dealing with the Christianization of Bulgaria dramatically highlight the first problem facing Boris when he decided to become a Christian. His decision plunged his kingdom into a grim crisis during which the khan was in grave danger of losing control over his subjects. This crisis was compounded of several factors which can be clarified only by an examination of the precise circumstances surrounding Boris' decision to become a Christian.

As has already been noted, Christianity began to penetrate the area controlled by the Bulgars as early as the seventh century. The new religion was introduced by war prisoners, merchants, and by Bulgars who had lived for a time in the Byzantine Empire and then returned to the Bulgar state. While this process of slow penetration continued, the Bulgar state remained officially pagan. As nearly as can be ascertained, the Bulgar khans for a long time paid no attention to the growing number of Christians in their realm. However, by the ninth century they could no longer overlook the fact that Christianity was becoming an important factor among their people. One account has it that during the reign of Khan Ormatog (814–831) there were even Christians in the khan's household, seeking, with some success, to influence major decisions.[25] The khans of the early ninth century attempted to solve this problem by persecuting the Christians, although apparently with no success.[26]

By the middle of the ninth century, then, when Boris became khan, Christianity was a force in Bulgaria of sufficient importance to concern the prince, and some decision about this new religion would soon have to be made. Factors other than the presence of Christians were also emerging to drive the khan toward a decision in favor of the official conversion of Bulgaria to Christianity. Boris' kingdom was made up of Bulgars and Slavs, the former actually being a minority group long accustomed to dominating the latter. Like his predecessors, Boris searched for forces which would unite these disparate and often hostile elements into a single nation.

A common religion was certainly a possible solution, and the promise of its efficiency as a unifying force must have led Boris to think in terms of imposing Christianity on his subjects. Perhaps he sensed that the only way to persuade the Slavic element in his kingdom to accept the authority of a Bulgar lord was to make that lord a Christian ruler, and he was probably convinced that Christianity would also enhance his power as head of the state. Knowing from the experience of his predecessors that the Bulgar nobles, the *boyars*, were jealous of the khan's authority, he perhaps hoped that the institution of a new religion and the creation of a new church in his realm would give him prestige enough to curb the *boyars* and power enough to rule over his subjects after the fashion of the Byzantine *basileus* or the Frankish *augustus*.

25. Theophylactus, *Historia Martyrii XV Martyrum*, Chs. 29–30, Migne, *PG*, CXXVI, cols. 192–93.

26. For evidence of persecution under Ormatog, see *ibid.*, Ch. 30, col. 193; Theophanes Continuatus, *Chronographia*, V, Ch. 4, ed. I. Bekker, *CSHB*, pp. 216–17; Ioannes Zonaras, *Epitomae historiarum*, XVI, Ch. 6, ed. T. Büttner-Wobst, *CSHB*, p. 408; Theodore of Studite, *Sermones Catechatici*, No. LXIII, Migne, *PG*, XCIX, col. 591. See also Gérard, *Les Bulgares*, pp. 162–78; Spinka, *A History of Christianity in the Balkans*, pp. 27–29; Dvornik, *Les Slaves, Byzance et Rome au IXe siècle*, pp. 99–101.

The religion of the Bulgars was surely a significant factor in the international policy pursued by the Bulgar khans. Beginning with the reign of Krum (802–814), the khans followed an aggressive, expansionist policy against the Byzantine Empire, the Serbs, the Croats, the Moravians, and the Franks. To succeed against so wide a variety of foes required alliances, and Boris certainly realized that his chances of winning favor from most of these potential allies were poor so long as he was a pagan. The acceptance of Christianity might contribute substantially toward engendering respect among foreign powers for a people long thought of as destructive, cruel barbarians, who were capable of such an act of savagery as using the skull of a dead Byzantine emperor for a drinking cup.[27] The success of the Moravians in winning Byzantine support (in 863) by agreeing to become Christians under the aegis of Cyril and Methodius could hardly have been lost on Boris or ignored in his diplomatic calculations.[28]

There were, perhaps, even personal forces at work pushing Boris toward conversion. One account tells that his sister had long been in Constantinople as a hostage, had been converted, and had returned to Boris' courts, where she exerted an influence on him.[29] Other sources speak of the presence at the Bulgar court of Greek monks who were seeking to persuade the khan to accept the true faith.[30] In view of the strong religious bent Boris demonstrated after his conversion, one might well conclude that he was personally attracted to Christianity quite aside from political and diplomatic considerations. It appears beyond question, then, that throughout the early years of Boris' reign there were numerous pressures recommending that the khan accept Christianity for himself and his people.

27. *Theophanis Chronographia*, ed. Carolus de Boor (2 vols.; Leipzig, 1883–85), I, 491.

28. See Dvornik, *Les légendes de Constantin et de Méthode vues de Byzance* (Prague, 1933); *idem, Les Slaves, Byzance et Rome au IX⁰ siècle*, pp. 147–83, 259–96; J. Bujnoch, *Zwischen Rom und Byzance. Leben und Wirken des Slavenapostel Kyrillos und Methodios (Slavische Geschichtsschreiber*, I) (Gratz, 1958); Franz Grivec, *Konstantin und Method, Lehrer des Slaven* (Weisbaden, 1960); and Zdenek R. Dittrich, *Christianity in Greater Moravia* (Gronigen, 1962), for a full discussion of the problem of the conversion of the Moravians and the activities of Cyril and Methodius.

29. Theophanes Continuatus, *Chronographia*, IV, Ch. 14, ed. I. Bekker, *CSHB*, pp. 162–63; Ioannes Zonaras, *Epitomae historiarum*, XVI, Ch. 2, ed. T. Büttner-Wobst, *CSHB*, pp. 387–88.

30. Theophanes Continuatus, *Chronographia*, IV, Chs. 14–15, ed. I. Bekker, *CSHB*, pp. 163–64; Georgius Cedrenus, *Compendium Historiarum*, ed. I. Bekker, *CSHB*, II, 152–53; Symeon Magister, *Annales: De Michaele et Theodora*, Ch. 22, ed. I. Bekker, *CSHB*, p. 664; Ioannes Zonaras, *Epitomae historiarum*, XVI, Ch. 2, ed. T. Büttner-Wobst, *CSHB*, p. 388.

With these rather powerful forces operating to drive Boris toward conversion, it seems that the khan would have been free to decide the time and the circumstance for the introduction of the new religion into his realm. The first years of his reign were marked by a series of triumphs, especially in the diplomatic field. No one, inside or outside his realm, seemed to be in any position to dictate to him, and the evidence suggests that Boris, of his own volition, had decided by the early 860's to accept Christianity at a time and under circumstances that would permit him to reap a diplomatic reward.

The tantalizing prize was the prospect of an alliance with Louis the German against Rastislav of Moravia. A German alliance, aimed at victimizing Rastislav, promised to give Boris greater freedom to extend his control over the Slavic world and to provide him with a strong ally against Bulgaria's greatest foe, the Byzantine Empire, which at the moment was deeply engaged in a crucial struggle with the Moslems. Boris apparently chose to accept Christianity as part of the price to be paid for a firm alliance with Louis the German. The treaty between Boris and Louis was agreed upon in a meeting at Tuln in 862, and shortly thereafter reports reached Rome that Boris was willing to accept Christianity, apparently under the guidance of German clergymen.[31]

However, Boris' clever attempts to capitalize on his conversion by extracting a diplomatic advantage for Bulgaria were unavailing. The Byzantine government discerned his game, and, acting to offset the Bulgar advantage, made an alliance with the sorely tried Rastislav. Soon thereafter, they sent Cyril and Methodius to Moravia as missionaries, thereby counteracting the influence of the German clergy operating there. The government of Emperor Michael III, fortunately freed from the Arab threat as a result of an important victory in 863, sent a military expedition into Bulgaria in 864. Surprised by these speedy moves and crippled because of a famine in his land, Boris surrendered to the Byzantine forces without a struggle. The skillful diplomacy of the Greeks apparently made his choice easier by allowing him to retain all his territory, insisting only that he give up his alliance with the Franks. Indeed, the chief condition imposed on Boris was that he accept Christianity under Greek auspices. With almost unseemly haste the final settlement was negotiated in Constantinople, and a group of Greek clergymen, led by a bishop, was sent to baptize Boris and to assume the burden of converting his subjects.

31. *Nicolai I. Papae Epistolae*, No. 26, ed. Perels, *MGH, Ep.*, VI, 293; *Annales Fuldenses, a.* 863, ed. Kurze, *MGH, SS. rer. Germ.*, p. 56; *Annales Bertiniani, a.* 864, ed. Waitz, *MGH, SS. rer. Germ.*, p. 72.

The whole process was completed by the summer of 865. Boris was a Christian and the conversion of his subjects was under way.[32]

This chain of events obviously negated whatever plans Boris had made in 862, 863 and 864 for the conversion of Bulgaria with the help of German missionaries. More significantly, the sudden shift of affairs permitted a foreign power to become involved within Bulgaria in a fashion which appeared to compromise Bulgar sovereign power and to subordinate the khan to an external authority. By 865, foreign priests, sponsored by a government that had just won a military victory over the Bulgars, were streaming into Boris' realm and telling his subjects to do strange things.[33] Officials in Constantinople were assuming that they had certain powers over Boris and his subjects.[34] In accordance with Christian usage, the khan had been persuaded to assume a foreign name, Michael, as a result of his acceptance of Emperor Michael III as his godfather.[35] This arrangement, however innocent in spiritual terms, had definite implications of Bulgar political subordination to a superior authority. For the moment there was no telling how far the influence of the Greeks over the Bulgars' internal affairs might extend.

To many Bulgars, and perhaps even to the khan, their defeat at the hands of the Byzantine forces in 864 was greater than any defeat the Bulgars had previously suffered. Earlier defeats had involved loss of territory, the payment of tribute, and the sending of hostages to the

32. The chief sources informing us (not very adequately) on the events leading to the conversion of Boris are Theophanes Continuatus, *Chronographia*, IV, Ch. 15, ed. I. Bekker, *CSHB*, pp. 163–65; Georgius Monachus (Continuatus), *Vitae recentiorum imperatorum: De Michaele et Theodora*, Ch. 16, ed. I. Bekker, *CSHB*, p. 824; Ioannes Zonaras, *Epitomae historiarum*, XVI, Ch. 2, ed. T. Büttner-Wobst, *CSHB*, pp. 387–89. For a careful analysis of these sources and their meaning, see Dvornik, *Les Slaves, Byzance et Rome au IX⁰ siècle*, pp. 184–89; Spinka, *A History of Christianity in the Balkans*, pp. 25–33; Gérard, *Les Bulgares*, pp. 183–205; and Runciman, *The First Bulgarian Empire*, pp. 102–5. See A. Vaillart and M. Lascaris, "La date de la conversion des Bulgares," *Revue des études slaves*, XIII (1933), 5–15, for a discussion of the problems connected with the date of the conversion.

33. At least Boris complained of this condition to Pope Nicholas I; see Nicholas, *Ep.*, No. 99, Chs. 6, 14–16, 54–55, 57, 66, 77, 94, 103–6, pp. 572, 575–76, 587, 588, 590–91, 593, 597, 599–600.

34. Photius, *Ep.*, No. 6, Ch. 20, ed. Valetta, p. 220, where Boris is referred to as the "spiritual son" of Photius (. . . πνευματικὲ ἡμῶν υἱέ).

35. Theophylactus, *Hist. Martyrii XV Martyrum*, Ch. 34, Migne, *PG*, CXXVI, col. 200; Georgius Monachus (Continuatus), *Vitae recentiorum imperatorum: De Michaele et Theodora*, Ch. 16, ed. I. Bekker, *CSHB*, p. 824; Theophanes Continuatus, *Chronographia*, IV, Ch. 14, ed. I. Bekker, *CSHB*, p. 163; Josephus Genesius, *Regum Liber IV de Michaele Theophilii Filio*, ed. C. Lachmann, *CSHB*, p. 97; Symeon Magister, *Annales: De Michaele et Theodora*, Ch. 25, ed. I. Bekker, *CSHB*, p. 665.

victor; this defeat had loosed upon the Bulgars the agents of a foreign power who engaged themselves—as we shall see in detail—in changing Bulgar society in profound ways. All of this had come about because Boris had already decided to Christianize his subjects and was now willing to accept foreign assistance in this task as a condition for a peace settlement.

The presence of these missionaries, a by-product of a military defeat, appeared to assure Greek predominance in Bulgaria and to preclude complete freedom of action for the Bulgars in the realm of diplomacy. Boris had suffered a serious setback by being forced to do—at a moment and under circumstances not of his choosing—something he had already decided to do: to become a Christian and to assume responsibility for converting his subjects. Put another way, his position would have been much more secure had he been free to "invite" German missionaries to his land under terms that would have permitted the world to think that Bulgaria was accepting Christianity out of free choice and with the assistance of missionaries who had entered Bulgaria by the grace of the khan. Because of his skill as a leader, Boris escaped the potential consequences of his subordination to a foreign power, but, for a brief time between 864 and 866, his position was indeed tenuous.

The seriousness of the crisis surrounding the conversion of the Bulgars in 864 probably resulted from a serious miscalculation by Boris. In spite of the fact that he felt many internal pressures forcing his nation toward conversion, he deliberately sought to exploit his willingness to accept Christianity as a diplomatic ploy, first to gain an ally and then to soften the exactions of a victorious foe. He seemingly failed to realize the significance the Christian world attached to the conversion of an entire people of some prominence in the contemporary world scene, and he therefore underestimated the extent to which outsiders would insist on being involved in Bulgar affairs in the name of Christianizing his land.

Perhaps Boris should not be blamed for his limited grasp of the situation. So far as we can determine, no Christian prince or prelate had taken any interest in the spiritual state of the Bulgars during the nearly two centuries prior to the reign of Boris, when Christianity was slowly penetrating the pagan land. However, the moment it became obvious that Boris was inclined to accept Christianity and convert his people, it became a matter of universal concern. Kings and emperors had maneuvered furiously to force Boris' hand, and then had vied to be on hand when Boris was ready for baptism. They hoped that by having assisted in the conversion process and the institution of the new religion they would be in a position to exercise a degree of control over the newly converted prince and his land, or that they could entrench their ecclesiastical representatives in his realm as agents capable of controlling the policy of Bulgaria in their favor. Everyone seemed to assume that the movement of the Bulgars toward conversion would result in a profound transformation of Bulgar society which would make that people more desirable as allies and more formidable as foes. No one could stand aside and permit the pagan Boris to proceed toward the conversion of his people at his own speed.

In spite of the fact that Boris enjoyed a reputation as a powerful ruler, he was not strong enough or skillful enough to control the actions of those outside his realm once they were convinced that his land was open to Christianity. Nor could he prevent foreigners from using his willingness to accept their aid in carrying forward the conversion process as evidence of Bulgar subordination to their overlordship. This sudden aggressive thrust by outsiders, justified in the name of assisting with conversion, introduced elements into the Bulgarian scene that seriously compromised the power of the prince, threatening—at least momentarily—to reduce him to a dependent position.

The crisis accompanying the decision to accept Christianity had another dimension which likewise threatened the ruler's power, and this was its effect on the people within the Bulgar state. Considerable confusion developed at all levels of the populace, centering around a conviction that the acceptance of a new deity and the repudiation of the old gods involved tampering with the foundations of the cosmic order, and that drastic consequences might result. This state of mind bred resentment, fear, and doubt among those being converted, and it contributed to the general atmosphere of crisis accompanying Boris' decision to accept Christianity.

Several sources relating to the conversion of the Bulgars suggest the existence of religious tension and uneasiness. Certain scraps of evidence also indicate that Boris himself had wrestled seriously with the religious implications of the acceptance of Christianity. A Greek chronicler insists that a vivid painting of the Last Judgment (by a Christian artist named Methodius, living at the khan's court) aroused in Boris a fear of eternal damnation and hellfire strong enough to help persuade him to become a Christian.[36] It was also said that Boris was convinced that the famine which afflicted his land in 864 (the year of his conversion) was caused by

36. Theophanes Continuatus, *Chronographia*, IV, Ch. 15, ed. I. Bekker, *CSHB*, pp. 163–64; see also Georgius Cedrenus, *Compendium Historiarum*, ed. I. Bekker, *CSHB*, II, 152–53.

the wrath of the Christian God and could be alleviated only by surrender to that God.[37] These instances are hardly sufficient for a valid generalization but they imply that the coming of the new religion posed disturbing questions for the Bulgars about the powers of their old gods and the possible dire consequences of a failure to take account of the Christian God.

The *boyar* revolt that occurred in Bulgaria as an immediate reaction to Boris' decision to impose Christianity on his subjects offers further confirmation of a state of uneasiness in the land. The following account of that revolt, provided by a western European source, contains some interesting reflections of the state of mind prevailing in Bulgaria during the initial stages of the conversion process:

> The king of the Bulgars ... received holy baptism. Because his nobles thought themselves injured, they incited the people against him in order to kill him. [Everybody] in the ten provinces gathered themselves around his palace. He, having invoked the name of Christ and being accompanied by forty-eight men all fervent Christians who remained with him, emerged against all that multitude. And then as he passed out of the gates of the city, there appeared to him and to those with him seven priests; each of them held a burning candle in his hand. And thus they led the way for the king and those who were with him. To those who had rebelled against him it seemed that a great palace burning over their heads was about to fall on them; and in front the horses of those who were with the king stood erect and struck the rebels with their front legs. So great a fear seized them that they neither tried to flee nor to defend themselves, but prostrated themselves unable to move.[38]

This account highlights the extremes to which opinion ran at the decisive hour of conversion: from belligerent opposition to abject surrender in the face of an outward display of the symbols of the new religion.

One might dismiss these scraps of information simply as fanciful attempts by later historians to explain the miraculous working of God so

---

37. Theophanes Continuatus, *Chronographia*, IV, Ch. 14, ed. I. Bekker, *CSHB*, p. 163; Theophylactus, *Hist. Martyrii XV Martyrum*, Ch. 34, Migne, *PG*, CXXVI, cols. 197–200; Georgius Cedrenus, *Compendium Historiarum*, ed. I. Bekker, *CSHB*, II, 151–52; Ioannes Zonaras, *Epitomae Historiarum*, XVI, Ch. 2, ed. T. Büttner-Wobst, *CSHB*, p. 388; Symeon Magister, *Annales: De Michaele et Theodora*, Ch. 22, ed. I. Bekker, *CSHB*, pp. 664–65.

38. *Annales Bertiniani*, a. 866, ed. Waitz, *MGH, SS. rer. Germ.*, p. 85. The revolt is also noted by Theophanes Continuatus, *Chronographia*, IV, Ch. 15, ed. I. Bekker, *CSHB*, p. 164; Ioannes Zonaras, *Epitomae Historiarum*, XVI, Ch. 2, ed. T. Büttner-Wobst, *CSHB*, pp. 388–89; and Symeon Magister, *Annales: De Michaele et Theodora*, Ch. 25, ed. I. Bekker, *CSHB*, pp. 665–66; these sources do not, however, supply such full details.

as to assure the spread of his true religion. They are corroborated, however, by the questions Boris sent to Pope Nicholas, many of which reflect concern and tension in the minds of the Bulgars as they began to face the implications of their conversion. Repeatedly, the khan asked the pope's opinion about the necessity for abandoning ancient practices, and the tone of these requests suggests that the new converts were torn by indecision and doubts as they proceeded to divest themselves of their time-sanctioned customs.[39] Boris and his subjects needed papal reassurance of the wisdom of their acceptance of Christianity; probably the khan also needed papal authority to help persuade his subjects that the abandonment of pagan religious practices was both necessary and safe.

In several other instances Boris sought papal direction for the exact way Christians should go about certain activities with which pagan religious practices were associated: preparation for battle, the supplication of the spirit world for relief from drought, praying at mealtime, and the disposal of animals killed in unusual ways.[40] In these cases the khan seemed to be fearful lest he and his subjects innocently anger their new God by some ritualistic indiscretion and thus bring disaster on themselves in matters absolutely essential to their daily lives. Perhaps the most poignant request made by Boris—one symbolical of all the uncertainty surrounding the acceptance of a new religion and the abandonment of the old—was his query about the propriety of praying for his dead pagan ancestors.[41] The khan seemed to have realized that the pope would answer that a Christian was not allowed to pray for dead pagans, yet the new convert felt compelled to raise this question on a vital matter so as once more to set his mind at rest that no catastrophe would descend on those who had abandoned their ancient gods for a new one. Throughout Nicholas' response there are indications that the new convert was uneasy, doubtful, and ready to grasp at anything for assurance that his recent religious choice was one that would benefit rather than harm him.

It appears, then, that there are grounds for concluding that the decision to become a Christian brought personal anxiety and uneasiness to the khan. Moreover, some of the *boyars* were seriously enough moved by the khan's decision to attempt regicide, which earned them the reward they must have known would result from failure: execution by the khan. It is perhaps not unwarranted to assume that the general populace shared

39. Nicholas, *Ep.*, No. 99, Chs. 33, 62, 79, 89, pp. 580–81, 589–90, 594, 596.
40. *Ibid.*, Chs. 34, 53, 56, 90–91, pp. 581, 587–88, 596.
41. *Ibid.*, Ch. 88, p. 596.

the misgivings and doubts of their superiors. Indeed, the tenor of some of Boris' questions to Pope Nicholas I strongly suggests concern among the mass of people over fundamental issues: whether the old gods would be displeased by being abandoned, whether the cessation of ancient usages would deprive men of accustomed benefits, and whether their clumsy, amateurish approach to the new deity would provoke wrathful responses ruinous to their fortunes.

This state of mind hardly made it easier for the ruler to sustain his authority. Coupled with the onslaught of foreign influences, this internal uneasiness undermined, at least temporarily, the sovereign's control over his realm, as is evident in the *boyar* revolt. Nor did the unsettled condition vanish quickly. When Boris abdicated his office (in 889) in favor of his son, Vladimir, a new effort was made by the *boyars*, with the new khan's cooperation, to return to paganism.[42] Apparently, resentment of the new religion had existed covertly for a quarter of a century, having posed a permanent problem for the khan that had demanded his constant vigilance.

Boris was able to survive the disturbances that gripped his realm at the moment of his decision to Christianize his people, but serious problems still awaited him. Shortly after his baptism, he was reminded by Photius that after he had been liberated from error and freed from darkness, it was his duty to turn his faculties to the beauty of divine worship.[43] To the khan, only recently relieved of the crisis that accompanied his conversion, this command pointed to what all sources indicate was the most onerous burden facing a newly converted prince: the institution among his subjects of the outward forms of the new religion and the instruction of his people in the basic tenets of the new faith. Of course, a newly converted king could expect aid in this task, but he was made to feel that the responsibility was primarily his. The whole burden of Photius' letter to Boris was to remind the newly converted prince of the extent of his obligation in guiding his subjects to a full understanding and proper practice of Christianity.[44] Pope Nicholas was no less positive in assigning the burden of the institution of Christian practice in Bulgaria to Boris.[45]

42. Regino of Prum, *Chronicon*, a. 868, ed. Kurze, *MGH, SS. rer. Germ.*, pp. 95–96; Theophylactus, *Hist. Martyrii XV Martyrum*, Ch. 47, Migne, *PG*, CXXVI, col. 213.

43. Photius, *Ep.*, No. 6, Ch. 2, ed. Valetta, p. 203.

44. *Ibid.*, Chs. 25–28, pp. 224–26.

45. Nicholas, *Ep.*, No. 99, Chs. 17, 35, 40, 41, 82, 84, 106, pp. 577, 581, 582–83, 595, 599–600.

Boris did not shrink from this obligation. From the time of his baptism until the end of his reign, a major portion of his energies was absorbed in instituting Christian practices and spreading Christian doctrine among his subjects. His efforts, quite clearly, were marked with success, for by the end of his reign the outward Christianization of Bulgaria was far advanced. Moreover, the sources definitely indicate his dedication to this task. Never is there a hint—for instance, in the many papal letters sent to Boris to try to win him back under Roman control after he had given his allegiance to Constantinople in 870—that the khan had been negligent in fulfilling his obligations to Christianize his subjects; and in some cases the popes openly admit his devotion to that cause.[46] Furthermore, in the course of his lifetime Boris earned a great reputation for personal piety, dedication to duty, and steadfastness in pursuit of the goal of converting his people.[47] It is especially noteworthy that the Bulgar khan enjoyed a very high repute in western Europe, where he might have been regarded with suspicion because of his defection to Constantinople after his temporary acceptance of Rome's spiritual guidance.

Perhaps the most dramatic proof of his personal contribution to the Christianization of Bulgaria came after his abdication in 889. That event was the signal for a pagan reaction, led by his son and successor, Vladimir, and supported by a faction of the *boyars*. The fate of the new religion was in the balance until Boris left his monastic retreat to save the day.[48] However, the same sources which testify to Boris' successes in implanting the Christian faith and practices also demonstrate the magnitude of his task. They conclusively indicate that the progress of the new religion depended on the ruler's ability to cope with several different problems simultaneously.

Boris' first problem was providing for the baptism of his people. He himself set the pattern by accepting baptism from a Byzantine bishop who had been sent into Bulgaria; and some members of his court circle were baptized at the same time.[49] This initial step still left the bulk of

46. *Iohannis VIII. Papae Ep.*, Nos. 66, 67, 182, 192, ed. Caspar, *MGH, Ep.*, VII, 59, 61, 146, 153–54.

47. *Liber pontificalis*, ed. Duchesne, II, 164; Regino of Prum, *Chronicon*, a. 868, ed. Kurze, *MGH, SS. rer. Germ.*, pp. 95–96; Theophylactus, *Hist. Martyrii XV Martyrum*, Chs. 34–36, Migne, *PG*, CXXVI, cols. 200–201; Theophylactus, *Vita s. Clementis*, Chs. 16–19, Migne, *PG*, CXXVI, cols. 1221–28.

48. Regino of Prum, *Chronicon*, a. 868, ed. Kurze, *MGH, SS. rer. Germ.*, pp. 95–96.

49. Theophanes Continuatus, *Chronographia*, IV, Chs. 14–15, ed. I. Bekker, *CSHB*, pp. 163–64; Symeon Magister, *Annales: De Michaele et Theodora*, Ch. 25, ed. I. Bekker, *CSHB*, p. 665; Ioannes Zonaras, *Epitomae Historiarum*, XVI, Ch. 2, ed. T. Büttner-Wobst,

the population to be brought to the baptismal font. Holding that it was his personal duty to assure this fundamental step in the Christianization of Bulgaria,[50] Boris was concerned with this problem for the remainder of his reign. Between the time of his conversion in 864 and his appeal to Rome in 866, the chief burden of baptizing Bulgars was borne by priests from the Byzantine world. Boris obviously tried to keep them under surveillance, for he complained to Nicholas of abuses perpetrated by these priests and asked for guidance in correcting the consequences.[51] After the Greek priests were replaced, priests from western Europe took up the burden. Again, Boris was concerned with the progress being made, since he sought to recruit additional clergymen for that purpose in the kingdom of Louis the German, as well as at Rome.[52] Twenty years later, Boris had not yet completely solved this problem. In 885 he greeted with open arms the disciples of Methodius, who had been forced to flee Moravia, and put them to work baptizing Bulgars in remote regions of the kingdom.[53] One can only conclude that from the moment of his conversion Boris felt he had to be alert for unbaptized subjects and to devise ways of bringing them to the baptismal font.

However, the baptism of the Bulgars presented complexities that extended beyond the mere task of finding priests in sufficient numbers to baptize every Bulgar. There were some who refused to become Christians.[54] Others apostasized after baptism and rose in rebellion against the ruler they held responsible for having caused them to be baptized.[55] Some, apparently, tried to flee the land to escape baptism.[56] This recalcitrant element in the population must have caused Boris no end of uneasiness, especially in the initial stages of the effort to baptize all Bulgars. With so many to lead to the baptismal font, Bulgaria was apparently attractive to clergymen with dubious credentials, for Boris complained that a

---

CSHB, p. 388; Theophylactus, *Hist. Martyrii XV Martyrum*, Ch. 34, Migne, *PG*, CXXVI, col. 200.

50. Nicholas, *Ep.*, No. 99, Ch. 17, p. 577.

51. *Ibid.*, Chs. 14, 104, pp. 575, 599.

52. *Liber pontificalis*, ed. Duchesne, II, 165; *Anastasii Bibliothecarii Ep. sive Praef.*, No. 5, eds. Perels and Laehr, *MGH, Ep.*, VII, 412; *Annales Fuldenses*, a. 866, 867, ed. Kurze, *MGH, SS. rer. Germ.*, pp. 65–66.

53. Theophylactus, *Vita s. Clementis*, Chs. 17, ff. Migne, *PG*, CXXVI, cols. 1224 *et seqq.*

54. Nicholas, *Ep.*, No. 99, Ch. 41, pp. 582–83.

55. *Ibid.*, Chs. 17–19, pp. 577–78; *Annales Bertiniani*, a. 866, ed. Waitz, *MGH, SS. rer. Germ.*, p. 85.

56. Nicholas, *Ep.*, No. 99, Ch. 20, p. 579.

Greek, who falsely claimed to be a priest,[57] and a Jew[58] were busily engaged in baptizing Bulgars. Not only was it necessary for the khan to discover such charlatans, he also had to worry whether the sacrament they had administered was valid.

Certain technical questions about the administration of baptism arose: the nature of baptismal sponsorship, the proper season for baptism, the number of times a year the sacrament could be administered, and fasting regulations on days of baptism.[59] Although nowhere explicitly stated, it appears likely that many of the questions posed by Boris in his letter to Nicholas were issues raised by people about to be baptized. For example, it seems logical to infer that Boris asked Nicholas about the legitimacy of the Bulgar custom of hanging a wooden pendant about the neck as a healing device because many about to be baptized had asked whether part of the bargain included giving up such sacred objects.[60] An abundance of such questions must have been a burden to the khan and his priests. Clearly, the baptism of large numbers was no simple task; rather, the process raised numerous questions and caused uneasiness everywhere.

Although the baptizing of the Bulgars continued slowly, the khan was faced with the problem of inculcating into the minds of his subjects the basic concepts of Christian dogma. It was no doubt the complexity of this task which prompted Boris to end his letter to Nicholas with a humble appeal that the pope instruct him as he would anyone not having true and perfect Christianity.[61] This sense of inadequacy could well have been induced in Boris by the stress his mentors placed on *knowledge* of the faith as a key to merit.

Photius was especially insistent in his pastoral letter that every prince must be responsible for guarding his subjects against heterodoxy. The proper discharge of this responsibility demanded that the prince know the tenets of the faith and that he see to it that his subjects learned about Christian doctrine. Lest out of ignorance Boris take this task too lightly, Photius deemed it best to instruct him in the fundamentals of the faith. Nearly a third of his tract to Boris consists of a summary of decisions by all of the ecumenical councils on matters of dogma. Nor did Photius neglect to insinuate the idea that heresy breeds contention and tumult

57. *Ibid.*, Chs. 14–15, pp. 575–76.
58. *Ibid.*, Ch. 104, p. 599.
59. *Ibid.*, Chs. 2, 69, pp. 569, 591–92.
60. *Ibid.*, Ch. 79, p. 594.
61. *Ibid.*, Ch. 106, pp. 599–600.

in a nation, providing Boris with a special reason for concerning himself with the responsibility of teaching the true faith.[62] As one reads the patriarch's presentation of the central tenets of Christian dogma, it seems possible that Boris may have felt smothered by doctrinal points beyond his comprehension. Photius, in fact, plunged him straight into the intricate questions which dominated the ecumenical councils—in addition to quoting him the Nicene Creed as the starting point for dogmatic knowledge. Nicholas I, although not so expansive on dogmatic matters, did not fail to remind Boris that there were many things for him to learn about the faith and to transmit to his people.[63]

The sources are extremely vague on the procedures employed to assure the instruction of the new converts in the rudiments of the faith, and their vagueness may indicate that this was a process that did not occupy the center of attention from the Bulgar point of view. Usually, the sources state only that priests went through the land preaching;[64] and the missionaries may well have taken it upon themselves to decide what dogmatic matters were suitable to their audiences. Both Photius and Nicholas made it perfectly clear that they did not place any great confidence in the khan's grasp of Christian doctrine. This, then, might suggest that when missionaries came to Bulgaria they were not inclined to look to the royal court for guidance, or even cooperation, in the task of teaching the Bulgars the essentials of the faith.

Boris' major concerns in his requests to Nicholas strongly imply that he did not see the Christianization process basically in terms of the instruction of his people in dogma. He seldom asked the pope anything that was concerned directly with dogma; his interest was almost exclusively with the external practices and with the disciplinary aspects of the new religion. This is not to imply that Boris was completely ignorant of Christian doctrine, for his questions indicate an acquaintance with the sacramental system, the nature of sin, the doctrine of immortality, and prayer.[65] However, the occasional references that demonstrate some doctrinal awareness must be matched with evidence of the khan's doctrinal naïveté. Boris' confusion on the nature of baptism and penance, on the

62. Photius, *Ep.*, No. 6, Chs. 2–22, ed. Valetta, pp. 203–23, esp. Chs. 2, 20, 21, pp. 203, 220–22.
63. Nicholas, *Ep.*, No. 99, Chs. 1, 106, pp. 566–67, 599–600.
64. *Anastasii Bibliothecarii Ep. sive Praef.*, No. 5, eds. Perels and Laehr, *MGH, Ep.*, VII, 412; *Liber pontificalis*, ed. Duchesne, II, 165, 185.
65. Nicholas, *Ep.*, No. 99, Chs. 9, 14–16, 65, 75, 78, pp. 573, 575–76, 590, 593–94, on the sacraments; Chs. 16, 24, 26, 28, 29, 31, 32, 83, 85, 98, pp. 576, 579, 580, 595, 598, on sin; Chs. 38, 56, 61, pp. 582, 587–89, on prayer; Ch. 88, p. 596, on immortality.

efficacy of prayer and the sign of the cross, and on the role of the priest in administering the sacraments[66] may well have prompted Nicholas' rather uncomplimentary remark that the Bulgars, like little children, must be fed on milk until they were old enough to handle solid food.[67] It undoubtedly convinced the pope of the advisability of urging Boris to check with bishops and priests in Bulgaria to clear up difficult points.[68]

These scraps of evidence lead one to conclude that although the Bulgar ruler may have honored in the abstract the admonitions addressed to him to instruct his people in the faith, he had no particular program for achieving this end. The lack of a program stemmed from the khan's inadequate grasp of the doctrinal side of the new faith and from his inclination to see Christianity as a ritual and an external discipline. Perhaps toward the end of his reign, after the conversion of Bulgaria had made considerable progress, Boris began to realize the need for a systematic effort to assume royal direction over the doctrinal instruction of his people. This realization may have been part of his reason for sending Bulgars to Constantinople for instruction[69] and for encouraging the founding of monastic schools for the education of native Bulgars.[70] Until these efforts bore fruit, doctrinal instruction was in the hands of foreign missionaries, who operated as they saw fit.

Although it seems true that Boris did not develop a program for doctrinal instruction, and that he was not inclined to see the Christianization of his land primarily in terms of dogmatic issues, doctrinal matters nevertheless constituted a major problem for the khan and forced him to engage in an arena where he was confused and uncertain. Boris became involved simply because the missionaries upon whom he had to depend insisted upon making Bulgaria a theological battleground and upon establishing adherence to a certain doctrinal line as a criterion for true conversion.

As early as 866, Boris revealed that he was confused by various versions of Christian truth. He wrote to Nicholas that "many Christians from diverse lands had come into [his] land, . . . speaking in various tongues, that is, Greek, Armenian, and so forth," and he asked the pope

66. *Ibid.*, Chs. 2, 7, 14–16, 33, 38, 53, 56, 61, 71, 74, 78, 104, pp. 569, 572–73, 575–76, 580–82, 587–89, 592–94, 599.

67. *Ibid.*, Ch. 4, p. 571.

68. *Ibid.*, Chs. 9, 56, pp. 573, 587–88.

69. Photius, *Ep.*, No. 255, ed. Valetta, p. 556.

70. Theophylactus, *Vita s. Clementis*, Ch. 18, Migne, *PG*, CXXVI, col. 1225; "Life of St. Nahum" in M. Kusseff, "St. Nahum," *Slavonic and East European Review*, XXIX (1950–51), 142–44.

to tell him "whether he should obey all of these according to the various meanings or what he ought to do."[71] Nicholas told him what to do: follow the guidance of the church of Rome. Boris accepted this advice for the moment, and his appeal to Nicholas resulted in a new crop of missionaries from Rome, who, with the help of Boris, expelled the Greeks.[72]

Nicholas definitely instructed his representatives to root out the error established by the Greeks.[73] That they followed papal instructions is dramatically revealed in an angry letter addressed by Photius to the eastern patriarchs, accusing the Latins of spreading heresy in Bulgaria.[74] Prior to writing this letter Photius had apparently had these teachings condemned by a local synod, and he tried to use this decision to influence Boris. A letter from Emperors Michael and Basil was sent to Boris, informing him that a synod had condemned the teachings of the Roman missionaries. This was obviously an attempt to undermine the confidence of the Bulgars in their new spiritual masters, as was the spreading of pamphlets among the Bulgars condemning the Latins.[75]

Having, however, failed to persuade Boris that his adherence to Rome involved him in heresy, Photius enlarged the conflict. He summoned the patriarchs of the east to a general council in 867 to condemn the Latin doctrines being spread in Bulgaria. As F. Dvornik has shown, this meeting was held primarily to undermine the Roman position in Bulgaria.[76] Latin sources indicate that the Greeks used the decisions of this council to weaken Boris' attachment to Rome.[77] And it seems likely that confusion about the source and the content of the true Christian doctrine had a bearing on Boris' ultimate decision to abandon his second set of missionary teachers. In 870 his legates appeared at a council in Constantinople and asked the assembled prelates to decide to which jurisdiction the Bulgars pertained. The council ruled in favor of Constantinople. Thereupon a new set of clergymen passed into Bulgaria to drive out the

71. Nicholas, *Ep.*, No. 99, Ch. 106, p. 599.

72. *Liber pontificalis*, ed. Duchesne, II, 164.

73. Nicholas, *Ep.*, No. 100, ed. Perels, *MGH, Ep.*, VI, 601; *Liber pontificalis*, ed. Duchesne, II, 165.

74. Photius, *Ep.*, No. 4, ed. Valetta, pp. 165–81; see especially Chs. 3 and 4, p. 168, for Photius' version of what happened in Bulgaria after the Roman missionaries arrived and expelled the Greeks.

75. Nicholas, *Ep.*, No. 100, p. 603. Nicholas knew of these matters because Boris turned the imperial letter and other inflammatory writings over to the papal legates in Bulgaria.

76. Dvornik, *The Photian Schism*, pp. 119–31.

77. *Liber pontificalis*, ed. Duchesne, II, 185; *Anastasii Bibliothecarii Ep. sive Praef.*, No. 5, eds. Perels and Laehr, *MGH, Ep.*, VII, 413.

Latins and to correct the errors that had so agitated the Greeks since 867.[78]

Still the Bulgars found no relief. For many years the papacy tried to win back the Bulgars, primarily by arguing that the new converts were being led into grave doctrinal errors which endangered the newly established faith. The papal argument was embodied in a series of letters sent by Pope John VIII to Boris[79] and to his chief confidants.[80] John's argument in all these letters was fairly standard. The Bulgars had begun on the right path toward orthodoxy under Rome's direction, but now that the Greeks had infested Bulgaria, the pope feared that the Bulgars would be led into diverse heresies, schisms, and errors. John denied any interest in governing the Bulgars but he intimated that the Greeks' motives may not be apolitical. He also cited cases of other peoples who had been doctrinally misled by consorting with the Greeks. To avert the menace of heresy—with all its implications for the salvation of souls— the Bulgars must return to Rome, the fountain of the true faith. One motive governs all these letters: to kindle among the Bulgars a distrust for the Greeks which might lead the khan and his nobles to repudiate them and take the initiative in returning to Roman jurisdiction. John must have been convinced that the Bulgars were sensitive to doctrinal issues and the problem of orthodoxy for he pinned his hopes of victory almost entirely on the doctrinal level.

Boris and his advisers were not, to our knowledge, moved by the papal letters, nor by the personal appeals of a papal agent who was sent to Bulgaria presumably to argue the same cause.[81] Perhaps more worrisome to the khan was a letter addressed by John to the Greek clergy in Bulgaria that threatened to excommunicate them if they did not depart immediately.[82] The news of such a drastic step may well have raised serious alarm among new converts, clinging to the word of their priests that the faith was the answer to their spiritual problems.

We can therefore say with some certainty that the implantation of Christian doctrine generated troublesome clashes between missionary groups in Bulgaria which required vigilance by the ruler. Although

78. *Liber pontificalis*, ed. Duchesne, II, 181–85, for the events of this council and the appearance of the new missionary force in Bulgaria.

79. *Iohannis VIII. Papae Epistolae*, Nos. 66, 70, 182, 192, 198, 298, 308, ed. Caspar, *MGH, Ep.*, VII, 58–60, 65–66, 146, 153–54, 158–59, 260, 266–67; *Fragmenta Registri Iohannis VIII. Papae*, Nos. 7, 37, pp. 277, 294–95.

80. *Iohannis VIII. Papae Epistolae*, Nos. 67, 183, pp. 61–62, 147.

81. *Ibid.*, Nos. 184, 190, pp. 147, 152.

82. *Ibid.*, No. 71, pp. 66–67.

evidence is far from conclusive, the problem may well have been more serious. Divergent dogmatic positions presented to the populace in rapid succession may have bred confusion through the land. That such confusion existed is implicit in the tenor of John VIII's letters. Given the penchant of the Bulgars to fret over propriety—dramatically manifested in Boris' requests to Nicholas—one might surmise that the problem of coping with divergent dogmas left the entire population worried and uncertain during the early years after Christianity became the official religion.

Although the teaching of Christian doctrine was a significant and difficult aspect of the Christianization of Bulgaria, the institution of the outward practices of Christian worship was of greater concern to Boris. His requests to Nicholas I are so completely concerned with this issue that one is tempted to conclude that Boris saw the conversion process primarily as an exercise in changing the modes of worship of his people. This would be too strong a position, however, for we have already seen—or will see—that Boris realized other matters were also involved in the conversion process. What his queries indicate is that the introduction of the Christian cult raised major problems and that the khan was constantly involved in the issues that emerged from the institution of Christian worship.

A summary listing of the several aspects of Christian religious worship and observance that had to be introduced into Bulgaria will give some indication of the magnitude of the task facing Boris and his missionaries. Churches had to be built.[83] Public services, new to the Bulgars, had to be introduced into these churches: the mass, baptism, communion, confession, public prayer, marriages, confirmation, preaching, singing, funeral services, processions, veneration of relics, the use of Christian symbols.[84]

83. The literary sources say little about this matter except to note that churches were built; e.g., *Anastasii Bibliothecarii Ep. sive Praef.*, No. 5, eds. Perels and Laehr, *MGH, Ep.*, VII, 412; Theophylactus, *Vita s. Clementis*, Ch. 23, Migne, *PG*, CXXVI, cols. 1229–31. A proper treatment of this subject would involve a more thorough investigation of recent archaeological findings than has been made for this paper; for helpful suggestions see Bogdan D. Filov, *L'Art antique en Bulgarie* (Sofia, 1925); André Grabar, *La peinture religieuse en Bulgarie* (Paris, 1928); and Dimiter Dimitrov, *Bulgaria: Land of Ancient Civilizations* (Sofia, 1961), and the bibliography indicated there.

84. Nicholas, *Ep.*, No. 99, Ch. 76, p. 593, for mass; Chs. 14–16, 69, pp. 575–76, 591–92, for baptism; Chs. 9, 55, 65, 71, pp. 573, 587, 590, 592, for communion; Chs. 11, 38, 56, 61, 74, 88, 100, pp. 574, 582, 587–89, 593, 596, 598, for prayer; Chs. 2, 3, 39, 48, pp. 569–70, 582, 586, on marriage; Chs. 35, 75, 78, pp. 581, 593–94, on confession and penance; Ch. 94, p. 597, on confirmation; Chs. 11, 14, 105, pp. 574, 575, 599, on preaching; Ch. 11, p. 574, for singing; Chs. 98–100, p. 598, on burial; Chs. 7, 8, pp. 572–73, for

New converts had to be taught how to comport themselves in the churches at these various ceremonies: how to dress, how to prepare for baptism and communion, how to take communion, how to pray.[85] They had to be acclimated to the obligation to attend church on Sundays and feast days, and to refrain from work, public activities, and private pleasures on these days.[86] Dietary laws had to be introduced.[87] A special set of regulations for the Lenten season had to be defined, a matter which apparently perplexed and irritated the Bulgars no end, if we can judge from Boris' repeated queries to Nicholas on the subject.[88] The Bulgars had to be taught the Christian manner of praying at meals, of invoking rain, of preparing for battle, of taking an oath, of arranging a betrothal, and of praying for the ill—matters that were often conducted outside the churches and individually.[89] Obviously, the Bulgars were striving to institute the whole range of Christian observances, a task that could have been completed for all Bulgaria only after a long time and only with monumental effort. A concomitant problem was the suppression of pagan practices of worship.

Formidable as all of this was, the sheer labor of acquainting the Bulgars with the basic forms of Christian worship was only part of the problem. In turning to Nicholas for advice, Boris provided abundant evidence that his labors to teach his people how to worship were complicated by a vast ignorance of Christian usage. His requests to Nicholas reflect the desperation of one who knows in a general way the Christian practices that should be inaugurated in order that the new deity may be honored properly, but who is often at a loss about the specific nature of Christian usage. He began his message to Nicholas by asking that "the Christian law" be sent to him, evidently expecting that Nicholas would be able to supply a simple guide that would inform the Bulgars of proper Christian usage. Nicholas could only reply that this would require "innumerable volumes."[90] Lacking a concise compendium to explain how the Christians

---

veneration of relics and the use of the cross. See also Theophylactus, *Vita s. Clementis,* Chs. 18, 22, 29, Migne, *PG,* CXXVI, cols. 1224–25, 1228–29, 1237–38, for the labors of St. Clement of Ochrida along these lines.

85. Nicholas, *Ep.,* No. 99, Chs. 7–9, 54, 55, 58, 65, 66, pp. 572–73, 587, 590–91.

86. *Ibid.,* Chs. 10–12, 34, 63, pp. 574–75, 581, 590.

87. *Ibid.,* Chs. 4–5, 42, 43, 56, 57, 60, 69, 90, 91, pp. 570–72, 583–84, 587–89, 591–92, 596; Photius, *Ep.,* No. 4, Ch. 5, ed. Valetta, pp. 168–70.

88. Nicholas, *Ep.,* No. 99, Chs. 44–48, 50, pp. 585–86; Photius, *Ep.,* No. 4, Ch. 5, ed. Valetta, pp. 168–70; Nicholas, *Ep.,* No. 100, ed. Perels, *MGH, Ep.,* VI, 603.

89. Nicholas, *Ep.,* No. 99, Chs. 33, 35, 40, 53, 56, 62, 67, 79, pp. 580–82, 587–91, 594.

90. *Ibid.,* Ch. 1, pp. 566–67.

worshipped, Boris could only search for advice on particular matters where his knowledge was inadequate; he could only ask Nicholas to tell him exactly how to do what he realized should be done. No doubt he frequently turned to missionary clergymen to resolve the problems that arose from his ignorance of Christian usage.

To analyze the full extent of the ignorance plaguing the Bulgar ruler as he struggled to institute the proper forms of Christian worship would require a discussion too lengthy for this paper, but a few examples drawn from his requests to Nicholas will suffice to reveal the nature of his quandary. Boris knew that Christians must observe fast days, but he had to ask Nicholas what days these were. He had trouble deciding who could carry the cross in processions. He wanted to know whether communion could be received daily during Lent. He was confused about what to do in cases where an unworthy priest had administered baptism. He fretted over the proper manner of praying while in military camp, presumably away from a church. He asked for a specific list of animals and birds that the Bulgars might eat. He did not know how to pray at mealtime when a priest or deacon was absent. The exact requirements for fasting were not clear in his mind. He asked Nicholas to tell him how to swear an oath. He was at a loss about how long a woman who had just borne a child should be kept from attending church. He requested specific advice on how many times a year baptism may be administered and what fasting conditions should be imposed on those being baptized. He asked Nicholas for a penitential.[91] All of this strongly suggests that there were nettlesome problems pertaining to Christian worship ever awaiting the king's decision. It also indicates that once the question of Christian propriety was resolved an effort would have to be made to correct the erroneous practices that had grown up as a result of Bulgar ignorance.

In some of these cases Boris' concern certainly extended beyond a need for information. He, and very likely his subjects, appear to have been beset by a fear that as neophyte practitioners of the Christian cult they might commit some minor or unintentional fault which would displease the Christian God and result in grave consequences. When Boris asked if it is lawful to receive communion daily during Lent, one suspects that he was concerned not so much with securing papal sanction for partaking of divine grace more frequently as with the possibility that an unusual departure from a ritualistic practice would affect him adversely.

91. *Ibid.*, Chs. 4, 7, 8, 14, 15, 38, 43, 53, 60, 67–69, 88, pp. 570–73, 575–76, 582–84, 587–89, 591–92, 596.

His keen concern about those days in which it was forbidden to do battle and about the precise preparations for battle reflects a fear that violation of Christian usages would end in defeat. When he sought to discover whether a risk might be involved if he uttered an improper prayer when he was in military camp and without the services of a priest, or if he prayed the wrong number of times a day outside the church, or if he simply made the sign of the cross over his meals when no priest was present, Boris suggested that his every supplication of the new deity involved grave concern lest erroneous usage might negate the efficacy of prayer or even anger Almighty God. One can almost visualize the perturbed state of mind that afflicted the Bulgars as they struggled to abide by the admonitions of Greek missionaries that they would be guilty of sin if they did not stand in church with their hands clasped to their breasts, if they took communion without wearing a belt, and if they entered a church wearing a linen headbinding.[92] The list could be lengthened; there was apparently no end of the instances in which a sincere convert felt timorous as he went about worshipping in a new way, hoping that he would not commit some mechanical fault which would provoke divine wrath.

There are veiled hints in Boris' questions which imply not only that ignorance and temerity impeded the institution of the Christian cult but also that a subtle form of resistance by the new converts complicated the entire process. The clue to this difficulty lies in certain cases where Boris asked the pope to render a judgment on a Christian usage about which the khan almost certainly knew the correct position. For instance, Boris asked Nicholas whether it is lawful to work and to judge cases in the courts on Sundays and feast days. In spite of evidence that his knowledge of Christian practice was not perfect, it is impossible to believe that the khan did not know the Christian usage on this point. Nor is it possible to think that the missionaries were spreading confusion on this matter. One must suppose that Boris needed an authoritative statement from Rome—perhaps accompanied by a rationale—concerning the sanctity of Sundays and feast days in order to convince some elements among his subjects who were reluctant to accept this particular usage. The same issue seems to have been involved when Boris asked Nicholas what insignia should replace the horse's tail, traditionally carried into battle by the Bulgars. Boris must surely have encountered enough Christian armies and heard enough from missionaries to have known what a Christian army should display as a battle insignia. Again, the khan's

92. *Ibid.*, Chs. 9, 34, 35, 38, 43, 53–55, 57, 61, 66, 90, 91, pp. 573, 581–84, 587–91, 596.

concern must have been to obtain a definite papal opinion that could be used for persuading his subjects to abandon a convention that did not conform to Christian usage.[93]

Boris' persistent questioning on matters of this order implies that one of his most difficult tasks in introducing Christian cult observances lay not in breaking down the resistance of adamant supporters of ancient religious usages but in justifying to sincere converts the religious significance of certain Christian practices. The issue appears to have been especially troublesome in cases where the new system of worship involved the abandonment of ancient habits of life that previously had had no special ritualistic significance. The khan apparently sought to resolve this issue by citing the word of a recognized authority, a word that he himself had invoked by asking Rome's position on specific situations that had been encountered in Bulgaria.

When his subjects wondered why they must become involved in a complex ritualistic procedure involving church-going, confession, penance, prayer, the freeing of prisoners and slaves, and almsgiving in preparation for battle, Boris and his priests could answer best by citing Rome's position on the matter. Those women who protested covering their heads in church could be confronted with a papal opinion buttressed by scriptural citations. The pope's commands may have helped to supply a persuasive reply to those men who felt no meaningful compulsion to refrain from the conjugal bed on Saturday night and Sunday as an aspect of honoring God. (In this particular case, the papal argument that such conduct constituted work on the Lord's day may have been harder to respect than papal authority.)

Boris seems to have encountered his greatest trouble with respect to Lenten observances. Apparently the Bulgars could see little reason why they must stop hunting, holding court, waging war, celebrating parties, and marrying during Lent in favor of fasting, penance, prayer, and church-going. The khan's careful and extensive questioning of Nicholas on Lenten observances indicates that the difficulty arose not from the new converts' opposition to the Christian usages suitable to Lent but from their inability to see the religious implications of eliminating customary pursuits as a mode of worshipping God. The presence of this spirit among the Bulgars strongly suggests that there was a constant demand upon those responsible for introducing Christian practices to explain the meaning of what converts were being asked to do. The Bulgars were not dumb, silent victims, ready to do what they were told;

93. *Ibid.*, Chs. 10–12, 33, pp. 574–75, 580–81.

at least in some cases, especially where they were asked to give up parts of their traditional modes of living, they demanded that the innovations make religious sense to them.[94]

In reviewing the whole range of activities involved in instituting the Christian religion in Bulgaria, one is inevitably struck by how often the critical issue seems to have rested with relatively minor matters of a highly formal nature. Boris' constant concern with these issues and Nicholas' meticulous care in providing explanations for what seem to be petty technicalities may well provide the secret to the Christianization process. There is no solid evidence to indicate that the great mysteries of the Christian faith or the subtle issues of dogma emerging from these mysteries vitally influenced the reception of the new faith in Bulgaria. There is abundant evidence that the Bulgars readily accepted and entered into the major forms of Christian public worship—the mass, baptism, communion, confession, prayer, burial rites, and the like; the only troublesome issue on this score was learning the correct manner of performing these rites. What disturbed them, provoked questions, and even engendered resistance was a whole range of minor practices which in the name of religion required them to put aside customs which previously had had little or no religious meaning, or which demanded the abandonment of traditional usages without an obvious substitute. The surviving sources leave no hint that the triune God or the *filioque* question or any other fundamental point embodied in the creed quoted to Boris by Photius acted as an obstacle to the conversion of the Bulgars. But Lenten regulations created no end of formidable problems. Everything suggests that the Bulgars viewed the mass as no loathsome innovation but rather accepted it quickly as a suitable substitute for pagan sacrificial and propitiatory rites. What agitated the new converts was the insistence of the missionaries that the new mode of worship be conducted without those activities that customarily had formed an integral part of their great religious ceremonies: judging cases, battle preparations, gaming, singing, etc. Probably the Bulgars felt no great hardship in substituting the Christian procedure of betrothal for their customary practice; the equivalence was fairly obvious. What left them frustrated was the insistence of the missionaries that they abandon their dead pagan kinsmen; and it was here the new religion left an empty spot in their lives.

One is thus drawn to the conclusion that the decisive element in the process of instituting Christian practices was the ability of the missionary forces to provide two things: substitute religious practices for the every-

94. *Ibid.*, Chs. 35, 44–48, 50, 58, 63, pp. 581, 585–86, 588, 590.

day, simple pagan usages not acceptable to Christians, and meaningful explanations which would persuade the Bulgars to abandon practices which had no religious significance but which ran counter to Christian usages. Conversion apparently did not involve the glorious rebirth which Photius and Nicholas spoke of so eloquently; it entailed a tortuous process of substituting Christian practices as recognizable equivalents for time-sanctioned pagan usages. The burden upon the ruler and his missionary forces was to make evident the equivalence between the old and the new. The process constantly ran the risk of asking the converts to abandon too wide a range of conventional usages that did not seem intimately linked to religious life as they understood religion. When the demand to suppress conventional modes of life extended beyond the religious comprehension of the converts, the missionary forces had to try to supply a rationale capable of persuading the Bulgars to conform to Christian standards. This necessity often arose when the Bulgars were asked to accept practices that had become attached to Christianity by virtue of its evolution in a Judaic-Roman environment for which there were no corresponding experiences or precedents in the Bulgar tradition.

This examination of the problems involved in the institution of Christian worship and the propagation of Christian doctrine among the Bulgars prompts one final remark. The task was obviously one that required a monumental expenditure of labor. It seems safe to assume that the entire process involved nothing less than the full concentration of the nation's energies for an entire generation. It is difficult not to admire those who were willing to persist in the face of so great a task. Obviously, the ruler was the vital force, alone capable of concentrating the needed energy on the work to be accomplished.

While contending with the numerous burdens associated with the institution of Christian beliefs, rites, and practices, Boris plunged into another problem that he obviously felt was critical to his undertaking. He sought to assure the development of a formal organization of the emerging Bulgar Christian community after a pattern that reflected current usage in the Christian world. This problem was complicated not only by the newness of Christianity in his realm but also by the necessary involvement of external elements which had to be respected in establishing an ecclesiastical organization.

There is no evidence to clarify the organizational pattern involved in Bulgaria when the first Greek missionary parties appeared in 864 and

865 to baptize Boris and to proceed with the work of conversion. The imperial government sent a bishop to Bulgaria to baptize Boris, but there is no suggestion that this move had any organizational significance.[95] Perhaps the Byzantine authorities only imitated for Bulgaria the procedure that had been employed in 863 in Moravia. In the latter case the imperial regime, backed by Photius, had commissioned two men to lead a missionary expedition into a land ready to accept the cross. These men were qualified for the task by their piety, learning, linguistic skill, and experience with people of Slavic origin and non-Christian faiths. Neither leader had high ecclesiastical standing or dignity at the time of the mission to Moravia; Cyril was a man of learning and a teacher, while Methodius was a monk. Nor did a prestigious rank seem necessary during the early stages of their work in Moravia.[96] If the same procedure held in Bulgaria, we can suppose that the original Greek mission was composed of a body of men led by one or two figures whose authority rested primarily on their reputation as pious, learned men of exemplary Christian life and on their designation as missionary chiefs by the imperial government and the patriarch. Photius made it clear to Boris from the outset that the spiritual head of the emergent Bulgar church was in Constantinople.[97] Nowhere in his pastoral letter did he indicate the need for the formal establishment of an ecclesiastical organization in Bulgaria.

Boris apparently was not satisfied with this arrangement, for in 866 he asked Nicholas I if it was lawful for his nation to have a patriarch, how such a patriarch ought to be ordained, and whether the king could constitute a patriarch. Obviously, he had begun to envisage a hierarchical arrangement of the most ambitious kind; and perhaps he was also a little overawed by the audacity of his request, for, further on in his letter, he requested information on how many true patriarchs there were and which was second after Rome. Nicholas quickly dismissed the possibility of a Bulgar patriarch, but in his responses to these questions he laid out a plan for the organizational evolution of the Bulgar church, at least as Rome saw it. He explained the true patriarchates in some detail and the reasons or rights upon which this dignity was based.

---

95. Theophanes Continuatus, *Chronographia*, IV, Ch. 14, ed. I. Bekker, *CSHB*, p. 163: "παρὰ τοῦ πρὸς ἐκεῖνον ἀποσταλέντος ἀρχιερέως ἀπὸ τῆς βασιλίδος τῶν πόλεων"; Ioannes Zonaras, *Epitomae Historiarum*, XVI, Ch. 2, ed. T. Büttner-Wobst, *CSHB*, p. 388: "καὶ ἀποστάλη μὲν ἀρχιερεὺς πρὸς αὐτόν. ὁ δὲ καὶ ἐμυήθη καὶ ἐβαπτίσθη."

96. For a discussion of the work of Cyril and Methodius, see the works cited in n. 28, above.

97. Photius, *Ep.*, No. 6, Chs. 20, 114, ed. Valetta, pp. 220–21, 247–48.

His remarks could hardly have encouraged Boris to believe that the Bulgars would soon, if ever, have their own patriarch. The pope stated clearly that under no circumstances could a king establish a patriarchate, nor even an archbishopric or bishopric. Nicholas would first appoint a bishop for Bulgaria, and this bishop would be granted the archiepiscopal honor by the pope as soon as the Christian population had increased to Rome's satisfaction. This archbishop could then consecrate other bishops for Bulgaria, and they, in turn, would be permitted to elect the first archbishop's successor. The first archbishop would not have to come to Rome for his *pallium*, but all his successors would be required to discharge this obligation before assuming their new position.[98] This plan left no question that Bulgaria was destined to remain a province fully subordinated to Rome.

Nicholas launched this program by commissioning two bishops to go to Bulgaria, Paul of Populonia and Formosus of Porto, bearing his famous responses to Boris' questions.[99] The pope obviously intended that these bishops would exercise the episcopal function for he commanded Boris to seek guidance from them on several matters.[100] However, it was not the pope's intention that either of these men would be elevated to a permanent position as head of the Bulgar hierarchy. He made this clear when he refused to honor Boris' request to make Formosus archbishop of Bulgaria, justifying his refusal on the grounds that it was uncanonical to transfer an already established bishop from one see to another.[101] The task of Paul and Formosus was to travel, preach, baptize, confirm, build churches—in short, to direct a missionary establishment.[102] Not long after their arrival another missionary bishop, Hermanrich of Passau, arrived from the East Frankish kingdom with a retinue of clergy and a supply of religious materials, but he left when he found that the Romans were in control.[103]

The sources are unanimous in reporting that Boris was pleased with the work of Paul and Formosus. However, the situation may not have

---

98. Nicholas, *Ep.*, No. 99, Chs. 72–73, 92–93, pp. 592–93, 596–97.

99. *Liber pontificalis*, ed. Duchesne, II, 164, 185; Nicholas, *Ep.*, No. 100, ed. Perels, *MGH, Ep.*, VI, 603; *Anastasii Bibliothecarii Ep. sive Praef.*, No. 5, eds. Perels and Laehr, *MGH, Ep.*, VII, 412.

100. Nicholas, *Ep.*, No. 99, Chs. 24, 26, 28–30, 50, 51, 81, 95, pp. 579, 580, 586, 594, 597.

101. *Liber pontificalis*, ed. Duchesne, II, 165.

102. *Ibid.*, p. 164; *Anastasii Bibliothecarii Ep. sive Praef.*, No. 5, eds. Perels and Laehr, *MGH, Ep.*, VII, 412.

103. *Annales Fuldenses, a.* 867, ed. Kurze, *MGH, SS. rer. Germ.*, p. 65.

been completely satisfactory from an organizational viewpoint. We have already noted[104] that the Greeks, having been driven out of Bulgaria upon the arrival of the Roman party, launched a counter-attack which sought to impugn the orthodoxy of the Latins. Boris, perhaps feeling the need for a stronger organization to combat this threat, sent a legate to Rome asking Nicholas that Formosus be elevated to the archiepiscopal rank and that more priests be sent to Bulgaria. Nicholas dispatched carefully selected priests, but he refused to accede to the request for the promotion of Formosus. Arguing that it was illegal to transfer the bishop of Porto to another see, he sent two more bishops to Bulgaria, Dominic of Treviso and Grimoald of Polimarti. He ordered Dominic and Formosus to proceed to Constantinople to conduct papal business; and Paul and Grimoald were charged with the conduct of the Bulgar mission.[105]

Hadrian II pursued Nicholas' organizational program—still without notable success in terms of Boris' interests. In 869 another Bulgar legate, Peter, came to Rome to request that a certain deacon Marinus be made archbishop of the Bulgars. If this was not possible, Boris asked that "someone from among the cardinals" be sent to the Bulgars to be examined as a candidate for archbishop, and the Bulgars would send him back to Rome for ordination if he met their approval. Since the "cardinals" at this time comprised clergymen of all ranks who were associated with certain churches in the city of Rome and who often served as functionaries in the papal curia, Boris' request seems to indicate an interest in obtaining for the leadership of the Bulgar hierarchy the services of a man closely associated with papal affairs and trusted by the pope. Because Marinus had already been assigned to Constantinople as a papal legate, Hadrian sent the subdeacon Silvester to the Bulgars as an archiepiscopal candidate. Boris promptly sent Silvester back to Rome, along with a second request that Formosus of Porto be made archbishop. The pope was still not willing to consent to Boris' wish to entrust the leadership of the Bulgar church to Formosus, who apparently had made a powerful impression on Boris. In response to the khan's request, Hadrian wrote that anyone else whom the Bulgars wished to be their archbishop would receive papal approval. While these negotiations were in progress, the leadership of the Bulgar mission remained in the hands of the missionary bishops previously sent from Rome. The chief figure was Grimoald, who had been commissioned to work in Bulgaria by Nicholas I; his working companion, Paul of

104. See above, p. 81.
105. *Liber pontificalis*, ed. Duchesne, II, 165; Nicholas, *Ep.*, No. 100, ed. Perels, *MGH*, *Ep.*, VI, 603.

Populonia, had returned to Rome in 869 in the company of the khan's legate, Peter.[106]

It may well have been that Rome's failure to constitute a hierarchy suitable to the Bulgars severely disappointed Boris, for by 870 he was beginning to waver in his allegiance to the see of St. Peter and to think of a return to the ecclesiastical jurisdiction of Constantinople. However, other pressures were also driving Boris toward Constantinople. The Greeks had made a powerful effort to convince him that the Latins were spreading heresy among his people. He was, moreover, faced with internal resistance, which the Greeks may have been exploiting, and so successfully that the khan felt the need to establish friendlier relations with the imperial court. Western writers insist that the Greeks used "gifts and promises" to weaken the Bulgar attachment to Rome, and "promises" may in some way have involved discussions of the organizational future of the Bulgars.[107] Whatever the reason, Boris sent a legation to Constantinople in 870 to ask the important general council, then in session, to decide whether Bulgaria's jurisdiction pertained to Rome or to Constantinople.[108] Despite a stout defense of Rome's claims in Bulgaria by papal legates, the council decided that Bulgaria pertained to the authority of Constantinople.[109]

This decision, obviously approved by Boris, once again reoriented the entire organizational evolution of the Bulgar church. The Latin clergy were expelled, and among those required to leave was Bishop Grimoald, apparently none the worse for his experiences, since it was reported that he had become rich while in Bulgaria.[110] A letter of Hadrian II, written in 871, indicates that Patriarch Ignatius had by that date appointed a bishop for Bulgaria;[111] and this seems to be confirmed by an inscription which speaks of a Greek bishop named Nicholas working in Bulgaria.[112] Greek priests again entered Bulgaria to carry on missionary

106. *Liber pontificalis*, ed. Duchesne, II, 185.

107. *Ibid.*, p. 185; Nicholas, *Ep.*, No. 100, ed. Perels, *MGH, Ep.*, VI, 603; *Anastasii Bibliothecarii Ep. sive Praef.*, No. 5, eds. Perels and Laehr, *MGH, Ep.*, VII, 413.

108. For the larger implications of this council, see Dvornik, *The Photian Schism*, pp. 145–58; Amann, *L'époque carolingienne*, pp. 483–89.

109. For a full account of the treatment of the Bulgar requests at the council of Constantinople, see *Liber pontificalis*, ed. Duchesne, II, 182–85; *Anastasii Bibliothecarii Ep. sive Praef.*, No. 5, eds. Perels and Laehr, *MGH, Ep.*, VII, 411–15.

110. *Liber pontificalis*, ed. Duchesne, II, 185.

111. *Hadriani II. Papae Epistolae*, No. 41, ed. Perels, *MGH, Ep.*, VI, 760.

112. H. Grégoire, "Une inscription datée au nom du Roi Boris-Michel de Bulgarie," *Byzantion*, XIV (1939), 227–34.

work. All this aroused the wrath of the papacy and prompted Popes Hadrian II and John VIII to engage in a long battle of words in an attempt to regain jurisdiction over Bulgaria.

We need not follow this struggle, since papal efforts had no significant impact on church organization in Bulgaria,[113] but the papal letters supply some evidence on the development of the ecclesiastical organization under Greek aegis. We have already noted that in 871 Hadrian II spoke of a Greek bishop residing in Bulgaria. In a letter written in late 872 or early 873, John VIII indicated that Ignatius had "sent there [to Bulgaria] some schismatic with the title of archbishop,"[114] who may well have been the "antistites" referred to by Hadrian II in his letter of 871. In another letter, written to Boris at about the same time, John spoke of the presence of Greek "bishops and priests" in Bulgaria.[115] Such evidence indicates that the Bulgars had finally got an archbishop, which may have been a concession made by Constantinople to gain the victory of 870. Moreover, bishops had been consecrated under the archbishop and were actively engaged in episcopal functions. This is confirmed by a letter from John VIII to Boris, in 878, ordering the deposition of "a certain eunuch, Sergius, a Slav by birth," who had been made bishop of Belgrade by George, "who had falsely assumed to himself the title of bishop."[116] A native episcopacy appears to be emerging and the division of Bulgaria into dioceses has begun. Nor is it impossible that Sergius had been one of those Slavs who had been educated in Constantinople about this time.[117]

There is further proof of the existence of several bishops in Bulgaria by 878 in a letter of John VIII addressed to "all Greek bishops and other clergy who are invaders of the *dioceses* of Bulgaria," threatening them with excommunication if they did not leave their offices within thirty days. Some of these churchmen had come from outside Bulgaria already holding the episcopal office, for John assured those who obeyed his command that they would be restored to their former sees.[118] It may have occurred to John that if he could not oust the Greek hierarchy then emerging in Bulgaria, he could at least influence it, for in June, 879, he wrote to Boris

---

113. See Dvornik, *The Photian Schism*, pp. 151 ff.; Runciman, *The First Bulgarian Empire*, pp. 114–23.

114. *Fragmenta Registri Iohannis VIII. Papae*, No. 9, ed. Caspar, *MGH, Ep.*, VII, 278.

115. *Ibid.*, No. 7, p. 277.

116. *Iohannis VIII. Papae Epistolae*, No. 66, ed. Caspar, *op. cit.*, p. 60.

117. Photius, *Ep.*, No. 255, ed. Valetta, p. 556.

118. *Iohannis VIII. Papae Epistolae*, No. 71, ed. Caspar, *MGH, Ep.*, VII, 66–67. A second letter dealing with the same matter was sent at the same time to Patriarch Ignatius; see *ibid.*, No. 68, pp. 62–63.

asking whether the khan wished to receive a papal legation and an apostolic visitation.[119] Apparently Boris felt no such need, for he did not request Rome's guidance. The ecclesiastical organization of Bulgaria was apparently taking a shape that was satisfactory to him.

One of the concessions John VIII extracted from the imperial government at the synod held at Constantinople in 879–880 in return for his recognition of the reinstallation of Photius as patriarch was the restoration of Bulgaria to Rome's jurisdiction. This decision was clearly an arrangement between Rome and Constantinople; Boris was not involved in any of the negotiations,[120] and he apparently refused to adhere to the decision taken in Constantinople. The imperial regime undoubtedly was aware of his devotion to Byzantium and therefore quite willing to concede to Rome nominal jurisdiction over Bulgaria.

Because Boris paid no heed to the decisions of 879–880, there was no exodus of the Greek hierarchy in favor of a new crowd of Romans. John may initially have intended that this would happen for he ordered Photius to see that "the bishops consecrated there and all lower clergy leave the country."[121] However, as Dvornik has shown, John eventually was willing to compromise the issue of allowing the Greeks to remain in Bulgaria provided they would admit his jurisdiction, come to Rome for installation in higher offices, and refrain from depending in any way on Constantinople. Photius and the imperial government were not averse to this arrangement,[122] but Boris provided the roadblock, refusing to accept Rome's jurisdiction. Papal appeals in 881 and 882 produced not so much as an answer.[123]

All of this would suggest Boris' satisfaction with the organization that had developed since 870. Probably by 880 the hierarchy in Bulgaria was sufficiently pliable to his will and so oriented to Bulgar problems that it felt no burning interest in the disputes and negotiations involved in establishing the jurisdiction to which Bulgaria belonged. Thus Boris could see no advantage in inviting a complete upheaval of the existing organization by permitting the pope to oust the Greeks and introduce a new and inexperienced leadership in Bulgar problems, especially since

119. *Ibid.*, No. 192, pp. 153–54.
120. For an analysis of this council see Dvornik, *The Photian Schism*, pp. 159–219; Amann, *L'époque carolingienne*, pp. 492–98.
121. *Iohannis VIII. Papae Epistolae*, No. 209, ed. Caspar, *MGH, Ep.*, VII, pp. 185–86.
122. Dvornik, *The Photian Schism*, pp. 210–13.
123. *Iohannis VIII. Papae Epistolae*, Nos. 298, 308, ed. Caspar, *MGH, Ep.*, VII, pp. 260, 266–67.

Rome had previously been reluctant to permit an independent hierarchy in Bulgaria.

Toward the end of his reign Boris took steps to increase the number of native clergy in Bulgaria. This move may at first have been intended only to complement the Greek hierarchy, but it is very likely that Boris already planned to create a Bulgar hierarchy that could ultimately replace the Greeks. We have noted that Boris had begun to send Bulgars to Constantinople for a monastic education, and presumably some of these Bulgars returned to serve as clergymen in their homeland (although we have no precise confirmation of this). At any rate, Bulgars trained in Byzantium would probably have been thoroughly Hellenized and thus little different in their outlook from the Greeks who had entered the Bulgar kingdom to serve in a missionary capacity. The Greek missionary forces also elevated some natives to the clerical rank, although this does not appear to have been a regular procedure.[124] Perhaps, then, it was especially significant that, about 878, Boris sent his second son, Symeon, to Constantinople to be educated and then to become a monk.[125] It appears not unlikely that already the khan planned that Symeon would ultimately return to Bulgaria to assume the role of patriarch, thoroughly prepared for that exalted task by the intellectual and spiritual experiences he had gained while associating with the circle surrounding the great Photius.[126]

About 885 a new and unexpected opportunity presented itself to Boris that permitted him to move toward the creation of a native clergy.[127] After the death of St. Methodius, a German-inspired reaction occurred

124. *Ibid.*, No. 66, p. 60; Theophylactus, *Vita s. Clementis*, Ch. 22, Migne, *PG*, CXXVI, col. 1229, which says that many priests in Bulgaria used Greek so poorly that they could not understand Scripture. This would suggest a more numerous native clergy by the end of the reign of Boris.

125. Luidprandus of Cremona, *Antapodosis*, III, Ch. 29, in *The Works of Luidprand of Cremona*, trans. F. A. Wright (New York, 1930), p. 123.

126. For a somewhat imaginative review of Symeon's career in Constantinople and suggestions on the purpose for which he was sent there, see G. Sergheraert (Christian Gérard), *Syméon le Grand (893–927)* (Paris, 1960), pp. 15–47.

127. The following section is based on Theophylactus, *Vita s. Clementis*, Chs. 14–29, Migne, *PG*, CXXVI, cols. 1217–40, and on the old Slavonic *life* of St. Nahum, the text of which is given, along with an English translation, by Kusseff in *Slavonic and East European Review*, XXIX (1950–51), 142–44. Kusseff's "St. Nahum," *ibid.*, 139–52, and "St. Clement of Ochrida," *ibid.*, XXVII (1948–49), 193–215, and I. Snegarov's "Les sources sur la vie et l'activité de Clément d'Ochrida," *Byzantinobulgarica* (Sofia, 1962), I, 79–119, provide careful analyses of these sources; they are especially useful because of their use of Slavic studies unavailable to the present author.

in Moravia. The Slavic-speaking disciples of this Apostle of Moravia were forced to flee, abandoning their effort to develop a Slavonic liturgy and a Slavonic literary tradition in Moravia. Some went directly from Moravia to Bulgaria, and many of these clergymen found a warm welcome in Bulgaria. Others were sent to the slave markets of Venice, where an emissary of Emperor Basil rescued them and returned them to Constantinople, and from there they were eventually transferred to Bulgaria. The biographies of two of these missionaries, Clement of Ochrida and Nahum, provide insight into Boris' use of the talents of these skilled missionary workers and illuminate his plans for a Bulgar hierarchy.

Upon their arrival in Bulgaria, Clement and Nahum were taken to Boris by the governor of Belgrade, who, according to Clement's biography, "knew that Boris was friendly to such men." The khan greeted them joyfully, placed them in the houses of Bulgar nobles, and asked them many questions. After a short time, Boris moved to make better use of Clement's talents. In the Macedonian area of his realm, where the population was predominantly Slavic, he divided a larger province so as to create a smaller territory, and commissioned Clement to be "teacher" (διδάσκαλος) over this area. The title suggests that Clement's role was that of a missionary leader; however, the description of his position indicates that he enjoyed a considerably larger authority, which permitted him to order affairs so as to expedite missionary work. A secular official, named Dobeta, was installed in the territory to share responsibility with Clement and to assist his missionary work, perhaps submitting to his authority in some matters. Boris provided Clement with houses in Devol, Ochrida and Glavinitze, commended Clement to the Slavic population of the area, and ordered them to support his work with material gifts. The entire arrangement suggests that Clement, representing the tradition of a Slavonic church established earlier in Moravia by Cyril and Methodius, was being given a jurisdiction independent of the Greek archbishop in Bulgaria and separate from the court. He was being used to rally Slavs to the new religion and to represent the Bulgar khan among these Slavs, where Bulgar overlordship may not have been popular.

For seven years Clement occupied himself spreading the Word in his area, laboring with a population given to superstition and ignorance. As a part of this effort, Clement established schools which taught reading and writing, and the number of students in these centers was reported to be 3,500. From those taught to read, Clement apparently singled out certain ones who became his constant companions, and their training was apparently more thorough. From these, selected pupils were eventually ordained lectors, subdeacons, and priests, perhaps in large enough numbers that they could be sent to serve elsewhere in Bulgaria. Clement and his disciples at the same time labored to create a body of theological and liturgical literature suited to the needs of the Slavs, who could not comprehend Greek. These efforts were a continuation of the work begun in Moravia by Cyril and Methodius; indeed, from the work of Clement and his disciples there soon evolved the first flowering of a Slavonic literary culture, which reached its full fruition during the reign of Symeon (893–927).[128] This cultural activity, prompted by the needs of a newly established religion, proved to be a powerful force in bridging the gap between the ruling Bulgars and the subject Slavs. As the fame of Clement spread—along with the religious works produced by his disciples—the importance of the Greek hierarchy in Bulgaria undoubtedly receded.

The outcome of the role in which Clement had been cast was inevitable. Shortly after Symeon became khan (893), the widely known and greatly respected Clement was elevated to the episcopacy, the first Bulgar-speaking man to be so honored. With this event, the native element in Bulgaria had moved to the forefront. The perpetuation of the tradition of Cyril and Methodius had produced a circle of ecclesiastical figures deeply schooled in Byzantine learning but possessed of the linguistic skills and the experience to put their talents to work in Bulgaria. Their presence made unnecessary any further dependence on Greeks as ecclesiastical leaders among the Bulgars. Boris' reception and utilization of the fugitives from Moravia in 885 was the initial step toward the establishment of a Bulgar patriarchate in 925.

But Clement was not the only man to serve the khan's effort to produce a native clergy. Nahum had spent the years 885 to 893 as a leader of scholarly activity at the newly established monastery of St. Panteliemon, near Preslav. The monks there were chiefly engaged in translations and copying, producing numerous works in the Slavonic tongue to serve the rapidly emerging native church. After Clement had been made a bishop, Nahum went to Clement's territory in Macedonia to serve as missionary leader and teacher. He built another important monastery on Lake Ochrida and made it an important educational center.

128. For a review of Bulgarian cultural activity in the reign of Symeon, see Sergheraert, *Syméon le Grand (893–927)*, pp. 88–115; also see pp. 180–89 for an excellent bibliography on the subject. Likewise suggestive are the remarks of Dvornik, *The Slavs: Their Early History and Civilization (Survey of Slavic Civilization*, Vol. II) (Boston, 1956), pp. 147–88.

Meanwhile Boris had taken his last step to shape the organization of the Bulgar church. After returning from his monastic retreat to thwart the efforts of his son and successor, Vladimir, to overturn the Christian establishment and restore paganism, Boris sought to give formal sanction to the ecclesiastical organization. In 893 he summoned an assembly of important men to approve a series of crucial decisions. The Slavonic rite was made official. Symeon, who had been living as a monk at St. Pantelie-mon, was made khan. Seven metropolitan sees were formally proclaimed: Drista, Philippopolis, Sardica, Provadia, Margum, Bregolnitsa and Ochrida, all to be under the archbishop of Bulgaria, whose see was now moved to Preslav, the new capital. Most of these cities or towns had been the centers of ancient provinces and had served as ecclesiastical centers between the years 864 and 893. Bishoprics already existed in several provinces.[129]

When Boris died, in 907, the organization of the Bulgar church had progressed far from its state of forty years earlier, when the khan had pleaded with Rome to designate a foreign archbishop to serve Bulgaria. It is obvious, however, that progress in this direction had created many problems that had been added to the burden imposed on the khan by the conversion process as a whole. The creation of an ecclesiastical organization had depended on foreigners; there had been the initial problem of securing adequate help from abroad. The missionary bishops, priests, and monks who could be recruited were then confronted by a population whose language and culture were strange, a condition that must have led to misunderstandings. Furthermore, the clergy that came to Bulgaria initially owed prime allegiance to superiors outside the Bulgar kingdom; and these superiors, in Rome and/or Constantinople, had preconceived notions of how an ecclesiastical organization should evolve in a missionary territory.

These ideas had often prevented the khan from promoting the organizational growth which he judged suitable to his realm, especially since the two major sources of missionary aid for Bulgaria were engaged in bitter competition for jurisdiction over Bulgaria. As a consequence, both had insisted on the exclusive right to proselytize among the Bulgars, a condition which had forced Boris to choose one or the other as the source of assistance. Each choice had resulted in the exodus of one group of missionaries and the appearance of a new group. Roman and Greek missionaries, whichever were in command, had to combat pressures from

129. Runciman, *The First Bulgarian Empire*, pp. 135–36; Sergheraert, *Syméon le Grand (893–927)*, pp. 51, 55–58.

the out-group, insisting that their work was tainted in some way. This contentious situation must certainly have compromised the authority of ecclesiastical leadership and thereby endangered the progress of the missionary effort. As far as can be determined from the evidence, neither the Roman nor the Greek missionary forces strove to develop a native clergy from which a native hierarchy could emerge. This crucial step had to await a happy accident, which put at the service of Boris a capable missionary group which was also willing to prepare native Bulgars for responsible ecclesiastical posts. Boris' skill in utilizing this new talent was a decisive turning point in the Christianization process in Bulgaria and a mark of his effective leadership of that process.

As one studies the problems connected with the establishment of an ecclesiastical organization in Bulgaria he becomes more sympathetically understanding of Boris' constant concern with this problem. Most authorities have accepted without question the position that Boris' pre-occupation with securing an autonomous ecclesiastical authority for Bulgaria was dictated by ambition and premature dreams of Bulgar glory.[130] Indeed, it is not difficult to arrive at such a conclusion when one finds Boris asking the pope, within two years after his conversion, how one goes about establishing a patriarchate. Yet in view of what has been established in the preceding pages as the practical problems that faced the Bulgar khan in establishing Christian doctrine and practice, it is also easy to realize how desperately Boris must have felt the need for an ecclesiastical superior of sufficient authority—and with intimate knowledge of the Bulgar situation—to resolve the many issues that arose from day to day as the new religion spread. It is inconceivable that a ruler so intimately involved in the conversion of his people would not have immediately sensed that the task would become easier if it were supported by an ecclesiastical hierarchy self-contained in Bulgaria and answerable to no external power whose interests in the Bulgars involved more than the conversion process. Although it is conceded that excessive ambition, grandiose dreams, and national pride played a large part in Boris' attempt to establish an independent Bulgar hierarchy, it seems likely that he also saw the practical necessity of a strong hierarchy as a vital aspect of an effective and successful missionary effort.

130. For example, Spinka, *A History of Christianity in the Balkans*, pp. 37–40; Slatarski, *Geschichte der Bulgaren*, I, 43–46; Dvornik, *Les Slaves, Byzance et Rome au IXᵉ siècle*, p. 190; Amann, *L'époque carolingienne*, pp. 477–78. Although agreeing with this view in general, Gérard (*Les Bulgares*, pp. 208–9) hints that Bulgar problems had some relationship to Boris' anxiety to secure an independent organization and to develop a hierarchy re-sponsive to his will.

In this respect he appears to have achieved an insight common to other successful missionary leaders of his era, e.g., Boniface, Ansgar, and Gregory the Great: that ecclesiastical authority was needed in the missionary arena almost as soon as the first pagan was baptized. To gain this end, Boris had to contend with an unusual situation: he was dependent on the aid of outsiders who were reluctant to permit the growth of a Bulgar hierarchy unless they were perfectly certain of that hierarchy's first allegiance. Had Boris been free to deal exclusively with either Rome or Constantinople, he might have secured an effective hierarchy without so much difficulty. And that hierarchy might have been allowed a greater degree of independence in responding to the unique problems in Bulgaria.

As the new religion took hold among the Bulgars, a fresh range of problems arose to complicate a situation already quite complex. The introduction of Christianity called into question the art of government as traditionally practiced among the Bulgars, and, by implication, it required a wide-ranging adjustment of existing usages to new concepts of government and to new situations produced by the mere presence of Christianity. To Boris fell the responsibility of making the changes demanded in establishing a Christian government for the Bulgars. Unfortunately, we can see only the dimensions of his problem; the meager evidence does not permit us to follow the political changes actually effected as efforts were made to adjust to the new religion. Still, what emerged as new political issues, regardless of their ultimate resolution, leaves no doubt that the conversion process called into question the basic concepts and processes of government that had prevailed in Bulgaria before the conversion.

The most striking political development suggested by a synthesis of all the sources is that the Christianization of Bulgaria demanded a vast expansion of the power of the khan. Certainly the internal evolution of the Bulgar state before 864 had witnessed the slow transformation of the khan's position from that of a war chieftain, commanding a loosely knit band of warriors in incessant pursuit of the prizes of war, into that of a genuine chief of state, with authority over a set territory, with power to judge, pronounce laws, punish, tax, and conduct a foreign policy—and with at least a primitive administrative system at his command. This gradual strengthening of monarchical government was apparently nourished by at least two powerful forces: the exigencies involved in wresting from formidable foes a territory that would serve as a homeland for the Bulgars, and the example of the more-advanced political systems

of these foes, especially the Byzantine Empire.[131] But with the baptism of Boris in 864, what had been a drift in Bulgar political life suddenly was presented to the khan as a necessity. Popes and patriarchs insisted that the new convert was responsible for converting his subjects, for protecting the purity of the faith among a population whose crudity endangered it, and for ordering all things in Bulgaria so as to expedite and assure the spread of Christianity. Implicit in their injunctions was a broad range of new powers for the khan, which promised to exalt his position beyond that enjoyed by his pagan predecessors.

The most eloquent testimony for the range of authority that a Christian prince could rightfully claim was the pastoral letter sent to Boris by Photius shortly after the former's baptism. For the enlightenment of his spiritual son the patriarch produced an elegant treatise on the duties of a Christian prince, replete with concepts drawn from the classical tradition. It has often been said that Photius' delineation of the prince's role could have meant little to the unsophisticated Bulgar khan. Indeed, the tract might have been more appropriate if addressed to an educated Byzantine prince (for whom it may well have been produced originally); yet one suspects that what Photius insisted Boris should do served but to suggest to the new convert what he might do to increase his royal power. Photius' epistle is therefore worth a brief description as an indication of the concept of authority a newly converted ruler earned by his journey to the baptismal font.

In his letter, Photius assumed the role of spiritual father to Boris, an office which demanded that he lead the newly initiated Christian to a fuller comprehension of the truth to which Boris had surrendered. The patriarch's task had a dual character: to acquaint Boris with the basic tenets of the faith and to provide him with a guide to those good works which are proper to a follower of Christ.[132] Photius insisted that "the excellent ornament of [his] labors"[133] understand that faith and good works are linked: "right faith produces noble habits, and purity of deeds proves that faith is fully divine."[134] Photius appears to have treated Boris

131. Slatarski, *Geschichte der Bulgaren*, I, 1–41; Gérard, *Les Bulgares*, pp. 136–82. Also see the interesting attempt of V. Beševliev, "Souveränitätsansprüche eines bulgarischen Herrschers im 9. Jahrhunderts," *Byzantinische Zeitschrift*, LV (1962), 11–20, to demonstrate that a ninth-century inscription from Bulgaria indicates that an effort was being made by the khan to imitate the powers of the Byzantine emperor.

132. Photius, *Ep.*, No. 6, Chs. 1–2, ed. Valetta, pp. 202–3.

133. *Ibid.*, Ch. 5, p. 204: "... ὦ καλὸν ἄγαλμα τῶν ἐμῶν πόνων."

134. *Ibid.*, Ch. 3, p. 203: "Καὶ γὰρ δογμάτων μὲν εὐθύτης πολιτείας προβάλλεται κοσμιότητα, πράξεων δὲ καθαρότης τῆς Πίστεως ἀπαγγέλλει Θειότητα."

as merely another catechumen; his explanation of the purpose of his letter made no mention of its being a guide for the exercise of royal power. Yet Photius inevitably had to consider that Boris was a prince, and therefore he developed arguments that Boris could interpret only as justifications for more and greater princely powers.

Having stated his general purpose, Photius devoted a long section of his letter to expanding the basic doctrines of Christianity.[135] He first set down the Nicene Creed; then he outlined the decisions of all the ecumenical councils, explaining the heretical ideas that had necessitated these councils. But the patriarch did not stop with a simple exposition of the content of the faith, he tried to convince Boris that this body of doctrine must be guarded against contrary opinions while it was being spread among the newly converted Bulgars. He therefore developed an argument suggesting how great would be the displeasure of God over any deviation from these truths, and how drastic would be the tumults, wars, contentions, and battles afflicting Bulgaria if heresy were to develop. His discourse led inevitably to one conclusion: upon the ruler falls the burden of guarding orthodoxy and preventing the disorders that emerge from heresy.[136]

As Boris pondered the strictures of his spiritual father, he must have envisaged, from his position as prince, a new area of authority that had not been his as a pagan. There had been handed over to him a body of truth whose sanctity must be guarded. By the very nature of the universe, diabolic forces would be laboring constantly to subvert that truth. If such subversion occurred, God would be displeased and the society over which the khan ruled would be rent with tumult and struggle. To prevent such catastrophes he was entitled, and duty-bound, to use whatever powers he could muster; indeed, the exercise of extraordinary powers was divinely sanctioned. As his subjects came to understand the pure faith, having grasped the evil consequences of heterodoxy, they would certainly acquiesce to whatever authority the prince needed to protect them from error and strife. In brief, the institution of the Christian faith in Bulgaria involved a special kind of responsibility for the prince, and a new range

135. *Ibid.*, Chs. 4–18, pp. 203–19.

136. *Ibid.*, Chs. 19–20, pp. 219–21. Photius speaks in such terms as these: "Ταύτην προσήκει καὶ τὴν ὑμετέραν θεοφρούρητον σύνεσιν, ἤδη πρὸς τὸν ἡμέτερον κλῆρον τῆς εὐσεβείας ἀφορῶσαν, εἰλικρινεῖ διαθέσει, καὶ γνώμης εὐθύτητι, καὶ ἀδιστάκτῳ πίστει ἀποδέχεσθαι καὶ στέργειν, καὶ μήτε δεξιᾷ μήτε ἀριστερᾷ, μηδὲ ἐπὶ βραχὺ ταύτης ἀποκλίνειν. . . . "Ἄρχουτος γὰρ ὡς ἀληθῶς μὴ τῆς ἰδίας μόνον σωτηρίας ποιεῖσθαι φροντίδα, ἀλλὰ καὶ τὸν ἐμπιστευθέντα λαὸν τῆς ἴσης ἀξιοῦν προνοίας, καὶ εἰς τὴν αὐτὴν τῆς θεογνωσίας χειραγωγεῖν τε καὶ προσκαλεῖσθαι τελειότητα."

of powers followed that could not be shirked by a Christian prince worthy of that rank. As protector of the faith, Boris had become something he had not been as a pagan ruler, and he was therefore constrained to act in ways that had not been proper to his office before he was baptized.

Having charged his pupil with new and grave responsibilities as the guardian of orthodoxy, Photius turned to a discourse on good works.[137] His argument turned on a simple proposition: having accepted the new faith, Boris was obligated to remold his life, to bear witness to his faith by the nature and quality of his deeds. Once again Photius wrote in terms that were applicable to all Christians,[138] outlining a moral code for Boris that was the same as for any other Christian. However, the patriarch could not escape the fact that he was instructing a prince, revealing his awareness of this fact when, at the very outset of his exposition, he admonished Boris to emulate Constantine the Great.[139] Thus his moral precepts repeatedly emerge as suggestions that pointed to ways in which careful observance of the new religion might enhance royal power—or as commands indicating new powers which the newly converted king should assume.

A few examples will suffice to illustrate the political overtones of Photius' moral advice. The patriarch was especially skillful in tempting Boris to think that a modification of his moral conduct would exalt him in the eyes of his subjects. "The habits of princes are as the law among subjects."[140] This means that if the prince by his example can induce his people to love one another, they will refrain from bloodshed, theft, adultery, false witness, fighting, and the desire for the goods of others.[141] If the prince can cause his subjects to pray and worship together, they will then be bound in a new kind of unity.[142] In the administration of justice, the spirit of Christian mercy, benevolence, and moderation will gain greater praise and respect than rigid adherence to the letter of the law.[143] Subjects will respect him who orders his desires and dominates his pleasures.[144] Kindness and pious feelings toward compatriots will win a prince

137. *Ibid.*, Chs., 21–114, pp. 221–48.
138. *Ibid.*, Ch. 24, p. 224: "'Αλλὰ ταῦτα μὲν ἀνθρώπῳ παντὶ πάσῃ δυνάμει παραφυλακτέον, ἄρχοντι καὶ ἀρχομένῳ νέῳ καὶ πρεσβύτῃ, πλουσίῳ καὶ πένητι. Κοινὴ γὰρ ἡ φύσις, καὶ κοινὰ τὰ προστάγματα, καὶ κοινῆς τῆς παραφυλακῆς καὶ ἐπιμελείας δεόμενα."
139. *Ibid.*, Ch. 22, p. 222.
140. *Ibid.*, Ch. 47, p. 233: "'Ο τῶν ἀρχόντων τρόπος νόμος γίνεται τοῖς ὑπὸ χεῖρα."
141. *Ibid.*, Ch. 23, pp. 223–24.
142. *Ibid.*, Chs. 25–27, pp. 224–25.
143. *Ibid.*, Chs. 42–43, 54, pp. 232–35.
144. *Ibid.*, Ch. 53, p. 234.

greater favor than successful conduct of war.[145] Anger, passion, distrustfulness, voluptuousness and drunkenness debase the power of a prince, but virtues will enhance his position.[146] As he followed Photius' discourse point by point, Boris could easily have convinced himself that a close observance of Christian morality would exalt his prestige and enhance his respect among his subjects. If his people came to admire his moral qualities, they would unquestioningly permit him to do what he pleased.

At times, Photius' letter probably suggested new political activities to which the khan must commit himself. Certainly it was clear that he must do whatever was necessary to spread the faith and to protect orthodoxy. If Christianity demanded good works as a complement to correct belief, then Boris was obliged to do whatever was necessary to "reform" the morals of his subjects; this would not only please God but would also make his subjects more appreciative of his virtues and more respectful of his power. The khan was unequivocally commanded to build churches for his subjects, a new activity that required new powers.[147] He was exhorted to examine the qualifications of those who advised him,[148] a command that implicitly broadened the princely power over administrative personnel and procedures. The administration of justice needed rethinking in the light of Christian principles,[149] and obviously such a review would broaden the khan's authority in this area. In fact, virtually all that Photius mentioned by way of moral instruction for his spiritual son contained an invitation for Boris to assume new authority in the interests of improving his own and his subjects' conduct.

There seems little question, then, that Photius—and no doubt the popes involved in the conversion of Bulgaria—thought in terms of an increase of royal power as a necessary concomitant of the Christianization of a pagan land. Did Boris react to this stimulus by seeking a more exalted role among his subjects? And was he able to increase his authority?

A response to these questions is difficult in the light of the sources. Some evidence can be cited to suggest that Boris assumed certain new powers as a consequence of the existence of Christianity in his realm. We have already noted the khan's role in summoning and dismissing missionary parties and in seeking to establish an ecclesiastical organization.

145. *Ibid.*, Ch. 56, p. 235.
146. *Ibid.*, Chs. 85–87, 91, 92, 94, pp. 241–43.
147. *Ibid.*, Ch. 27, p. 225.
148. *Ibid.*, Ch. 57, p. 235.
149. *Ibid.*, Chs. 39–41, pp. 231–32.

Boris sought from Pope Nicholas "worldly laws," evidently for the purpose of clarifying his regal position.[150] He wielded his power arbitrarily to punish false clergymen who sought to prey upon the Bulgars during the conversion period,[151] and to crush those who revolted in protest against the introduction of Christianity.[152] These measures suggest autocratic action in the cause of the new religion. He was at least tempted to take severe steps against those who resisted conversion or rejected the faith once they had received it.[153] When it came time to provide a missionary setting for Clement, Boris moved boldly to dismantle an existing administrative district and place part of it under the authority of a missionary leader.[154] To say the least, such a procedure appears unusual, and it is indicative of the khan's power to act as he chose.

These scraps of evidence hardly prove that the Bulgar khan became *basileus* or *autocrator* immediately after Christianity was introduced into his realm, but they indicate that the presence of the new religion and the issues raised by it gave the khan an opportunity to extend his authority into fresh areas. These opportunities, coupled with the vision of authority suggested by Boris' mentors, especially Photius, may indeed have been significant in shaping a stronger central government in Bulgaria than had existed prior to the Christianization of that land. The glorious reign of Boris' son, Symeon, would also seem to bear out this conclusion.

While hinting that Boris may have been inspired to autocratic political conduct by Christian ideals and religious problems, the evidence more strongly suggests another and perhaps more troublesome political consequence of the conversion process. The document that draws us closest to Boris himself, the letter of Pope Nicholas, repeatedly implies that the introduction of Christianity raised great confusion in the khan's mind about the conduct of ordinary, routine political processes. He appears to have believed that a Christian prince is bound to act differently than he did when he was a pagan, and that time-sanctioned political practices had to be recast to fit a Christian style of statecraft. These beliefs or inclinations appear to have bred uncertainty in the khan's mind that drove him to seek guidance on what should be done to refurbish his government to meet Christian standards.

The major political concerns reflected in Boris' requests to Nicholas

---

150. Nicholas, *Ep.*, No. 99, Ch. 13, p. 575.
151. *Ibid.*, Chs. 14–16, pp. 575–76.
152. *Ibid.*, Chs. 17–19, pp. 577–78.
153. *Ibid.*, Chs. 18, 41, 102, pp. 578, 582–83, 599.
154. Theophylactus, *Vita s. Clementis*, Ch. 17, Migne, *PG*, CXXVI, col. 1224.

can be grouped under a few broad headings. By far the most prominent issue centers around the administration of justice. In this connection, Boris was troubled on three points: he repeatedly asked the pope to define the position he, as judge, should take toward certain criminal groups in society; he was concerned about punishments proper for various kinds of crime; and he was worried lest conventional judicial procedures violate the Christian religion.

In seeking information about how various lawbreakers should be judged, Boris was often concerned with types of criminals that had been present in Bulgar society long before Christianity had entered the land. He asked Nicholas to tell him what should be done with fugitives from battle, those who refuse to fight, parricides, those trying to flee the country, murderers of relatives, adulterers, those guilty of incest, rapists, animal thiefs, kidnappers, those who castrate others, false accusers, poisoners, and slaves who accuse their masters.[155] We must assume that Bulgar custom and law had long ago established that those who were guilty of these acts were criminals, and Boris knew—under the old order—what to do with them; but for some reason he felt that conventional usages had been outmoded by the coming of Christianity. The fact that he asked what should be done with such common types of criminal action forces one to conclude that he was ready to change ancient usage to fit new standards. Nicholas must have interpreted his requests in this fashion, for he sent Boris a code of laws[156] and constantly directed the khan to this document for specific instructions on revamping the Bulgar judicial system.

The coming of Christianity introduced a new range of crimes and confronted the khan with the problem of the judicial treatment of his subjects who were found guilty of these new offenses. Boris now needed to know what should be done about apostates, those who flee the country to escape the new religion, those who refuse to become Christian, those who copulate with their wives during Lent, bigamists, married priests, adulterous priests, those who try to force widows to become nuns against their will, criminals who seek asylum in churches, those who divorce their spouses, suicides, false missionaries, and troublesome preachers.[157] From

155. Nicholas, *Ep.*, No. 99, Chs. 22–26, 28–32, 52, 84, 85, 97, pp. 579–80, 586, 595, 597–98.

156. *Ibid.*, Ch. 13, p. 575. M. Conrat, "Römisches Recht bei Papst Nikolaus I," *Neues Archiv*, XXXVI (1911), 724, argues that this code was a Lombard law code enlarged by certain Carolingian capitularies; he denies that it was the Code of Justinian, as some have suggested.

157. Nicholas, *Ep.*, No. 99, Chs. 18–20, 41, 50, 51, 70, 71, 87, 95, 96, 98, 104, 105, pp. 578, 579, 582–83, 586, 592, 595–99.

a modern point of view, Boris encroached upon private ground, for he compounded criminals and sinners, and at one point asked Nicholas how he should treat sinners in general.[158] However, what is more significant than these niceties is the fact that the introduction of the new religion thrust upon the ruler the responsibility for rendering justice on matters previously unknown in Bulgar society. Again, the conversion process had introduced complications into the ordinary processes of government and had left the ruler uncertain of his responsibility.

Not only did Boris want to know his position vis-à-vis the perpetrators of a wide range of criminal acts, he also worried about the punishment he should mete out to criminals. Apparently convinced that a mark of Bulgar barbarity was its savagery in punishing lawbreakers, Photius had cautioned the khan against imposing weighty punishments according to the exact letter of the law.[159] It seems almost certain that the new convert was moved by this admonition and that he was gravely concerned lest customary Bulgar severity in punishing criminals violate Christian teaching. At one place in his letter to Nicholas, Boris submitted a sample of Bulgar justice for papal evaluation: if a thief or a robber is apprehended and denies what is charged against him, the judge strikes his head with a rod and pierces his sides with iron picks until he tells the truth.[160] He asked the pope to tell him if this is a just treatment of a criminal.

In two other cases he asked for a judgment on Bulgar treatment of criminals by making a personal confession to the pope. Boris had apprehended a "lying Greek who claimed to be a priest" performing baptism; he judged him, and then punished him by cutting off his ears and nose, lashing him, and expelling him from the country. He begged the pope to tell him whether he should do penance for such conduct.[161] Boris then recounted that when some of his subjects had rebelled against him for having introduced Christianity into the land, and had sought to kill him, he had killed the nobles involved and their progeny. His chief concern was whether his conduct as judge had been sinful.[162]

In each of these three instances the Bulgar penal code is held up for scrutiny, and Boris would hardly have raised these issues had he not felt that the new religion demanded less severe punishments. We must presume that in all his requests for guidance in dealing with criminals he was

158. *Ibid.*, Ch. 83, p. 595.
159. Photius, *Ep.*, No. 6, Chs. 42–44, ed. Valetta, pp. 232–33.
160. Nicholas, *Ep.*, No. 99, Ch. 86, p. 595.
161. *Ibid.*, Chs. 14, 16, pp. 575, 576.
162. *Ibid.*, Ch. 17, pp. 577–78.

also seeking to discover the approved Christian punishments as replacements for the savage habits of the Bulgars. Nicholas apparently sensed Boris' sentiment, for he repeatedly counseled his protégé to temper the law with mercy and moderation. The law code he sent to Boris provided specific information for establishing a new penal code.

In the matter of justice, finally, Boris was concerned with the propriety of certain judicial procedures as he was forced to cope with new factors introduced by Christianity. The new religion required that he cease holding courts and imposing death sentences on Sundays, feast days and during Lent.[163] The customary ways of extracting confessions from accused criminals were no longer permissible;[164] and the khan was now expected to entrust to the clergy the final authority in deciding certain kinds of cases, especially those involving marriage problems,[165] sexual abuses,[166] and rights of asylum for criminals.[167] This latter requirement inevitably involved the clergy in the routine procedures of the courts. However, Boris was given to understand that the ruler had no right to judge clerics in any matters,[168] so clerical discipline necessitated the creation of another judicial system in Bulgaria. The conventional form of oath-taking had to be changed to fit Christian usage, thereby introducing a foreign element into judicial administration.[169] These cases were not sufficiently numerous to warrant the conclusion that the whole procedure for the administration of justice had to be scrapped, but they suggest that enough modifications had to be made that they disturbed accustomed patterns and caused confusion.

Another area of political concern for Boris lay in the area of foreign relations. He worried over several matters relating to the waging of war, reflecting a fear that improper procedures would provoke divine wrath and lead to defeat. He asked Nicholas to tell him if there were certain days or seasons when it was not proper to engage in war.[170] He requested guidance on what battle insignia was proper for a Christian army and what kinds of preparation were suitable prior to a military engagement.[171] He wondered if he could still send his agents through the land to check

---

163. *Ibid.*, Chs. 12, 45, pp. 574–75, 585.
164. *Ibid.*, Ch. 86, p. 595.
165. *Ibid.*, Chs. 28, 50, 51, 70, pp. 580, 586, 592.
166. *Ibid.*, Chs. 29, 50, 51, pp. 580, 586.
167. *Ibid.*, Chs. 24, 26, 28, 95, pp. 579, 580, 597.
168. *Ibid.*, Chs. 70, 83, pp. 592, 595.
169. *Ibid.*, Ch. 67, p. 591.
170. *Ibid.*, Chs. 34, 36, 46, pp. 581, 585.
171. *Ibid.*, Chs., 33, 35, pp. 580–81.

that all his subjects had the horses, arms, and other necessities required for battle.[172] The khan was greatly concerned over battle preparations; and he even asked Nicholas to tell him what ought to be done when, in the midst of prayer, a messenger brings news of an enemy's approach.[173] Obviously, the khan and his warriors had been accustomed to trust that the gods would assure their victory, and they wanted to be sure that their new God was properly and adequately placated so that their military fortunes would continue to flourish. One suspects that, at least for a time, the changes in military procedures necessitated by Christianity caused the Bulgars to enter battle somewhat less confidently than in former days, when there had been no new-fangled usages to respect.

Boris also felt a need to clarify the procedures involved in making peace.[174] He asked Nicholas to instruct him in how to make and keep peace with foreigners who came seeking it. Nicholas interpreted this request to mean that Boris was concerned about pacts with pagan nations, and he responded by telling Boris to make sure that a treaty in no way compromised the faith. Indeed, Boris was concerned about Bulgar relations with pagans for he specifically asked about diplomatic dealings with them. And he was troubled about his rights and responsibilities in cases where a pact with a Christian people was broken by the other party.

Again it would appear that the introduction of the new religion had cast doubts on existing political usages and had raised serious questions about the validity of Bulgar commitments to neighboring peoples. Our limited knowledge of Bulgar foreign relations suggests that Boris' questions touched on vital matters: the treaty with the Greeks in 864, Bulgaria's hostile policy toward the Moravians prior to Boris' conversion, the treaty of 862 with the East Franks, and Bulgar relations with several Slavic tribes adjacent to the Bulgar frontiers. If Christianity demanded a new code of diplomacy, Boris may have felt that the Bulgar position must be changed as it pertained to some of her neighbors. One suspects that the khan was hopeful that his adhesion to the new religion and his willingness to observe Christian principles in his foreign policy would elevate his status in the eyes of the great powers of his generation: the Christian states of Byzantium and the East Franks.

Still another political issue posed by the conversion of Bulgaria was the problem of the relationship between the Church and the state. Our discussion of Boris' efforts to establish a church organization has already made

172. *Ibid.*, Ch. 40, p. 582.
173. *Ibid.*, Ch. 34, p. 581.
174. *Ibid.*, Chs. 80–82, pp. 594–95.

it clear that the khan was convinced it was a matter of urgency to institute the Church as a corporate entity in his realm. Boris obviously felt free to use his secular authority to manipulate this new organization emerging in his realm. He punished religious leaders whom he felt were acting in error;[175] he expelled missionary bishops and priests who no longer suited his needs;[176] he commanded his noble supporters to provide hospitality for Clement in the newly formed missionary district and ordered those living in that district to support his efforts.[177] The Roman missionary Grimoald could hardly have grown rich in Bulgaria except through the generous support given him by Boris.[178] The khan was at least inclined to exert his power to correct the religious shortcomings of his subjects and to compel them to observe his version of the Christian law.[179] All these cases indicate that Boris was willing and even eager to assume considerable authority over the religious establishment and to shape it according to his own lights.

It is equally obvious, however, that he could not act with complete freedom, that he was confronted with irresistible pressures to create a privileged place for the clergy in his realm and to accept considerable clerical involvement in political life. An examination of his efforts to create a church organization clearly indicates that he was heavily dependent on the will of ecclesiastical officials outside Bulgaria to secure bishops and priests as missionaries. From Nicholas' pastoral letter come clear indications that the missionary leaders came to Bulgaria primed to act positively in political affairs. The pope was good enough to respect Boris' plea for a secular law code, but he ordered that the book be returned to Rome with his legates, Bishops Paul and Formosus, so that the law would not be misinterpreted by Bulgars ignorant of its meaning. Obviously the bishops were charged with guiding Boris' use of the law in the conduct of his affairs,[180] and Nicholas repeatedly ordered Boris to refer judicial cases to the bishops.[181]

If Boris respected these orders, the clerical influence on the administration of justice was destined to be great. The Bulgar ruler was cautioned

175. *Ibid.*, Chs. 14–16, 104, 105, pp. 575–76, 599.
176. See above, pp. 81–82, 93–94.
177. Theophylactus, *Vita s. Clementis*, Ch. 17, Migne, *PG*, CXXVI, col. 1224.
178. *Liber pontificalis*, ed. Duchesne, II, 185.
179. Nicholas, *Ep.*, No. 99, *passim*; nearly every passage in this letter implies that the khan intends to use papal advice as a guide for the correction of the living habits of the people over whom he ruled.
180. *Ibid.*, Ch. 13, p. 575.
181. *Ibid.*, Chs. 24, 26, 28–30, 50, 51, 95, pp. 579, 580, 586, 597.

against assuming the right to judge the clergy, even when priests were involved in such flagrant sins as adultery, or obviously guilty of such infractions of canon law as marriage;[182] and the bishops were to be consulted in any case where there was a question of the suitability of a peace treaty.[183] Boris respected this command to involve the clergy in foreign affairs in at least one case, for he turned over to the papal legates certain letters unfavorable to Rome's cause which he had received from the Byzantine court.[184] Nor is there any reason to believe that the Greek clergy involved in Bulgar affairs during Boris' reign were any less timid than the Roman clergy in claiming an important role in guiding the khan's political actions. In short, the acceptance of Christianity brought powerful men to Bulgaria with strong convictions about the importance of the clergy in a Christian state and about the ideal configuration of a Christian political order.

Unfortunately, we cannot accurately weigh the influence of the Christian clergy in shaping Bulgar political life during the conversion period. Admittedly, Boris could have disregarded the repeated advice of Nicholas to rely on the bishops in formulating political actions, yet the very nature of the khan's situation makes this appear unlikely. Boris was trying to impose a new religion in the face of hostility from some of the *boyars*, which would seem to dictate close cooperation with the clergy and a respect for their claims to be involved in politics. He was also courting the allegiance of the Slavic elements in his realm and trying to overcome their hostility to the overlordship of the Bulgar ruling caste. The clergy, especially after the adoption of the Slavonic liturgy, was the khan's prime link with the Slavs. Boris was personally concerned that his conduct reflect the Christian ethos and that his people become Christians. To him this meant a change in old usages in favor of a Christian way of acting; almost every request he put to Nicholas bespeaks his seriousness in pursuit of this end.

Given the urge to act as a Christian, Boris had no recourse but to ask the missionary leaders for practical guidance in ways that were genuinely Christian; he was dependent on them for the enlightenment he felt he and his people required. The conversion process raised many problems of a political nature; Boris was ignorant of the Christian way of resolving these issues and had to depend on the missionary leaders for a suitable response. Thus the khan's intense search for the Christian way, coupled with the

182. *Ibid.*, Chs. 70–71, 83, pp. 592–93, 595.
183. *Ibid.*, Ch. 81, p. 594.
184. Nicholas, *Ep.*, No. 100, ed. Perels, *MGH, Ep.*, VI, p. 603.

admitted limitations on himself and his Bulgars, created an atmosphere that was conducive to a rapid advance of the clergy in political affairs. As the bishops moved to the center of the political stage, they must certainly have established a privileged place for themselves in society. Perhaps a fitting symbol of what happened in Bulgaria is contained in a western chronicler's account of how Boris suppressed a revolt by surrounding himself with clergymen and staging a religious procession.[185] This incident suggests strong reliance by the khan on clerical support in politics and it implies considerable involvement of the clergy in the processes of government. If the church made important advances in shaping political life, we might assume that considerable tension arose among the *boyars* who had been crowded aside. And perhaps even the great khan on occasion felt compromised by the involvement of ecclesiastical figures in the details of political life.

These reflections on the political consequences of the Christianization of Bulgaria lead one to give considerable weight to a remark that Boris made to Nicholas I. In recounting how some of his subjects had rebelled when he had introduced the new religion, Boris told the pope that the conspirators said their khan did not give them good laws, and therefore they wished to kill him.[186] One suspects that the rebels were right, if he interprets "good laws" to mean the kind of law that had been customary in Bulgaria. Inspired by the new religion, the khan set out to modify the political structure of his land in several significant ways. He caught a new vision of his own authority; he found new causes for charging his subjects with breaking the law; and he introduced new punishments for old crimes. Either by choice or by necessity, he listened to new advisers, some of whom probably knew little about Bulgar political usages but who could answer the ruler's incessant demands for knowledge of the true Christian way. He took a new view of those who were friends and enemies of the Bulgars.

All of these innovations were probably sufficient to unsettle political life in Bulgaria and to cause apprehension among those not yet convinced that the Christian style of politics represented a great advance. In short, conversion was not just a religious matter; it led to a profound unsettling of the political order in Bulgaria.

The intrusion of the new religion into Bulgaria likewise called into question conventional patterns of moral behavior. As a result, Boris and

185. *Annales Bertiniani, a.* 866, ed. Waitz, *MGH, SS. rer. Germ.*, p. 85.
186. Nicholas, *Ep.*, No. 99, Ch. 17, p. 577.

those associated with him in the conversion of the Bulgars were forced to question the many moral practices that prevailed among the Bulgars and to ponder ways of effecting changes in behavior. Implicit in this matter, then, was the need for a profound transformation of the mores of the society.

The sources leave little doubt that the missionary forces entering Bulgaria constantly reminded the new converts of the inadequacies of the traditional code of conduct. At several places in his letter, Nicholas I stressed that the Bulgars would have difficulty living up to Christian standards because of the crudity of their present mode of life.[187] And Photius began his letter to Boris with an austere reminder that the acceptance of the new faith called for a moral regeneration, by implication condemning the existing morality of the Bulgars.[188]

Somewhat surprisingly, the Bulgars appear to have taken the criticisms to heart. Throughout Nicholas' letter there are constant allusions to the fact that Boris approached Rome in a spirit of humility, bred of his realization of the moral shortcomings of his people. In a sense, he put his sentiments into words at the very end of his requests to Nicholas when he begged the guidance of the pope for a people "not having a true and perfect Christianity."[189] When Clement and Nahum came to Bulgaria, after having fled Moravia, there was a clamor among the Bulgar nobles to be allowed to speak to these teachers and to learn from them a more perfect manner of life; apparently the presence of saintly missionaries awakened in men an urge to learn a new way of life.[190] The introduction of Christianity thus brought into Bulgaria critics of the existing morality, and at the same time bred among Bulgars a sense of inadequacy and an urge for change.

But the missionaries came not only to show the Bulgars the inadequacies of the traditional morality, they apparently insisted that their converts accept a new morality. Indeed, this may have been the major theme in their formal presentation of Christianity. Nicholas I and Photius spoke in almost identical terms on the issue of moral regeneration in the opening sentences of their pastoral letters to Boris. Nicholas wrote: "Let it be known that the law of the Christians consists of faith and good works. For faith is the first of all virtues in the habits of believers. . . . However, good works are no less demanded of the Christian."[191] After pointing out

187. *Ibid.*, Chs. 4, 16–17, 47, pp. 570–71, 576–77, 585–86.
188. Photius, *Ep.*, No. 6, Chs. 2–3, ed. Valetta, pp. 202–3.
189. Nicholas, *Ep.*, No. 99, Ch. 106, p. 599.
190. Theophylactus, *Vita s. Clementis*, Ch. 16, Migne, *PG*, CXXVI, cols. 1221–24.
191. Nicholas, *Ep.*, No. 99, Ch. 1, p. 569.

to Boris the need to understand the Christian faith, Photius argued: "However, it must be said that virtues and good works must not be separated from faith; instead the good man ought to perfect and unite the one and the other. For right faith produces noble habits, and purity of deeds proves that faith is fully divine." [192]

These pronouncements were not idle comments, for Nicholas made it clear that the missionary leaders he was sending to Bulgaria would inform Boris in detail on everything that pertained to the fundamental Christian law. [193] It was reported of these papal missionaries that "they began to teach the people with saving warnings" and "with the grace of God caused the customs of the Bulgars to be changed over to the ways of the Christian faith, as they had been instructed by the most holy pope." [194] Another source says that Nicholas answered Boris' plea for help (in 866) "not only by giving the true faith but also [giving] a manner of living." [195]

It thus appears beyond dispute that missionary forces arrived in Bulgaria prepared and even determined to guide the crude Bulgars into new patterns of behavior. It is much more difficult to ascertain the specific content of their preachments on morality. Virtually the only source that treats this matter in detail is the pastoral letter of Photius, two-thirds of which is given over to moral strictures. This elegant, sophisticated discourse, exhorting Boris to "illustrate his faith through actions," [196] often strikes a note that seems far removed from the Bulgar scene and asks of Boris a mode of behavior beyond his simple talents. Yet, despite its exalted tone, it touches on a range of moral problems that may well have been at issue in Bulgaria. It thus seems permissible to cite its content as a guide to the major themes stressed by missionaries in their effort to alter Bulgar conduct in the name of the new law to which the Bulgars had become subject through baptism.

Photius presented Christian morality to Boris, in part, as a series of prohibitions. Implying that the barbarian prince—and, by inference, all new converts—were apt to be accustomed to various acts that were considered sins by Christian standards, he sought to convince Boris to abandon these ways; and his admonitions were grounded in the Ten

192. Photius, *Ep.*, No. 6, Ch. 3, ed. Valetta, p. 203.

193. Nicholas, *Ep.*, No. 99, p. 568.

194. *Liber pontificalis*, ed. Duchesne, II, 165.

195. *Anastasii Bibliothecarii Ep. sive Praef.*, No. 5, eds. Perels and Laehr, *MGH, Ep.*, VII, 412.

196. Photius, *Ep.*, No. 6, Ch. 22, ed. Valetta, pp. 222–23: "ἀρεταῖς κοσμεῖν τὴν πίστιν, καὶ τῇ πίστει τάς ἀρετάς λαμπροτέρας ἀπεργάζεσθαι." The following section is based on *ibid.*, Chs. 21–114, pp. 221–48.

Commandments, with which he presumed the khan was familiar. From these prohibitions sprang a wide range of acts that a Christian, and especially a Christian prince, must shun. He must guard against excesses and improprieties in dress, bodily adornment, and motions. Silly laughter and obscenity ought to be shunned, and accusers and sycophants. Those who have power must avoid all abuse by that power of the powerless, and must guard against the employment of power to induce fear. Envy, pride, arrogance, deceit, vengefulness, anger, blind passion, voluptuousness, lust, bestiality, and drunkenness are dreadful offenses, bound to displease God and to destroy the authority of a prince. Whoever is in a special position in society must take great care in establishing friendships, since men will constantly press for the honor of enjoying his friendship. Once friends are made, however, every Christian has a grave moral responsibility to respect them, to treat them fairly, and to be mindful of what they have done for him. A prince is constantly in danger of using his great power to command others to a sinful action, but such conduct must be avoided at all costs. If Boris understood Photius, he must have been led to believe that leading the Christian life involved the abandonment of many actions, and a purgation of one's life that eliminated specific faults.

The patriarch was equally forceful in casting Christian morality in positive terms. If Boris hoped to do good works, he must learn to love God and his fellowmen. From this would flow numerous positive virtues: respect for parents, avoidance of shedding blood, respect for the good of others, refusal to bear false witness, avoidance of adultery. The good Christian should learn to pray, to devote himself to divine worship, and to follow the guidance of his priest. He must be merciful to those who offend him. If he is in a position of power, the good man must judge with mercy and punish with moderation, and for such a man it is especially crucial that he learn the nature of true justice and act accordingly. He should learn to control his desires and moderate his pleasures. Kindness, fairness, prudence, willingness to bear adversity, charity, generosity with one's material goods, readiness to assume labors, faithfulness to promises, beneficence, and honor toward friends mark the man who does good works in the Christian sense. Photius repeatedly made it clear that the attainment of these virtues and the consequent winning of the favor of God depended upon one's efforts. Every new Christian must understand that Christian virtue demanded an heroic struggle with the dark forces that inhabited the world, that lurked in the human soul, that distracted man from his task of earning, by his good works, the merits necessary for salvation. Again, if Boris grasped Photius' line of argument, he must have envisaged his moral responsibility not only in terms of refraining from certain acts but also in undertaking new kinds of actions that would demonstrate his willingness to do good.

If one accepts Photius' letter as the prototype of the manner in which the missionary forces confronted the Bulgars on the level of personal morality, he may wonder what the Bulgar reaction was to the double demand to purge old customs and accept new standards and patterns of behavior. The evidence does not supply any convincing proof that the Bulgars became deeply immersed in the positive side of Christian morality. No doubt the institution of the Christian cult, as previously described, altered outward modes of conduct in various ways, but mere conformance to its demands would not necessarily have involved deep moral issues. As has already been suggested, the Bulgars may have accepted Christian liturgical practices as substitutes for pagan rites; and the sources provide little indication that Christian worship evoked a new level of spiritual awareness which manifested itself in a new morality. Perhaps it was only a quest for moral regeneration that later persuaded Boris and a few of his subjects to retreat to the cloister. On the whole, it seems that the positive content of Christian morality did not deeply stir the moral sensibilities of the new converts.

What concerned the Bulgars on the moral level was whether, and to what degree, traditional moral usages differed from or violated Christian norms. This issue dominated Boris' requests to Nicholas. The khan almost never demonstrated any concern for discovering ways to put into effect Christian modes of behavior that would have been new to his people; almost never did he ask Nicholas to inform him of ways to attain the kind of moral excellence of which Photius had discoursed so eloquently. Incessantly he sought from the pope opinions about the propriety of particular Bulgar customs in terms of Christian standards. His inquiries range over a wide variety of matters, from marriage usages and sexual mores to bathing practices and the style of pants befitting true Christian life.[197] The mixture of serious moral issues and banalities in Boris' requests points toward a proscriptive concept of morality.

The moral problem before the new converts was, essentially, discovering and expurgating from habitual conduct certain kinds of behavior that

197. Nicholas, *Ep.*, No. 99, Ch. 6 (bathing), 21 (fugitive slaves), 33 (battle insignia), 35 (battle preparations), 39 (degree of kinship in marriage), 42 (royal eating customs), 43 (dietary regulations), 44, 47 (hunting), 49 (dowry), 51 (bigamy), 56 (prayers for rain), 59 (pantaloons), 63–64 (sexual mores), 79 (pendants for healing), 96 (divorce), 97 (slavery), 100 (disposal of the bodies of dead soldiers), pp. 572, 579, 580–88, 590, 594, 597–98.

violated the law observed by Christians. When that purification of prohibited usages was achieved, the converts would consider themselves
morally fit as Christians. As he grasps the intent of Boris' concern over the
moral life of his people, one suspects that the missionary preachers were
leaning heavily on Old Testament concepts of strict adherence to a formal
moral code in their efforts to Christianize Bulgar behavior. Put another
way, it appears that the Bulgars took Photius' prohibitory admonitions
much more seriously than his positive approach to the moral life that
flowed from Christian spiritual values.

As he sought to provide intelligible and practicable answers to this
barrage of questions for a judgment on Bulgar moral practices, Nicholas
seems to have sensed that Boris' concern with these matters was too great.
The pope was not only liberal in approving ancient Bulgar modes of conduct, he took special pains to assure Boris that whatever the Bulgars had
done without sin before baptism could be done without sin after baptism.[198] Surely he emphasized this consoling principle to assure Boris that
the introduction of Christianity did not require the abandonment of every
manner of conduct to which the Bulgars were accustomed, and that the
new converts did not have to strain over every item of their traditional
code of morals to discern the propriety of each. But it appears that the
Bulgar reaction was exactly this. When the missionaries descended on their
land, calling for the newly baptized to abandon their old ways of life in
favor of the new law, some of the most fervent Bulgars, including the khan,
questioned the propriety of many aspects of the conventional morality.
No doubt these same pious souls were not slow to call into question the behavior of their compatriots who were not moved by the appeals of the
missionaries to take upon themselves the observance of the new law.

It would appear, then, that the conversion process disturbed the
moral order in Bulgaria, which leaves the momentous question of the
practical consequences of this disturbance. Did the Bulgar effort to abide
by Christian moral law by purging their lives of specifically prohibited
usages have any significant effect? The sources are mute; the historian
cannot demonstrate the degree to which moral practices were altered in
the newly converted society. All that Boris' requests to Nicholas indicate
is that in their daily lives most Bulgars still followed their old customs even
though they were being admonished to change. But one can at least
suggest the possibility of serious tension in Bulgar society over moral
conduct.

The evidence affirms that serious doubts had been cast on the validity

198. *Ibid.*, Ch. 49, p. 586.

of ancient moral standards. These doubts must surely have weakened, or perhaps even destroyed, the one element that gives any moral code its ultimate force: the unquestioning assumption of those bound by it that its provisions are valid. This condition points toward the dissolution of the old morality. The sources further attest the inability of the new converts to comprehend the positive content of Christian morality. Inevitably one is forced to envisage a situation where many Bulgars (probably the most enthusiastic converts) found themselves deprived of confidence in the old morality and fairly ignorant of the new. Such a situation could have bred moral anarchy, and perhaps Photius sensed this possibility when he so strongly stressed the need for moral excellence in a prince as a model for the rest of society. Or such a condition may have led to constant and painful soul-searching of moral issues by serious men, just as Boris had reflected uneasiness about his personal conduct in his requests to Pope Nicholas. However, this is all conjecture; the sources tell virtually nothing of changes in morality during the conversion era.

While grappling with the manifold problems accompanying the institution of the Christian religion and the adjustment of Bulgarian institutions and customs to its demands, Boris had one more major challenge to face. The sources repeatedly indicate that Christianity was presented to the Bulgars in such a way as to imply that its survival in that backward land depended upon the ability of the khan and his subjects to achieve a higher level of culture. Put another way, the acceptance of Christianity brought the Bulgars more intimately into contact with a new range of culture and made it imperative that they strive to possess this new culture not so much for its own sake but in order to comprehend the essential features of the Christian message.

In attempting to assess the cultural impact of Christianity on Bulgaria, one is first struck by the degree to which the Bulgars were belittled by those involved in introducing the new faith into the land. It has already been noted that those who offered Boris advice on the content of the faith, on its proper practice, on the arts of government suitable to a Christian society, and on the moral life proper to the sons of the Christian God were quick to assume that the Bulgars knew little of these matters, that the new converts were children who needed milk before they could feed on solid food.[199] This assumption was even more prevalent in matters that touched upon cultural life.

199. See above, pp. 78, 84–88, 106–10, 114.

The letters of Photius, Nicholas I, and John VIII are permeated with statements indicating their low opinion of the intellectual capabilities of the Bulgars; the two popes agreed with Photius' characterization of the Bulgars as a "barbarous people."[200] Repeatedly and consciously, they cast their admonitions and instructions to the Bulgars in terms which implied they were simplifying matters so as not to overstrain the limited mental abilities of the new converts.[201] Each of these potentates was quick to blame the repeated switch of ecclesiastical allegiance by the Bulgars on Bulgar simple-mindedness, which made the new converts easy prey for more subtle and sophisticated men.[202] Nicholas often advised Boris to seek the advice of the Roman bishops in his land, for "they hold the keys of knowledge";[203] the pope clearly implied that Boris and his Bulgars suffered from a lack of knowledge. The pope would not even run the risk of allowing the Bulgars to keep the law code he sent them, for he was fearful that after his bishops left there would be no one capable of using it correctly.[204]

Although they may have done so unconsciously, the Bulgars reacted to the appearance of the culturally advanced missionaries as if to confirm their barbarous condition. Boris admitted to Nicholas that he was confused by the conflicting versions of Christianity presented in his land and that he was puzzled about what to do with "the profane books" brought to him by Moslems; he must have felt that his knowledge was too limited to cope with such complexities.[205] His eager reception of the learned Clement and Nahum, and his effort to employ their talents in developing a system of education and a literary culture in Bulgaria, suggest a strongly felt need to overcome Bulgar cultural crudity.[206] So also does Boris' decision to send his son and some of his subjects to Constantinople for a monastic education.[207]

200. Photius, *Ep.*, No. 4, Ch. 3, ed. Valetta, p. 168: "βουλγάρων ἔθνος βαρβαρικὸν."
201. For example: Nicholas, *Ep.*, No. 99, Chs. 4, 16, 17, 47, pp. 570–71, 576–77, 585–86.
202. Photius, *Ep.*, No. 4, ed. Valetta, pp. 165–81; Nicholas, *Ep.*, No. 100, ed. Perels, *MGH, Ep.*, VI, 601, 603; *Iohannis VIII. Papae Epistolae*, Nos. 66, 67, 182, ed. Caspar, *MGH, Ep.*, VII, 58–62, 146. The western version of the appearance of the Bulgars before the Council of Constantinople in 870 is based upon the assumption that the simple Bulgars had been beguiled into defecting from Rome by the Greeks; see *Liber pontificalis*, ed. Duchesne, II, 182–85; *Anastasii Bibliothecarii Ep. sive Praef.*, No. 5, eds. Perels and Laehr, *MGH, Ep.*, VII, 411–15.
203. Nicholas, *Ep.*, No. 99, Chs. 9, 106, pp. 573, 599–600.
204. *Ibid.*, Ch. 13, p. 573.
205. *Ibid.*, Chs. 103, 106, pp. 599–600.
206. Theophylactus, *Vita s. Clementis*, Chs. 16–17, Migne, *PG*, CXXVI, cols. 1221–24.

The Bulgars appear to have seized any opportunity to submit themselves to the cultural influences of their spiritual mentors, an attitude that could only have reinforced what the outsiders already felt—the Bulgars were "ignorant and brutish." [208] The Bulgars even capitalized on their reputation for naïveté and crudity. When, in 870, Boris decided to turn away from Roman supervision over his newly converted land and accept Greek tutelage, he sent his legates to Constantinople to present the matter to the council then in session. Upon gaining a hearing before the papal legates and the eastern patriarchs, the Bulgar spokesman stated his case completely in terms of Bulgar ignorance of the laws and precedents of the Church. He asked only that his august and sacred audience decide the proper jurisdictional disposition of his native land, then he let his more learned judges argue the case and ultimately decide it the way they wished. [209]

In their totality, these cases strongly suggest that the conversion process suddenly deflated the Bulgars in the opinion of both the contemporary world and the Bulgars themselves. Whereas before 864 the Bulgars had been treated as formidable warriors, desirable allies, and skilled diplomats, after 864 and the coming of Christianity they were universally treated as ignorant, crude suppliants who needed guidance in extracting themselves from their helpless state. In their own eyes they had committed themselves, by their choice to become Christians, to a course which forced them to admit their inadequacies and their former sins of omission and commission. Indeed, the Bulgars actually possessed about the same order of strength and power after 864 as before, but neither the world around them nor they themselves viewed the situation in this perspective after 864. The introduction of Christianity revealed their cultural backwardness, and it set the Bulgars the monumental task of making themselves culturally worthy of the new religion.

The full proportions of this task are not entirely clear from the sources; nor does this paper encompass a period long enough to trace in full the cultural uplifting of the Bulgars as a result of the introduction of Christianity. However, the sources for the first stage of the conversion process during the reign of Boris indicate that the outside world confronted the

---

207. Luidprandus of Cremona, *Antapodosis*, III, Ch. 29, in *The Works of Luidprand of Cremona*, trans. Wright, p. 123; Photius, *Ep.*, No. 255, ed. Valetta, p. 556.

208. Theophylactus, *Vita s. Clementis*, Ch. 21, Migne, *PG*, CXXVI, col. 1228: "ἀμαθέστατοι καὶ . . . κτηνωδέστατοι."

209. *Liber pontificalis*, ed. Duchesne, II, 182–85; *Anastasii Bibliothecarii Ep. sive Praef.*, No. 5, eds. Perels and Laehr, *MGH, Ep.*, VII, 411–15.

Bulgars with the broad outlines of a new culture which that barbaric people had to master in order to comprehend Christianity in the fullest sense, and to draw from it the richest spiritual benefits. The cultural task facing the Bulgars was never stated in the form of a specific program; rather, those who addressed themselves to the problems facing the new converts repeatedly presented their arguments and appeals in terms which suggested only the broad cultural areas in which the Bulgars must acquire skill and knowledge. Even to understand their mentors fully, the Bulgars would have had to develop greater competence in a variety of cultural pursuits.

The first and most pressing task that faced the Bulgars was a mastery of Scripture. There is hardly a chapter in Nicholas' long letter to Boris which does not utilize a scriptural passage as a device for clarifying the course of action demanded of the new converts or for illustrating the exact content of Christian teaching. The letters of Pope John VIII to Boris are no less generous in the use of Scripture, and no doubt the missionary workers in Bulgaria turned with equal frequency to scriptural passages to instruct the Bulgars. Occasionally the scriptural references are only partially quoted or are paraphrased, which placed upon the reader of the papal letters the burden of seeking out the full text—assuming he had an interest in reading the original version. There is no direct evidence that the Bulgars possessed the linguistic ability to read a Latin or Greek version of the Bible; however, because of the great number of Latin and Greek letters sent to Bulgaria and Boris' specific request for law codes, penitentials, and missals in Latin,[210] we must assume there were men of learning at the Bulgar court who were capable of utilizing the Bible in Latin and Greek.

The Bulgars were faced not only with the task of mastering the literal words of Scripture in order to grasp the full meaning of Christianity, they were also confronted with the whole problem of its allegorical interpretations. Nicholas I imposed this burden on Boris in specific terms. In response to a query of whether the Greeks were right in prohibiting anyone from receiving communion unless he wore a belt, Nicholas said he was ignorant of any such command in Scripture, unless the Greeks were referring to the Lord's order: "Let your limbs be bound up" (Luke 12:35). The pope continued: "In truth this testimony of the holy gospel

---

210. Nicholas, *Ep.*, No. 99, Chs. 1, 13, 75, 76, pp. 568, 575, 593. For some interesting comments on the linguistic situation in Bulgaria in the pre-conversion period, see Beševliev and Grégoire, "Les inscriptions protobulgares," *Byzantion*, XXV–XXVI–XXVII (1955–56–57), 853, ff.

must be fulfilled not according to the letter, but according to the spirit,"
and he thereupon proceeded to enlarge on the allegorical meaning of
the passage, quoting at length from a letter of Pope Celestine.[211]

On numerous occasions elsewhere in his responses to Boris, the pope
himself used Scripture allegorically to illustrate the precepts he wished
to convey to the Bulgars.[212] It is worth comment that Nicholas often
reverted to this technique when Boris called upon him to pass judgment
on a pagan practice. One suspects that he hoped to offer the khan a solution to one of his most pressing concerns; namely, the establishment of a
standard against which to judge the propriety of pagan usages. The
Bulgars had only to read the spiritual meaning of the Bible, as the pope
so often did, and their doubts would be cleared away. However, to the unlettered Bulgars the art of interpreting "the spiritual sense" of Holy Writ
may indeed have been difficult, requiring far greater learning than they
possessed during the first generation of their membership in the Christian
community.

If the first burden placed upon the untutored Bulgars by their spiritual
guides was the learning of Scripture, certainly the second was the mastery
of a new law. More accurately, one should say new laws, for the various
documents addressed to the Bulgars from Rome and Constantinople refer
to a variety of laws so complex that the Bulgars could well have been
utterly confused, as Boris often admitted. Keeping in mind what has
already been demonstrated in the attitude evinced by Christian spokesmen toward the inferiority of many Bulgar legal and moral usages, there
seems to be little doubt that the Bulgars were expected to put into practice
new rules that would govern all aspects of their society. Moreover, part
of their obligation as Christians was the discovery of these new laws.
Although Pope Nicholas was at times inclined to condone Bulgar customs,
at least temporarily,[213] he did not hesitate to inform the new converts of
their ultimate responsibility: "Now, however, in the same fashion that
you have changed from the old men to the new, so likewise you should
change from the former customs to our custom in all things." [214]

But what was *morem nostrum*? In terms of Nicholas' letter, as it is supported by other documents sent to Bulgaria, the new law was a combination of many laws with which the Bulgars must acquaint themselves.

211. Nicholas, *Ep.*, No. 99, Ch. 55, p. 587.
212. For example: *ibid.*, Chs. 1, 2, 7, 17–20, 33, 40, 41, 50, 95, pp. 568–69, 572–73,
577–83, 586, 597; and *Iohannis VIII. Papae Epistolae*, No. 66, ed. Caspar, *MGH*, *Ep.*, VII,
59.
213. Nicholas, *Ep.*, No. 99, Ch. 49, p. 586.
214. *Ibid.*, Ch. 59, p. 588.

Scripture itself was a prime source of the Christian law, and Nicholas and Photius repeatedly drew on scriptural commands as sanctions for their instructions to the neophyte Bulgars. It is probably this source which Photius had in mind in admonishing Boris to observe the "divine law," and what Nicholas meant when he spoke of "the sublime mandate of God." [215] Nicholas also repeatedly referred Boris to a code of secular law as his guide in shaping a Christian polity for his realm, in most cases directing the khan to the collection of *leges mundanas* which he had sent to Bulgaria. [216] It has been shown that this collection was a Lombard law code with certain Carolingian capitularies added; [217] however, the code had been influenced by Roman law, so that the Bulgars were led toward familiarity with that great body of law. Nicholas on two occasions made specific references to Roman law, clearly indicating that he presumed a Christian kingdom would utilize the code of Justinian. [218] One must suppose that Photius' numerous references to the law and its proper application were based on the presumption that the Bulgars would adopt the Roman law, probably in the form then employed in the Byzantine Empire. [219]

Equally numerous in the sources are references to the canon law, and to become adept in this body of law the Bulgar khan had to turn to several sources. Nicholas referred to "sacred canons" or "sacred rules" (*regulae*) on many occasions, which almost always meant the enactments of church councils. [220] John VIII also directed Boris to these sacred canons as a source of information on Rome's position in the ecclesiastical world. [221] And, of course, Photius' whole discussion of the disposition of past heresies rested on the decrees of the seven ecumenical councils, which the patriarch presented to Boris in capsule form. [222] However, Boris could not learn canon law simply by mastering conciliar statutes.

215. Photius, *Ep.*, No. 6, Ch. 75, ed. Valetta, p. 238: "... θεῖος ... νόμος"; Nicholas, *Ep.*, No. 99, Ch. 49, p. 586.

216. *Ibid.*, Ch. 13, p. 575, for the reference to the law code Nicholas sent to Bulgaria; Chs. 12, 19–29, 31, 32, 49, 52, 84, 85, 95, pp. 574–75, 578–80, 586, 595, 597, for allusions to the use of that law.

217. See above, n. 156.

218. Nicholas, *Ep.*, No. 99, Chs. 2, 39, pp. 569, 582.

219. Photius, *Ep.*, No. 6, Chs. 38, 42, 43, 50, 54, 59, ed. Valetta, pp. 231–36.

220. Nicholas, *Ep.*, No. 99, Chs. 4, 9, 28–30, 39, 48, 69, 93, 95, pp. 571, 573, 580, 582, 586, 591, 597. In two cases the reference is to *apostolicis regulis* (Ch. 72, p. 592) and *apostolica decreta* (ch. 79, p. 594).

221. *Iohannis VIII. Papae Epistolae*, Nos. 66, 192, 198, ed. Caspar, *MGH, Ep.*, VII, 60, 154, 159; *Fragmenti Registri Iohannis VIII. Papae*, No. 7, ed. Caspar, *MGH, Ep.*, VII, 277.

222. Photius, *Ep.*, No. 6, Chs. 5–18, ed. Valetta, pp. 204–19.

Nicholas frequently indicated to him that various popes had laid down important decretals and that the Bulgars would have to familiarize themselves with this body of law.[223] The popé sent Boris a penitential which introduced the Bulgars to another facet of the customs of the Christians.[224] He also implied that Boris would have to familiarize himself with monastic rules,[225] which became a greater necessity when monastic communities were established in Bulgaria.[226] Finally, Nicholas occasionally made vague illusions to *mos ecclesiae* and *lex Christianorum*, implying a body of Christian customs which was not written down.[227]

As the Bulgars became aware of the many sources of the law which would guide them to Christian life in the fullest sense, they perhaps began to appreciate what Nicholas meant at the opening of his letter: "If one attempted to explain [the Christian law] fully, innumerable books ought to be written." [228] It is obvious that the introduction of the new religion placed before them the need to master an immense body of legal enactments. This would be no easy task, as Nicholas warned when he ordered that the secular code he sent to Bulgaria be returned to him lest it fall into inexperienced hands and be abused.[229] Compilations of law would have to be acquired, and for this the Bulgars would have to depend on the generosity of outsiders or upon the labors of copyists who sought out the necessary texts in Rome or Constantinople. This material would then have to be studied and interpreted, and its numerous provisions would have to be applied to particular problems in Bulgaria somewhat after the fashion of Nicholas' responses to Boris' questions. At least in the beginning, the foreign priests in Bulgaria seem to have been called upon to perform this task, as Nicholas so often advised. Nonetheless, the mastery of the new law was a supreme cultural challenge to the new converts who hoped to become Christians in the real sense.

No less formidable were the theological issues. Quite aside from the rudiments of the faith which the new converts were expected to learn as catechumens,[230] those who sought to guide the neophytes to Christian

223. Nicholas, *Ep.*, No. 99, Chs. 10, 14, 15, 39, 55, 68, pp. 574–76, 582, 587, 591.
224. *Ibid.*, Ch. 75, p. 593.
225. *Ibid.*, Ch. 87, pp. 595–96.
226. Theophylactus, *Vita s. Clementis*, Ch. 29, Migne, *PG*, CXXVI, col. 1237; "Life of St. Nahum," trans. Kusseff, in *Slavonic and East European Review*, XXIX (1950–51), 142–44.
227. Nicholas, *Ep.*, No. 99, Chs. 1, 9, 51, pp. 569, 573, 586.
228. *Ibid.*, Ch. 1, p. 568.
229. *Ibid.*, Ch. 13, p. 575.
230. See above, pp. 78–80.

truth made it clear that the Bulgars would have to master a formal body of theology of no mean proportions. Nicholas quoted frequently from the fathers, always indicating that they were unerring guides to Christian truth. Among those he cited were John Chrysostom, Gregory the Great, Augustine, Jerome, and Ambrose.[231] Photius directed Boris' attention to such figures as Gregory of Nyssa, Origen, Didymus, Evagrius, and Athanasius.[232] Photius' résumé of the seven ecumenical councils drew attention to the theological issues involved in Arianism, Nestorianism, Monophysitism, Monotheletism, and Iconoclasm, and, more vehemently, to the orthodox doctrines posited to combat these heretical movements.

The learned patriarch repeatedly made it clear that a body of literature had developed in connection with each of these heresies and that only a mastery of this literature would assure an understanding of the errors of figures like Arius, Nestorius, Eutyches, and Theodore of Mopsuestia, and of the teachings of the heroic doctors who refuted them.[233] Nicholas called attention to the Novitian and Manichean heresies, without expanding on the particulars.[234] John VIII addressed Boris on the heretical group known as "pneumatomachii Macedonii," and on Arianism.[235] And when he warned Boris to beware of Greek heresy in general, he probably had in mind the *filioque* dispute, which raged around the Bulgars throughout the period of their conversion.[236] It was thus made evident that the Bulgars must immerse themselves as quickly as possible in patristic learning and in the polemical literature surrounding theological disputes if they were to get to the essence of Christian doctrine. The simple creed quoted to them by Photius was only the beginning of their theological education.

The demands of the liturgy probably posed another cultural challenge. We have already discussed the introduction of the rudiments of Christian worship in Bulgaria as a part of the conversion process, but suggestions in the sources indicate that the Bulgars were expected to go beyond the basic practices of the cult. Photius urged Boris to give attention to public services so that God would be rightly honored and the public good would

231. Nicholas, *Ep.*, No. 99, Chs. 3, 5–7, 10, 15, 43, 61, 64, 68, 71, 90, 99, 100, 104, pp. 570–74, 576, 587, 589, 590–92, 596, 598, 599.

232. Photius, *Ep.*, No. 6, Chs. 8, 14, ed. Valetta, pp. 207, 212–13.

233. *Ibid.*, Chs. 5–18, pp. 204–19.

234. Nicholas, *Ep.*, No. 99, Chs. 78, 90, pp. 594, 596.

235. *Iohannis VIII. Papae Epistolae*, No. 66, ed. Caspar, *MGH, Ep.*, VII, 56–60.

236. *Ibid.*, p. 59. For the Bulgar involvement in the *filioque* dispute, see Nicholas, *Ep.*, No. 100, ed. Perels, *MGH, Ep.*, VI, 603; and Photius, *Ep.*, No. 4, Chs. 10–22, ed. Valetta, pp. 172–75.

be served. Moreover, he commanded the khan "to build temples to God and the saints according to ecclesiastical law." [237] The force of this command may have contributed to the building of the impressive churches whose remains have been unearthed on the site of the fortress-city of Pliska (the capital of Bulgaria in Boris' time) and at Preslav. [238] What survives of the ecclesiastical structures in these cities indisputably indicates that the coming of the new religion and its liturgical demands resulted in important architectural and artistic innovations. Nicholas I likewise made clear the need for the Bulgars to elaborate their ritualistic practices, giving them instructions for observing the numerous feast days of the Church. [239]

When Boris asked how the Bulgars should prepare for battle, the pope advised them "to go to the churches, say prayers, forgive sinners, attend solemn masses, offer oblations, make confession of sins to priests, effect reconciliations and communion, open the prisons, dissolve the chains of slaves, and especially [those of] the broken and the crippled, give freedom to captives, and give alms to the poor." [240] All these acts of piety demanded some liturgical form with which the Bulgars were probably not familiar. By implication, many other aspects of life also had to be given a ritualistic dimension if the Bulgars were to act as Christians in the fullest sense. From some source, the Bulgars had to learn the proper manner in which to perform the rites which would give a Christian flavor to all of their activities. Perhaps it was this need that prompted Boris to ask Nicholas for a Roman missal. [241]

The various letters addressed to Boris abound in historical references, usually employed as examples to clarify the meaning of Christianity to the new converts. The Bulgars could hardly avoid the conclusion that they must inform themselves of a past heretofore foreign to them if they were to comprehend their new faith properly. Nicholas turned the attention of the Bulgars directly to scriptural history when, in response to Boris' inquiry about the propriety of hunting in Lent, he instructed the khan to look to "sacred history." [242] Repeatedly, throughout his responses, he utilized historical incidents from the Old and the New Testaments to

---

237. Photius, *Ep.*, No. 6, Chs. 26–27, ed. Valetta, p. 225.

238. See Dimitrov, *Bulgaria: Land of Ancient Civilizations*, pp. 33–38; Sergheraert, *Syméon le Grand (893–927)*, pp. 89–94.

239. Nicholas, *Ep.*, No. 99, Chs. 4, 10–12, 69, pp. 570, 574–75, 591–92.

240. *Ibid.*, Ch. 35, p. 581.

241. *Ibid.*, Ch. 76, p. 593.

242. *Ibid.*, Ch. 44, p. 585.

explicate and illustrate the conduct proper for a Christian.[243] Pope John VIII chose to demonstrate the primacy of Rome by recounting the New Testament version of the establishment of the Roman see.[244] There could have been little doubt among the Bulgars that they had the task of mastering sacred history as a part of their new cultural burden.

Almost as frequent in the literature addressed to the Bulgars were allusions to church history. Nicholas I called Boris' attention to the history of martyrs and confessors, referring not only to their feast days but also to such intriguing bits of information as the great numbers who had fled their native lands in the face of persecutions.[245] In his lengthy account of the seven ecumenical councils, Photius repeatedly introduced Boris to the great bishops, priests, and monks who had defended orthodoxy and to the wicked heretics who had threatened it. It would appear that he expected the Bulgars to desire and seek more information about these giants whose efforts had shaped the destiny of the Church. His whole account of the calling of the councils and the circumstances which required that they be held was cast in a chronological framework which invited his reader to think in terms of church history.[246] And Nicholas answered Boris' query about the origin of the patriarchates with a brief historical discourse which also invited further investigation.[247]

When the Bulgars went to the council of 869–870 in Constantinople to discover whether their land pertained to the jurisdiction of Rome or of Constantinople, they were subjected to a disputation that hinged on the history of the land they now possessed; and it must have appeared that they had to acquaint themselves with that history if they were to sustain their rights in the future. Pope John VIII likewise reminded the Bulgars of their land's distant past.[248] Occasionally the letters of Nicholas and John referred to episodes in papal history which emphasized the importance of knowing that history as well: the conversion of England by Gregory I, the dispute between Pope Felix and the Patriarch Acacius, the career of Pope Damasus. In all these cases, history was employed as an educative

243. For example, *ibid.*, Chs. 18, 20, 33, 38, 42, 43, 46, 47, 50, 51, 82, 89, pp. 577–86, 594–96.

244. *Iohannis VIII. Papae. Epistolae*, No. 67, ed. Caspar, *MGH, Ep.*, VII, 61.

245. Nicholas, *Ep.*, No. 99, Chs. 5, 11, 20, pp. 571, 572, 579.

246. Photius, *Ep.*, No. 6, Chs. 6, 8, 10, 12, 14, 15, 16, 17, ed. Valetta, pp. 204–7, 209–18.

247. Nicholas, *Ep.*, No. 99, Ch. 92, pp. 596–97.

248. *Liber pontificalis*, ed. Duchesne, II, 182–85; *Iohannis VIII. Papae Epistolae*, No. 71, ed. Caspar, *MGH, Ep.*, VII, 66–67.

device to which the neophytes must turn if they expected to understand the new truth to which they had subscribed.[249]

Even secular history was brought into the picture. Photius introduced Boris to the various emperors who ruled at the time of the ecumenical councils and implied a significant role for each.[250] The patriarch suggested that Boris model his life after Constantine the Great, and that he could learn something about the danger a king's concourse with women holds by studying the fate of Alexander the Great with the Persians.[251] Nicholas referred Boris to Constantine's struggle with Maxentius and to Hadrian's dealings over Jerusalem. He also suggested that the Bulgars learn something of Roman customs.[252] John VIII warned the khan against following the footsteps of the Goths down the path to heresy, as had occurred in the time of Emperor Constantius II.[253] Even these few cases must have suggested to the unlettered Bulgars their need to absorb some of the history of this world so that they might grasp the ways of their God in determining the destiny of men. Their own tales of the past, which appear to have been recounted when they prepared for battle and when they celebrated marriage feasts,[254] may well have appeared inadequate.

We have some indications that the cultural vistas opened to the Bulgarians by the coming of Christianity prompted action even during the time of Boris. In composing his encomium to Clement, Theophylactus wrote:

> O good pastor, . . . you educated us in holy scripture which you interpreted in your tongue, and into ways of justice, and in the work of justice you have led us! Through you the whole kingdom of Bulgaria learned of God; you strengthened the churches with hymns and psalmody; through you the monks were led by the lives of the fathers to the ascetic life; through you the priests were taught to live according to the canons.[255]

This paean was prompted by the kind of work to which Clement devoted himself with the support of the khan. Finding himself among people "ignorant and beastly," Clement first undertook to introduce the

249. Nicholas, *Ep.*, No. 99, Chs. 6, 15, 64, pp. 572, 575–76, 590; *Iohannis VIII. Papae Epistolae*, No. 71, ed. Caspar, *MGH, Ep.*, VII, 66.
250. Photius, *Ep.*, No. 6, Chs. 6, 9, 11, 14, 16, 17, ed. Valetta, pp. 206, 209, 211, 212, 216.
251. *Ibid.*, Chs. 22, 92, pp. 222, 242.
252. Nicholas, *Ep.*, No. 99, Chs. 33, 92, 95, pp. 580–81, 597.
253. *Iohannis VIII. Papae Epistolae*, No. 66, ed. Caspar, *MGH, Ep.*, VII, 59–60.
254. Nicholas, *Ep.*, No. 99, Ch. 35, p. 581.
255. Theophylactus, *Vita s. Clementis*, Ch. 29, Migne, *PG*, CXXVI, col. 1237.

Bulgars to the simple tasks of learning to read and write.[256] Then, following the example of St. Methodius, he provided materials for the use of
Bulgar priests, "many of whom found Greek difficult to understand." [257]
In the Bulgar language, he prepared prayers, simple sermons for all occasions, compendia of miracle stories, the lives and journeys of the prophets
and apostles, stories of the martyrs, saints' lives, and "in short all kinds of
things pertaining to the church. . . ." [258] The monastery which Clement
built at Ochrida was the center of this cultural activity, all of which was
aimed at making available to the Bulgars some of that vast cultural
heritage that other spokesmen for Christianity insisted the Bulgars must
comprehend if they were to comprehend their new religion. Clement's
work in Bulgaria was a symbol of the cultural impact of the new religion
on the backward Bulgars. Its continuation by Nahum [259] and others led
directly, and quickly, to the impressive achievements of the reign of
Symeon, which assured that the impact of higher culture would have a
permanent effect on Bulgaria.

It is almost impossible to estimate the immediate effects on Bulgar
society of the sudden confrontation of that society with so vast a cultural
challenge. It seems clear beyond dispute that the coming of Christianity
dramatically posed a cultural problem for Bulgar leadership. We have
seen that those who undertook the guidance of the conversion process
took the position that the Bulgars were backward, and that they proceeded
to set forth a number of areas where the new converts would have to
achieve competence in order to be called good Christians. The Bulgars
reacted by taking positive steps to narrow the gap between their inferior
culture and the superior cultures beyond their boundaries. Until their
efforts had borne fruit, in a generation or two, they must have lived in a
cultural limbo of tensions and uneasiness.

Their old modes of thought and expression could hardly have been
fully satisfactory. They had learned, in broad terms, that they must
master theology, law, history, scriptural scholarship, poetry, music, and
art in order to function as genuine Christians. Yet the specific content of
these many areas of Christian learning was beyond them; it existed in
languages they did not know. And their spiritual mentors had provided
only broad clues to its existence, leaving for them the task of acquiring

256. *Ibid.*, Ch. 18, cols. 1224–25.
257. *Ibid.*, Ch. 22, col. 1229.
258. *Ibid.*
259. "Life of St. Nahum" (cited above, n. 226), pp. 143–44. For a good discussion of
the activity at Nahum's monastery, see Sergheraert, *Syméon le Grand (893–927)*, pp. 49–53.

the appropriate specific materials. For the moment, they were at the mercy of outsiders for cultural guidance, outsiders who had suddenly become the élite in Bulgaria—and who had probably conducted themselves in a fashion appropriate to their role. Their presence must have engendered great dissatisfaction among the dispossessed élite of an earlier day.

All of this would again suggest that the coming of the new religion created serious strains upon the very roots of Bulgar society, that the very assumptions upon which Bulgar life was based were badly shaken by the somewhat vague but dynamic cultural forces that entered Bulgaria with the cross.

In reflecting on the events surrounding the initial stages of the conversion of the Bulgars, one is compelled to conclude that the introduction of Christianity marked a sharp division in Bulgarian history. Although the sources are far too inadequate to permit a full reconstruction of the situation, they strongly suggest that during the quarter century between Boris' decision to accept the new religion and his retreat to a monastery the accustomed pattern of life was seriously disturbed on many levels. New beliefs, practices, and ideas crowded into the land to create new standards against which the old ways had to be measured. Religious usages, political institutions and processes, legal practices, and moral customs that had enjoyed acceptance among the Bulgars from time beyond memory began to undergo modifications intended to adjust them to a new set of criteria of acceptability. The process of change was further accentuated by the introduction into the Bulgar social order of elements heretofore absent from the scene: a new élite group in the clergy, a new form or organization for that group, new intellectual, literary, and art forms, and even a new written language. The presence of so many forces of change makes it impossible to avoid the conclusion that all levels of Bulgar society felt the effects of conversion in a substantial way.

It would be illuminating if the historian could accurately measure the intensity and the tempo of change brought on by the appearance of Christianity in Bulgaria. Unfortunately, the surviving sources that deal with the internal history of Bulgaria preclude any adequate estimate on this score, but it seems safe to say that the forces of change did not proceed at a revolutionary pace: there was no concerted assault on an old order that aimed at entirely replacing it with an entirely new system. Indeed, the most informative sources—especially the letter of Nicholas I—strongly suggest that a spirit of timidity presided over the changes occurring in

Bulgaria. Boris' mood, as reflected in the questions he placed before Nicholas I, was conservative, restrained, almost reluctant to face the demands implicit in the new order. Yet Boris was certainly in the vanguard of the agents promoting modifications of the existing order, far more devoted to movement toward a new order than was a significant faction of *boyars*, who had for so long buttressed princely power with their support and helped provide leadership for Bulgar society.

Yet if the change was not revolutionary—in the sense that it did not involve a conscious assault on an old order with a view toward reconstituting a completely new order—it was intensive enough to disturb society deeply. The evidence suggests that change occurred in a rather patternless fashion, involving only particular usages and practices which were discovered to be incompatible with Christian usage. Boris was not interested in altering the Bulgar system of justice in its entirety so that it would conform to an abstract system with which he had become acquainted by virtue of Christian influences; rather, he felt compelled to modify the old manner of treating certain criminals and to search out a new basis for treating certain acts against the social and political order. He did not seek to impose a new moral code on his people but to discover whether, according to the new dispensation, it was morally proper to wear old-fashioned breeches, to copulate with one's wife on Saturday night, to prepare for battle in the accustomed way, and to pray for one's pagan ancestors.

Probably this order of change began at the moment of his baptism, and on an elemental level—where a mechanical conformance to directions was more clearly involved than a conscious realization of the implications of action. By the act of baptism the new convert was forced to change his manner of worshipping in a significant way. This first step into a new world created situations which called into question the propriety of ancient patterns of conduct. The new convert committed himself to attend mass, which immediately required that he dress differently, stand differently in the church building, desist from conversing with his neighbor while in the sacred precincts, and learn new formulas for addressing his deity. He partook of the sacrificial feast at holy communion as a part of his new religion, but only after he had made preparations which kept him away from the conjugal bed the night before and altered his eating habits on the day of communion. His baptism imposed on him the obligation to respect Sundays and holy days, but this requirement interfered with the execution of public justice, battle preparations, work patterns, and amusements. All of this necessitated changes in conduct.

Thus the most rudimentary practices of Christian worship, even when imposed upon a simple, unlettered populace, caused ripples of change to move across the existing patterns of life. Each ripple caused new disturbances, which were added to the existing turbulence, until the ripples became waves which swept away large portions of the old order. In this process there was neither pattern nor program, as is clearly reflected in the letter which Boris addressed to Pope Nicholas I, a letter composed of a confusing hodgepodge of questions, few of which appear to have any logical connection with any other. Boris' requests seem to represent the true measure or result of the introduction of Christianity into Bulgaria: the new religion generated a hectic, pell-mell, disruptive process of change that touched many aspects of life and called into question a wide variety of customary actions.

One is tempted to suggest that this kind of change creates more acute tension in a society than does a conscious, planned effort at revolution, but, regardless of one's response to this philosophical issue, it is beyond dispute that the appearance of the new religion in Bulgaria acted as an acid that ate at the texture of society to compel change. None of this change was planned or even conceived; all of it occurred in a confused way.

The evidence that Christianization bred change in Bulgaria prompts a new range of questions. What motivated Bulgars, as Christians, to try to change their accustomed ways? What was there about the introduction of a new religion—more specifically the Christian religion—that nourished an urge to move into new patterns of conduct? Why did not Christianity serve simply as a substitute for the old religion, without becoming a dynamic influence leading to change? One would like to say, with Photius and Nicholas I, that the new faith miraculously irradiated the stupid, beastly Bulgars with a new, divinely inspired wisdom that permitted them to comprehend clearly the folly of their old ways and that provided them with the will and the knowledge to act differently. However, there is little evidence to suggest that God spent his illuminating powers very generously on the Bulgars at the moment of their conversion. The quest for answers to these questions must turn in other directions.

In the manner of the modern modes of explaining human conduct, one is tempted to say that change occurred in Bulgaria because those who held power saw an opportunity to improve their positions as a consequence of the conversion of the Bulgars. *Cui bono?* It is difficult to escape the fact that the Bulgars stood to gain in the world of diplomacy by accepting the faith of their most dangerous adversaries and their most promising allies. In

Christianity Boris probably saw a source of greater authority for the khan, and therefore a mode of strengthening the monarchy in his land. The Bulgars' knowledge of the wealth, splendor, and power of Christian Byzantium (and perhaps, to a lesser degree, of Christian Rome and Christian Germany) undoubtedly bred an urge to share in those material benefits that appeared to come only to Christians. Christianity also certainly appeared as a potential binding force, capable of relieving the tension which existed between Bulgar masters and Slavic minions—the latter constituting the vast majority of the population of the Bulgar state. One can hardly escape the conclusion that baptism promised a rich harvest of tangible benefits that were as appealing as the spiritual fruits of which the great ecclesiastical authorities so often preached. It may well be, then, that change in Bulgar society was promoted by leaders who sought to gain positive advantages from the new religion which would improve their position as overlords in Bulgaria.

However, a thorough reading of the sources with a view to discovering what happened in Bulgaria and to the Bulgars during a crucial quarter of a century suggests another dimension to the problem of change. Religious inspiration was one of the many forces that prompted the new converts to alter their conduct and their attitudes. As best one can capture Boris' mentality, it appears certain that he was a religious man. He lived in a world where the power of the divine presided over every facet of human life: the administration of justice, diplomacy, daily conduct, preparation for battle, or the way one dressed. Every aspect of life involved acts which might please or displease the divine power, and thus shape the course of one's existence. Conversion involved a commitment to a new deity whose deportment toward men was fundamentally no different than that of the gods they had previously honored. The chief appeal for the new converts was their conviction that this new deity was more powerful than other gods, that he could work greater benefits and inflict more terrible disasters than the others. This belief imposed upon the new converts the absolute necessity of conforming to the law of the Christian God. They were compelled by the logic that ruled their basic religious outlook to discover and to abide by the rules imposed on men by the Christian God.

It is this quest that permeates Boris' requests to Nicholas and that appears to control his religious conduct in the few cases where there is evidence of that conduct. In short, conversion did not fundamentally change the religious outlook of the Bulgars; it involved the substitution of a new deity for old ones. The consequence of this fundamental fact was the need to adjust the outward conduct of life to a new law, to learn what pleased and displeased the new deity so as to assure the continued flow of divine bounty and to avoid the ever-present possibility of divine wrath. Basically, the urge to change Bulgar society flowed from a primitive, unsophisticated religious impulse. But that crude impulse was powerful enough to unleash forces that touched society at every level and in every aspect of human conduct.

The drive to transform existing cultural patterns that was generated within Bulgar society was clearly accentuated by the conduct of the missionaries who brought the new faith to Bulgaria. Their contempt for Bulgar patterns of behavior was manifest, as unmistakable as the condescension that pervaded the letters of Photius, Nicholas I, and John VIII.

The disdain of the missionaries for the pagan culture of the Bulgars was matched by their complete confidence that baptism would infuse the Bulgars with a new range of talents which would permit them to overcome their previous shortcomings. They believed that barbarism was a condition imposed by paganism and argued that the Bulgars were crude, ignorant, and savage because they worshipped inferior gods. The saving waters of baptism would wash away both sin and ignorance; the new convert would suddenly acquire a vast new range of intellectual and emotional powers which would make it possible for him to absorb all the essentials of the civilization enjoyed by those who worshipped the true God. Thus the missionaries, especially the Greeks, felt free to confront the Bulgars with the complete range of Christian civilization in the full expectation that the regenerated Bulgars could absorb it. They proceeded on the conviction that all the worldly aspects of their culture were inevitable consequences of the Christian faith. They never doubted that the splendid art, literature, theology, political institutions, wealth, and comforts of the civilized world were natural by-products of the benevolence of the Christian God. They made no distinction between culture and Christianity; to them there was only Christian culture, superior to all other cultures because it was Christian. Now that the Bulgars had become Christians, there was no reason why they could not absorb Christian culture in the fullest sense.

With a confidence that a modern historian—schooled to think of cultural patterns as derived from and dependent upon factors other than divine pleasure—finds almost unbelievable, the missionaries confronted the new converts with a demanding yet majestic goal. They argued, in effect, that all the Bulgars had to do was *will* to become civilized, and it would be so. Conversion itself gave the Bulgars the powers required for living like Christians; that is, to live as men did in Constantinople and

Rome. Buoyed by such assurances, which certainly must have softened the missionaries' deprecatory attitude toward ancient Bulgar culture, the Bulgars were encouraged to reach for a new mode of life. What their basic religious attitudes and their native aspirations for power, wealth, and acceptance drove them to undertake was reinforced by what their mentors urged them to undertake. And success had been assured them.

One is inclined to argue, then, that the most profound consequence of the conversion process was the creation in Bulgaria of a state of tension which could be released only by an effort to modify accustomed patterns of behavior. The coming of the new religion created fresh opportunities for the exercise of power and influence inside and outside Bulgaria. Christianity confronted each convert with the critical problem of making peace with a deity whose chief attribute was his greater power to control human destiny. The acceptance of Christianity let loose in Bulgaria persuasive spokesmen for the idea that the approach to the baptismal font had at one stroke created the need for a complete change of habits and had provided every convert with the full range of powers needed to acquire all the amenities of civilized life.

As these forces were generated in Bulgaria, they acted as a powerful reagent, casting doubts on the propriety of ancient ways, breeding new aspirations, and creating new norms for conduct. The only way to escape from these pressures was to alter conduct. And yet change itself was fraught with doubts: a lingering fear that abandonment of old ways could court danger, a constant uncertainty whether new patterns of behavior were being properly carried out, a sense of frustration when the new wisdom which allegedly came with baptism was not immediately and clearly operative when problems arose, and a feeling of inferiority in the presence of the proud minions of Christian civilization.

And what of the prince in this confusing world, at the vortex of all these forces? To him was promised the richest harvest of power, wealth, and influence—plus an especially exalted place in the world to come—if he could bring his subjects to a full acceptance of Christianity; no less an authority than Photius gave this assurance, and in the most inspired language. Against this sweet temptation was the threat of a terrible loss if his subjects refused to follow him into the Christian camp; the *boyars* who revolted in 865 dramatically posed the possible consequences of failure. As a man who was moved by powerful religious sentiments, the khan had to face the constant danger that a false move in dealing with the new God might unleash divine retribution so terrible that his nation would be ruined. In his role as the head of a people, he had to think constantly in terms of the displeasure the Christian God might feel if his subjects failed, in even the most minor matters, to act in a Christian way.

This terrible responsibility drove the khan to an incessant involvement in the particulars that surrounded the institution of the new religion. It was he who had to confront most directly the missionary forces, who haughtily belittled the past accomplishments of the Bulgars and who treated them as children. Moreover, he was compelled to contribute to this deflation of the Bulgars by humbly requesting guidance from the mighty guardians of the Christian faith and civilization on the most simple questions relating to religious matters, giving credence to the notion of the helplessness of the new-born children of the Christian God.

It is inescapable that the decision to lead a people to Christianity imposed a Herculean task on a prince, one that involved every aspect of his princely office. Perhaps this burden completely occupied a prince during the early years of the conversion period, leaving little time and less energy for the other considerations associated with his office. Yet it was equally true that the progress of a conversion process hinged absolutely on the prince's decisions and actions. Even though he was a prisoner of his decision, he became the decisive agent in enacting that decision.

In Bulgaria, Boris played a vital role in every major aspect of the Christianization process. He defined and enforced the new rules that governed the conduct of his Christian subjects. He decided from whence the missionaries would come. He chose the path which the organizational growth of Bulgaria would take. He determined the configuration of Bulgarian attachments to the rest of the Christian world. He controlled the ecclesiastical personnel who labored to Christianize his people. He took the harsh steps necessary for curbing the forces that opposed the conversion of Bulgaria. He made the ultimate decision which determined the adoption of a unique ritual, in the native tongue, for Bulgaria. The fate of Christianity in Bulgaria would have been perhaps radically different without the intimate involvement of the prince in the conversion process.

Having concluded that the introduction of Christianity exerted a profound influence on Bulgar society, one is then tempted to generalize upon the experiences of the other nations that were also drawn into the Christian orbit during the early middle ages. But such generalization is not valid because the situation in Bulgaria was unique; its conversion process was affected by factors that were not present in other areas into which Christianity spread. The bitter rivalry for jurisdiction between Rome and

Constantinople constantly influenced the progress of Bulgar Christianity. The penetration of foreign influences into Bulgaria was particularly strong prior to the actual conversion. The division between Bulgars and Slavs within the state was a special situation. The Byzantine world was at that moment sensitized to missionary problems to a degree that was never quite repeated, with the Byzantine government and church devoting special energy to the Bulgars. The personality of Boris was another unique ingredient in Bulgaria. All these factors created a situation which had no exact parallel elsewhere; and they make argument by analogy dubious or unsound.

However, the Bulgar case perhaps invites a new examination of the meager sources that pertain to the Christianization of Europe in the early middle ages with a view toward more firmly establishing the nature of the impact of the new religion on pagan, barbarian societies. The Bulgar experience may suggest or prompt a more careful screening of the kinds of sources that can be easily overlooked when the conversion process is examined primarily from the missionaries' point of view. Perhaps the sources that relate to the conversion of other peoples can yield additional evidence on the precise problems faced by a pagan society and its ruler in the early stages of the conversion process.

On the basis of the Bulgar case, it would appear that the religious mentality of the new converts was highly significant in determining the progress of Christianity. The attitudes of the new converts toward their missionary leaders and toward the culture represented by these missionaries appear to have been crucial factors in shaping the impact of Christianity and in determining the reaction of the converts to the religion. The interaction between local political conditions and the new ecclesiastical order cannot be slighted. The impact of particular Christian usages— liturgical, moral, disciplinary—on the ordinary conduct of daily life should be scrutinized more thoroughly, for the Bulgar experience strongly indicates it was in this area that conversion had the most profound and disturbing effect. Closer attention should be paid to the degree to which missionaries succeeded in impressing upon a newly converted society an awareness of its inferiority to the Christian, civilized world.

It is entirely possible that a new look at the entire range of missionary history in the early middle ages from these perspectives would not prove as informative in clarifying the impact of Christianization on a pagan society as it is in the Bulgar case. However, until such an investigation is made, with the Bulgar example firmly in mind, it seems permissible to presume that in a nation whose ruler had decided to Christianize his people a profound change had begun to affect all aspects of society from the moment that missionary work had begun. Although the new converts may not have become fully Christianized for many years, their lives were altered in a substantial way from the very beginning of the conversion process. Certainly Boris and his colleagues would affirm that this had been their experience in Bulgaria.

THE PISAN CLERGY AND AN AWAKENING OF HISTORICAL INTEREST IN A MEDIEVAL COMMUNE

Craig B. Fisher

University of California, Davis

THE PISAN CLERGY AND AN AWAKENING
OF HISTORICAL INTEREST IN A MEDIEVAL
COMMUNE

In the first third of the twelfth century the city of Pisa witnessed a remarkable flourishing of historical interest. This interest brought forth diverse works: three annalistic works of limited extent, a number of poetic inscriptions, a collection of historical and geographical material, and two extended historical poems—one of epic proportions. These form a group of works unique in extent and diversity for that period. They are of considerable importance as the first instance of a well-developed historical interest and tradition in a medieval Italian commune, if we pass over the century-earlier Venetian annals and the Milanese ecclesiastical histories. In addition, they offer an invaluable source for the study of communal attitudes in a period when other sources for the ideology of the commune are very limited. This study will try to discover the reasons for the appearance of such an historical interest and to determine its principal characteristics.

Pisa had attained considerable prosperity and power by this period, not only in Italy but also in the Mediterranean area.[1] As late as 1011, Pisa had still been on the defensive, suffering in that year a raid by Saracen corsairs. But by 1034 her ships had attacked the Saracen city of Bona in North Africa. In 1087 the Moslem ruler of al Mahdiya was forced to pay tribute after most of his capital had been captured by the Pisans and Genoese. And in the campaign of 1113–1115 the Pisans, with western allies, were able to destroy—at least temporarily—Saracen power in the Balearic Islands, an expedition which was to be Pisa's most impressive military achievement. The new successes and prosperity of Pisa were made apparent in this period by the construction of a magnificent cathedral, which had few contemporary architectural rivals. In 1081, as a final sign of her power, Henry IV gave official recognition to the communal government of Pisa, and soon her magistrates proudly bore the title of

1. The general histories of Pisa of the sixteenth and seventeenth centuries by Roncioni and Tronci are of little value since all statements must be verified. G. Volpe's *Studi sulle istituzioni comunali a Pisa* (Pisa, 1902), in *Annali della r. scuola normale superiore di Pisa*, XV, is still a classic but it is primarily concerned with institutional history beginning with the second half of the twelfth century. Consequently, William Heywood's *A History of Pisa, Eleventh and Twelfth Centuries* (Cambridge, 1921) is still the best general treatment of this period, though it is by no means definitive.

143

consuls. A feeling of pride in these accomplishments undoubtedly animated the Pisans, but to account fully for this sudden historical interest and importance, we must find further motives.

The authors of the historical works we have mentioned, as we shall see, were from the Pisan clergy, primarily from the cathedral chapter of canons. The cathedral clergy maintained a library which could have provided some sources for the earlier history of Pisa, but it also gave these writers some assurance that their works would be preserved. The reorganization of the cathedral chapter and the restoration of its property in the general reform pattern of the eleventh century had given new life to the cathedral library and school.[2] Although it can be assumed that the monasteries of Pisa also had libraries, little is known of their collections; and there is no evidence of private, secular libraries in Pisa at this period. While the commune of Genoa had an archive that preserved a chronicle of the city in the second half of the twelfth century, nothing is known of a similar city archive at Pisa in the period we are considering. Further, the cathedral clergy was an educated, literate group which could compose and appreciate historical works. Although some of the laity—at least those associated with the profession of the law—were able to read Latin, their first chronicles from the middle of the twelfth century betray their lack of literary refinement.[3] Thus the cathedral clergy, as a community with a library and with the requisite culture, was the one group in early twelfth-century Pisa capable of producing historical works of literary value.

The principal concern of these clerical authors was not so much with ecclesiastical developments as with secular and military events. Military history, for these writers, was not lacking in spiritual significance; on the contrary, victories were regarded as the handiwork of God, especially in this age which had witnessed the beginning of the crusades. Even so, the interest of these clerics in the communal rather than the ecclesiastical history of Pisa is unusual. The primary cause for this secular interest of the clergy was the political influence which the Pisan church gained in this period by its elevation to the rank of an archbishopric. In the early period of the Italian communes the secular authority over the territory

2. The chapter of canons at Pisa had already been received under papal protection with Victor II, but the history of the Pisan church during the period of the investiture controversy is obscure. However, the effects of reform on a cathedral chapter can be seen in the neighboring diocese of Lucca; see E. Kittel, "Der Kampf um die Reform des Domkapitels in Lucca im 11. Jahrhundert," *Festschrift Albert Brackmann dargebracht* (Weimar, 1931), pp. 207–47.

3. Chroniclers such as Maragone of Pisa and the Genoese Caffaro employed a simple prose style completely without literary pretensions.

outside a city was closely connected with the ecclesiastical jurisdiction of the city's prelate.[4] The promotion of Pisa from a bishopric to an archbishopric, with the subordination of other bishoprics to its authority, was therefore not only a change in ecclesiastical administration but also a change in political significance for the commune of Pisa.

In September, 1118, Pope Gelasius II, fleeing from Rome to seek refuge in France, delayed his trip for more than two weeks at Pisa. The papal biographer mentions the honorable and solemn reception given the pope by the entire populace and clergy, noting that before departing from the city the pope "negotiated with complete freedom certain things pertaining to his office."[5] On September 26, 1118, Gelasius II consecrated the new cathedral church of Pisa, its imposing proportions a monument to the progress and ambitions of the church and the city-state of Pisa. More importantly, however, the pope also raised the see of Pisa to metropolitan rank over the bishoprics of the island of Corsica. This action was actually a reconfirmation of earlier papal grants which had fallen into disuse, but Pisan contemporaries seem to have regarded it as a completely new grant.

Because this event formed a constant though often not explicit background for the historical works of the clergy in our period, the long preliminaries and the instability of this elevation should be considered in some detail.[6] The first step toward this new ecclesiastical dignity was taken by Gregory VII in 1077. Gregory, planning to bring Corsica within the jurisdiction of the Roman church as a phase of his program of centralization, had appointed Landulf, bishop of Pisa, papal legate to carry through a reform of the Corsican churches.[7] In 1078 the Roman pontiff changed the legatine assignment from a temporary office to a position to be enjoyed by the future bishops of Pisa, increasing the secular rights of the legate over the island but retaining final authority for the Roman see.[8]

Gerard, successor to Landulf as bishop of Pisa from 1080 to 1085, was not as zealous for the cause of the reform papacy and tended to cooperate

---

4. Volpe, *op. cit.*, pp. 9–10.
5. "quaeque sui officii, libertate plenaria tractans." L. Duchesne, *Le Liber Pontificalis* (Paris, 1955), II, 317. In view of subsequent developments, the phrase *libertate plenaria* is interesting since Calixtus II will speak of *necessitas* as the reason for Gelasius' actions at Pisa. To be sure, the papacy was dependent on Pisa and Genoa for its escape to southern France.
6. A. Felbinger, "Die Primatialprivilegien für Italien von Gregor VII. bis Innocenz III. (Pisa, Grado, und Salerno)," *Zeitschrift für Rechtsgeschichte. Kanonistische Abteilung*, LXVIII, 95–163.
7. Gregory VII, *Register*, V:2 and 4, *MGH, Epistolae selectae*, II, 349–52.
8. *Ibid.*, pp. 414–15 (*Reg.*, VI:12).

with Henry IV.[9] After a vacancy, the Pisan see was received by Daimbert, about 1088. Daimbert's background was questionable; he had been consecrated deacon by Wezel, the schismatic archbishop of Mainz from 1084 to 1088, but Urban II hastened to defend the new Pisan bishop from the more zealous local reformers.[10] In 1091 the pope renewed legatine jurisdiction over Corsica for the Pisan bishops on the condition that Pisa continue to display its fidelity to the Roman church.[11]

On April 21, 1092, Urban II elevated the Pisan bishops from the temporary role of legates of the Roman church to archbishops with metropolitan jurisdiction over the Corsican churches. As justification for his action, Urban referred to Pisa's recent successes:

> Surely the dispensation of the divine majesty has deigned to make illustrious in our times the glory of the city of Pisa by her triumphs over the Saracens and to advance the city in the promotion of secular concerns, so as to exalt her over the other cities of the province. For this reason we, the executors and fellow workers of the divine piety, have decreed to glorify her in spiritual matters as well.[12]

Along with the metropolitan position, Urban II granted Daimbert the *pallium*. The document of this grant was kept in the Roman archives and duly copied at Pisa.[13] To the grant of metropolitan rights, Urban II later added the legatine office over the island of Sardinia.[14] Daimbert retained this new title of archbishop for the remainder of his rule. As a devoted follower of Urban II, he was frequently in attendance at the papal court not only in Italy but also in France. In 1099, Daimbert was leader of the Pisan forces on the First Crusade, and he remained in Jerusalem as the Latin patriarch of the city. However, during the years of the archbishop's absence from Pisa, the newly granted jurisdiction probably fell into abeyance; it was later maintained that in the last years of Urban II

9. N. Zucchelli, *Cronotassi dei vescovi e arcivescovi di Pisa* (Pisa, 1907), p. 43.

10. Migne, *Patrologia Latina*, CLI, 295, 333–35.

11. "quandiu in ea quam hodie exhibet Ecclesiae Romanae fidelitate perstiterit." *Ibid.*, col. 331.

12. "Divinae siquidem majestatis dispositio Pisanae urbis gloriam nostris temporibus, et Saracenorum triumphis illustrare, et saecularium rerum provectibus promovere, ut prae comprovincialibus exaltare dignata est. Eapropter et nos divinae pietatis prosecutores et cooperatores, eam in spiritualibus quoque glorificare decrevimus, sicut praedecessores nostros multis olim fecisse scriptorum ecclesiasticorum testimoniis comprobatur." *Ibid.*, col. 345.

13. P. F. Kehr, *Italia pontificia* (Berlin, 1908), III, 321.

14. In the bull of Innocent II, 1138: "legationem quoque Sardiniae, a praedecessore nostro papa Urbano praedecessoribus tuis concessam." *PL*, CLXXIX, 362.

and during the pontificate of Paschal II the Corsican bishops had been consecrated by the pope himself.[15] Although there is no evidence of a formal document demoting the Pisan prelate to bishop, Peter, the successor of Daimbert (probably in 1104), no longer used the title of archbishop in his documents.[16]

Gelasius II's action in September of 1118 was therefore more than a confirmation of Urban's grant; coupled as it was with the consecration of the new cathedral, it symbolized the beginning of a new period of greatness for the Pisan church and commune.[17] Peter immediately adopted the newly granted title, which was to be used in the future by all his successors. He also proceeded to exercise his office directly, going with a papal legate and members of the Pisan clergy and laity to Corsica to consecrate the newly elected bishop of Mariana and to receive obedience and oaths of fidelity from the other Corsican prelates.[18] The metropolitan position appeared to be assured.

The new position, however, could not be regarded with equanimity by Pisa's maritime neighbor, Genoa, which also had ambitions in Corsica. Calixtus II, returning to Rome from France, visited Pisa in May of 1120. On this occasion the pope consecrated the new archbishop, Azzo, formerly a cardinal, renewed the grant of metropolitan jurisdiction over Corsica, and consecrated three altars in the cathedral. During the consecration of the altars, the Genoese, who had recently opened hostilities against the Pisans, attacked the city,[19] probably to impress on the pope the seriousness of the rivalry between the two cities.

15. In the bull of Calixtus II, 1121, *PL*, CLXIII, 1192.

16. The titles used by Daimbert and Peter can be readily found in *Regesto della chiesa di Pisa*, ed. N. Caturegli, *Regesta chartarum Italiae*, Istituto storico italiano per il medio evo (Rome, 1938), XXIV.

17. Gelasius' actions are recorded in the Pisan *Gesta triumphalia*, ed. M. Gentile, in Muratori, *Rerum Italicarum Scriptores²*, VI:2, 94, and by Peter of Monte Cassino, in J. Watterich, *Pontificum Romanorum Vitae* (Leipzig, 1862), II, 110. There is also a Pisan note, *Historia consecrationis*, ed. Muratori, in *RIS¹*, III:1, 404–5. The great interest of its author in listing relics and his mention of the podestà, however, place the composition of this note no earlier than the thirteenth century.

18. *RIS²*, VI:2, 94–95.

19. Calixtus II mentioned his confirmation of the metropolitan position in his bull of 1121, Migne, *PL*, CLXIII, 1192. Further details can be found in a fourteenth-century chronicle of Pisa, Archivio di Stato, Lucca, MS 54, fols. 31*v*–32. Since this portion of the chronicle has not been published, I will quote the pertinent passages: "e in Pisa intro a di v di magio, ricieuto chon grande honore da tutto il populo pisano . . . e con canti, inni, e laude la chiesa magiore visito, e poi allo palasso del arciveschovado poso. dipo pochi di Athne piagentino arcidiacono chardinale prima che fusse cardinale lo elese arciveschovo di Pisa, e a di x di magio prezente lo consegro in arciveschovo. . . . dell isula di Corsicha li

The Genoese soon turned to other weapons against Pisa. A delegation, led by Caffaro, later the chronicler of Genoa, was sent to Rome. The Genoese archives have retained a most incriminating document which gives the outcome of the efforts of this city's first embassy at the papal court.[20] On June 16, 1120, shortly after Calixtus returned to Rome, the Genoese embassy agreed to pay by mid-November fifteen hundred marks of silver to the pope and his court, as well as fifty ounces of gold to Roman clerics, and it guaranteed a military alliance if Pisa should begin war against the papacy. After the Genoese had met these conditions, the pope was to forbid—under anathema—the consecration of the bishops of Corsica by a Pisan or any other bishop, reserving such consecrations for the Roman church. There is no evidence that the Genoese fully complied with the agreements, but the document of June records that advance sums were paid to the pope, clerics, and individual Roman nobles.

Even more incriminating is the fact that on January 3, 1121—two months after the payments were to have been completed—Calixtus issued a document to the Corsican bishops which freed them from subordination to Pisa and again placed them directly under the Roman see.[21] Calixtus argued in this document that Urban II had made the grant because of the service and devotion of Pisa but further under the exigencies of that time. Gelasius II had confirmed the grant under an even more pressing compulsion, and he, Calixtus, had followed the example of his predecessor. Moreover, Calixtus contended that this special privilege for Pisa had been the direct cause of war between Pisa and Genoa, and that, as a consequence, the papacy was being charged with the responsibility for beginning the conflict. Further, Calixtus claimed that the people of Rome resented the diminution of the prerogatives of the Roman see and were causing trouble. And finally, he stated that the clergy and laity of Corsica sought to end their subjection to Pisa.

Pressure from these diverse groups and the desire to restore the prerogative to the papacy caused the pope to rescind the privileges of Pisa,

---

veschovi consegro allui e a suoi suciessori, e in perpetuo li brevilegio. e preghato dall arciveschovo e da calonaci [canonici] pisani consegro nella chieza magior di Pisa tre altari . . . dipoi si parti di Pisa per essere a Roma. e acompagnato fue da due consuli pisani e molti altri cavalieri pisani fine alla cita di Roma." The Genoese attack is mentioned in Caffaro, *Annali genovesi*, ed. L. Belgrano, Fonti per la storia d'Italia (Rome, 1890), XI, 16–17.

20. *Ibid.*, p. 20, n. 1.
21. Migne, *PL*, CLXIII, 1192–94.

whose prelate was no longer granted the title of archbishop in papal documents. The issue arose again at the Lateran Council of 1123 when, after the judgment of a special court, the pope (in a bull dated April 6) renewed his prohibition of the consecration of Corsican bishops by Pisan prelates.[22]

A new pope followed a new policy on the Pisan ecclesiastical claims. Shortly after his entry into office, Honorius II began negotiations to bring an end to the continuing war between Pisa and Genoa. On July 21, 1126, he issued a bull that returned the right of consecrating Corsican bishops to the archbishop of Pisa.[23] In reviewing the course of the controversy, the pope placed the blame for the war on the Genoese:

> The Genoese, envying the honor of the Pisan people and not bearing with equanimity the increase of the power of that people, on the occasion of this affair began war against the Pisans.[24]

According to Honorius, Calixtus II, "a lover of peace," had been swayed by the arguments of the Genoese and had withdrawn the consecration privilege, but the war between the two peoples had not ceased. And when, after three summonses, the Genoese had not presented valid grounds against Pisan consecrations in Corsica, the pope turned the case back to the special court which had judged it under Calixtus. The judges said they had been led in their earlier decision by "divine love"; their new decision was that the earlier privileges giving the metropolitan position over Corsica to Pisa should be maintained, especially since the position had been taken from the Pisan prelate "without proper judiciary order." Honorius then consulted the cardinals, who agreed (with the single exception of a deacon) to the reinstatement of the Pisan archbishop "even against the will of the bishops of this island." The leading Roman barons also agreed, and Honorius II proceeded to confirm the earlier privileges, principally reiterating Urban II's grant of 1092.

The Pisan-Genoese war continued until peace negotiations were effected by Innocent II. The result of these talks, in 1133, was a new

22. For this incident in the council, see Caffaro, *op. cit.*, pp. 18–20. The bull is in Migne, *PL*, CLXIII, 1287–90.

23. Migne, *PL*, CLXVI, 1261–65.

24. "Januenses autem honori Pisani populi invidentes, et eorum incrementum aequo animo non ferentes, hujus rei sumpta occasione guerram contra Pisanos moverunt. Unde caedes, incendia, et multae Christianorum captivites, peccatis exigentibus, contiguerunt, et debacchandi in Christianos Saracenis multa crevit audacia." *Ibid.*, col. 1261.

settlement of the Corsican question. The principle of a parity of positions was established: each city would have metropolitan rights over three of the six Corsican bishoprics. The two archbishops were then granted, as compensation, additional suffragan bishoprics on the mainland, and Pisa also received two bishoprics and legatine authority in Sardinia.[25]

The final confirmation of this settlement is to be found in the bull of Innocent II, dated April 22, 1138, which set the practice for the future.[26] One phrase of the bull is worth underscoring. To the metropolitan authority, Innocent II added symbolic honors, "so that the city of Pisa might be further honored, a city which through heavenly favor has frequently obtained victory over the enemies of the Christian name and has subjugated many of their cities."[27] An equality of position in Corsica was the only feasible solution to the problem at a time when the two city-states were almost equally powerful. In the thirteenth and fourteenth centuries, when Pisa fell behind in competition for the Mediterranean, the Genoese gained possession of Corsica, and the Aragonese of Sardinia. But the Pisan prelate still bears the title "primate of the islands of Corsica and Sardinia, and *legatus natus.*"[28]

In all of the papal documents that favored the Pisan church, the simple political reality that the island of Corsica lay within the Pisan sphere of in- fluence—even though it was not directly subject to the mainland city—is almost completely overlooked. Instead, the papacy maintained two other arguments for its grants: first, the grants were a compensation for the fidelity of the Pisan church to the Roman church in the troublesome times of those decades; secondly, since divine will was granting Pisa an expansion of its power—and especially victories over the infidels—the papacy was bound to honor the Pisan church and city in whatever way it could.

The first argument must have had particular significance for the Roman church, but the second was undoubtedly of more importance for the Pisans. It would be the pride and the intent of the Pisan writers to trace this divine favor which had already given the city secular power and prosperity—and that was now given as the justification for elevating the Pisan church to a higher ecclesiastical rank.

25. Kehr, *op. cit.*, III, p. 324 (number 23).

26. Migne, *PL*, CLXXIX, 361–62.

27. "ut Pisana civitas, quae coelesti favore de inimicis Christiani nominis victoriam frequenter obtinuit, et eorum urbes plurimas subjugavit, amplius honoretur." *Ibid.*, col. 362.

28. G. Picotti, "Pisa," *Enciclopedia cattolica* (Vatican City, 1952), IX, col. 1563.

Annals

The earliest of these historical works is a short collection of notes that its editor, Novati,[29] called *Annales antiquissimi*. This collection was found at the end of a manuscript which contained commentaries on the Canticle of Canticles and the Apocalypse. The writer collected extremely terse entries for ten years, between 1105 and 1117 P.S.[30] Most of the entries deal with the struggles of the Pisans and the Saracens, but notices of fires and earthquakes have sometimes been added. Although it is usually impossible to identify the sources of early chroniclers, it was a common practice for annalists of those centuries, when writing local annals with no earlier collections at hand, to be able to muster information from the most diverse sources for about a century before the time of their writing. The *Annales antiquissimi* gives no clues to its author's identity other than that he must have been a Pisan who made his notes some time after the Pisan year 1117—which ended March 24, 1117, in the regular calendar. It was probably composed before September, 1118, since the visit of Gelasius II was not recorded. And its author was a cleric, if we can judge from the religious character of the rest of the manuscript.

The other two annalistic works, the *Fragmentum auctoris incerti* and the *Gesta triumphalia*, though they have been edited separately and given distinct titles by modern editors, were designed as companion pieces.[31] The *Fragmentum* carries short entries from as early as 688; the *Gesta* begins with the campaign of the Pisans in the First Crusade and continues with rather lengthy accounts of major events in some of the succeeding years. Since the *Fragmentum* does not reduplicate any of these events—except for two very short notices about the First Crusade—it can be assumed that the *Fragmentum* was a later work for supplying earlier annalistic background and certain events of minor importance after 1099. The *Gesta*

29. F. Novati, "Un nuovo testo degli 'Annales pisani antiquissimi' e le prime lotte di Pisa contro gli arabi," *Centenario della nascita di Michele Amari* (Palermo, 1910), II, 13. The annals are to be found in MS 79 of the Biblioteca Governativa of Cremona, fol. 99*v*.

30. The Pisan calendar of the middle ages began the year with the Annunciation, March 25, but one year in advance of the then generally accepted chronology. Rather than transfer all dates into the common chronology, I shall use the P.S. to distinguish a date in the Pisan style.

31. *Fragmentum auctoris incerti*, ed. M. Gentile, in Muratori, *RIS*[2], VI:2, 99–103; also in Muratori, *RIS*[1], VI, 107–110, and Ughelli, *Italia sacra*, X, 97–99. *Gesta triumphalia*, ed. M. Gentile, in Muratori, *RIS*[2], VI:2, 89–96; also in Muratori, *RIS*[1], VI, 100–106, and Ughelli, *op. cit.*, X, 91–96.

detailed the more important events, which the author had witnessed or heard of in his own time.

There are indications that these two annals were originally composed, in their first versions, between March and September, 1119. The *Fragmentum* ends with the year 1136 P.S., the *Gesta* with 1120 P.S. The thirteenth-century scribe who copied them ended both with *et cetera*, indicating that the manuscript from which he was making his copy lacked endings for these two works. Because the *Fragmentum* records all the main entries of the *Annales antiquissimi*, the former must have been written after the shorter work of 1117. Further, the *Fragmentum* must have been originally written before September, 1119, the date of Archbishop Peter's death. The *Fragmentum* contains obituary notes for the Pisan bishops from the time of Guido, in 1076, to Roger, in 1132. While the earlier notices supply the month and the day of death, probably taken from a necrology, the entries for Peter and his successors give only the year.[32] This change in the style of the obituary notices indicates that the first version of the *Fragmentum* was composed before Peter's death in September, 1119.[33]

The *Gesta* probably ended, in its first version, with the events of March, 1119. It proceeds directly from the end of the Balearic campaign, in 1115, to events of 1118: the death of Paschal II, the visit of Gelasius II to Pisa and his constitution of the Pisan church as metropolitan over Corsica, the death of Gelasius II and the succession of Calixtus II, and finally the journey to Corsica of Archbishop Peter—with the papal legate, the canons of the Pisan church, and a consul of Pisa—to assume the newly restored metropolitan rights in the first quarter of 1119. That the greater part of the *Gesta*—which was devoted to the Balearic campaign—was not written before the events of 1118–1119 can be further determined by the title of archbishop which the author gave Peter,[34] a title which the Pisan prelate did not assume until after the papal visit in the fall of 1118.

The Pisan author of the *Gesta* had a purpose in ending his account with the effective exercise of metropolitan jurisdiction over Corsica. The papal documents reiterated that the promotion of the Pisan church was in part a reward for a city that had won significant victories over the infidel Saracens through divine favor. The *Gesta* opens with the significant sentence: "For the sake of a memorial, it has been our care to write down those things which God Omnipotent has deigned to bring about through

32. P. Scheffer-Boichorst first noticed this change in his "Die ältere Annalistik der Pisaner," *Forschungen zur deutschen Geschichte*, XI (1871), 509.

33. See Zucchelli, *op. cit.*, p. 53, for the month of Peter's death.

34. *RIS*², VI:2, 91.

the Pisan people." [35] The succeeding accounts of Pisan victories over the Moslems in the First Crusade and then in the Balearic campaign would have made legitimate, in the author's regard, the claim of the Pisan church and city to advancement in the ecclesiastical realm, even as the popes were recognizing the new position. Thus the Pisan writer turned to the most spectacular and recent campaigns after the time of the First Crusade, ending his work with the papal award for this period of noteworthy victories and the effective exercise of Pisan ecclesiastical rights over Corsica.

From the papal document copied for the Pisan church archives or from the testimony of older clerics, the writer must have known that the action of Gelasius II in 1118 was a reinstatement rather than a completely new deed. Yet neither he nor the later chroniclers of Pisa referred to the earlier grants of Pisan ecclesiastical jurisdiction over Corsica or to the archiepiscopal position of Pisan prelates before 1118. Certainly the actual occupation of such a jurisdiction in the presence of a papal legate during the following spring would have more meaning for the future than an obsolete document in the archives. Furthermore, this exercise of the new jurisdiction may have called for a recording, especially since there is a possibility that Gelasius did not issue a formal privilege. The *Gesta* mentions no specific privilege, nor is there any such document in the papal or Pisan archives. [36]

Both the *Fragmentum* and the *Gesta* were later augmented. Notices were added to the *Fragmentum* for the 1130's—a period beyond the scope of this study—but the *Gesta* was continued shortly after 1119. The present conclusion of the *Gesta* is an incomplete entry for the last part of 1119 (1120 p.s.). [37] The question is to determine what has been lost from the end of the *Gesta* and when this terminal addition was made to the first version of the chronicle.

The *Gesta* was used as a source by Maragone in the 1160's and by an anonymous Pisan chronicler in the fourteenth century. While Maragone often pared down the long entries of the *Gesta*, the later chronicler translated the earlier source into Italian almost verbatim. Both of these later chronicles have a gap of thirteen years between the entry for 1121 p.s. and 1134 p.s.; and it is probable that the notice for the year 1121 p.s.

35. "Ad memoriam habendam cure fuit nobis ea scribere, que Deus Omnipotens per Pisanum populum dignatus est efficere." *Ibid.*, p. 89.

36. The *Historia consecrationis* (above, n. 17) states that Gelasius confirmed the position, "tam privilegio, quam ore proprio," but the account is suspect. This *Historia* was included by the fourteenth-century Pisan chronicler, Archivio di Stato, Lucca, MS 54, fols. 31–31v.

37. *RIS²*, VI:2, 96.

(1120) was the final entry of the *Gesta*. When the text of Maragone is compared with the text of the later Italian chronicler, it is found that the chronicler used Maragone for the later part of his chronicle but not for the earlier part, and that for the entry of 1121 P.S. both were dependent on a third work, the *Gesta*.[38] The later Pisan chronicler records a detail that is not in Maragone's account, the return of the Genoese to Porto Venere; and he also included in his notice "through the grace conceded by God and by the Virgin Mother of Christ," a phrase that is used elsewhere in the *Gesta*.

Further, in the two points on which the authors are at variance, Maragone was wrong while the later chronicler was correct—Maragone dating the episode 1122 P.S. and the later writer dating it 1121 P.S. The latter was correct. Caffaro of Genoa stated that peace had been established between Pisa and Genoa in September, 1120 (1121 P.S.), and he listed no further hostilities until 1122.[39] Maragone was also incorrect in mentioning the consecration of an altar to Mary for the consecration of 1120 was of *three* altars—and a ceremony that was performed by the pope himself.[40]

38. *Maragone*	*Anonymous*
MCXXII. Ianuenses	Nelli anni MCXXI li gienovesi avendo facta armata di ghalee, e per li pisani senti di quelle l armare provideno d armata, e presto e
venerunt ad fauces Arni cum galeis xxii; Pisani, stantes ad consecrationem altaris Sancte Marie,	venendo sopra la focie d Arno con xxii ghalee, lo populo pisano essendo in nella chiesa catedrale alla consecratione di tre altari,
iverunt contra illos, et pugnando eos	sentendo la venuta delli genovesi, subito l armata si parti di Pisa e andono a trovare li gienovesi. e funo a battaglia, e per gratia concieduta da dio e dalla vergine
vicerunt, et sex galeas ceperunt, et alias fugaverunt,	madre di Christo sconfisseno li pisani le xxii ghalee, conpigliandone vi; l altre si ridusseno a Porto Veneri.
et cum magno triumpho Pisas redierunt.	
RIS², VI:2, 9.	Archivio di Stato, Lucca, MS 54, fol. 33.

39. Caffaro, *op. cit.*, p. 17.

40. Above, n. 19. The accuracy of the dating of this short note indicates that it was taken from what had probably been a contemporary account. The biographer of Calixtus II, Boso, incorrectly placed the dedication of the cathedral in honor of St. Mary during the visit of this pope rather than during the stay of his predecessor, Gelasius II. Watterich, *op. cit.*, p. 119.

To determine the date of the additions to the *Gesta* more closely and to ascertain why the author ignored the presence of Calixtus II at the consecration—and even his visit to Pisa when he confirmed the position of the Pisan archbishop—we must consider the sequence of events in 1119 and 1120. In the early months of 1119—probably in March when sailing was possible—Peter, the archbishop of Pisa, had gone to Corsica with a papal legate to exercise his metropolitan authority. The *Gesta* and the annals of Caffaro both mention a Genoese act of piracy in May of that year, and the Pisan *Gesta* gives the subsequent negotiations between the two communes and the successful retaliatory expedition of the Pisans in August, a victory not mentioned by Caffaro. The last entry of the *Gesta* mentions a skirmish near Pisa in May, 1120, during Calixtus II's visit to Pisa.

Then in June of the same year, Genoese ambassadors to the papal court entered into an arrangement with the pope designed to end Pisa's ecclesiastical power over Corsica. This settlement was probably supposed to remain secret, but with the many Pisan connections in the papal court it is likely that the Pisan church was informed of the negotiations against its interests. During the summer the Genoese sent an expeditionary force against Pisa, probably in the favored season for such campaigns, late July or early August. This last incident was treated by Caffaro in detail,[41] but the Pisan annals have no further entries that would throw light on Pisan-Genoese relations in the decade of the twenties. According to Caffaro, the Pisans made peace with the Genoese, "according to the will of the Genoese," in September of 1120. It is probable that the Genoese expedition had been planned so that the final defeat of the Pisans and the resulting peace would open the way for the papal bull of January, 1121, which released the bishops of Corsica from the jurisdiction of Pisa.

The Genoese had been successful militarily and diplomatically in 1120, and further incidents of a warlike character did not occur until 1122. The Pisan chronicler may have omitted a major Genoese victory during the summer, but he could have presented the peace settlement of September without losing too much honor for Pisa. And the omission of any reference to the visit of Calixtus II to Pisa is comprehensible if the Pisan chronicler was aware of the negotiations which were being undertaken against the interests of the Pisan church. It therefore seems likely that the *Gesta* was continued between June, 1120, when papal-Genoese negotiations were well advanced, and September, 1120, when Pisa and Genoa made a temporary peace. Thus the composition of these three relatively short Pisan chronicles can be placed within a span of three years: between 1117,

41. Caffaro, *op. cit.*, pp. 16–17.

when the *Annales antiquissimi* was probably written, and 1120, when the *Gesta* received further entries.

The author or authors of these short works cannot be identified. It was thought that the biographer of Paschal II also composed the *Gesta triumphalia*,[42] for in his biography of Paschal he had mentioned the Balearic campaign, deferring a special work on that event until later,[43] but the identification of the biographer as the author of the *Gesta* has already been rejected on stylistic grounds.[44] Furthermore, such an identification cannot reconcile the strongly Pisan outlook of the *Gesta* with the probable Roman background and sympathy of the papal biographer.[45] However, it is interesting to note that in the reign of Gelasius II or Calixtus II a writer at the papal court was sufficiently interested in the Balearic campaign to plan a separate work on the subject.

Although it is impossible to identify the authorship of these Pisan chronicles, it is most likely that they were Pisan clerics, since the *Annales antiquissimi* was written in a manuscript of commentaries on certain biblical books and since the outlook of the author of the *Fragmentum-Gesta* was definitely oriented toward the Pisan church. It is also likely that the authors came from the group of canons of the cathedral church. The *Gesta* emphasizes the role of the canons: they had helped the archbishop and the papal legate frustrate attempts to negotiate with the Saracens before the final fall of Majorca, and they had been present at the important exercise of the new metropolitan position in early 1119.[46] Because the

42. Duchesne, *op. cit.*, II, 308, n. 26.

43. "Quid autem egregia Pisanorum industria et admirabilis pertinentia per eundem domnum papam Balearibus insulis Effize et Maiorice contulerit, quem apparatum, quas copias supplementumque, quemve legatum ipsi habuerint, quo consule, sub quo imperatore militaverint, cuius vexilli inditia secuti fuerint, quisve eorum fortiter fecerit, quot navibus et quomodo ierint, quid naufragii quidve laboris in reficiendis ratibus passi sint, illud etiam gloriosum ammirandumque subsidium quod non desperaverint, quomodo etiam evulsis captivis direptis spoliis subversis urbibus victores redierint, quia digno volumine comprehendere disposui, suo loco suo tempori distuli." *Ibid.*, p. 301.

44. Calisse, in his edition of *Liber Maiorichinus* (Fonti ... Italia [Rome, 1904], XXVIIII, x, n. 3), denied any connection; and J. March, in his edition of *Liber Pontificalis* ... ([Barcelona, 1925], pp. 63–69), came to the same conclusion on the basis of stylistic differences.

45. The author of the *Gesta* had been present in the expedition: "Quapropter spem nobis omnem posse capi repellebat." *RIS*[2], VI:2, 91. However, the Roman cardinal, Boso, papal legate for the campaign, would have taken some of his clerics with him. It should be remarked that it is now thought the biographer of Paschal II was not a cleric but a "constable" at the head of the papal militia; see March, *op. cit.*, pp. 47–51. March's view has been accepted by C. Vogel, the editor of the supplementary volume in the re-edition of Duchesne, *op. cit.*, III, 16–18.

46. *RIS*[2], VI:2, 92, 95.

Pisan canons would have been concerned for the rank of their bishop, they would have had this further reason for recording the events of these years.

These first annalistic works from Pisa show the extremely localized interest of their authors. They were concerned only with events which had immediate importance for Pisa—except for the notice of the incident of Sutri in 1111 and certain obituary notices, mainly of the emperors through Conrad II (which were included in the *Fragmentum* from an earlier collection).[47] While the terse entries of the *Annales antiquissimi* and the *Fragmentum* indicate no attempt by the author at a conscious selection of material, the *Gesta* shows that its author chose his material and that he was trying to present a viewpoint and a program in his historical work. At the beginning of the work he announced his intention of recording the deeds God accomplished through the Pisan people; but he did not begin with the earliest campaigns of the Pisans against the Saracens, he began with the incidents of the First Crusade.

The notice of the chronicler concerning the First Crusade is a striking example of the effective use of half-truth that one often finds unhesitatingly employed in the proud days of the early communal historians. Almost two-thirds of the entry is devoted to matters that are not directly related to the Pisans—to celestial apparitions and a list of the leaders of the crusading army—but the first portion purports to give the role of the Pisan fleet of one hundred and twenty ships under the leadership of the archbishop, Daimbert:

> In the progress of the expedition they conquered and plundered Lucata and Cefalonia, extremely strong cities, since these had been accustomed to hinder the route to Jerusalem. Moreover, in the same journey, the Pisan army seized Maida, an exceptionally powerful city, and besieged Laudocia with Bohemund and Gibellum with him and Raymond, count of St. Gilles. Passing on from these places, they came to Jerusalem, which was taken and held by the Christians in the year one thousand and one hundred; staying there for some time and re-building the impoverished city, the Pisans returned to their own land.[48]

47. Specific notices about the Pisans before the eleventh century seem to have been drawn from a southern Italian source, as we shall note later.

48. "Profiscendo vero Lucatam et Cefaloniam urbes fortissimas expugnantes expoliaverunt, quoniam Ierosolimitanum iter impedire consuevarent. In eodem autem itinere Pisanus exercitus Maidam, urbem fortissimam, cepit et Laudociam cum Boamundo et Gibellum cum ipso et Raimundo Comite S. Egidii obsedit. Inde igitur digressi, venerunt Ierosolimam, que anno millesimo centesimo a Christianis capta fuit et retenta fuit; ibique Pisani morantes per aliquantum temporis, et inopem urbem rehedificantes ad propria regressi sunt." *RIS*[2], VI:2, 89.

Perhaps more has been left unsaid here than can be justified in honesty. The chronicler mentioned the capture of Leucas and Cephalonia, but did not mention that these were Christian cities under the Byzantine emperor. At the time of the crusade, the Pisans were still on good terms with the Normans of southern Italy, and the Pisan attack on the Greek islands of Leucas and Cephalonia—as well as on Zante and Corfu, which Anna Comnena added as victims of the Pisan raid[49]—would therefore have been in the interests of the Normans, who were hostile to the Byzantine power and eager to gain control of the islands in the Adriatic straits. But it may have been that the attacks were meant to provide harbors for wintering the Pisan fleet, or were merely occasions for plundering.[50] By 1119, moreover, Pisa was much more friendly toward the Byzantine emperor, so that mention of the Greeks would have been impolitic—as well as contrary to the crusading aspect of the expedition. Anna Comnena also mentioned a sea battle near Rhodes in which the Greek fleet defeated the Pisans, who then escaped in a storm, but there is good reason for doubting the full veracity of this account.[51] However, a Venetian account mentions a naval victory of Venetian over Pisan ships, the latter seeming to have been a secondary fleet that had followed the main expeditionary force, in the same waters off Rhodes.[52] The Pisan chronicler also mentioned a third city, Maida, which cannot be identified, but perhaps it was on Cyprus for Anna Comnena claimed that the Pisan fleet—after its defeat and escape—tried to attack Cyprus but was driven off by the Byzantine governor of that island.[53]

At last, in September of 1099, the Pisan fleet reached Laodicea, then held by the Byzantines, and began to help Bohemund in his siege of the city. When the other crusader leaders, especially Raymond of St.-Gilles, apprised Daimbert of the politics of the situation, the archbishop withdrew his fleet. The leaders of the crusade, together with the archbishop, and

49. *Recueil des historiens des croisades, Historiens grecs*, I:2, 78–79.

50. The account opens with the year 1099 p.s. It is impossible to be certain whether the Pisans set out in the late summer of 1098 and wintered in the Greek islands, or started in the early spring of 1099. Most historians now hold for the earlier date of departure; see S. Runciman, *A History of the Crusades* (Cambridge, 1953), I, 299.

51. *RHC, Historiens grecs*, I:2, 80–81. For one thing, Anna Comnena placed the battle some four years later than it should be.

52. In the *Translatio S. Nicolai ad Venetiam, RHC, Historiens occidentaux*, V, 258–59. The battle took place while the Venetians were wintering on Rhodes between October 28, 1099, and May 27, 1100. Thus the Pisan force could not have been the main fleet, which had already passed on to Syria in the late summer of 1099.

53. *RHC, Historiens grecs*, I:2, 82.

probably accompanied by the leaders of the Pisan fleet, then proceeded to Jerusalem. There is no other mention of a siege of Gibiloth at this time; the city was finally taken only four years later.

After hardships along the way, Daimbert and the Pisans reached Jerusalem shortly before Christmas, 1099—five months after Jerusalem had been conquered by the crusaders.[54] Yet the Pisan account, with its. extremely vague chronology, did not preclude the Pisans from having participated in the capture of the Holy City. Daimbert soon became patriarch of Jerusalem, and at an unspecified time—in 1100 or possibly 1101—the Pisan fleet returned with little profit or glory. Moreover, when Daimbert was divested of his office of patriarch in 1102, one of the charges leveled against him was the slaughter of Christians in the Greek islands.[55] There is a strong possibility that Pisan ships were later in active alliance with Genoese vessels in supporting the armies of Christian territorial rulers,[56] but the chronicler of the *Gesta* was doubtless interested only in the official expedition, "official" in that it had been led by the archbishop of Pisa—an especially important criterion for the clerical writer. And in order to make the exploits of that campaign worthy of being the first notice in the *Gesta triumphalia*, he had to do some careful historical writing.

The First Crusade was to be paralleled by the crusade against the Saracens in the Balearic Islands—this time a more purely Pisan-directed campaign, and in both accounts the reigning popes are mentioned at the beginning of the notices. The popes are not cited as having led or instigated the crusades, but it is noted that both campaigns were undertaken during their reigns,[57] and thus the directing roles of both popes are implied but not accentuated.[58] The account of Henry V's holding the pope at Sutri, which has been placed between the notices of the two Pisan expeditions, could have served as a foil to emphasize Pisa's loyalty toward the papacy. While the notice of the First Crusade is rather short, the account

54. Runciman, *op. cit.*, I, 300 ff.

55. Albert of Aachen, *RHC, Historiens occidentaux*, IV, 599–600.

56. The question is not of significance here. But Albert of Aachen consistently mentioned Pisans and Genoese together in the campaigning of the first decade of the century. As will be pointed out later, in this period the two cities had not yet developed the great hatred which would later make them such bitter competitors, and there was no reason why they would not cooperate in such Syrian campaigns, which were private ventures and not officially directed by the communal governments.

57. "Ecclesie Romane presidente D. Papa Urbano II" and "presidente in urbe Roma beate memorie PP. Pascale II," *RIS²*, VI:2, 89, 94.

58. I pass over the article of B. Nelli, "I papi e le imprese di Pisa contro i Saraceni nei secoli XI e XII," *Bollettino storico pisano*, VI (1937), 284–321, because of its completely uncritical approach.

of the Balearic expedition is lengthy; and the author frequently mentioned instances of divine intervention in the latter campaign but not in the earlier crusade.

Aside from several perfunctory mentions of divine intervention, divine power appeared as the decisive force at several crucial points. "Divine fire" had sparked the minds of the Pisans and the peoples of other Tuscan cities to undertake the campaign against Majorca.[59] Negotiations between the Spanish count of Barcelona and the Saracen king for less than complete surrender had been nullified "by the inspiration of the Lord and by the probity and prudence of the archbishop of the Pisans, the Roman legate, and the canons of the Pisan church."[60] Majorca fell on February 22, 1115:

> The divine power, foreseeing the fervor of the Pisans and wishing to have pity on the wretchedness of the captives, conceded that the magnificent city be seized by the hands of the Pisan citizens.[61]

There can be no doubt that the *Gesta triumphalia* was to be regarded as the "Gesta Dei per Pisanos." The Pisans thus become the instruments of the power of God, so that the subsequent elevation of the Pisan bishopric to metropolitan status over Corsica was a logical consequence of the divine role played by the Pisans, even as papal statements of this period made explicit. The new and exalted position of Pisa was therefore not the result of Pisan ambition and pride but the consequence of the realization that the Pisans, through their exploits, had shown themselves to be the chosen instruments of God. The careful collection of historical notices of the earlier history of Pisa, especially of her campaigns against the Saracens, was further substantiation of the special position of the Pisan people as Christian warriors against the forces of Islam.

The work of Pisan chroniclers seems to have aroused the interest of a member of the cathedral clergy in the neighboring church of Lucca. Sometime between 1112 and 1118 a scribe at Lucca added a necrology to an older, eleventh-century manuscript of the Ado martyrology.[62] Later,

59. "divinus ignis Pisanorum civium animos et aliarum Tuscie urbium populos contra Majoricam accendit." *RIS*[2], VI:2, 90.

60. "de Domini inspiratione et Pisanorum Archiep., et Romani Legati Ecclesieque Pis. canonicorum probitate atque prudentia." *Ibid.*, p. 92.

61. "divina potentia providens fervorem Pisanorum, et volens misereri miserie captivorum, urbem magnificam . . . per manus Pisanorum civium capi concessit." *Ibid.*, pp. 92–93.

62. The manuscript is in the cathedral chapter library of Lucca, Biblioteca Feliniana, pluteo viii, cod. 618. The martyrology extends from fol. 5 to 139, the necrology from fol.

this manuscript must have seemed an appropriate place for preserving some historical notices, for on sheets added at the beginning of the codex a scribe copied out most of the Pisan *Fragmentum auctoris incerti* up to the entry for 1100 P.S.[63] Then two notices of Luccan victories over Pisan forces, in 1104 and 1105, were carefully recorded.[64] This is an extremely rare instance of the influence of one city's historical writing upon another in this early period.

INSCRIPTIONS

Unusual witnesses to a sudden awakening of interest in history at Pisa are the historical inscriptions, most of which were fashioned in the decade after the Balearic campaign.[65] Their inspiration could have come from antique monuments and from commemorative inscriptions of other Italian churches, but the great number of inscriptions at Pisa, their unusual historical interest, and their classical style testify to a unique intensity of an appreciation of the past and of an immortalization of the present during these years in Pisa.

Most of these inscriptions are found on the western facade of the cathedral, a location which clearly suggests authorship under the auspices of the cathedral clergy, and the dating of the monumental framing of these inscriptions is therefore of some importance. The building of the cathedral was begun in the Pisan year 1063, but the dates for its stages of construction and its completion are extremely uncertain. In 1118 the church received a papal consecration, which would indicate that the basic structure—executed by the architect-builder Busketus—had been completed, but excavations have shown that the nave was later extended to

---

139v to 151. That the manuscript originally belonged to the chapter can be seen both by the entries of donations in the necrology and by papal letters copied at the end of the codex: fols. 151v–152 and the letters of Alexander III from 1175–76 for the canons of Lucca. The necrology can be dated between 1112 and 1118 because the notice of the death of Bishop Rangerius (1098–1112) is in the same hand as most of the other notices, while the entry for Bishop Rudulf (1112 to December, 1118), which also records the election of his successor, was written in a different hand.

63. *Ibid.*, fol. 2v.

64. *Ibid.*, fol. 4, edited as an addition to the *Fragmentum* in *RIS*², VI:2, 102.

65. The excellent article of G. Scalia, "Epigraphica pisana: Testi latini sulla spedizione contro le Baleari del 1113–15 e su altre imprese anti-saracene del secolo XI," *Miscellanea di studi ispanici*, VI (1963), 234–86, presents most of these inscriptions in a most thorough manner.

the west for the distance of three interior bays. Sanpaolesi has concluded, on the basis of artistic styles, that the present monumental western facade was built after 1120; that the first story of this facade, which encompasses the inscriptions, was completed by the builder Rainaldus before 1145; that the upper, more elaborate stories were finished by about 1170; and that work on the facade was brought to an end around 1180, with the installation of the bronze doors of Bonanno.[66] Thus most of these Pisan inscriptions had probably received their final settings in the facade by 1150; and it is likely, but not absolutely certain, that some of them had been displayed on the original facade before 1120.

The exterior decoration of the cathedral shows that in this period there was an interest in ancient inscriptions. In facing the structure with marble the builders inserted many fragments of ancient inscriptions with no attempt either to set them off artistically or to obliterate them.[67] The mention of Ostia and Sardinia in these inscriptions gives an idea of the source of some of this fine marble taken from ancient structures.[68] The most extensive and important of the ancient Pisan inscriptions—which commemorates Lucius Caesar, the patron of Colonia Julia Pisana and grandson of Augustus—was eventually included in the facade of the cathedral.[69] While repairs on the western portals were being made in 1604, after a fire, this inscription was found, cut in half vertically and with the lettering turned to the wall, forming portions of the architraves of two of the doorways. If the bronze doors of Bonanno were finished about 1180, the marble doorways would have been fashioned in the immediately preceding years, precisely during one of the rare periods when Pisan politics had turned from a pro-imperial policy to one of opposition to the imperial legate, Christian of Mainz.[70] Under such circumstances, this important imperial inscription may have been given its new, reversed position. There

66. P. Sanpaolesi, "La facciata della cattedrale di Pisa," *Rivista dell' istituto nazionale d'archeologia e storia dell'arte*, new series, V–VI (1956–57), 300 ff, 322–23, 261. There are several studies of the critical dating of this cathedral and especially of the facade. An early and important article, which placed the construction of the final facade within the thirteenth century, is R. Papini's "La costruzione del duomo di Pisa," *L'arte. Rivista di storia dell'arte medioevale e moderna e d'arte decorativa*, XV (1912), 345–65.

67. *Corpus Inscriptionum Latinarum*, XI:1, Nos. 1414, 1415a, 1416, 1420, 1422–25, 1429, 1437, 1443, 1447a, 1448, 1506, 1509, 1510. There may have been some significance in the inversion of No. 1423, which reads IMP CAESARI. These inscriptions have been treated in detail by C. Lupi, *Le antiche iscrizioni del duomo di Pisa* (Pisa, 1877).

68. For Ostia, see *CIL*, XI:1, Nos. 1415a and 1447a. No. 1414 may have come from Sardinia, according to N. Toscanelli, *Pisa nell'antichità* . . . (Pisa, 1933), II, 338.

69. *CIL*, XI:1, No. 1420.

70. Heywood, *op. cit.*, pp. 197 ff.

is a possibility that such a long inscription, and others on the walls of the church, had helped inspire the canons of the twelfth century.

Rangerius, bishop of Lucca, writing a biography of Anselm of Lucca at the end of the eleventh century, also showed an interest in ancient monuments.

> The ancient Romans could not suffer their magnificent deeds to be hidden by time. And at first they set forth their lifelike forms in bronze and marble as an incitement to praise. Soon, when even the most extensive marketplaces would not contain the *tituli*, the letter more fittingly and in briefer compass took on the task.[71]

Other churches at this time—at Lucca, Rome, and elsewhere—also set up occasional inscriptions as epitaphs or to commemorate the construction or restoration of churches or altars, so that only in their number and their historical content are these Pisan inscriptions unique.

There are eleven Pisan inscriptions to be considered, and they fall into two groups, distinguished by meter: eight are in elegiac distich and three in dactylic hexameter. This divergence in meter divides the earlier inscriptions in distich form from the later in hexameter. The elegiac distich, especially favored by Ovid, was a common verse form in the eleventh century, and most Roman verse inscriptions of that century were composed in this meter. Rangerius of Lucca used it for his life of Anselm, and a Pisan writer, copying a geographical and historical collection (which we will discuss later), composed a poem in this meter in his introduction during the winter of 1118–1119. But in the 1120's, when the Pisan epic, the *Liber Maiorichinus*, was being written, the more grandiose dactylic hexameter was employed. It is possible that through the influence of this latter work the new verse form replaced the former in inscriptions.

Unfortunately, a consideration of the epigraphical style of the inscriptions gives little aid in dating them. The lettering ranges from severely squared block lettering, perhaps influenced by the Roman style, to curved uncials, often in a single inscription, so that there is no real uniformity. Further, probably not enough inscriptions were made in this period to

---

71.   Romani veteres ingentia facta suorum
        Tempore celari non potuere pati.
    Ac primo vivas ex aere et marmore formas
        Ad stimulum laudis proposuere suis.
    Mox ubi iam titulos fora maxima non capiebant,
        Apcius et brevius littera cepit opus.

MGH, Scriptores, XXX:2, 1155, ll. 9–14 of the prologue.

establish a definite development of epigraphical style, and the style of lettering in some cases seems to have been determined by that of an earlier inscription, next to which the new one was to be placed. Consequently, style is not trustworthy for establishing a relative dating for many of these inscriptions.[72] The eleven inscriptions span three quarters of a century, from about 1075 to 1150, but at least seven of them can be placed in the second and third decades of the twelfth century by other than epigraphical evidence.

The earliest inscription is a four-line commemoration of the construction of the cathedral at the time of Guido of Pavia, bishop of Pisa from 1061 to 1076,[73] and it may have been composed during the lifetime of Guido.[74] The reference in the last line to king and pope would seem to indicate a time before the open hostility of Henry IV and Gregory VII; but the inscription is small, mediocre in execution, and similar to others of its genre.

The next inscription is without parallel among other Italian inscriptions of this period. In twenty-six lines it gives a chronicle of some early events in the history of Pisa.[75] After an introduction of ten lines, it recounts

72. The inscriptions of the facade of the cathedral have been dated to the first half of the twelfth century by A. Vanni, "Di alcune iscrizioni della primaziale Pisana," *Studi storici*, IV (1895), 228; and Papini, *op. cit.*, pp. 345 ff., has also placed them in the twelfth century. Scalia's article (cited above) carefully treats the epigraphy of most of these inscriptions.

73.   Quam bene quam pulchre procul haud est edes ab urbe,
         Que constructa fuit civibus ecce suis,
         Tempore Widonis Papiensis presulis huius,
         Qui regi fama est notus et ipsi pape.

Scalia, *op. cit.*, p. 236. Also see R. Maiocchi, *Guido da Pavia* (Pisa, 1909).

74. Scalia, *op. cit.*, p. 236 n. 6, takes the "presulis huius" and "est notus" as indications that the bishop was still alive.

75.   Ex merito laudare tuo te, Pisa, laborans
         Nititur e propria demere laude tua.
         Ad laudes, urbs clara, tuas laus sufficit illa,
         Quod te pro merito dicere nemo valet.
         Non rerum dubius successus neque secundus
         Se tibi pre cunctis fecit habere locis:
         Quare tanta micas quod te qui dicere temptat,
         Materia pressus, deficiet subito.
         Ut taceam reliqua, quis dignum diceret illa
         Tempore preterito que tibi contigerint?

         Anno Dominice Incarnationis MVI.

         Milia sex decies Siculum, prostrata potenter,
         Dum superare volunt, exsuperata cadunt.

—four lines to each—the plundering of Pisan territory, the victory of the Pisans over Sicilian Moslems at Rhegium in 1006 P.S., the defeat of Spanish Saracens by a Pisan fleet near Sardinia in 1016 P.S., and the Pisan sacking of African Bona in 1034.[76] The composition of this inscription can be placed with some accuracy between the *Annales antiquissimi*, written shortly after 1116, and the *Fragmentum* of mid-1119.

The four events recorded in the inscription are the first four of the *Annales*.[77] Despite its florid (and partly ambiguous) poetic version, the inscription adds no details to the terse annals but rather omits facts, so that it was most likely based on the *Annales*. But it was written before the *Fragmentum* because the former—just as the *Annales*—mentions a single expedition to Sardinia in 1016 P.S., while the latter adds a second campaign in the following year. If it had been written as early as a generation

---

Namque tuum Sicula cupiens gens perdere nomen
Te petiit fines depopulata tuos.
Unde, dolens nimium, modicum disferre nequisti,
In proprios fines quin sequereris eos.
Hos ibi conspiciens cunctos Messana perire,
Cum gemitu quamvis, hec tua facta refert.

Anno Dominice Incarnationis MXVI.

His maiora tibi post hec, urbs clara, dedisti,
Viribus eximiis cum superata tuis
Gens Saracenorum periit sine laude suorum.
Hinc tibi Sardinia debita semper erit.

Anni Domini MXXXIIII.

Tertia pars mundi sensit tua signa triunphi,
Africa, de celis presule rege tibi.
Nam, iusta ratione petens ulciscier, inde
Est, vi capta tua, urbs superata Bona.

Scalia, *op. cit.*, pp. 252–53, and Table I.

76. The campaign against Bona was always given the date 1035 P.S. by Pisan chroniclers, but the inscription gives the year 1034. Vanni, *op. cit.*, pp. 244 ff., therefore maintained that the dates of the inscription had been given in the common reckoning, not the Pisan, so that visitors to Pisa would appreciate the dating. Scalia, *op. cit.*, p. 245, has noted that this last date of the inscription was not designated as a dating from the Incarnation and may therefore be on the basis of the Nativity, which would place the year in the general form of reckoning. Scalia remarked that the inscriber did not have space for the full dating formula. But why could not the inscriber or his informant have simply made an error?

77. "Anno mill. quinto civitas pisana capta fuit a saracenis. Mill. VI. pisani vicerunt saracenos ad regium. Mill. XVI. pisani vicerunt mugertum regem in sardiniam. ·Mill. XXXV. pisani vicerunt bonam urbem africe." Novati, *op. cit.*, p. 13.

before the *Annales*,[78] we would expect that more details for each campaign, or possibly even more campaigns, could have been remembered from the earlier period.

The inscription praises Pisa, noting that the city's honor had been lost and then regained by a successful revenge. The first ten lines form an introduction of praise for Pisa's position, gained by a "not uncertain but favorable course of events." Pisa moves from the defensive, having been attacked by the enemy, to the offensive in two naval battles in Italian waters and to ultimate and justified revenge in sacking an African city. These four events represent the full story of Pisa's vengeance and her initial rise to maritime power; mention of later campaigns would have been superfluous. Therefore, this inscription was not intended as the first of a series of chronicle inscriptions but as a separate account.

It is true that these four events are the only ones known from the *Annales* before the beginning of the construction of the Pisan cathedral, but there is no mention of the Pisan church in the inscription, so that these events were not regarded as a series of successes leading up to the new building venture. The inscription was definitely intended for the cathedral, since it was inscribed so that the commemorative inscription of Bishop Guido could be fitted into the upper right-hand corner, but the chronicle inscription is larger and much more elegantly executed than Guido's earlier dedication.

The remarkable feature of this poem is that its dominating motive of revenge and praise carries absolutely no religious tone. The Saracens are named, but the Pisan war against them is not characterized as a religious venture, nor justified on the basis of religion; it is merely a matter of a just revenge for the initial attack on Pisa. Except for its obvious connection with Guido's inscription and its location on the facade of the cathedral, the inscription shows no sign of an ecclesiastical origin.

Another inscription, probably erected about the same time as the chronicle inscription, shows a similar lack of religious ideas. This is a triumphal celebration of the Balearic campaign, intended for the *Porta Aurea* at Pisa:

> For outstanding citizens this is called the Golden Gate, on which the honor of nobility thus declares: You may regard this city as the general splendor of empire, a city which is wont to strike the fierce

78. Scalia, *op. cit.*, p. 261, has dated the inscription to 1087–90, or probably a few years earlier; or even during the period of Bishop Guido. He has assumed that the phrase "Ut taceam reliqua" refers to another major victory, such as that against Palermo in 1064, but probably not to the campaign against al Mahdiyah in 1087.

necks of wicked men. Extremely shameful was the madness of Balea of Majorca, and conquered Ibiza has experienced what this city could effect. One thousand one hundred and fifteen years from the time when the Virgin Mary conceived God, the Pisan people as a victor laid low both cities. And the unrivalled slaughter gives faith to these words. "Delight in justice, you who judge the land." [79]

The date in this inscription indicates that the poem was composed shortly after the Balearic campaign, since 1115 p.s. was the year of the victory.[80] Aside from the form of dating, there is no indication that this commemorates a war of Christians against Moslems. The enemy was the "madness of Balea," and the justification was not revenge but the "general splendor of empire" of a city accustomed "to strike the fierce necks of -wicked men." The justification is more subtle—and more in the Roman tradition—than revenge, but it is just as secular. This inscription was probably composed by a cleric, since it is unlikely that a layman could have fashioned such a Latin poem in those years, but it should be noted that the inscription is much smaller and more poorly executed than the chronicle inscription—the inscriber had even omitted an entire line, which was inserted later.

These two inscriptions show that in the years immediately succeeding the Balearic campaign, expeditions against the Moslems in the western Mediterranean were not yet regarded as crusades but rather as evidence of Pisa's strength. The change in this attitude appears with the *Fragmentum-Gesta triumphalia*. Starting the *Gesta* with the First Crusade, its author for the first time recasted into crusades not only the Balearic campaign but

79.   Civibus egregiis hec aurea porta voca[tur].
             In qua sic [dic]tat nobilitatis honor:
             Hanc urbem decus imperii generale putetis,
                 Que fera pravorum colla ferire solet.
             Maioris Balee rabies erat improba multum:
                 Illa quid hec posset, victaque sensit Ebus.
             Annis mille decem centum cum quinque peractis
                 Ex quo concepit virgo Maria Deum,
             Pisanus populus victor prostravit utramque.
                 Hisque facit strages ingeminata fidem.
             Diligite iustitiam qui iudicatis terram. (Wisdom 1:1)
Scalia, *op. cit.*, p. 272, and Table IV. The inscription is now in the facade of the church of La Madonna dei Galletti.
80. Scalia, *op. cit.*, p. 258, has maintained that the phrase "annis ... peractis" refers to the succeeding year, 1116 p.s. It is true that the final citadel was taken April 3, 1116 p.s., but the major victories were won in 1115 p.s.: the great land battle before Balea in August (after Ibiza had been captured) and the capture of the city of Balea in March.

the earlier expeditions as well. In the *Fragmentum*, campaigns against the Saracens are won "gratia Dei," a phrase that is not found in the earlier *Annales antiquissimi*. This new attitude will appear in later inscriptions and in the epics that will be written in succeeding years.

A further indication of Pisa's tremendous pride of accomplishment in the years after the Balearic campaign is the appearance of a *porta aurea*. The naming of this gate shows that the Pisans felt that their city could begin to rank itself with the older capitals of the Mediterranean, Rome and Constantinople; however, because this inscription has been moved from its original position, it is difficult to determine for which city gate it was intended. It may have been the gate near the church on which the inscription is now located, the gate that stood on the south side of the city where a bridge led to Kinzica, the suburb across the Arno.[81] The interesting problem is to try to determine the reason for the Pisans' having given this particular name to one of their gates. Since it is unlikely that in this period such a gate would have been extensively decorated in real gold, or would have received such a name simply from its southern location, the name would probably have been adopted in imitation of such a gate in another city.

Other Italian cities of that time had a gate called the Golden Gate.[82] At Benevento, the former arch of Trajan was used as a gate in the northern walls of the city and was called the Golden Gate. At Capua, an eastern gate bore this name; and Pavia and Ravenna also had their golden gates. But it is not very likely that Pisa, with the ambitions it nourished in these years, would look to such cities. Jerusalem had a *porta aurea* in the twelfth century, a gate in the eastern wall of the city that led directly into the precincts of the Temple.[83] Pisa had a gate that led directly from the west to its cathedral, but there is no indication in its inscription that this gate had a similar religious importance. Rome also had a golden gate in the twelfth century, the most western of her gates, formerly called the *Porta Aurelia*,[84] and here we have a closer parallel to the *Porta Aurea* of Pisa. Both were situated on the ancient *Via Aurelia*, the land route between

81. See J. Ross and N. Erichsen, *The Story of Pisa* (London, 1909), pp. 119–20.

82. G. Gerola, "Porta aurea–porta aureola," *Atti del reale istituto Veneto di scienze, lettere ed arti*, LXXXIX (1929–30), 391–419.

83. *Ibid.*, pp. 401–2. See Saewulf's account of 1102–3 in *Palestine Pilgrims' Text Society*, IV:2, 41.

84. For all that is known about this gate, see Ian A. Richmond, *The City Wall of Imperial Rome* (Oxford, 1930), pp. 221–22. The twelfth-century *Mirabilia* of the city of Rome gives the gate its name of *Porta Aurea* for the first time; R. Valentini and G. Zucchelli, *Codice topografico della città di Roma*, III, Fonti . . . Italia, XC, 18.

Rome and Pisa along the coast, and in the twelfth century both gates would also have been the main entries to the two cities from their ports— Pisa having a harbor of its own on the coast and Rome using Civitavecchia as its port. There is no indication that the *Porta Aurea* at Rome was regarded as a triumphal entrance to the city. However, Constantinople had a triumphal portal that was called the Golden Gate.[85] Since the fourth century, the emperors of Constantinople had entered the city after victorious campaigns by a special gate in the southwest corner of the city walls. By 1115, the Pisans had recently established themselves in the capital of the Byzantine Empire[86] and it is quite possible that they became acquainted with the significance of this Byzantine gate. It would therefore seem likely that either the Roman or Byzantine gates—or both—served as examples for the Pisans' celebration of their Balearic triumph.

The next five inscriptions to be considered are epitaphs, and the first is the epitaph of a princess of Majorca.[87] Although the *Gesta* recounts not her death but her conversion to Christianity,[88] it is surprising that the epitaph does not mention her conversion but ends with the plea that the passerby pray to God for her soul—an indication that she had died a Christian. There are no indications that it was originally intended to accompany the inscriptions on the cathedral's facade, but it is now located outside and beneath the frame of the chronicle inscription. This short epitaph gives no material for a dating of its composition except that it must have been after the Balearic expedition, during which the princess was captured by the Pisans.

---

85. See A. van Millingen, *Byzantine Constantinople: The Walls of the City and Adjoining Historical Sites* (London, 1899), pp. 59–73. The inscription can be restored: HAEC LOCA THEVDOSIVS DECORAT POST FATA TYRANNI. AUREA SAECLA GERIT QVI PORTAM CONSTRVIT AVRO. *Ibid.*, p. 60.

86. Pisa had gained a special quarter in Constantinople by 1112; Heywood, *op. cit.*, p. 54.

87.   Regia me prol[es] [g]enuit, Pise rapuer[unt]:
           His ego cum nato bellica pr[eda] fui.
           Maiorice regnum tenui. Nunc condita s[ax]o
           Quod cernis iaceo, fine potita meo.
           Quisquis es, ergo, tue memor esto conditionis
           Atque pia pro me mente precare Deum.

Scalia, *op. cit.*, pp. 273–74, and Table V.

88. The capture of the princess and her coming to Pisa are recounted in the *Gesta*, *RIS*², VI:2, 93. Scalia, *op. cit.*, pp. 281–82, raises the possibility that she was the queen of Mugehid, captured in 1016. But why would a new epitaph have been prepared for the latter more than a hundred years after her capture?

Another epitaph, that of a certain Ugo, was probably originally in the cathedral but later was placed in the Campo Santo.[89] Ugo's epitaph refers specifically to the Balearic campaign:

Toward the setting sun there was by chance an impious race which the sacred powers command be uprooted from the earth. The people of Pisa, sent for such vengeance, had this youth among its leaders.

There were several persons named Ugo in the Balearic campaign, according to the *Liber Maiorichinus,* so it is impossible to be more specific in identification. Ugo, from the family of the Visconti of Pisa, was mentioned as a leader of the campaign, but no reference is made in the *Liber Maiorichinus* to his youth, and it would seem that Ugo Visconte had been a more mature man. Further, the family name of Visconti would probably not have been omitted from an epitaph of one of its members.[90] Though the young man apparently did not die in battle but after his return, pride in his activity and the fact that there is no mention of other campaigns would place the epitaph in the years immediately following the Balearic victory. The importance of the epitaph is the religious justification that

89.   Ugo, [maiorum] Pisarum nobilis unus,
        Quem [nunc defunctum] subdita tumba tegit,
    Coniugi[o fidus feli]x cum coniuge vixit:
        Illa per[equatas] reddidit inde vices.
    Forte s[ub occidu]o fuerat gens impia sole,
        Quam [mundo evell]i numina sacra iubent.
    Pisarum [populus vindic]tam missus ad istam
        Inter [ductores hunc hab]uit iuvenem.
    Iste fu[it iuvenis, quo] nullus gratior a[lter]
        Sensu [doctrina c]onsiliove fuit.
    Temporibu[s iuv]enis, sed erat probitate s[enili],
        Frena iuventu[ti] de probitate ferens.
    Pectoris audacis sibi laudes arma[que querens],
        Miserat Hispanos mortis in ora te[nus]:
    Deiecit Mauros gladioque furente per[emit],
        Captorumque ducum colla superba tra[hit].
    Tempore, quo Gemini tolerant inc[endia solis],
        Et mensis media parte remissus [abit],
    Tunc predictus Ugo sub [tempore desiit esse];
        Perpetuo vivens nulla pericla [timet].

The poem has been reconstructed by F. Patetta in "Il preteso epitaffio di Ugo Visconte morto nella spedizione dell'anno 1087 contro i pirati saraceni di Mehdia," *Atti della reale accademia delle scienze di Torino,* XLVI (1910–11), 574.

90. Patetta, *ibid.,* pp. 575 ff., suggested that the dead man might have been a Visconte, but he left the final identification open.

was given the expedition. Along with the motive of revenge is the characterization of the Saracens as the *gens impia* and the command of the sacred powers. This epitaph is the first of the inscriptions that shows the new crusading concept, and it should be dated 1119 or shortly afterwards.

In the rebuilding of the cathedral's western facade, about 1120, special prominence was given to poetic inscriptions commemorating the ·architect-builder Busketus; they were placed directly above the chronicle inscription. Little is known about this early builder of the cathedral, but a Busketus who is mentioned in Pisan documents from 1101 to 1111 may well be the same person.[91] The four-line poem, which was inscribed on his sarcophagus, may thus be dated in the second decade of the twelfth century.[92] The poem shows that its author was less interested in the beauty of Busketus' work than in his engineering feat of managing enormous weights. When the sarcophagus was relocated on the new facade, it was felt that this small inscription could no longer be easily read, so it was repeated in larger lettering on a new stone above the sarcophagus.[93]

But a much more elegant epitaph for the builder was also set up above the previous inscription.[94] This sixteen-line poem shows a much

91. Papini, *op. cit.*, p. 350, n. 1.
92.   Quod vix mille boum possent juga juncta movere,
          Et quod vix potuit per mare ferre ratis,
          Busketi nisu quod erat mirabile visu,
          Dena puellarum turba levabat onus.
A. da Morrona, *Pisa illustrata nelle arti del disegno* (Pisa, 1787), I, 22.
93. There is a photograph of these inscriptions in Papini, *op. cit.*, p. 355. The new inscription was fashioned in a definitely later epigraphical style, perhaps about 1145, when this portion of the facade was being finished.
94.   Busketus iacet hic [qui motibus] ingeniorum
          Dulichio [fertur] prevaluisse duci
        Moenibus iliacis cautus dedit ille ruinam
          Huius ab arte viri moenia mira vides.
        Calliditate sua nocuit dux ingeniosus
          Utilis iste fuit calliditate sua.
        Nigra domus laberintus erat tua Dedale laus
          At sua Busketum splendida templa probant.
        Non habet exemplum niveo de marmore templum
          Quod fuit Busketi prorsus ab ingenio.
        Res sibi commissas templi cum lederet hostis
          Providus arte sui fortior hoste fuit
         Molis et immense pelagi quas traxit ab imo
          Fama columnarum tollit ad astra virum
         Explendis a fine decem de mense diebus
          Septembris gaudens deserit exilium.

Ibid., p. 345, n. 1.

deeper appreciation of Busketus, and not only as a builder but also as an architect. What decidedly set this inscription apart from those we have considered are its classical allusions. In no less than ten lines it develops extended contrasts between Busketus and two men of Greek antiquity. The destructive ingeniousness of Ulysses is contrasted with the useful skill of Busketus, and the dark, labyrinthine palace built by Daedalus with the gleaming temple of Busketus.[95] The Greek contrasts may have been inspired by the Pisan belief in their descent from Greek colonists, but they also definitely show that the poet had more than a casual acquaintance with ancient literature and a very real desire to compare the modern and the ancient, to the advantage of the modern.

Another epitaph of this period also illustrates a new or sudden interest in antiquity. This is the epitaph of a consul, Henricus, which is now located in the exterior marble facing of the western wall on the north transept of the cathedral.[96] The contrast with the antique, especially with Rome, is most striking. The poem begins:

> Her whom you, Pisa, follow in the fortune of battle, namely Rome,
> may you follow in the praise of your famous consul.

Then, in six lines, Henricus is compared with ancient worthies: Cato, Hector, Cicero, Fabricius, and Regulus. There was a Consul Henricus among the leaders of the Balearic campaign, but the poem does not mention that specific action. Rather, it would seem that the consul had been imprisoned by the enemy and had died in captivity. His captors are not

---

95. In the inscription Ulysses is called "Dulichius dux," a phrase used by Ovid, *Metamorphoses*, XIV, 226, and *Remedia amoris*, 272. The poet probably learned from Ovid, *Metamorphoses*, VIII, 157 ff., that Daedalus built the house of Minos, and from Virgil, *Aeneid*, V, 588 ff., that the house was called the labyrinth.

96.   Quam sequeris belli fortuna, laude sequaris
               Romam, Pisa, tui consulis egregii.
          "Claruit Henricus," dic, dic "virtutibus altis,
               Nomen cuius erit semper in ore meis."
          Hic tibi nempe Cato fuit, Ector, Tullius alter,
               Mente, manu, lingua, par tribus unus homo.
          Fabricius castis sprevit temporibus olim
               Munera: contempsit hic et in orbe levi.
          Regulus iste tibi, captus tua bella gerendo,
               Blanda, minas, mortem, spernere, ferre, pati
          Preposuit pro te; mutans, non vivere perdens.
          Clauditur hic, mundi climata corde tenens.

From F. Patetta, "Appunti sopra alcune iscrizioni medievali pisane," *Atti della reale accademia delle scienze di Torino*, LII (1916–17), 1034–35.

identified, and it is likely that the noteworthy lack of any reference to the Saracens means that he had been captured by the Genoese during the wars between the two cities in the 1120's—his earthly remains could have been recovered and placed with the epitaph. The later epitaph of Busketus and that of Henricus, because of their strong classical tone, can probably be ascribed to the same period in the 1120's, and thus are slightly later than the inscriptions already noted. The same classical tone and comparisons are also found in two Pisan epics that were written in this same decade of the twenties.

The last three inscriptions are characterized by the use of the dactylic hexameter; and they, too, are of a later date, probably composed in the 1130's and 1140's. They represent changing attitudes but they show a continuing interest in history and monumental inscriptions.

The longest of these, which mentions the beginning of the construction of the Pisan cathedral in 1063 P.S. and relates the campaign against Palermo in 1064, is embedded in the facade of the cathedral between the central and northern portals.[97] Its location, form, and lettering are very similar to that of the long chronicle inscription, and this later inscription

97. Anno quo Christus de virgine natus ab illo
     Transierant mille decies sex tresque subinde,
     Pisani cives, celebri virtute potentes,
     Istius ecclesie primordia dantur inisse.
     Anno quo Siculas est stolus factus ad oras,
     Quo simul armati, multa cum classe profecti,
     Omnes maiores medii pariterque minores
     Intendere viam primam sub sorte, Panormam.
     Intrantes rupta portum pugnando catena,
     Sex capiunt magnas naves opibusque repletas,
     Unam vendentes, reliquas prius igne cremantes,
     Quo pretio muros constat hos esse levatos;
     Post hinc digressi parum, terraque potiti,
     Qua fluvii cursum mare sentit solis ad ortum,
     Mox equitum turba peditum comitante caterva,
     Armis accingunt sese, classemque relinquunt.
     Invadunt hostes contra sine more furentes,
     Sed prior incursus, mutans discrimina casus,
     Istos victores, illos dedit esse fugaces:
     Quos cives isti ferientes vulnere tristi
     Plurima pre portis straverunt milia morti,
     Conversique cito tentoria litore figunt,
     Ignibus et ferro vastantes omnia circum.
     Victores, victis sic facta cede relictis,
     Incolumes multo Pisam rediere triumpho.

Scalia, *op. cit.*, pp. 263–64, and Plate II.

was apparently designed as a companion to the earlier. These similarities have led Scalia to date both inscriptions in the same period,[98] but there are strong arguments against such a conclusion. First, there is the difference in meter, a significant difference when we note that all eight poems we have already considered and dated roughly before 1130 were composed in the elegiac distich. Secondly, while there is no mention of Rome or antique heroes, the poem is filled with classical *loci*[99] and therefore shows the poetic style especially of the *Liber Maiorichinus*, also written in dactylic hexameter in the third and fourth decades of the century.

A confusion of the dating of events in the inscription also seems to indicate a later composition. The inscription combines the beginning of the cathedral with a campaign against Palermo under the date 1063 p.s. There is no other evidence for the year in which the building was begun, but the expedition against Palermo took place in 1064, according to non-Pisan sources, and both the *Annales antiquissimi* and the *Fragmentum* give the year 1065 p.s.[100] Maragone, who composed his chronicles of Pisa about 1150, copied the inscription and thus dated the campaign 1063 p.s.,[101] which date then passed into Pisa's later chronicle tradition. Maragone's entry indicates that the inscription had been erected before

98. *Ibid.*, p. 261.

99. *Ibid.*, p. 262, n. 29.

100. The date of the expedition of the Pisans to Palermo. M. Amari, *Storia dei musulmani di Sicilia* (Catania, 1933–39), III, 104–5, dated the expedition to 1063 in accord with this inscription. Amari also used the account of the Sicilian chronicler Gaufredus Malaterra (*RIS*², V:1, 45), which was written at the end of the eleventh century; but Malaterra, with his disdain for the Pisans, is not completely trustworthy. However, Amato of Monte Cassino, in his *Storia de' Normanni* (ed. V. de Bartolomaeis, Fonti . . . Italia, LXXVI, 255–56), stated that the Pisans came to Palermo while the duke of Sicily was besieging the city. (The manuscript gives Bari instead of Palermo, but see n. 2, p. 255; the chapter headings at the beginning of the book mention Palermo instead of Bari, p. 222.) Duke Robert besieged Palermo unsuccessfully in 1064 (Malaterra, *op. cit.*, pp. 46–47). Malaterra placed the Pisan expedition in the year before the duke's siege of Palermo. Because of Malaterra's prejudice against the "mercenary and gain-seeking" Pisans, there is no reason for not following Amato's account where Robert asks for and receives aid from the Pisans at Palermo. Therefore the date of the expedition should be 1064 (1065 p.s.). It should be noted that the Normans are not mentioned in the inscription. For the *Annales*, see Novati, *op. cit.*, p. 13, and for the *Fragmentum*, *RIS*², VI:2, 101.

101. *RIS*², VI:2, 5–6. Scalia, *op. cit.*, p. 255, along with Novati, tried to vindicate the dating by observing that the date is reckoned from the Nativity, and therefore 1063 (1064 p.s.), and further that "Transierant" as pluperfect would refer to the succeeding year 1064 (1065 p.s.). For further proof, Scalia referred to the date in the inscription of the *Porta Aurea*, but see n. 80 above. Scalia did not mention that the date of the Marseilles inscription would then also have to be reinterpreted in this way; see n. 102. But why did the poet of the Palermo inscription resort to such complexity?

1150—this portion of the facade had probably been finished by 1145. And the *Fragmentum*, with its correct dating of the campaign, may serve to locate it after 1119. The author of the inscription was intent on connecting the beginning of the cathedral with the Palermo campaign and was thus forced to change the date of the latter event.

The account of the campaign, while very terse in the chronicles, is detailed in the inscription, and some of its details are substantiated by non-Pisan sources. The poet had an excellent source, but the very accuracy of his account makes it all the more puzzling that he did not identify the enemy. Palermo was ruled by the Arabs in 1064, but they are not named in the poem. Further, there are no crusading features; in fact, no motives or justifications, not even revenge, are given for the expedition. By 1072, Palermo had been taken from the Moslems by the Normans of southern Italy. In 1133, Pisa began a war with Roger of Sicily that did not end until 1137. In 1135, a Pisan campaign sacked the Norman-controlled maritime city of Amalfi, and in 1137, when peace was concluded, the Pisans were aiding Lothair in laying siege to Salerno. During this war with the Normans, a poet recounting an earlier campaign against Palermo might have intentionally omitted identifying the earlier enemy as Saracens to have left open a more stimulating comparison between the Palermo campaign of 1064 and the contemporary expeditions against the Normans. Thus the omission of any identification of the enemy in the earlier campaign is best explained by placing the composition of the inscription about 1135.

The second inscription in hexameter is the epitaph of the Pisan dead who were buried in the church of St. Victor at Marseilles.[102] According to the inscription, the Pisans, during their return to Pisa, interred their

102.   Verbi incarnati de virgine mille peractis
               Annis, his centum bis septem connumeratis,
               Vincere Maioricas, Christi famulis inimicas,
               Temptant Pisani Maometi regna profani.
               Marte neci dantur multi: tamen hii sociantur
               Angelice turbe celique locantur in urbe.
               Terra destructa, classis redit equore ducta,
               Et vi divina redeunt victrice carina.
               O pia victorum bonitas! Defuncta suorum
               Corpora classe gerunt Pisamque reducere querunt.
               Sed simul adductus ne turbet gaudia luctus,
               Cesi pro Christo tumulo clauduntur in isto.

Scalia, *op. cit.*, p. 268, and Plate III. The epitaph had originally been set up in the porch of the church; it is now in the Musée Calvet at Avignon.

dead at this monastic church. In this period the monastic order of St. Victor was second in the western Mediterranean region only to Cluny itself. In 1107, the Pisan bishop, Peter, granted the monastery of St.-Andrea—in Kinzica, the suburb of Pisa across the Arno—to the monastic community at Marseilles.[103] Therefore, close ties already existed between Pisa and this church in southern France, and Pisans may well have been buried there, possibly those killed in the Balearic campaign.

This particular epitaph, however, could not have been set up at the time of the return of the Pisan armada to Italy because the inscription's date of 1114 is incorrect both in the Pisan calendar and in other contemporary reckonings. For the Pisans, the Balearic campaign extended from 1114 to 1116. Though the inscription of the *Porta Aurea* gives 1115 P.S. as the year of the actual victory, the return had not begun until after Easter, April 18, 1116 P.S. According to the more general reckoning the expedition would have occurred in 1113–1115; consequently the date of the inscription, 1114, is incorrect. The *Gesta triumphalia*, in narrating the Balearic campaign, gives the year 1114 P.S. at the beginning of the account and ends the chapter with the year 1116 P.S. But later chroniclers, such as Maragone, simply gave the date of the beginning of the campaign. The epitaph's error in dating can probably be attributed to a fairly late composition, long enough after the event that the author would not have realized that the campaign had occupied two full years. The ideas of the poem would also seem to indicate a later date than the triumphal inscription of the *Porta Aurea*. Almost every line emphasizes the Christian character of the expedition. Although it is unlike the inscription of the city gate in that it was designed for a church, this epitaph clearly shows the results of an elaboration of the Christian crusading aspects of the campaign.

The last inscription is a three-line poem commemorating the architect Rainaldus.[104] It was placed in the facade of the cathedral to note the rebuilding of at least the lower portion of the western facade before 1145. The inscription, as the last of those to be found on the facade of the cathedral, is the final sign of an enthusiasm for such public monuments in this period.

These eleven inscriptions attest not only to considerable interest in history, an interest which in this instance reached its climax around 1119,

---

103. Kehr, *op. cit.*, III, 353.
104.   Hoc opus eximium tam mirum tam pretiosum
                  Rainaldus prudens operator et ipse magister
                  Constituit mire sollerter et ingeniose.

Scalia, *op. cit.*, p. 250, n. 70.

they also reflect the development of ideas and taste in this period. The historical inscriptions before 1119 show no religious or crusading motivations, but after that year the crusade idea—first developed by the author of the *Gesta triumphalia*—influenced these short historical notes. On the other hand, a strong classicism appears in the inscriptions of the 1120's, a classicism we shall find again in the *Carmen in victoriam Pisanorum* and in the *Liber Maiorichinus*, also composed in that decade.

GUIDO'S COLLECTION

A collection of diverse material—geographical, political, historical, and legendary—drawn from earlier works is the next aspect of historical interest at Pisa to be considered for it gives an idea of the sources that were available in these fields to a scholar of the early twelfth century—in addition to the works which particularly caught his interest.[105] Guido's work, or collection, has no original passage except the prologue, which raises a number of complex questions.

> Here begins the prologue of Guido's book, composed from diverse histories for the several benefits accruing to the reader. "Since nature itself has instituted a certain society among all men, and since no society could continue to exist without a gathering together of property and labor, we ought to bestow not the least portion of our property, tasks, and studies on the society of mankind."

After a continuation of such generalities, with quotations from Lucan and Ambrose, the prologue continues:

> "Therefore, I, Guido, urged on by my knowledge and abilities, have determined to bestow a certain small portion, gained by long labor, of my endeavors and studies upon the society of mankind and the community of living, so that, agreeing with the conclusions of those who have written on service, I may incite by my example others to this task and exertion in the present, and in the future I might attain the prize toward which I labor and direct my attention." Here ends the prologue.

105. Bibliothèque royale de Belgique, MS 3095. C. P. Bock has given a rambling description and discussion of this manuscript in *Annuaire de la bibliothèque royale de Belgique*, XII (1851), 41–212. Scalia, *op. cit.*, pp. 283 ff., has located a fifteenth-century copy of another collection—probably made by Guido—in the Vatican Codex Latinus 11564; see J. Ruysschaert, *Codices vaticani latini, codices 11414–11709* (Vatican City, 1959), pp. 313–14.

A short table of contents follows, and then a poem:

Happy are they who can merit such great gifts that they may think their deeds live after death. This book teaches you in what relationship the land and sea are placed and the succession of kings. Here you can find kings placed in their order; it spreads out to view peoples, wonders, beasts, and histories. From these Guido has left behind these beautiful documents; for which he shall be perpetually commemorated. In the name of our Lord, Jesus Christ, God Eternal. In the one thousand one hundred nineteenth year from His Incarnation, in the twelfth indiction.[106]

This introduction is composed of a number of sections: Guido's prologue, a table of contents, a poem on the work, an invocation, and a date. The date at the end of this introduction seems to refer to the year in which the manuscript was written, not to the year in which Guido made his collection,[107] and there are indications that this manuscript is not the autograph of the compiler, Guido.[108] Furthermore, Guido's prologue, written in the first person, is at the beginning of the manuscript but is separated from the date by a poem, which refers to Guido in the third

---

106. "Incipit prologus libri Guidonis compositi de variis historiis pro diversis utilitatibus lectori proventuris. 'Cum inter omnes homines societatem quandam natura ipsa constituit, nec ulla sine rei vel operae collatione possit constare societas, in humani generis societatem rerum nostrarum, operum et studiorum non minimam partem conferre debemus. . . . Unde ego Guido, inductus pro scientia mea et viribus, statui in humani generis societatem et vitae communionem operum ac studiorum meorum quandam conferre particulam longo conquisitam labore, ut eorum qui de officiis scripsere studiis concordans, re ipsa et exercitio et in praesenti et caeteros meo incitem exemplo, et in futuro, ad quod laboro et intendo, consequar praemium.' Explicit prologus. . . .

>Felices tam magna queunt qui dona mereri
>Ut sua post obitum vivere facta putent.
>Terra fretumque simul qua consistunt ratione
>Et regum seriem vos liber iste docet.
>Hic reperire potes positos ex ordine reges,
>Gentes, monstra, feras, pandit et historias;
>Ex quibus haec Guido documenta decora reliquit
>Per quae perpetuo commemorandus erit.

In nomine Domini nostri Jesu Christi Dei eterni. Anno ab incarnatione ejus millesimo centesimo xviiii indictione xii."

Edited in *Bulletins de l'académie royale des sciences et belles-lettres de Bruxelles*, X:1 (1843), 469–71. I have compared it with the edition of J. Schnetz, *Itineraria Romana* (Leipzig, 1940), II, 113–14, and have made some revisions from the manuscript.

107. Bock, *op. cit.*, p. 49, regarded the date as the year of Guido's collection; he promised to give evidence later but did not do so.

108. *Ibid.*, pp. 44–48.

person, and which, consequently, has been added to Guido's original introduction. The date would therefore not refer to Guido's original work but to this particular copy. This date can give only a *terminus ante quem* for Guido's work, and it places the copying of Guido's work in the winter of 1118/1119, since the manuscript was written at Pisa.[109]

There are several indications that the manuscript came from Pisa. In one of the itineraries a *nota* has been placed next to the list of Tuscan cities, including Pisa, a cross has been located next to Jerusalem, and a further *nota* has been added in the margin beside seacoast cities of Palestine —cities in which a Pisan would have been interested after the First Crusade.[110] A list of Italian cities contains a notice about the foundation of Pisa, and it is repeated in a second list.[111] Further, two passages about Pisa have been inserted in the original text of the *Excidium Troiae*.[112] Finally, a Pisan historical poem, the *Carmen in victoriam Pisanorum*, is in this manuscript, although as an addition that was made after the manuscript had been completed.[113]

Guido, the compiler of the original work, was probably a deacon of the cathedral clergy of Pisa in the first decades of the twelfth century. In these years a monk named Guido was writing at Monte Cassino. Peter, a monk of the same monastery, wrote that he, Peter,

> composed a chronicle of the kings of the Trojan nation, and of the consuls, dictators, and emperors. He collected an itinerary from all

109. The Pisan date extends from March, 1118, to March, 1119; the indiction from September, 1118, to September, 1119.

110. Bibliothèque royale de Belgique, MS 3095, fols. 24*v*, 20, 18*v*.

111. "Pisa, quae civitas praedicta in Tuscia a Pelopide Tantali filio constructa et edificata est, apud eam exulans." *Ibid.*, fols. 5, 33*v*. The source for this statement was probably Servius' commentary on Virgil's *Aeneid*, X, 179. Perhaps the augmented version of Servius' commentaries had been misread: "sane Pisas antiquitus conditas a Peloponneso profectis, vel ab his qui cum Pelope in Elidem venerunt." Has someone read "exilium" instead of "elidem"? The medieval writer must have learned from another source that Pelops was the son of Tantalus. Solinus, 2.1, names Pisa "a Pelopidis." Guido had access to Solinus' work, and inserted a passage from Solinus (2.23) in fol. 3*v*.

112. *Ibid.*, fols. 136, 137. In the first passage a catalogue of Tuscan forces, drawn from the *Aeneid*, X:166–200, has been added, along with a notice of the foundation of Pisa by Pelops, in exactly the same sentence as in the itineraries. In the second passage Pisa is only named. Both changes have been edited by E. Atwood and V. Whitaker in the critical notes to *Excidium Troiae* (Cambridge, 1944), pp. 41, 44. The editors used the late thirteenth-century Codex Riccardianus 881, not an exact copy of Guido's manuscript but very similar.

113. See Mommsen, *MGH, Auctores antiquissimi*, XI, 497. I will later consider the relationship of the *Carmen* to the original manuscript.

the ancient books and dedicated it to Guybaldus the abbott of Monte Cassino . . . also a history of the Trojan nation from the beginning of the world down to his own times.[114]

The description fits, as we shall see, the major portion of the collection now being considered. Since it is known that Peter assumed authorship for some of Guido's work, it is possible that Peter's description refers to what had originally gone under the name of Guido of Monte Cassino.[115]

However, another Guido lived in Pisa in these same years. He appears in Pisan documents from November, 1115, to February, 1116,[116] and is probably the Guido of the Balearic campaign who was described as "deacon by rank, versed in the material of the *trivium*" by the *Liber Maiorichinus*.[117] The material of this collection would fall within the field of the medieval *trivium*. Also, because the scribe of this manuscript did not identify Guido, the compiler, with any epithet of city or monastery, and because this manuscript was copied at Pisa, we can surmise that the copyist and Guido were Pisans. Our rather circumstantial conclusions are therefore that Guido, a deacon of the Pisan church who had participated in the Balearic campaign, returned from the expedition with new horizons of interest, gathered historical-geographical material between 1115 and 1118, and that this collection was copied in a Pisan manuscript in the winter of 1118/1119.

The compilation has been assembled from diverse earlier works. There are indications that for at least a portion of his work Guido used a source from southern Italy, material that was probably composed there in the middle of the tenth century. Guido included a list of the princes of Benevento, which ends with the year 948—not the death-date of the last prince mentioned (Pandulfus, who died in 980) but the date when the list was written.[118] Also, the list of the Lombard, Frankish, and German

114. *RIS*[1], IV, 537. "Chronicam Regum gentis Trojanae, et Consulum, Dictatorum, et Imperatorum composuit. . . . Itinerarium ex omnibus veteribus libris collegit, et Guybaldo Casinensi Abbati dicavit . . . . Ystoriam gentis Trojanae a principio mundi usque ad sua tempora."

115. W. Smidt, "Guido von Monte Cassino und die Fortsetzung der Chronik Leos durch Petrus Diaconus," *Festschrift Albert Brackmann dargebracht* (Weimar, 1931), pp. 318–21. Smidt, p. 298, is of the opinion that Guido of Monte Cassino did not compose this collection. A list of the works of Guido of Monte Cassino is to be found in Peter the Deacon's *De viris illustribus casinensibus*, *RIS*[1], VI, 53.

116. G. Scalia, "*Oliverius e Rolandus* nel *Liber Maiorichinus*," *Studi mediolatini e volgari*, IV (1956), 299 n. 41.

117. Calisse, *op. cit.*, p. 26, l. 530.

118. Bibliothèque royale de Belgique, MS 3095, fol. 75; see *MGH, SS*, III, 213.

kings of Italy parallels other such lists until the entry of Otto I, in the middle of the tenth century, when the list in our manuscript begins to show considerable divergences from the others.[119] Finally, the itineraries Guido used show a reworking by a southern Italian. To the original itinerary of an unknown writer of Ravenna have been added short notices that deal with the foundation of certain cities, their political importance, and their patron saints.[120] The itinerary covers the territory of the Roman Empire at its greatest extent, yet, aside from a notice added to Pisa, only southern Italian cities and cities of the eastern Mediterranean have these additional notes.

Such considerations would seem to point to a Latin source in the Byzantine Empire and tradition, written in the middle of the tenth century when parts of southern Italy were still dominated by Constantinople. This southern Italian origin of one of Guido's sources also answers a problem that deals with the source for the earliest entries of the Pisan *Fragmentum auctoris incerti*. This chronicle has five notices, between 867 and 937, which do not directly concern Pisa but deal rather with Benevento, Bari, Apulia, and Capua.[121] The southern manuscript may have had a short chronicle which Guido did not consider worth copying but which was used by the Pisan chronicler in 1119.[122]

The second book of Guido's collection is also of interest. Here Guido made selections from the rich medieval encyclopedia, Isidore's *Etymologiae*. He selected terms dealing with civil and military ranks, public buildings, private homes, social classes, and the rings worn by Romans to signify their social rank.[123] Such a selection is significant in showing the lively interest an early twelfth-century Pisan had for the institutions and terms of the ancient Romans, an interest similar to that which gave rise to the usage of *consul* for the new urban magistrates in the Italian cities.

119. *Ibid.*, fol. 62*v*. These lists have been edited and compared by Waitz, *MGH, Scriptores rerum langobardicarum et italicarum*, pp. 504–19.

120. *Ibid.*, fols. 4–7, ed. Schnetz, *op. cit.*, II, 113–42.

121. *RIS*[2], VI:2, 99–100. All of these entries can also be found in the chronicle of Lupus Protospatarius (*MGH, SS*, V, 52 ff.), whose extended chronicle of southern Italy ends with 1102. It is to be noted that none of the dates of Lupus and the *Fragmentum* exactly correspond. The Pisan chronicler had to convert the dates to the Pisan style, and medieval scribes were notoriously careless with Roman numerals.

122. Scheffer-Boichorst, *op. cit.*, p. 510, suggested that the manuscript could have been brought to Pisa as booty or by a Pisan merchant in the tenth century. The *Fragmentum* (*RIS*[2], VI:2, 100) has the entry "DCCCCLXIX. Fuerunt Pisani in Calabria." But nothing is really known about these early activities of Pisans in southern Italy.

123. "De regnis militiaeque vocabulis," *Etymologiae*, IX:3; "de aedificiis publicis," XV:2; "de habitaculis," XV:3.1–8; "de civibus," IX:4; and "de anulis," XIX:32.2–6.

Bock has interpreted this part of the collection as an indication that Guido was attempting to justify imperial government and feudal institutions against the ecclesiastical hierarchy.[124] But Guido was interested in Roman government in general, not specifically in the emperors, and Isidore made no mention of feudal institutions. To be sure, Guido did not excerpt from Isidore passages that dealt with the ecclesiastical hierarchy, but as a cleric he was undoubtedly already acquainted with that material. He was interested in the Roman institutions of the city-state, an interest which requires no elaborate explanation for Pisa in this period.

Guido's collection shows the rather imperfect and impractical sources for history and geography in his age. The first and third books of the collection are devoted to geography. There are several itineraries and geographical works that deal primarily with the Mediterranean region and specifically with Italy and Rome, but there has been no attempt by the compiler to bring the earlier works up to date. Such a composition would scarcely have been of real use for merchants or even for travelers of the twelfth century. This section shows that Guido was not writing for a secular audience but for a literary group for whom almost anything evoking the ancient world was of interest—such as the small circle of clergy in Pisa interested in history and ancient Rome.

The fourth book is concerned with what we may call history. It includes the world history of Isidore's *Etymologiae* and it is supplemented by short extracts from Paul the Deacon's *Historia Langobardorum*, with its list of the kings of Italy through Henry IV, and by a second world chronicle, an abridged version of Isidore's adaptation of the Eusebian chronicle—to which has been appended a list of Beneventan dukes.[125] Both chronicles give only a very slight framework for world history since they consist mainly of lists of monarchs, with very few events noted. Between the two chronicles has been inserted the rather long Pisan historical poem, the *Carmen in victoriam Pisanorum*.

The fifth and final book of Guido's compilation is devoted to ancient history: the romance and letters of Alexander the Great; Dares Phrygius' story of the Trojan War; the *Excidium Troiae*, which brought the tale from the last days of Troy to Aeneas' descendant, Romulus; and Paul the Deacon's *Historia Romana*.

Guido's work thus shows us the material that was available in geography—and especially in history—in early twelfth-century Italy. A late

124. Bock, *op. cit.*, p. 98.
125. Isidore, *Etymologiae*, V:39. The others are edited in *MGH, Scriptores rerum langobardicarum*, pp. 506–16; *MGH, Auctores antiquissimi*, XI, 498–501; and *MGH, SS*, III, 211–13.

eleventh-century manuscript, used at Rome in the early twelfth century for recording recent events, shows in its very similar list of historical works that such an historical collection was typical of this period.[126] It should be noted that earlier history is not represented by the greatest works of Roman historians, Livy, Sallust, or Tacitus, but by drastically abridged and modified works from the earlier middle ages, and by romances whose legendary character could not as yet be separated from the more authentic material.

The manuscript of Guido's collection contains the *Carmen in victoriam Pisanorum*. It would appear that the poem was added to the manuscript slightly later: the general style of the handwriting, which is bold with large, thick letters, differs from the style of the rest of the manuscript— although the individual letters do not indicate a different paleographical period. The poem occupies the final six sides of a gathering of eight folios between the first and second chronicles of the fourth book, thus directly following the list of the kings of Italy. The original copyist of Guido's collection must have left these sheets blank. They would have formed an appropriate place for a chronicle of Pisa, and it is possible that the copyist intended to insert such a chronicle later. As he was copying his manuscript in the winter of 1118/1119, he may have known that a succinct chronicle, the *Annales antiquissimi*, had recently been written, and that a fellow Pisan was considering a more elaborate chronicle of the city, the *Gesta-Fragmentum*, to be written sometime between March and September, 1119.

THE "CARMEN IN VICTORIAM PISANORUM"

This poem, celebrating the expedition of the Pisans against the African cities of al Mahdiya and Zawila in 1087, deserves more attention than has usually been given to it.[127] The identity of the author cannot be

126. Vatican, Codex Latinus 1984, and described in detail by Bethmann, "Die ältesten Streitschriften über die Pabstwahl," *Archiv der Gesellschaft für ältere deutsche Geschichtskunde*, XI (1858), 841–49. Incidentally, this Roman manuscript has the important *Annales romani*, the first section of which was written shortly after 1121.

127. Editions: *Bulletins de l'académie . . . de Bruxelles*, XI:1 (1843), 524–45, an uncritical edition; Edélstand du Méril, *Poésies populaires latines du moyen age* (Paris, 1847), pp. 239–51, a more critical edition and the best-edited (I shall use this edition exclusively); L. T. Belgrano, *Atti della società ligure di storia patria*, IV (1866), CCXVI–CCXVII, a poor and erroneous copy of the first edition; Federico Patetta, "Studi storici e note sopra alcune iscrizioni medievali," *Memorie della regia accademia di scienze, lettere ed arti in Modena, sezzione di lettere*, series III, VIII (1909), 195–207, the editor attempted to edit Belgrano's

determined, but, given the general cultural factors of this period, we can assume that he was a member of the clergy. Some of the closing stanzas of the work also seem to identify him as a cleric of the cathedral. Though he had mentioned that the church of St. Sixtus was constructed from the profits of the campaign,[128] his real concern was for the gifts to the cathedral and its clergy:

> But upon you, Queen of Heaven, famous Star of the Sea, they bestow all costly and exceptional treasures; whence your church will be eternally resplendent, gleaming with gold, jewels, pearls, and cloths. To the clerics who remained behind they gave with common counsel two portions for perpetual service. Thus you desired, O Queen, thus you asked of your Son, whose aid you gained for them in all their toils.[129]

Scholars have been almost unanimous in stating that this long historical poem was written shortly after the event it celebrates; only Amari has made a rather vague reference to "the beginning years of the twelfth century."[130] It is certain that the writer either personally participated in the expedition or learned about it from a campaigner or a contemporary account. The accuracy of the geography and details of the campaign is too thorough to permit a very late date for the composition. The Pisan account can be checked with the short notices of the German chronicler,

---

text critically without reference to du Méril's text; and the most recent but not the best work, Fedor Schneider's *Fünfundzwanzig lateinische Rhythmen aus der Frühzeit* (Rome, 1925), pp. 39–42. The poem is to be found in two manuscripts: the early twelfth-century Brussels manuscript, already mentioned, and a manuscript at the university library of Breslau, No. IV, Fol. 33, fols. 105–8—a later copy of the Brussels manuscript and consequently of no real value in establishing the original text.

128. It is interesting to note that a church dedicated to St. Sixtus was also built at Genoa after the campaign; Caffaro, *op. cit.*, p. 13, n. 4, in a notice added in the margin of Caffaro's manuscript.

129.   "Sed tibi, Regina coeli, stella maris inclyta,
        donant cuncta pretiosa et cuncta eximia;
        unde tua in aeternum splendebit ecclesia,
        auro, gemmis, [et] margaritis et palliis splendida.
        Clericis qui remanserunt, perpetuo servitio,
        donaverunt partes du[as] communi consilio;
        sic volebas, tu Regina; sic rogasti filium
        cujus illis praebuisti in cunctis auxilium."

Du Méril, *op. cit.*, p. 251.
130. *Op. cit.*, III, 173; but he gave no reasons for his statement.

Bernoldus,[131] as well as with the entry in the Pisan *Fragmentum*.[132] But as a special corroboration of the account, Arabic sources—which were certainly not available to the Pisan poet—agree with his account even in details of minor importance. The Arabic chroniclers stated that both Pisans and Genoese participated in the campaign, that the attack took place after the eclipse of August 1, 1087 (the Pisan account mentions the day of St. Sixtus, August 6), and that the Arab king Tamim, after the city had been seized, retired to his castle and finally made peace by a cash settlement—all these events are found in the *Carmen*. A later Arabic writer even added the insignificant note that the Moslem garrison on the island of Pantelleria had sent messages by pigeons to the African king—another episode which was noted by the Pisan. It is further interesting that an Arabic poet wrote a long elegy, or *qasida*, on the fall of the cities, only portions of which have survived in a later chronicle.[133]

Although the Pisan author is found to have been the most accurate after his account is compared with other early accounts, certain passages seem puzzling if it is assumed that the poem was written immediately after the campaign of 1087. Relatively few individuals are named in the

131. Under the year 1088: "His temporibus Pisani et Genuenses et alii multi ex Italia Affricanum regem paganum hostiliter invaserunt, et depraedata eius terra, ipsum in quandam munitionem compulerunt, et eum deinceps apostolicae sedi tributarium effecerunt." *MGH, SS*, V, 447.

132. There are two other sources, but they are not trustworthy. The *Chronica monasterii casinensis* (*MGH, SS*, VII, 751), compiled in this portion by Peter the Deacon, makes the expedition into a crusade under the inspiration of Victor III. This account, and its tendency to exalt the pope, was first pointed out by A. Fliche, "La crise religieuse depuis la mort de Grégoire VII jusqu'à l'avènement d'Urbain II (1085–1088)," *Revue des cours et conferences*, XXIV (1922–23), 1410. Carl Erdmann, *Die Entstehung des Kreuzzugsgedankes* (Stuttgart, 1935), p. 285, n. 2, opposed Fliche's judgment and regarded the poem as "the clearest document of the popular crusade concept of that time" (p. 274). He tried to substantiate the account of the chronicle by reference (p. 284, n. 1) to Smidt's study; namely, that this section of the chronicle of Monte Cassino had been written by Guido and not by Peter, who was rather notoriously untrustworthy in other details. But Smidt (*op. cit.*, pp. 312–13) does not say who might have written this entry, although he thinks that the notice directly preceding it was written by Peter. However, the most plausible argument was given by Fliche, so this account cannot be used. The other source is Malaterra, *RIS*², V:1, 86–87, but this has already been attacked by Amari (*op. cit.*, III, 170). We have already found that Malaterra was not completely reliable in his accounts of the Pisans; the details of this entry of 1087 are also designed to exalt the Sicilian duke by contrast with the Pisans.

133. An Italian translation of the pertinent Arabic passages is to be found in M. Amari, *Biblioteca arabo-sicula, versione italiana* (Turin–Rome, 1880–81), pp. 112, 160–61. (This is the quarto edition, supplementary to *RIS*².)

poem, and these are carefully identified, such as *Pantaleo malfitanus, inter Graecos Sipantus.* However, the clerical leader of the expedition, Benedict, is given only the vague title of *presul.* The lack of any further identification is significant because, so far as the infrequent documents of this period of Pisan history permit conclusions, the see was vacant between May, 1085, and the accession of Daimbert sometime in 1088.[134] These years were troublesome for many Italian bishoprics, and there is always the possibility that a Benedict had been unsuccessful in maintaining himself as bishop of Pisa. However, it is unlikely that a leader of so successful a campaign would have left no trace of his activities in Pisa. It is therefore more likely that this Benedict was bishop of another Italian see, perhaps Modena.[135] Benedict of Modena was an active supporter of the exiled Anselm of Lucca, and his name is to be found in the necrology of the Luccan church;[136] he is also the only bishop in Italy in 1087 whom we know was called Benedict.[137] It is especially curious, then, that the poet did not identify the prelate.

However, it is likely that the author had intended to discover the identity of the leader.

> *Sed hoc sprevit Benedictus astutus*
> *Dei nutu illuminatus luce Sancti Spiritus.*

The *Carmen* was written in rhyming lines of fifteen syllables each, but the poet has not perfected his work: there are more than twenty lines which have one or two syllables lacking or have more than the prescribed number. Only in the first line (above) is there an error of more than two syllables—here the line lacks four syllables.[138] The answer could be that

134. Zucchelli, *op. cit.*, p. 44.

135. *A History of the Crusades*, ed. K. Setton (Philadelphia, 1955), I, 52. Krueger wrote that Benedict was bishop of Modena but did not give his source.

136. Part of the Luccan necrology has been edited by H. Bresslau, *Neues Archiv*, III (1877), 138. In Rangerius' *Vita*:

> A Mutina Benedictus adest, facundia cujus
> Utilis Aeclesiae per loca multa fuit.

MGH, SS, XXX:2, 1301.

137. According to P. B. Gams, *Series episcoporum ecclesiae catholicae . . .* (Regensburg, 1873).

138. Du Méril (*op. cit.*, p. 243) edited the lines thus:

> sed hoc sprevit Benedictus astutus, Dei nutu
> (et sacra) illuminatu(s) luce Sancti-Spiritus.

Then he noted that the rhyme was imperfect. However, the Breslau manuscript, fol. 106, makes it especially clear that "Dei nutu" should begin the new line and not end the previous one; the rhyme would be restored with "astutus" and "Spiritus."

the poet had left room for the insertion of a place-name to identify the see of Benedict but for some reason had not added that information before the poem was copied in the manuscript of Guido's collection. His apparent inability to identify the prelate would seem to indicate that he was not composing his poem immediately after the campaign.

Another puzzling statement was made with reference to the date of the landing and first attack of the Pisans:

> This was the ancient, noble feast of Saint Sixtus,
> which is ever a day of victory from heaven for the Pisans.[139]

The day of St. Sixtus was indeed famous in the annals of Pisa, and also infamous, for on that day in 1284 the city suffered its most disastrous defeat at the hands of the Genoese, in the battle of Meloria. However, if the poet was writing shortly after 1087 he could scarcely have regarded the date as famous, for the only other victory of that day that he could have known was the defeat of the Saracens by the Pisans at Reggio, in 1005.[140] On the other hand, the day of St. Sixtus recurred in the Pisan annals of the early twelfth century, for the great expedition to the Balearic Islands left Pisa on August 6, 1113, and on that same day, in 1119, the Pisans defeated the Genoese at Porto Venere. Certainly the day of St. Sixtus could have been considered more justly a day of Pisan victories after 1119 than directly after 1087. Thus the remark about the day of St. Sixtus would seem to indicate that the composition of the poem cannot be placed immediately after the campaign but instead at the end of the second decade of the twelfth century. A final factor, which by itself is in no way conclusive, is that the poem was first copied as an addition to a manuscript that is dated in the winter of 1118/1119.

These three considerations, taken together, would suggest that the poem was written sometime around 1120 rather than directly after 1087. In a much less specific manner, this later date would also appear more likely because of the increased interest in Pisan history that began after the Balearic campaign of 1113–1115 and grew toward 1120, as we have seen in the chronicles and inscriptions.

With this later dating, the *Carmen* also has significance in terms of the external problems of the commune of Pisa about 1120. Communal writers

139.   Hoc fuit antiquum festum sancti Sisti nobile,
        qui sunt semper Pisanorum de coelo victoriae;
Du Méril, *op. cit.*, p. 243.

140. In the *Fragmentum*, *RIS*², VI:2, 100. Calisse, *op. cit.*, p. 13, n. 1, also mentioned victories of 1003 and 1070, but the specific days of these battles have been taken from Roncioni, by no means a trustworthy source for such information.

always rather begrudged sharing honors with other communes for military successes, especially when the other commune was not by tradition a distant friend or a subject neighbor. It is therefore with some surprise that one notes in the *Carmen* that the Pisan poet appears to have been careful to give the Genoese a share in the honor. At the beginning of the campaign, "the Genoese assembled with wondrous power and join themselves to the Pisans with amiable love."[141] The poet closely paired the Genoese and Pisans on four other important occasions during the campaign.

This apparently emphasized cooperation of Genoese and Pisans is all the more surprising because the two communes had no strong tradition of friendship; there had been friction between these neighboring sea powers on several occasions before 1087—in 1016, 1065, and 1077,[142] and in 1113 the Genoese refused to join the Pisans in the Balearic campaign.[143] There was open hostility between the two communes from 1119 until 1130—but with a short truce from September, 1120, through 1121. Thus, while there had been friction in the eleventh century, serious conflict broke out in 1119, when Pisa tried to establish its domination over Corsica through ecclesiastical sanction.

A change of attitude between the two communes can be seen clearly in the *Gesta triumphalia*. When the first part of this chronicle was written, probably in the summer of 1119, the writer in the parallel annals of the *Fragmentum* duly noted not only the few instances of early hostility with Genoa but also the occasions of alliance between the two communes. In recounting the Balearic campaign in the *Gesta*, he did not think it worth remarking that Genoa had refused to join the Pisans in the campaign, but the later writer of the *Liber Maiorichinus* mentioned the Genoese refusal in some detail. Thus in 1119 the chronicler showed no particular animosity toward the Genoese; however, when he resumed his writing to give the incidents of the recent opening of war between the communes, his attitude toward Genoa had changed—though he still showed a degree of mutual respect at least between the governing classes of the two communes. He maintained that the Devil had prompted the envy of the Genoese for Pisa's new ecclesiastical position.

---

141.   Convenerunt Genuenses virtute mirabili,
                      et adjungunt se Pisanis amore amabili;

Du Méril, *op. cit.*, p. 242.

142. *RIS*², VI:2, 100–101.

143. According to the *Liber Maiorichinus*. Calisse, *op. cit.*, p. 9, ll. 88–93.

However, the wise men among the Pisans did not wish to give hearing to these silly rumors, considering as they did that the Genoese people were ruled and led by the law and governance of wise men. But after the judgment of God it happened that, through the force of their deserts, the insanity of the Genoese had as leader and companion foolishness and madness. For, after God and the Roman church with the peculiar right of the Roman pontiff had with dignity and magnificence elevated the Pisan church, the Genoese, spotted with most wretched malice and rendered insane with the loss of all reason, think it of little moment to break the tie of friendship with the Pisans, and they in no wise hesitate from shattering the oaths of peace for so long mutually retained.[144]

A piratical action by the Genoese opened the war in May, 1119, and the first phase of the conflict ended, after two campaign summers, on September 14, 1120, with a peace favorable to Genoa. The war was not resumed until 1122. The *Carmen*, if written shortly after August, 1119, would express the ideas of at least a portion of the Pisan clergy at this first period of war and peace with Genoa, but hatred for the rival commune was not yet as thorough as it would become in the later *Liber Maiorichinus*. A Pisan clerical poet could still advocate peaceful cooperation with neighboring Genoa through his historical work. The general intention of the author would have been to point out that when the two communes had been singularly cooperative, as in the campaign to North Africa in 1087, they could be highly successful against the Saracens, enemies not only because of piracy and commercial rivalry but also through religion.

Relative to the contemporary situation around 1120, the author would have tended to favor a resumption of friendship between the two Christian communes, now embarking on fratricidal war, so that they could engage in further successful and more honorable action against the non-believing Saracens. Looking back from that time, the poet would have found the campaign of 1087 the most recent and best known instance of

144. "His autem fatuis rumoribus Pisanorum sapientes auditum prebere nolebant, cogitantes Ianuensem populum sapientum jure atque moderamine regi et conduci. Sed de iudicio Dei factum est ut, eorum exigentibus meritis, Ianuensium vesania ducem et comitem haberet fatuitatem et insaniam. Nam quoniam Deus et Ecclesia Romana de proprio jure Romani Pontificis digne ac magnifice sublimaverat Ecclesiam Pisanam, Ianuenses, livore pessimo aspersi et omni sensu perdito amentes effecti, Pisanis amicitie vinculum frangere vilipendunt, atque sacramenta pacis diu ad invicem habita frangere nullatenus renuunt." *RIS*², VI:2, 95.

cooperation between the two cities. It may be argued that this conjecture implies more sophistication and restraint by the poet than can normally be expected from medieval writers, but it must also be remembered that this was not yet the garrulous thirteenth and fourteenth centuries when so little was left implicit in historical works.

The *Carmen* is of interest not only as expressing the view of the poet in foreign relations but also in giving a hint of his attitude toward internal politics. In the narrative the leaders of the expedition are Benedict, the consuls and nobles of Pisa, and the leaders of the allied groups. And yet no less than a tenth of the poem—a section prominently inserted in the crucial battle—is devoted to Ugo Visconte, who died during the assault.[145] Though he is not named in counsel with the bishop or elsewhere as a Pisan leader, he is regarded by the author of the poem as the foremost citizen, as "head of the city":

> O our leader and prince with heart most brave! a king like the most noble king of the Greeks, who acted thus when he heard the answer of Apollo; for, that his people might be triumphant, he freely underwent death.[146]

Immediately after recounting Ugo's heroic death, the poet expressed his loyalty:

> We will be faithful and peaceful in your house, and we will live among yours as guardians and stewarts; no one shall ever raise his boldness against your offspring, because you, dear friend, have given your soul for Pisa.[147]

---

145. Du Méril, *op. cit.*, pp. 247–48.

146.   O dux noster atque princeps cum corde fortissimo!
         Similatus rex Graecorum regi nobilissimo,
         qui sic fecit ut audivit responsum Apollinis;
         nam ut sui triumpharent sponte mortem subiit.

Loc. cit. The allusion appears to be to Codrus, king of the Athenians, but no classical source in Latin connects Codrus with Apollo. Also of interest is the fact that in the Isidorian chronicle, copied in the same manuscript of Guido's collection with the *Carmen*, the scribe omitted the first three words of the entry: "Codrus Atheniensium rex sponte se hostibus offerens interimitur." Then he crossed out the entry, which he had erroneously placed directly after the name of King David (fol. 68).

147.   Erimus in domo tua fideles et placidi,
         et vivemus apud tuos tutores et bajuli;
         nullus unquam contra tuos levabit audaciam,
         quia tu, Care, pro Pisa posuisti animam.

Loc. cit.

There would seem to be more than patriotic devotion in these lines, but, unfortunately, too little is known of Pisan internal politics at the beginning of the twelfth century, so the implications of the poet remain somewhat obscure. The *vicecomes* of Pisa had been the deputy of the margrave of Tuscany, and as such had shared with the bishop rule over the city. By the first half of the twelfth century the Visconti family, which held the position by heredity, had been forced to share this rule with the communal government, until in the middle of the century they unsuccessfully attempted to overthrow the commune in order to regain domination.[148] The lines of this poem show that the family power of the Visconti already needed support and protection, and that the poet, as a member of the Pisan clergy of the cathedral church, was concerned with maintaining the older, feudal power of the *vicecomes*.

The poet's attitudes on the outbreak of hostilities between Genoa and Pisa and on the position of the Visconti family betray the outlook of a reactionary program of returning to the previous policies of the city-state. Such an approach of hearkening to the past could be expected from a member of the higher clergy of Pisa, who represented the secular political outlook of the established ecclesiastical foundation. There is little evidence of social changes in Pisa at this period, but from the development at Milan in the later eleventh century—a development most likely paralleled at Pisa—it is apparent that the appearance of communal government was an expression of the rise to political power of a more recent aristocracy which gradually replaced the leadership of the older and more restricted nobility of the city, a nobility by long tradition attached to the religious institutions of the city, especially the episcopacy. In this same period, because of the elimination by the Italian maritime cities of the threat which Moslem corsairs had presented in the Mediterranean, the Italian maritime centers entered into fiercer rivalry with one another, a rivalry which was marked in the twelfth and thirteenth centuries by an increasing incidence of serious wars. In a sense, the poet of the *Carmen in victoriam* was reacting against both of these new developments in turning to the past for his perfect example of the old traditions.

In keeping with the classical tone of Pisan inscriptions of this period, the author made allusions to ancient Rome and Greece. The remote similarity of the campaign to North Africa by the Pisans and Genoese

148. Volpe, *op. cit.*, pp. 3–4. A. Schaube thought that Ugo's death, in 1087, had occasioned a renewal of civil struggles, *Handelsgeschichte der Romanischen Völker* (Munich-Berlin, 1906), p. 56.

with the Punic wars of the Romans could not but attract the poet. The first four lines establish the simile:

> I, who am to write the history of the illustrious Pisans, call up remembrance of the ancient Romans. For now Pisa extends the wondrous praise, which in times past Rome received by conquering Carthage.[149]

The allied force from medieval Rome which joined the Pisans evoked the victory of great Scipio. But while the campaign in general recalled the Punic war, the poet preferred to choose an extremely obscure example from Greek history as a simile for the death of Ugo Visconte, a simile which he handled rather ineptly. Also, the destruction of the fortifications and ships of al Mahdiya recalled not the fall of Carthage to the Romans but the sack of Troy by the Greeks.[150] Apparently the Pisans were already aware of the legendary Greek descent of their city, as they could find it told in Servius or in Guido's compilation. Thus Greek similes would naturally have significance.

Though some classical similes are used by the poet, the more numerous and elaborate similes are drawn from the Old Testament. Immediately after the comparison with Rome's Carthaginian campaigns, the expedition is likened to the deeds of Gideon against the Midianites. The only direct speech of the entire poem, that of the bishop before the walls of the African cities, has references to Jericho, Goliath, and Maccabaeus. The booty taken by the Pisans was not unlike the spoils the Hebrews took from the Egyptians. And when on the return voyage the fleet discovered a spring on an island where it had stopped for water, the spring was compared to the water which Moses had brought forth from the rock.[151] Thus the basic comparison is not with the Romans or Greeks but with the Hebrews, the "chosen people" of God in the Old Testament.

The author had not the slightest doubt that the real leader of the expedition had been God, and the example of Gideon was the simile for this verity:

149.   Inclytorum Pisanorum scripturus historiam,
              antiquorum Romanorum renovo memoriam;
              nam extendit modo Pisa laudem admirabilem,
              quam olim recepit Roma vincendo Cathaginem.

Du Méril, op. cit., pp. 239–40.
150. Ibid., pp. 242, 247, 248.
151. Ibid., pp. 240, 244, 250, 251.

First I praise the most powerful hand of the Redeemer, by which the Pisan nation destroyed a race most impious. This is completely similar to the miracle of Gideon.[152]

The bishop called to their attention Maccabaeus, "confident not in the strength of an extremely strong man, but in the majesty alone of God most powerful."[153] The major battle had been left to the judgment of God; it is therefore not surprising to find the Christian army aided in the fray by St. Michael, St. Peter, and by the angel who had smitten the army of Sennacherib.[154] As did the chronicler of the *Gesta*, the poet regarded the Pisan people as the chosen people who carried through their victories over the infidels by the hand of God.

THE "LIBER MAIORICHINUS"

From these same years and from the same clerical circle interested in the history of Pisa came the last and most important work of this period, the *Liber Maiorichinus*, perhaps the finest literary work ever to come directly from Pisa.[155] This long epic—one-third the length of the *Aeneid*—with its dactylic hexameter verse and its numerous literary allusions, was undoubtedly inspired by Virgil's epic. Pisa, now taking the role of ancient Rome, should have an epic to parallel the great saga of her predecessor.

It was long believed that the author of the *Liber* was a certain Laurentius Veronensis (or Vernensis), but Henricus, a Pisan canon, is now generally regarded as the poet. The earliest manuscript, of the twelfth century, and the first entry of this work in the catalogue of the cathedral

152.   Manum primo redemptoris collaudo fortissimam,
                    qua destruxit gens Pisana gentem impiissimam;
                    fit hoc totum Gedeonis simile miraculo,

Ibid., p. 240.

153.   nec confidens in virtute cujusquam fortissimi,
                    sed in majestate sola Dei potentissimi.

Ibid., p. 244.

154. *Ibid.*, pp. 245–46.

155. Editions: Ughelli, *Italia sacra*, X, 127–72; Muratori, *RIS*[1], VI, 111–62; Migne, *PL*, CLXIII, 513–76; and Calisse (cited above, n. 44, which edition will be used here). The epic previously bore the name *Liber Maiolichinus*, but the proper title would be *Liber Maiorichinus*. See G. Scalia, "Intorno ai codici dell 'Liber Maiorichinus,'" *Bullettino dell' istituto storico italiano*, LXIX (1957), 272, n. 1.

chapter library leave the work anonymous.[156] But two manuscripts of the fourteenth century identify the author as a certain Laurentius,[157] and the manuscript used by Ughelli and then by Muratori in their early editions of the poem more specifically names the author as Laurentius Veronensis (or Vernensis), a deacon of the archbishop of Pisa, Peter.[158]

No record of such a Laurentius has been found in the fairly plentiful Pisan documents of the first half of the twelfth century. Marchetti suggested that Laurentius may have revised the epic in the thirteenth or fourteenth century,[159] but since Scalia has shown that the supposed later revision was done by the author himself, and not in the following centuries, the role of Laurentius is still in doubt.[160] Roncioni, a not-too-reliable sixteenth-century historian of Pisa, several times mentioned his use of an epic poem on the Balearic expedition written by an "Enrico, cappellano dell'arcivescovo di Pisa." When the ecclesiastical archives were searched for a Henricus of the early twelfth century, more substantial evidence appeared. Among the canons of the cathedral chapter was found a Henricus, who appeared as a priest in documents after 1108, as *plebanus* after February, 1116, and in documents of 1133 and 1134 as *presbiter et custos et plebanus de Calci*—a document of March, 1134, being the last in which his name appears.[161]

Henricus was a leading canon of the cathedral chapter, as is implied from the fact that his name as witness directly follows that of the arch-presbyter in the documents. As *custos* in his late years, he became the keeper of the treasury of the cathedral chapter, and most likely the custodian of the cathedral library as well. From the many details of

156. This manuscript, formerly of the Roncioni collection, is now in the library of the University of Pisa; Calisse, *op. cit.*, pp. xxxvi ff. For the catalogue entry, see Scalia, "Intorno ai codici," pp. 264–65.

157. The Florentine manuscript at the Biblioteca Laurenziana, Rediano 202 (formerly 173), also contains the *Gesta triumphalia* by the same hand, and the *Fragmentum*; Calisse, *op. cit.*, pp. xxxi ff. The other manuscript is in the British Museum, Additional MS 10315, *ibid.*, pp. xxxv–vi.

158. *Ibid.*, p. xvii.

159. *Ibid.*, pp. xxiv–v. The argument was first put forward by Serafino Marchetti, "Intorno al vero autore del poema 'De Bello Maiorichino,'" *Studi storici*, II (1893), 261–69, 295–313. Calisse has repeated the same argument without giving sufficient credit to Marchetti.

160. G. Scalia, "Per una riedizione critica del 'Liber Maiorichinus,'" *Bullettino dell' istituto storico italiano*, LXXI (1959), pp. 91–92.

161. These dates, originally given by P. Pecchiai in "Notizie su l'autore del 'Liber Maiolichinus,'" *Archivio Muratoriano*, I (1913), 126–28, have been revised by Scalia, "Per una riedizione critica," pp. 108 ff.

the campaign which the poet was able to supply it can be assumed that—unless he had an exceptionally detailed source of information—he was present on the expedition. Only one Pisan cleric named Henricus appears in a rather significant role in the course of the epic. The siege of Majorca had become protracted and the army could see no victory in the near future, but on the day before the capture of the first series of walls a certain Henricus, *plebanus*, received a prophecy of the fall of the city.[162] Elsewhere, when the poet named a member of the Pisan clergy, he always added a laudatory epithet; but here, where he may have been referring to himself, he gave only the office.

This is also the only instance of prophecy in the poem, and the poet may well have thought of the role of the poet in terms of the classical *vates*.[163] The poet wrote in the first person only in dedicating the epic to Christ, and consequently there is no further evidence that might identify him as Henricus. However, knowing the position of Henricus in the cathedral clergy of Pisa and the role of the Henricus in the poem, we can assume with a degree of certainty that the cleric was the author of the *Liber Maiorichinus*.

Still, a positive identification is not of especially great significance for this study. We could surmise that such a poet came from the cathedral clergy. The sparse facts which can be added to our knowledge of the author from the documents give no insights into his character or personality. The author has concealed himself so thoroughly in the epic that there is no way of being certain of his identity. Even more, his anonymity seems to have been intentional since even the earliest manuscripts do not appear to have borne his name. There is a striking contrast between the introduction to Guido's miscellaneous collection—where the compiler wrote at length of his service to his fellowmen and carefully gave his name

162.   Presbiter Henricus plebanus luce sub ista
         Letitie didicit presagia cuncta future.
         Talis facta viro vox auribus: "Accipe," dixit,
         "Astra volunt hodie Pisanos urbe repelli.
         Cras vespertinis horis intrabit in urbem
         Plurima passa manus vincens pro velle Tonantis."
         Hoc et idem Karoli defuncti spiritus inquit
         Fratri: "Ne timeas, venient ad prelia sancti,
         Innumerique aderunt subeuntes menia tecum,
         Telaque non poterunt tibi me comitanti nocere."

The revised version of ll. 3165–72, edited by Scalia, "Per una riedizione critica," pp. 57–58.

163. Marchetti, *op. cit.*, pp. 312–13.

as the collector of a work which actually showed no creativity or origi-
nality—and the *Liber Maiorichinus*, which is a significant literary and
historical monument—where the author effaced himself. Under these
circumstances it would be most fitting not to refer the work to the authorship of a certain Henricus, canon of Pisa's cathedral, but to ascribe it to
the circle of clergy who at this time regarded themselves as the spokesmen
for the glorious achievements of the city-state of Pisa.

The original version of the poem can be dated around 1125, and the
revision was undertaken in the first half of the 1130's. Scalia has shown
that the epic was slightly revised by its original author, and he has conjectured that the poem was written within approximately twenty years of
the expedition, before 1135.[164] When the poet mentioned the arrival of
the fleet at Torres, Sardinia, on the journey west, he stated it was there that
"Constantine used to have his residence, a famous king, much celebrated
by all the populace of Sardinia."[165] The poet's use of the imperfect tense
in referring to Constantine could have meant simply that Constantine was
judex at the time of the visit by the Pisan fleet, or it could have implied
that Constantine had ceased to be judge when the poet was writing.
Unfortunately, information on the judges of Torres is rather sketchy.
There are two dated documents of Constantine, for 1082 and 1120;
moreover, his successor in 1147 mentioned that he, Gonnarius, had
already reigned for twenty years.[166] This rather vague note would place
the end of Constantine's reign before 1127, but, because of the vagueness
of the document, we cannot conclude that Constantine died in that year.

Later in the epic the author stated that Obertus, "the flower of the
deacons," could give the words of a speech by the archbishop to anyone
who might ask him.[167] This statement implies that Obertus (or Ubertus)
was still alive at the time of both the original work and the revision, and
that, for at least the first version, he was a deacon. A deacon of this name
is found in Pisan documents between 1108 and September, 1125, and in
a document of October, 1127, an Ubertus is named with the office of
canon of the cathedral and cardinal-priest—probably the same cleric who
became archbishop of Pisa in 1132.[168] Since the poem gives him the office

164. G. Scalia, "*Oliverius e Rolandus*" (cited above, n. 99), pp. 299–300.
165.   Constantinus habebat
          Sedes, rex clarus, multum celebratus ab omni
          Sardorum populo. (ll. 196–98)
166. D. Scano, "Serie cronologica dei giudici sardi," *Archivio storico sardo*, XXI:3–4
(1939), 95–96.
167. Lines 851–53.
168. Scalia, "*Oliverius e Rolandus*," p. 299, n. 41.

of deacon, it must have been first written before his elevation to cardinal-priest, between September, 1125, and October, 1127. This possible *terminus ante quem* refers to the middle of the third decade.

There is a final method for establishing a dating of both the first version and the revision. The poet has used the familiar form of address, the second person singular, on many different occasions. Inanimate objects, the future reader, Christ, saints, and some persons active in the campaign are thus addressed. He used the form for ten persons in the expedition—eight of whom were knights, of whom four, a Provençal and three Saracens, died during the siege.[169] There is only one person in the poem, aside from the author, who must have been alive when both versions of the epic were composed, and this is Obertus, who is referred to not in the second but in the third person.

These considerations indicate that the poet employed the familiar form of address for the departed, not for his living contemporaries. The Pisan archbishop, Peter, is also addressed in the second person.[170] The epithets he was granted seem further to imply that the bishop was no longer alive: "venerable for your blessed merits," "with hallowed voice," and "holy prelate."[171] Such phrases were not commonly used for a contemporary or living prelate. Thus the use of the familiar form and the epithets both indicate that the poem was first composed after the death of Peter, after September, 1119.

The termini for the first version of the *Liber* are therefore September, 1119, and September, 1127—probably toward the end of that interval. The lengthy and polished epic would have taken some time to complete. The poet was probably gathering his material even during the campaign, but he did not finish it until ten years after the expedition. Another cleric of the Pisan church is addressed in the familiar form, the priest, Gratianus. He is mentioned in this manner not in the original version but in the revision of the epic. Gratianus is found in Pisan documents from 1107 to

169. Pisans: Bishop Peter, ll. 39–48, 1390; Gratianus, a priest, ll. 2091–94, revised; Lambertus Uberti, ll. 1025–32; Macelinus, l. 1145; Vivianus, ll. 1804–8; Ildebrandus Matti, ll. 2857–58. Provençal: Dalmatius, ll. 1992–2005. Saracens: Ander, l. 1729; Raymundus Midan, l. 1918; Atila, l. 1929.

170. It is true that one of the two instances was changed into the third person in the revision, ll. 39–48.

171. "meritis venerande beatis," l. 39; "voce sacrata," l. 86; "sanctus . . . presul," l. 340; "sanctus . . . antistes," l. 3271; "magno cum presule," l. 1392, became "sancto cum presule" in the revision. It should be further noted that the poet referred to Peter as *presul*, *antistes*, or *pontifex*; he never used the terms *episcopus* or *archiepiscopus*, which could have been fitted into the meter. Was he being purposely vague in the period after 1121, when the title was in dispute?

June 26, 1129;[172] his name was entered in the Luccan necrology of this period under January 31.[173] Thus he died in January, 1130, or possibly in January of the succeeding year. The poet made his revision of the epic, therefore, no earlier than January, 1130.[174] If the poet was Henricus, who must have died shortly after his disappearance from Pisan documents in March, 1134, the revision would have been made in the first half of the 1130's.

A summarization of these conclusions will outline the probable sequence of events. A canon and priest of the cathedral, Henricus, joined the expedition to the Balearic Islands. Interested in recording the event, he made notes during the campaign, and several years after his return, about 1125, he finished the initial version of the epic. About 1130 he became custodian of the chapter treasury and library, which induced him to undertake a minor revision of the work. He died around 1135. It is only through such approximations that we can seek to establish the chronology of the *Liber*. But the chronology indicates that the poem was the last of the historical and literary works to issue from the cathedral chapter in this period of intensified interest in the exploits of Pisa.

For the poet, the Balearic campaign had the guidance of God. The first three lines of the original version of the epic, however, are strikingly similar in tone to the poem placed on the *Porta Aurea*:

We have written down the strength and warlike deeds of the Pisan people, their harsh toils on land and sea, the slaughter of the Moors, and the kingdoms plundered and subjected.[175]

172. Scalia, "Per una riedizione critica," p. 93, n. 3.

173. S. Baluzius, *Miscellanea novo ordine digesta* (Lucca, 1761), I, 431.

174. Another revised passage of the poem gives an equivocal factor for dating. Roger, formerly bishop of Volterra, was archbishop of Pisa from 1123 to 1131. During the Balearic campaign, as bishop of Volterra, he acted as the temporary guardian of Pisa. In the earlier version the poet had referred to Roger in only one passage (ll. 3116–17):

> Volscorum presul meriti Rogerius alti,
> Viribus insignis, factis et origine pollens,

With his revision, possibly after the death of Roger in 1131, the poet expanded the passage in the revision of lines 136–37:

> O satis eximio felix Antonia patre
> Nempe tue regionis hero generaliter urbis
> Cura datur, patrie qui pellat et arceat hostes.

That Antonia was regarded as a secondary name for Volterra is attested by Giovanni Villani, *Chroniche*, I, 55.

175.   Pisani populi vires et bellica facta
             Scripsimus ac duros terre pelagique labores,
             Maurorum stragem, spoliata subactaque regna.   (ll. 1–3)

Yet, despite the nonreligious temper of these lines, the rest of the epic makes it clear that the poet regarded the expedition as divinely led.[176] As with the other Pisan writers of this period, history was inconceivable without the operative force of God. On two occasions the poet made reference to divine support and surveillance,[177] but, in a subtle manner, most references to the effective intervention of the deity are given in the numerous speeches attributed to different members of the expedition; and the stronger statements are given not to clerics but to laymen. Of several examples, the most striking are to be found in the speech of Atho, one of the Pisan consuls:

> What is determined by the nod of the Lord is realized to be basically remote from human reason. . . . That is certainly the power of the Thunderer, for He destines the deeds of this world in accord with His wish, and with affectionate judgment He is master over every cause. . . . The Lord, not our own desire, has led us to this place; may the man who serves Him well hope and without doubt expect that he will never be cheated in his truly best interests.[178]

The Pisan army answered the taunts of the Saracens at Majorca: "We have come from our fatherland under the highest lord, Christ, with whose help we shall conquer the city of Balea."[179] In a letter to the ruler of Majorca the Pisans had early envisaged the campaign as a combat which would be judged only by God. The Balearic king later concluded the reception of a Pisan embassy with a call to God's judgment.[180] This same

176. It should be noted that the poet changed these opening lines in his revision (the italics are mine):

> Arma, rates, populum, *vindictam celitus actam*
> Scribimus ac duros terre pelagique labores,
> Gerionea viros sese per rura terentes,
> Maurorum stragem, spoliata subactaque regna.

177. Lines 1469 *et seqq.*, 2819–21.

178.
> Quod Domini nutu disponitur, a ratione
> Funditus humana cognoscitur esse remotum.
>   . . . vis est ea nempe Tonantis,
> Nam pro velle suo mundanos destinat actus,
> Arbitrioque pio causa dominatur in omni . . .
> Istuc nos Dominus duxit, non nostra voluntas;
> Qui famulatur ei bene speret et indubitate,
> Quod vera numquam fraudabitur utilitate.
>   Lines 308–9, 313–15, 326–28

179.
> Venimus a patria summo sub principe Christo,
> Cuius ob auxilium Balee superabimus urbem,   (ll. 3096–97)

180. Lines 915–16, 2934.

idea had been voiced by the author of the *Carmen*. Also, as in the *Carmen*, the heavenly host was to aid the crusading army, but while the earlier poet saw the divine forces, saints, and angels in the very midst of the fray, the poet of the *Liber* placed the assurance of their presence in the speech of the papal legate before the decisive battle.[181] Of course, the speeches cannot be read as true verbatim accounts, but the impression is most effectively given that the Pisans—and not only the clerics—regarded themselves as on a divine mission and relied on and trusted in the divine omnipotence. And yet, as with any medieval historical narrative, the strongest declaration of the power of God can be immediately followed by a most detailed account of human accomplishments.

To the Pisan poet the Balearic expedition was a true crusade, sanctioned by the clergy. His attitude is best expressed in a debate which he has placed at a crucial time, when, after initial successes, the Christian leaders feared the arrival of Saracen reinforcements, while the king of the islands was ready to negotiate. The Spanish and French counts argued for a truce, claiming that the Pisans were intent on praise and empty pomp and that the Pisans followed the clerics, who, not being warriors, should not incite others to battle.[182] The Pisans answered that they had come to eliminate the enslavement of Christians for the future as well as for the present and that the counts should fulfill their oaths.

> We obey the clerics, because the command for fighting came from the sacred rank. For the pope of the apostolic see has commanded battles, and, having followed his bidding, we can never change so great a design.[183]

If we compare this statement of the poet with the earlier inscription of the *Porta Aurea*, or even with the *Gesta*, it will be noted that the poet gave the expedition much more the character of a crusade than either of the earlier works. The *Porta Aurea* inscription mentioned neither the liberation of the captive Christians nor the clerical leadership of the expedition.[184] For the author of the *Gesta*, the liberation of the captives was the primary objective of the campaign, but the role of the clergy or papacy was not

181. Lines 2232–48.
182. Lines 2708–29.
183.   Paremus cleris, quia venit ab ordine sacro
              Iussio pugnandi. nam iussit prelia papa
              Sedis apostolice, cuius precepta sequuti
              Tantum propositum nusquam mutare valemus.   (ll. 2761–64)
184. Above, n. 89.

overly emphasized.[185] The expedition in the *Liber* bears all the outward signs of a crusade. The Pisans took the crosses, "celestial signs," from the hand of their bishop on Easter, 1113.[186] The poet thereby gave the official initiative to the Pisan bishop rather than to the papacy. However, he then placed the leadership in the hands of the pope. A delegation was sent to Rome where the pope bestowed the "Roman standards" on the military leaders, standards which were later referred to, in the course of battle, as the "banner of the apostolic see."[187] For the Pisan bishop, the pope sent a cross, along with the power of absolution.[188] The papal cross would imply that the Pisan prelate was to act as the spiritual lieutenant of the papacy, the leader of the crusade.

While the author did not further qualify this aspect of the bishop's leadership, a document from Barcelona shows clearly that the count of Barcelona regarded Peter as the representative of the papal see, at least before the arrival of the papal legate, Boso.[189] After joining the army in the spring of 1114, Boso remained with the expedition. However, he was not given a really decisive role by the poet; rather, the legate followed the lead of the bishop of Pisa.[190] Papal leadership brought absolution to the crusaders who would die in battle. The papacy also gave the campaign the express mission of liberating the captive Christians. Though the papal legate would later side with the Pisan clergy for a complete victory,[191] Paschal II seems to have envisaged the less ambitious goal for the expedition. Otherwise, the papacy supported the crusade with its benediction and the prayers of western Christendom.[192]

With this image of a crusade, which the poet was so eager to develop, it is surprising that he made absolutely no mention of either the *reconquista* or the First Crusade. The parallel between the Pisan crusade and the crusade to Jerusalem was doubtless in the mind of the poet, yet the comparison was never explicitly stated. Certainly his readers were not

185. For the *Gesta*'s account of this incident and the role of the clergy, see *RIS*[2], VI:2, 92.

186. Lines 39 *et seqq.*

187. Lines 74, 1688.

188. Lines 74, 79–81.

189. In Calisse's edition of the epic, p. 138: "qui dompni apostolici in predicto exercitu vicem gerebat,"

190. Lines 1590–91, 3271, 3279.

191. Line 3271.

192. It would be tempting to place the fashioning of this important role for the pope sometime shortly after July, 1126, when the regranting of Pisan metropolitan position showed that the contemporary pontiff favored Pisa.

supposed to regard this as a sign of the limited horizon of the Pisan author, they were rather to be impressed with the extent of the new, Pisan crusade.

The poet's perspective was dominated by the comparison with ancient Rome. As we have seen for the authors of the epitaphs and the *Carmen*, the only comparison that was worthy of the new position of Pisa and suitable for the author's contemporaries was with ancient Rome.

> If the current age would well consider warlike Pisa extending her double power over sea and lands, [they would realize that] Pisa is accomplishing what would be fitting for another Rome.[193]

In keeping with the Roman metaphor, the poet passed over Biblical similes. Although Biblical references were gathered by the author of the earlier *Carmen*, here they are to be found in only two speeches, those of the cardinal-legate and Deacon Guido.[194] But similes were frequently drawn from ancient Greek and Roman history. In the *Liber* the Pisans were compared to the Romans as often as to the Greeks—the poet did not attempt to stress the Greek origin of the city of Pisa by favoring Greek references, as had the author of the *Carmen*. The epic poet has also carefully chosen suitable similes, displaying at once a wider and more sound acquaintance with ancient history than the earlier author had shown.[195]

The classical tone of the epic is very strong. The poet was obviously most concerned with keeping his poetic vocabulary and style in the tradition of the great Latin epics, for he used very few words or phrases that are not found in the classical poetry of Rome. His most important model was the most famous of Latin epics, Virgil's *Aeneid*.[196] Of only slightly less importance for the poet were Ovid's works, especially the *Metamorphoses*.[197] And mention should also be made of his obvious acquaintance with Lucan's *De bello civili*.[198]

193.   Si bene belligeras pensent nova secula Pisas
            Per mare per terras geminas extendere vires,
            Hoc Pise faciunt Romam quod utramque deceret.   (ll. 778–80)
194. Lines 2221–22, 652–60.
195. Lines 179–80, 206–7, 227–29, 445–47, 717–18, 1160–62, 2165, 2380–82, 2485–88.
196. Fourteen borrowings of phrases from the *Aeneid* had been discovered; see M. Manitius, *Geschichte der lateinischen Literatur des Mittelalters* (Munich, 1931), III, nn. to pp. 673–74. I have found four additional phrases.
197. Aside from individual words to be found only in Ovid, there are at least seven borrowings from the *Metamorphoses* and one from the *Heroides*.
198. There are several possible loans of vocabulary, but the poet's simile of the Roman siege of Massilia is most striking:

Yet, even though the poet displayed a rather wide acquaintance with classical works, he used them mainly for vocabulary and a very few phrases. Only two of these phrases contain more than two words and they seem to have been obvious literary allusions. The poet began his description of Balea, the chief city of Majorca and the city whose capture was the main achievement of the campaign, with the line *Urbs antiqua fuit*, a significant allusion to the *Aeneid*, where Virgil used the words to introduce his first mention of Carthage.[199] The parallel of the destruction of Carthage by Rome and of Balea by Pisa must have been intended by the poet of the *Liber*. The second quotation is the phrase *fama tanti mali*.[200] Virgil used this expression at the crucial point in his epic, directly after Turnus had slain Pallas, and the "rumor of such an ill" came to Aeneas to incite him to avenge his fallen friend—a motive which carried the epic to the concluding death of Turnus. The Pisan author used it for the news of the piratical depredations by the Saracens of the Balearic Islands, news which incited the Pisans to vengeance and the destruction of Saracen power there.

This striking use of such allusions is only one indication of the literary ability of the poet. It is unfortunate that medieval poets of this period, writing in a literary language which passed out of vogue before the vernacular tongues, are given so little attention as really significant literary figures.

It has been suggested, by Calisse, that the *Liber* shows an increasing awareness of an Italian identity in the use of the classical name *Latini*.[201] But the author's attitude toward other cities of the Italian peninsula would not seem to indicate any strong feelings of a common Italian identity or any desire to share the glory of the campaign. A Catalonian document of this period mentions that the expedition was composed not only of Pisans but also of the people of Rome, Lucca, Florence, Siena, Volterra, Pistoia, Lombardy, Sardinia, Corsica, "and other innumerable nations."[202] The poet was, to say the least, niggardly in giving credit; he mentioned help from other cities in Italy in only one sentence:

> Massilie quondam Rome violenta potestas,
> Cui mare, cui tellus et plurima regna patebant,
> Ut superaret eam sane non celsius ullum
> Edificavit opus.   (ll. 2485–88)

It shows an acquaintance with the *De bello civili*, III.

199. *Aeneid*, I:12; *Liber*, 1552.
200. *Aeneid*, X:510; *Liber*, 30.
201. Calisse, *Liber Maiorichinus*, pp. xv *et seqq.*   202. *Ibid.*, p. 138.

Meanwhile certain men come from a distant race, and Rome along with Lucca sends assistance for the battle. Only the Genoese fatherland denied aid for the war and hinders Pisan activity as much as possible.[203]

Only two Sardinian military leaders are mentioned as joining the fleet, and the presence of the bishop of Cagliari was later noted only incidentally.[204] The Luccan auxiliaries retired from the campaign during the first year, before the Balearic Islands were approached. Lucca was the traditional enemy of Pisa on the mainland, and some of this animosity can be seen in the speech given by the poet to a Luccan knight who berates his fellow townsmen:

These men regret having come, they who are accustomed to work the fields and always to lean on the curved plows, and who spend all the seasons turning over the clods. And now, when they cannot plant their seed in the furrows or sink into the new wine trodden by their feet, night and day they complain of these delays and accidents.[205]

While the Luccans were held up to ridicule, the Genoese were attacked with more subtle abuse: In its account of the earlier Pisan victories over Mugehid near the beginning of the eleventh century, the *Liber* omits any reference to Genoa although the earlier *Fragmentum* had explicitly mentioned Genoese cooperation in these battles.[206] The negotiations between Pisa and Genoa for aid in the Balearic campaign are treated in the *Liber* with mention of Genoese deceit and fraud, her hindering of Pisan activity, and her dejection at the rapidity of the gathering of reinforcements at Pisa.[207] Further abuse was given Genoa in the incident of the accidental landing of a Genoese merchantman in the Pisan camp in Spain. The Genoese spokesman referred to the friendship between the Genoese and

203.   Interea veniunt quidam de gente remota,
                  Romaque cum Luca mittunt solatia pugne.
                  Auxilium bello Ianuensis sola negavit
                  Patria, quamque potest Pisanos impedit actus.   (ll. 133–36)
204. Lines 202–5, 1590.
205.   Hos piget venisse quidem, qui rura solebant
                  Vertere, qui curvis incumbere semper aratris,
                  Cunctaque consumunt vertendo tempora glebas.
                  Et modo, cum nequeant sua semina tradere sulcis
                  Aut conculcato pedibus procumbere musto,
                  Nocte dieque moras istas casusque queruntur,   (ll. 394–99)
206. Lines 924 *et seqq.* See *RIS*[2], VI:2, 100.
207. Lines 89 *et seqq.*, 135–36, 1168–69.

the Moslems of the Balearic Islands, but he was also forced to admit the
power of Pisa:

> All the seas are open to the Arno-born, and in their elation they begin
> to demonstrate to the nations new lust for battle.[208]

An interesting corroboration of this ambitious attitude of Pisa from the
viewpoint of a rival city-state can be seen in the account of a Venetian
monk at the time of the First Crusade. He spoke of the Pisans,

> who had attained such a haughtiness of pride that they had fashioned
> for themselves an imperial ship and imperial banners and were claim-
> ing that they were conquering the entire world. . . . They said that,
> just as territorial lords, they would go wherever they wished to the
> shame [of the Venetians].[209]

The alliance of the Pisan army and its contingents from other Italian
cities with the military forces of the counts of southern France and northern
Spain, while it was necessary for the successful outcome of the expedition,
did not lead to completely friendly relations between such diverse partners.
This alliance raises problems for the original intention of the Pisans and
for a significant change in the scope of the expedition; it also involves the
question of the credibility of the poet as an historian. Manfroni has
attacked the veracity of the poet, charging the Pisan with excessive
imagination, praise of the noble families of Pisa, abuse of the Genoese,
and with being at variance with the facts presented by Spanish documents.[210] The first charge is too vague to dwell on, and Manfroni has not
elaborated it. As will be pointed out, the poet praised the Pisan nobility
but with important qualifications. The abuse of the Genoese is patently
true, but it shows only the bias of a writer who was composing an epic
during a war between Pisa and Genoa—and it should be noted that
Manfroni was decidedly pro-Genoese and anti-Pisan in his own book.

The most serious charge, as Manfroni seemed to indicate by discussing
it at length, is the last: a contradiction between the *Liber* and the Spanish
documents. Manfroni indicated that Pisa had made arrangements for an
alliance with the western counts before the campaign began, and that

---

208.   Pervia Sarnigenis sunt equora cuncta, novosque
             Gentibus incipiunt tumidi monstrare furores.   (ll. 472–73)
    209. *RHC, Historiens Occidentaus*, V, 285: "qui in tantum superbiae fastum ascenderant,
quod navim imperialem et signa imperialia sibi fecerant, et seipsos totum mundum
devincentes appellabant . . . dixerunt se, sicut dominos terrae, quocumque vellent, ad
eorum dedecus, ituros."
    210. C. Manfroni, *Storia della marina italiana* . . . (Livorno, 1899), I, 169. Manfroni
called the epic a "poemetto."

the poet had therefore falsified the account when he stated that the Pisan armada, sailing toward the Balearic Islands and being diverted from its course by a storm, came to Spain only by chance and then gained the alliance of the counts.[211] Manfroni's charge was ill-advised, and other considerations tend to substantiate the account of the early poet-historian.

Alliances with foreign princes had previously been made by Pisan expeditionary forces. In 1064, Pisan ships had attacked Palermo in conjunction with the land forces of the Norman duke. In 1092, Pisans and Genoese had gone to help Alfonso against Valencia, [212] so unsuccessful a campaign that it found no mention in Pisan annals—although it may have been a semi-private venture and probably not directed by the bishop of Pisa. In the First Crusade the Pisan fleet had joined forces with the crusading counts in the Holy Land; and that crusade occasioned the first extended military campaign known in Pisan history, a campaign that possibly lasted two full years and necessitated two winters overseas. Only one other campaign before the Balearic is known in any detail, the attack on al Mahdiya in 1087, in which there had been no alliance with a major feudal army. This attack had been a surprise raid, according to the Arabic sources, and most of the Saracen forces were in another region.[213] The

---

211. "Infatti, mentre il poeta sostiene che il primo impulso alla spedizione partì nell'anno 1113 da papa Pasquale II e che per puro caso i Pisani si unirono ad alcuni principi di Spagna, i documenti spagnuoli provano che Berengario II, conte di Barcellona, venne in Italia a cercarvi aiuti contro i Saraceni di Spagna e si fermò a Pisa ed a Genova, facendo larghe promesse; anzi un documento ricorda, non appar ben chiaro se una promessa o una concessione di privilegi commerciali ai Genovesi, in cambio di aiuti da loro promessi od inviati." *Loc. cit.* The poet did not maintain that the pope had instigated the expedition; the count of Barcelona was not Berengar II but Ramon-Berengar III.

The document, dated 1118, appears in A. Capmany y de Montpalau, *Memorias historicas sobre la marina* . . . (Madrid, 1779), II, appendix, pp. 1–2; but, despite some ambiguity, the concession is for the men of Barcelona, not for the Genoese: "Haec est charta donationis, quam facit Raymundus Comes Barchinonensis hominibus Barchinonae. Manifestum est enim, quod ego Raymundus Comes Barchinonensis, pro commovendo exercitu ad liberandam Ispaniarum Ecclesiam, cum hominibus meis de Barchinona per mare navigio Januam et Pisas adivi. In reditu vero . . . illos mecum detinui. Quocirca . . . dimittimus . . . eis novum usagium quod ego Comes posui in Barchinona; videlicet quintam de omnibus galeis quam accipere soliti eramus, pro tot et tantis servitiis ac laboribus, quos pro me terra et mari perpessi sunt." Ramon-Berengar visited Genoa and Pisa in the spring of 1116 (see n. 218). The grant was for the men of Barcelona who had given the count service, not the Pisans or Genoese. Capmany (*ibid.*, pp. 4, 22) specifically noted the Pisan initiative in the Balearic campaign.

212. Heywood, *op. cit.*, p. 44. The campaign was against Rodrigo Díaz de Vivar, the Cid.

213. Amari, *Biblioteca*, pp. 112, 160.

Pisan and Genoese forces stormed the suburb and most of the city on August 6, and, having won captives and tribute from the Arabic ruler, they left the citadel in enemy hands and hastily returned to Italy. It is likely that earlier campaigns against Arabic strongholds in North Africa had been comparable raids, with no idea of a prolonged siege but planned rather as a surprise attack, the gathering of whatever plunder was available, and a speedy withdrawal before the Saracen soldiers or ships could rally—precisely the technique of the earlier Moslem corsairs.

The movements of the Pisan armada suggest that the Balearic campaign had begun as such a plundering expedition. It left Pisa on August 6, 1113. Apparently it arrived in Sardinia shortly afterwards, took on board some of the Sardinian lords, and was probably carefully provisioned, since the armada remained at the island until the last days of August. Perhaps it was also awaiting favorable winds, since in this season the west wind is strong off northern Sardinia.[214] On the night of August 30, having set sail from Sardinia, the Pisans were suddenly overtaken by a storm, and on the following day they reached what they thought was Majorca but what proved to be the coast of Spain. There they negotiated with the Catalan and Provençal counts, and, after more than three weeks, again set sail for the Balearics, on September 24. The winds proved unfavorable, so that by the end of September the armada had to turn back to Barcelona for the winter season.

This itinerary clearly shows that the Pisans had not made a previous agreement with the western counts, an "agreement" which the poet, normally well acquainted with politics, is supposed to have been unaware of or to have suppressed. If the Pisans had made arrangements to ally themselves with the western counts, the armada would not have gone by way of Sardinia but by the usual route along the coast of southern France. Further, the western military forces would have been readied for service. In the Mediterranean during the ancient period, the season for naval operations was from about May 26 to September 14—even more restricted than the trading season.[215] In the middle ages this period would still have applied since naval technology had not yet made any considerable advances. In fact, it was evident that the armada could not safely make the trip south from Barcelona toward the Balearics in late September. The fleet had not left Sardinia until the end of August, allowing itself only a short period to attack Majorca, gain what concessions could be wrung

214. Koninklijk Nederlands Meteorologisch Instituut, *Middellandse Zee* (The Hague, 1957), p. 9.

215. E. Semple, *The Geography of the Mediterranean Region* (New York, 1931), p. 580.

from the Saracen ruler, and return to Pisa—or more likely to the Christian portion of the Spanish coast for the winter.

This maneuver required surprise, so that the Saracen king of Majorca could not gain reinforcements in men or ships. When the Balearics had been inadvertently passed, the Pisan commanders must have considered a stronger attack in alliance with a western feudal army which could lay siege to Balea over the winter. This plan was frustrated by contrary winds, so that the Pisan forces had to winter in Spain, and this delay explains the complaints and the withdrawal of the Luccans, who had probably not counted on a prolonged campaign. As a consequence, the element of surprise for the attack on the Balearics had been lost; a larger force was now required, reinforcements were brought from Pisa, and the feudal forces of the western counts were probably augmented. The plundering campaign had assumed new proportions, and the alliance of Italian and French-Spanish forces required more effective mediation than either the bishop of Pisa or the count of Barcelona could supply. In the spring, Boso, as papal legate, arrived at the armada's base. That the legate had not sailed with the Pisan fleet in August of the preceding year indicates that the Pisans had not reckoned on a significant alliance with western forces.

On June 24, 1114, the armada was finally prepared to leave under favorable winds, but the element of surprise had been lost. The armada had to face strengthened garrisons, which appreciably prolonged the sieges of Ibiza and Balea, and it had to fear the arrival of a large Arabic fleet from Denia in southern Spain, or from North Africa. Fortunately for the Christians, the Saracen fleet did not appear—at least not until after the city of Balea, including the citadel itself, had been taken and the armada had departed, shortly after April 18 (Easter), 1115. The Arabic sources mention the arrival of a major Saracen fleet at Majorca directly after the withdrawal of the Pisan forces, and they state that the Christian armada suffered great losses in a severe storm [216]—it was still early in the year, before the best sailing season had come.

The itinerary and initial movements of the Pisan fleet show there had been no pre-arranged alliance with the western counts and that the narrative of the poet appears to be fully substantiated—except that he did not mention the original plan of a short campaign. What evidence is there, then, for an earlier alliance of the Italian cities and the western counts? A twelfth-century biography of the archbishop of Barcelona, Oldegarius, says that Count Ramon-Berengar III of Barcelona went to Italy to see the

216. Al-Makkari, *The History of the Mohammedan Dynasties in Spain*, abr. and tr. by P. de Gayangos (London, 1843), II, xlviii.

pope and that he stopped at Genoa and at Pisa.[217] However, this voyage was undertaken after the Balearic campaign, in the first half of 1116.[218] As a consequence, Manfroni's principal attack on the poet of the *Liber* cannot be maintained.[219]

The change in the scope of the campaign—especially the alliance with a large contingent of westerners—may very likely have caused the Pisan author some misgivings. He frequently mentioned the activities of the western allies, but there is always the possibility that he has not given full credit to their role in the success of the expedition.

In the debate between the counts and the Pisans, serious differences in the attitudes of the two parties were evident. The poet countered the counts' accusations of greed not by any attempt to vindicate Pisa's economic prospects but with the counter-charge that while the Pisan soldiers were pursuing the siege the westerners were making money by plundering the rural areas and selling to the Christian army. Further, the poet charged that the counts were guilty of venality in their relations with the Moslem ruler and at least guilty of greed in preferring to hold Moslem prisoners for ransom rather than dispatching this dangerous enemy.[220]

The poet also showed a peculiar lack of respect for the western clergy who joined the crusade. While many members of the Pisan clergy were given roles, and while the bishop of Cagliari was incidentally noted, no mention was made of the Spanish clergy. The presence of the bishop of Barcelona is attested by the *Gesta*, and a Spanish source mentions his death in the crusader camp.[221] The attitude of the western counts toward the expedition and toward the Moslems lacked the more intense religious fervor of the Pisan crusaders under clerical direction. The former must

217. E. Florez, *España sagrada* (Madrid, 1859), XXIX, 475–76.

218. No dates are given in the *Vita*, but the count was trying to get papal support for Oldegarius, who had been elected to the see of Barcelona in 1115, after the Balearic campaign. The papal letters to Oldegarius and the count are dated May 23, 1116 (*PL*, CLXIII, 405–7). Ramon-Berengar did not get farther than Pisa because of the enmity of Henry V, who had been in Italy since March, traveling about the Po valley; the road to Rome was unsafe since early April because of the strife among the Roman nobles. Therefore, the count of Barcelona probably came to Italy in April or May, 1116, during the sailing season.

219. It is surprising that G. Volpe, in his review of Calisse's edition of the epic, unquestioningly accepted Manfroni's charge; *Archivio storico italiano*, series 5, XXXVII (1906), 98.

220. Lines 2116, 2129–31; 1973–74, 2698–99; 2844–72.

221. In the *Vita Sancti Ollegarii, España sagrada*, XXIX, 474: "cum praedicto autem legato ipse Barchinonensis et alii pontifices, et magna pars cleri, tam ceterarum urbium et oppidorum quae per loca marina sita sunt, ad excidium Majoricae perrexerant."

have regarded the expedition with more practical experience in dealing with the infidels and must have foreseen the dangers in leaving the Balearic Islands without a strong government, a danger that was immediately realized after the Pisan withdrawal when the Almoravides seized the islands. Yet, to the Pisan writer, such considerations were signs of bribery, or at least of a lack of religious conviction.

In keeping with his general attitude toward the western counts, the poet, although noting that the count of Barcelona had been given the military leadership of the entire army,[222] did not stress this role of the count but rather used the count as the main spokesman for the unappreciated attitudes of the western troops. However, Raymond de Baux, from the region of Arles, was not incriminated along with the other western leaders but was specially favored by the poet, probably mainly because of his continued friendship with Pisa and its mercantile interest in southern France.[223] Otherwise, the western forces were either given slight attention or were occasionally vituperated—especially for the refusal of the counts to participate in the last stages of the siege until they saw that the Pisans would otherwise take all the booty.[224]

For the author of the epic, a Pisan cleric, acquaintance with the different attitudes of another region had not contributed to a better understanding or tolerance but may well have led to such attitudes' being regarded as possibly subversive if widely circulated among the secular society of Pisa itself. This possible polemic for the contemporary Pisan audience may have been the reason for the greater detail given by the poet to ecclesiastical leadership and his greater emphasis of the religious and crusading aspects of the expedition.

The *Liber Maiorichinus*, with its extent and its depth of treatment, is most important for the light it sheds upon the city-state of Pisa, upon her traditions and history, her politics, and her aspirations in the first half of the twelfth century. The consular period—the late eleventh and twelfth centuries—is so inadequately known from the generally terse chronicles of

222. The speech of the Pisan consul to Ramon-Berengar:
> Te sociare sibi belli sociumque ducemque
> Agmina nostra volunt; . . .
> Lines 271–72 (also see l. 3091)

223. Especially lines 2869–70. Calisse, *op. cit.*, p. 23, n. 3, has made this lord a Spanish knight from Balsio, but this is actually Raymond de Baux, the brother-in-law of Ramon-Berengar of Barcelona.

224.   . . . renuit dux bella Pyrenus;   (l. 3295, but)
> Hinc comes accelerans alia de parte Pyrenus
> Iudeos omnes sub deditione receptat.   (ll. 3339–40)

contemporaries and from the few laconic public documents that a work such as this epic is of unusual significance for controlling the conjectures of modern scholars, conjectures which differ more widely in proportion to the paucity of documents.

The epic first gives a general idea of the importance of tradition and history for the Pisans of that time. While Italian historians of the thirteenth and fourteenth centuries wove fabulous tales around the origins of their cities—the most notable instance being Florence—historians of the twelfth century generally showed little or no interest in such embroidering. The author of the *Liber* was no exception; his only mention of the origin of Pisa was of secondary importance, occasioned by an attempt to explain a second name for the Arno river, the Alpheus. He noted that this other name, as well as the name for Pisa itself, had been brought to Italy by a settler from Greece, where the city Pisae was on the Alpheus river.[225] This information came from Servius' commentary on the *Aeneid*, but it is interesting to note that the author did not mention the legend of Pelops' foundation of Pisa—a legend noted in Guido's geographical collection.[226] Pisan historians of more curious centuries would simply combine both stories, but our poet seemed to have had no great concern for such tales except as they provided a new term, *Alpheus*, which he could use to relieve the monotony of repeating *Pisanus*. The comment of a recent writer that our poet glorified Pisa for its ancestry from Rome and that he found Pisa "not an unworthy daughter of the ancient mother" is only a misunderstanding that perhaps arose from the influence of fascist ideas.[227]

The poet's concern for Pisa's more recent past was also rather limited. He has the Pisan elders incite the war spirit of the city through evoking the successful campaigns of Bona and Palermo[228]—which he could have found noted in the *Fragmentum*. The departure of the fleet from Pisa on

225.   Accepit has Sarnus, greco vocitatus ab amne
        Alpheus, cui Pisa vetus, nunc lapsa, cohesit,
        Ex qua Pisanus, qui Pisas condidit istas,
        Italie fluvio nomen donavit et urbi.   (ll. 138–41)

Servius' commentary on *Aeneid*, X, 179, reads in part: "Alpheus fluvius est inter Pisas et Elidem civitates Arcadiae, ubi est templum Iovis Olympici: ex quibus locis venerunt qui Pisas in Italia condiderunt, dictas a civitate pristina." Note that Servius did not mention that the original city had fallen into ruin. Was the poet of the *Liber Maiorichinus* drawing a parallel for Pisa with the Troy–Rome legend?

226. Above, n. 111.

227. G. Chiri, *La poesia epico-storica latina dell'Italia medioevale* (Modena, 1939), p. 43.

228. Lines 32–35.

August 6 reminded him of the Pisan victory over the "Poeni" on the same day, that is the Saracens of North Africa.[229]

His most interesting reference to an historical event in Pisan history was to the campaigns against Mugehid. Mugehid, a Moslem king from Spain, had attempted to seize Sardinia but had been driven off by the Pisans and Genoese. This event had an especially vital importance for Pisa not only since it seemed to foreshadow the campaign to the Balearic Islands, which had been ruled by Mugehid, but because it was Pisa's principal claim to a protectorate over both Corsica and Sardinia. It was under the stimulus of rivalry with the Genoese for these islands that the account of the victories over Mugehid was elaborated in the annalistic tradition of Pisa. This process was already beginning in the early twelfth century. In the *Annales antiquissimi* and in the cathedral inscription, only the campaign of 1016 P.S. was mentioned.[230] In the *Fragmentum*, a second victory of 1017 P.S. had already been added, and with additional information which seems to indicate a legendary motif: that Mugehid immured living Sardinians in his fortifications.[231] The author of the *Liber* further elaborated the basic story, adding, for instance, the detail that Mugehid had been king of Denia and the Balearic Islands, a detail attested by Moslem chroniclers.[232] The importance of the victory over Mugehid for the author of the *Liber*, as for the poet of the cathedral inscription, was Pisa's consequent claim to the island.[233]

229.   In qua Pisani de Penis marte subactis
                 Annales recolunt votiva laude triumphos,   (ll. 161–62)
Both the *Annales antiquissimi* and the *Fragmentum* give the day of St. Sixtus.

230. Above, nn. 75, 77.

231. *RIS*², VI:2, 100. For the two battles with Mugehid, an Arabic source placed the conquest of Sardinia by Mugehid in the Moslem month that corresponded to August 19–September 17, 1015, and the expulsion of Mugehid toward the end of the Moslem year, which fell on June 9, 1016 (Amari, *Biblioteca*, p. 111). But these dates permit only one campaign for Mugehid. The Pisans and Genoese would have had time to arm and meet Mugehid in battle only in the spring of 1016. The two battles of 1016 and 1017 P.S., found in the *Fragmentum*, are explained if we remember that the Pisan year ended on March 24. The Italian ships probably left toward the end of the Pisan year, returning at the beginning of the next year. The *Annales antiquissimi* has only one battle, for 1016 P.S. The author of the *Fragmentum* probably found a notice of the victorious fleet's return in 1017 P.S. in another source. Without more precise dates, he assumed there had been two battles and two campaigns for Mugehid.

232. Line 924. See the note to this line.

233.   Indeque tota manent Pisanis subdita regna
                 Sardinie. docuere senes quecumque retexo.
                 Quesiti Sardi non hec tibi vera negabunt.   (ll. 959–61)

The epic adds further information after the second battle against Mugehid: the Moslem's wife and son were captured by the Pisans, and the son, Alanta, was sent to the German king, who gave the child to a favored Pisan, who returned him to Mugehid and entered into an Arabic brother-friendship with Mugehid. This friendship was retained in the Pisan family until a grandson of the original Pisan used this connection with the Moslem rulers of the Balearic Islands to gain an audience.[234] Such an account would appear to be legendary, the first of many similar embroideries which wove the backgrounds of leading Pisan families into the Pisan historical past, but the kernel of truth was considerable. It is known from Arabic sources that Mugehid was king of Denia and the Balearics, that he undertook an unsuccessful campaign to Sardinia in 1015–1016, and that in the campaign his son, Ali, was captured by the Pisans.[235] It is also known from German sources that Henry II received part of the plunder from this campaign through the good offices of the papacy.[236] These independent sources make no mention of the role of a particular Pisan family in these affairs, but it is difficult to imagine another source for the surprisingly accurate historical details known by the poet. It would seem that family traditions, at least in the twelfth century, were not as mendacious as they would later become.

The epic gives material for a treatment of Pisa's political organization for coping with the problems presented by the long and difficult campaign.[237] In the constitution of this expeditionary commune, the bishop assumed a role of leadership, a role that was based upon his feudal position at Pisa, upon his religious leadership—backed by the papacy and expressed in the religious nature of the crusade—and also based upon his moral leadership as the Pisan who could act above feuds and personal animosities. It is not surprising that he is found exhorting the crusaders at the most crucial moments of the campaign;[238] in the *Carmen*, Benedict

---

For the significant change in the punctuation of the middle line, for the period following instead of preceding "Sardinie," see Scalia, "*Oliverius e Rolandus*," p. 296, n. 31. For the cathedral inscription, see above, n. 75.

234. Lines 957, 962–68.

235. Amari, *Biblioteca*, pp. 91–92, 111–12.

236. Thietmar, *MGH, SS*, III, 850, where the expedition was organized by the papacy, while the Pisans were not mentioned by name. Of the booty, the pope "imperatori suam transmisit partem, quae mille libris computabatur." There is no mention of the son of the Saracen king.

237. G. Volpe has also made a political analysis in his review (above, n. 219) of Calisse's edition, *op. cit.*, pp. 96–114.

238. Lines 346–76, 795–850, 1575–89, 3281–92.

had played a similar role. The bishop was the moderator and the peace-maker, as he had been earlier in communal affairs in Pisa.[239] He was the final authority for relations between the commune of Pisa and other political powers. The treaty of alliance with the non-Italian rulers had to be deferred to the bishop;[240] and the Spanish and southern French counts would have regarded his power as more legitimate than the power of the Pisan magistrates. In the camp that was set up during the siege of Majorca, the *patres* were located near the tent of the bishop "so that they might more quickly come to him when they were often summoned."[241]

But the monarchy of the bishop was by no means absolute. Sympto-matic of his limited power was the fact that even the poet did not give the original concept of the expedition to the bishop but rather carefully stated that, on news of the continued piratical actions of the Moslems of the Balearic Islands, the elders of Pisa incited the youths to action, with the result that the bishop began to bestow the crusader crosses.[242]

The really commanding and decisive group among the Pisan cam-paigners was the *patres*. Unfortunately, the poet never stated with any precision who the "fathers" were, but, from his various suggestions, they seem to have included the officials of the commune: the consuls and some of the *proceres*, the nobility. This not fully definable group may be regarded as the consular aristocracy of the early commune, the restricted assembly of the wealthy, politically powerful, and socially supreme class which was the very basis of the emerging Italian communes.[243] The epic clearly shows that this was the assembly which made the plans and gave the com-mands, and that violations brought more than civil punishment. As the Pisans departed from Sardinia on the voyage to Spain, the *patres* gave leadership to two pilots, but "the commands of the *patres* lay disregarded, and order was turned upside down"[244] when each ship tried to out-

239.   Civibus hic presul multum de pace locutus,
              Plurima per paucos incassum semina fudit;
              Sed tamen e multis fructum percepit eorum. (ll. 208–10)
See Daimbert's act of mediation in F. Bonaini, *Statuti inediti della città di Pisa* (Florence, 1854), I, 16–18.
240. Lines 337–38.
241.   Ut citius veniant ad eum cum sepe vocentur. (l. 2096)
242. Lines 30–41. The Arab king sent a letter to the Pisans "In qua pontificem, patres, populumque salutat." (l. 889)
243. See Volpe, *Studi . . .* , pp. 128 ff.
244.   Iussa patrum contempta iacent, convertitur ordo. (l. 214)
In another instance, the ships land and the sailors go unarmed in search of booty "contempto patrum iussu" (l. 2674); as a consequence, some are cut off from the ships and slain.

distance the others. It seemed almost a natural consequence that the Pisan fleet was then overtaken by a great storm, which God finally decided to calm. Thus a violation of the orders of the *patres* was a violation of law and nature that brought speedy retribution.

The elected officials of the commune had been the consuls of Pisa since the last quarter of the eleventh century. For the Balearic campaign

> they empowered twelve men from the summit of the nobility, to whom was granted the power of consul and duke, so that they might zealously rule all men, that their interest might be pure and they might dispose of each of the military necessities, and also that in constructing the ships they might be able to lend aid, thus preparing men and fleet.[245]

In the subsequent account of the campaign, the consuls act both as military leaders and as judicial and administrative officials.

Along with the elected consuls appeared Ugo, the *vicecomes*. As in the *Carmen*, he enjoyed the special favor of the poet, who not only praised his military accomplishments but also made strong statements about his power in Pisa: "who presides over the Pisan city in place of the count."[246] Later, during the siege of Majorca, Ugo performed courageous deeds before the walls of the capital. For a short time he single-handedly held off the attack of the Moslems. In this courageous action he seemed to imitate the renown of his ancestor, celebrated at the siege of al Mahdiya. However, the later Visconte was not killed in the battle but lived to lead the final assault on the last remaining citadel.[247] It is significant that Ugo Visconte never played an overtly political role in the *Liber*.

The term *populus* was used, in one sense, to refer to all the Pisans, and in another sense to refer to the Pisans who were not to be counted among the *patres*. The assembled *populus* constituted the commune on the expedition, and there are frequent mentions of such assemblies at all crises of the campaign. As was usual with these assemblies in the early stage of the commune, the *populus* simply listened to the propositions or opinions of the leaders, and was then asked only for its approval. While the Pisans

245.   Inde duodenos de culmine nobilitatis
              Constituere viros, quibus est permissa potestas
              Consulis atque ducis, regerent ut gnaviter omnes,
              Purus et istorum disponens singula sensus
              Congrua militie, ratibus quoque conficiendis
              Queque iuvare queant homines classemque pararent. (ll. 49–54)

246.   At vice qui comitis Pisana presidet urbe, (l. 760, or)
              Ugo, qui Pisis comitum vice preditus extat, (l. 1403)

247. Lines 2825 *et seqq.*, 3315 *et seqq.*

were still in Spain—preparing for departure after the Luccans had threatened to withdraw and return home—one of the Pisan consuls proposed and received the oath of the citizens. The oath, as elsewhere throughout Europe in the early history of the commune, was the formal submission of the individual to the group and its goals.[248]

Another group in the commune was the clergy, and although in most instances the poet gave them only the duty of praying and exhorting, he had them bring about the decision at the critical moment. One incident illustrates this role of the clergy, as well as the composition of the popular assembly. The city of Majorca had been entered and only the inner fortress was yet to be taken. The Spanish lords counseled for a pact with the Moslems.

> While they are discussing such ideas, the people, quickly summoned into a single assembly, consider the peace treaty. . . . The clergy is present, even as are the noblemen. The greatest strife arises; the points of difference expose divided opinions. One side urges for the pact; another side longs for battle. The clergy encourages the men wishing to fight; the saintly pontiff along with the cardinal holds for battle; the ranks favor them.[249]

248.   Surgens Henricus post hec Vinithone creatus
Ortatur cives bellum firmare, priusque
Una cum patribus sese iurare fatetur.
Dicta fides sequitur, iurant equaliter omnes.   (ll. 683–86)

249.   Talia dum referunt, cetum properanter in unum
Accitus populus pacis de federe tractat. . . .
Clerus adest, proceresque simul, contentio crescit
Maxima, divisas pandunt certamina mentes.
Pars trahit ad pactum, pars diligit altera pugnam.
Collaudat clerus partem pugnare volentem,
Sanctus et antistes cum cardine prelia censet,
Hisque favent acies.   (ll. 3264–65, 3267–72)

I have taken the rather intriguing line 3266 out of sequence:

> Ecclesie pastor suscepit iura cathedre.

Calisse should have realized that his manuscript had omitted a line before this; namely, the line which appears in the later manuscripts:

> Fulgebatque dies qua plenus dogmate sancto

The "ecclesie pastor" is not be looked for among the crusaders; it is St. Peter. As the *Gesta* stated, the date of the assault directly after this conference was "solemnitate cathedre Apostolorum Principis" (*RIS*[2], VI:2, 93), that is, February 22. Scalia, "Per una riedizione critica," p. 89, has duly noted it as a revision but failed to remark its significance.

The Pisans finally decided upon complete victory. It will be remembered that the *Gesta* recounted the same incident, using the more specific term "canons" for the poet's "clergy." Thus on occasion the Pisan clergy could exert political as well as devotional influence.

In military matters the author distinguished between the knights and the footmen, *equites* and *pedites*. The first, naturally, were the nobility. And as the cathedral clergy were closely connected with this aristocratic class, the writer did not hesitate to fill his account by naming many individuals of this class and by noting their personal exploits. In the great pitched battle between the crusaders and the Moslems immediately after the landing at Majorca, he listed no less than sixty-four Pisan knights by name, often giving the family or father's name.[250] To give his account of this battle a classical flavor, the author paired each knight with a Moslem, for whom he composed a name. And yet there is an interesting passage in the account of the earlier campaign against Mugehid which seems to have been pointed against the knighthood of the poet's time:

> Then no one from the nobility was ashamed to force with his strength oars through the sea's waves. If the breeze had been slight or had given out, a common power provided for the desired courses.[251]

In his care and attention for naming the leading figures of the Pisan nobility the poet made his work the very expression of the aristocratic commune. Despite his exaltation of the nobility, the poet by no means disparaged the common soldier. There are long passages that describe the Pisans' skill in the construction of siege equipment, the *pedites* are always mentioned in the battles, and some commoners are mentioned by name. It was also observed that the knight on horseback was ineffective in entering the breached walls,[252] and that most of the fighting at close quarters was done by the foot soldiers.

Without doubt, the true heroes of the *Liber Maiorichinus* were the Pisan people, the "holy people."[253] Unlike the epics with which the poet was familiar, such as the *Aeneid*, though he names many individuals he does not give a characterization of any. The epithets are all stock phrases, none

250. Lines 1647–1967.
251.　　　　　Tunc non erubuit quisquam de nobilitate
　　　　　　　Viribus equoreas remos urguere per undas:
　　　　　　　Si levis extiterat vel tota remanserat aura,
　　　　　　　Optatos cursus robur commune replebat.　(ll. 930–33)
252. Lines 2262–64.
253.　　　　　"Pisanus populus Christi virtutibus auctus,"　(l. 266, and)
　　　　　　　Circuiens properat captam gens sancta per urbem,　(l. 3341)

give the individual a distinctive personality; and individuals are usually named in a frequency that is proportionate to their place in the political and social hierarchy. The ordinary Pisan knight is mentioned only once. The Pisan consuls and the counts are named about four times in specific incidents, as is Ugo Visconte. The person most frequently named by the poet is the bishop, Peter; however, after putting these details together we gain no real picture of the bishop. Nothing is mentioned of his appearance; nothing is given of his background or of his family. As were all other Pisans in the epic, he was simply the idealized personification of his office and the duties of his position.

The entire epic displays this schematic approach. The Moslems are evil, even if evil in different ways. The allies of the Pisans are good as long as they follow the Pisans. All the Pisans are good; there is not even any real dissension among the Pisan citizens. An instance of serious discord which had been mentioned by the author of the *Gesta* was suppressed by the poet of the *Liber Maiorichinus*.[254] Thus the author has elevated his account from a simple narrative of the expedition to a portrait of the activity of an ideal commune, Pisa, on an ideal campaign, a crusade.

The *Liber Maiorichinus* was the last and finest work to appear as a result of the short-lived but intense interest in historical writing which was awakened at Pisa around 1120. The epic brought to final development the characteristics of the historical writing of that period. Its authorship in the small group of the cathedral clergy of Pisa and the apparently intentional anonymity of its author also characterize the other works which we have considered. Its depiction of a close cooperation between secular and clerical leadership within the new commune is a further outgrowth of clerical pride in the new archiepiscopal dignity of the see of Pisa. Its idealization of Pisa's foreign campaigns into expeditions undertaken by the "imperial" power of Pisa—as the chosen people of God against the infidel—is the final elaboration of the crusading ideal.

For a brief period, a revitalization of the cathedral chapter, a new ecclesiastical dignity and leadership for the see of Pisa, and the strength of the crusading ideal had formed a favorable constellation for a flourishing of historical writing. By the middle of the century the reform stimulus which had aroused the cathedral chapter of Pisa had spent itself. The archbishop and the communal government were increasingly at odds over the leadership of Pisa, while the new archiepiscopal dignity was proving

254. The expedition had landed in Corsica at Capalbo, the last stopping point before its proposed arrival at Majorca: "Quo in loco fere omnibus discordantibus ad pacem reductis," *RIS*², VI:2, 90. Compare this with the lines quoted in n. 239 above.

to be illusory. The commune's foreign policy was engaged in serious rivalry with the nearly equal strength of Genoa and with the growing power of neighboring communes of the interior—as well as in the complexities of the imperial program of Frederick Barbarossa. Maragone, the Pisan chronicler of the second half of the century, shares in none of these characteristics of the earlier historical literature of Pisa. However, for a brief period, and at an earlier time than in most other Italian communes, the obscurity of the early development of communal Italy was dispelled by an awakening of historical interest which produced annals, inscriptions, and epics glorifying the deeds of medieval Pisa.

ANDREA BANCHI, FLORENTINE SILK MANUFACTURER AND MERCHANT IN THE FIFTEENTH CENTURY

Florence Edler de Roover

ANDREA BANCHI, FLORENTINE SILK MANUFACTURER AND MERCHANT IN THE FIFTEENTH CENTURY

Very little has been written about the Florentine silk industry. Pagnini, in his book, *Della Decima*, devotes almost twenty pages to the subject and quotes several passages from a fifteenth-century treatise on the production of silk fabrics which was published later (in 1868) with notes by Girolamo Gargiolli.[1] The following year another Gargiolli published the *libro segreto* of the silk merchant, Gregorio Dati, who died in 1435.[2] The statutes of the Arte di Por Santa Maria, to which all silk merchants and manufacturers belonged, were edited by Umberto Dorini, who also wrote a slender volume on the silk industry in all of Tuscany.[3] Dorini envisaged a larger work but he never carried out his project.

It has been repeatedly asserted that in the course of the fifteenth century the production of silk fabrics took the place of the manufacture of woolen cloth as Florence's leading industry. If so, it would seem that this development merits detailed study. In the guild statutes, communal legislation, and other official records there is probably enough material for a study similar to the important study of Alfred Doren on the woolen industry.[4] But the modern economic historian is not content to limit himself to official records. He knows that these give a somewhat unrealistic picture of an industry because guild and communal statutes deal only with regulation and overlook anything that is not susceptible to regulation. What is needed to supplement them are business records: account books and letters of manufacturers. These are fairly plentiful in Florentine archives for the woolen industry, but Doren failed to use them. They are less numerous for the silk industry; however, several sets of related account books for the fifteenth and later centuries are extant.

1. Gian Francesco Pagnini, *Della Decima e di varie altre gravezze imposte dal Comune di Firenze, della moneta e della mercatura de' fiorentini fino al secolo XVI* (Lisbon-Lucca, 1765–66), II, 106–24; *L'arte della seta in Firenze: trattato del secolo XV*, ed. Girolamo Gargiolli (Florence, 1868).

2. *Il libro segreto di Gregorio Dati*, ed. Carlo Gargiolli (Bologna, 1869).

3. *Statuti dell'Arte di Por Santa Maria del tempo della Repubblica*, ed. Umberto Dorini (Florence, 1934); U. Dorini, *L'arte della seta in Toscana* (Florence, 1928). Another brief study is by Piero Pieri, *Intorno alla storia dell'arte della seta in Firenze* (Bologna, 1927).

4. Alfred Doren, *Studien aus der Florentiner Wirtschaftsgeschichte*, I, *Die Florentiner Wollentuchindustrie vom XIV. bis zum XVI. Jahrhundert* (Stuttgart, 1901).

Probably the most interesting set for the fifteenth century is that of the silk merchant and manufacturer, Andrea di Francesco Banchi. Eighteen volumes dealing with his business and private affairs from 1425 until 1467 have survived. Banchi died in 1462 but his partnership was continued for five more years, as he provided in his testament. The books are found in the archive of the Spedale degli Innocenti, in Florence.[5] This foundling hospital or orphanage was created and supported by the guild of silk merchants. As a result, it became the custom for some merchants, especially those who died without heirs, to make substantial legacies or even to leave their entire estates to the hospital. This custom explains the presence of merchant account books in the hospital's archive.

ANDREA BANCHI'S CAREER

Andrea Banchi belonged to a family of silk merchants (*setaioli*). His grandfather, Banco di Ser Bartolo, matriculated in 1328 as a *setaiolo* in the Arte di Por Santa Maria, or the Arte della Seta (Silk Guild).[6] All of Banco's six sons joined the guild, but the three eldest died early and without heirs. Andrea's father, Francesco, the fifth son, became a member of the Silk Guild on July 24, 1364, and served as consul of the guild in 1378.[7] He and his two brothers, Lodovico and Michele, owned three adjoining shops (*botteghe*) in Via di Por Santa Maria, where most of the silk shops were located.[8]

Andrea di Francesco di Banco was born September 20, 1372, and lived to be a nonagenarian, dying on October 12, 1462. Nothing is known about his early years. His father and his uncle Lodovico both died of the plague in 1390. Andrea probably worked from 1390 onward for his only surviving uncle, Michele. On February 4, 1401, while his uncle was consul

5. Archivio dello Spedale degli Innocenti di Firenze, Estranei, 73–88, 645. "Estranei" is the term applied to all the records of outsiders that came into this archive, chiefly through bequests, and it will be used henceforth without repeating Archivio. . . . I wish to thank Dr. Gino Corti for calling my attention to the Banchi account books and for his considerable aid in research and transcription.

6. Archivio di Stato, Florence (henceforth ASF), Arte della Seta, No. 7 (Matricole, 1328–1433), fol. 16.

7. *Ibid.*, fol. 62*v*.

8. *Bottega* means both a shop where finished goods are sold and a workshop where production takes place or where raw materials are issued to workers for processing. *Fondaco* has several meanings, but in the Banchi records it meant a rather large storeroom and work area from which materials were apparently issued to workers. Andrea Banchi eventually had both a *bottega* and a *fondaco*.

of the guild, Andrea applied for membership as a *setaiolo* and was matriculated on April 28.[9] Andrea apparently continued to work for his uncle, possibly as a junior partner, until Michele's death in 1413.

Since his uncle Michele left only minor sons, Andrea turned to other relatives to find a partner. He chose a first cousin once removed, ten years his junior, Priore, son of Mariotto di Lodovico Banchi. Their partnership was for three or four years and was renewed once. It probably did business in the shop Andrea had inherited from his father. For unknown reasons the partnership was dissolved by the end of 1420, rather abruptly. What the capital was and whether there were any profits is not known. In his private ledger (*libro segreto*) Andrea stated that by January 1, 1421, he was to receive as his share of the liquidation 4,054 florins.[10] However, the liquidation dragged on longer than expected. By 1425 he had received only 3,819 florins; further payments were made through 1432, as the last receivables were slowly collected.[11]

Andrea was probably wise to separate from his cousin Priore since the latter did not have the making of a successful businessman. He went into partnership with other relatives, failed, and lost most of his estate.

While in partnership with Priore, Andrea married—perhaps in 1418. His wife, Dianora, whose family name has not been found, brought him a dowry of 1,025 florins, which was fairly high.[12] Their first child, a daughter christened Beatrice and called Bice, was born in 1419; a second daughter, Caterina, arrived in 1424; and a son, Piero, followed in 1427. A son and a daughter born later both died in infancy. The family lived on the left bank of the Arno in the Via de' Bardi in the parish of Santa Lucia de' Magnoli.

From 1421 until 1428 Andrea Banchi carried on without a partner. In the shop in Via Por S. Maria he sold silks at retail. Soon he began producing silk fabrics as well. References to industrial account books in his early catasto reports, especially the Book of Weavers (Libro di tessitori), make this clear.

According to Andrea's return (*portata*) for the tax (*catasto*) of 1427, the taxable value of his property, including real estate, shares in the public debt (*Monte Comune*), and business investments (after a deduction of 1,000

9. ASF, Arte della Seta, 7, fol. 15v.
10. Estranei, 73, Libro segreto d'Andrea Banchi proprio, fol. 3.
11. *Ibid.*
12. That dowries of 1,000 florins or more were a sign of superior means in the early 1400's is pointed out by Lauro Martines, *The Social World of the Florentine Humanists* (Princeton, 1963), pp. 199–200, 204.

florins for five mouths [*bocche*]), was 7,441 florins, on which he was taxed 37 florins 10s. 2d. *a oro*.[13] This placed him in the upper 2 per cent of the taxpayers, which means that he had been quite successful in business and had accumulated a small fortune. Of course, he was no longer young, having reached the age of fifty-five. In addition to his house in the Via de' Bardi and his shop in Via Por S. Maria, Andrea's real estate consisted of a farm in the parish of Montaguto Pegolotti, near Grassina, and one at Sant'Elero di Putigliolo on the Ema Torrente. He also listed a piece of land with a small house in Santa Maria all'Antella.

He reported that his capital in the silk shop amounted to 5,202 florins, plus 413 florins 14s. 10d. in accumulated profits. He estimated his profits from January to July, 1427, at 200 florins, which was probably too low.

TABLE 1

SILK MANUFACTURERS TAXED 25 FLORINS OR MORE IN THE
1427 CATASTO (IN FLORINS)

Manufacturer	Taxable Wealth	Tax
1. Francesco di Francesco della Luna	34,987	175
2. Benedetto di Giuliano di Bartolo Gini . . .	27,601	138
3. Parente di Michele di Ser Parente	13,448	67
4. Andrea di Francesco Banchi	7,441	37
5. Bernardo di Bartolomeo del Benino	6,785	34
6. Giovanni d'Andrea Minerbetti	5,777	29

SOURCE: Biblioteca Nazionale, Florence, MSS Magl. XIII.72.2, fols. 34v–36v; Lauro Martines, *The Social World of the Florentine Humanists*, pp. 369, 372, 373, 375, 376.

According to the records of this first catasto, there were between forty-five and fifty silk shops, with partnerships outnumbering single proprietorships almost three to one.[14] At this time very few *setaioli* were richer than Banchi, for only three were assessed more than he. The wealthiest *setaiolo* was Francesco della Luna; next came Benedetto Gini; third in rank was Parente di Michele di Ser Parente (Table 1).

Banchi's capital investment in his business was higher than that of most silk manufacturers in 1427, yet he was in business alone and did not

13. ASF, Archivio del Catasto, No. 64 (Quart. S. Spirito, Gonfalon Scala, 1427), fols. 18v–20. The catasto was a combined property and income tax for which very detailed returns had to be filed by the heads of households. Attached to many *portate* are financial statements of business firms.

14. Pagnini (*Della Decima*, IV, xxiv) states that there were more than forty-five silk shops in 1427; my list totals forty-seven.

have to share profits with partners nor pay interest on any deposits, as was the practice in Florence. One of the silk firms, Bartolo di Domenico Corsi and Company, had a capital of 8,600 florins and an additional 1,000 florins in deposits. There were four partners, three Corsi brothers and Bernardo di Bartolomeo Gherardi.[15] The firm of Benedetto Gini (Table 1) had a capital of 5,400 florins, and three partners.[16] Many partnerships had a capital of about 3,000 florins, including Piero d'Adoardo de' Bardi and Company, Tommaso e Simone di Lapo Corsi and Company, and Gregorio di Stagio Dati and Company. Numerous others had a capital of around 2,000 florins. These are all firms of *setaioli grossi*, who were producing silk cloth. A retail silk merchant (*setaiolo minuto*) might have only 200 or 300 florins of capital; for example, in 1427 Lorenzo di Bartolo di Segna had 300 florins invested in his retail silk shop.[17]

Like other merchants of his time, Andrea Banchi acquired farms and other real estate as he prospered. Between 1440 and 1446 he purchased six farms (*poderi*), seven pieces of land and a vineyard, a house next to his residence in Via dei Bardi, and a storeroom or warehouse (*fondaco*) near his silk shop, the latter from a luckless cousin, Mariotto di Mariotto di Lodovico Banchi.[18] On one of the pieces of land, at Montaguto Pegolotti, purchased in August, 1444, for 60 florins, Banchi built a castlelike villa called La Rocca.

During the 1420's Andrea lent various sums of money to businessmen in the form of *depositi a discrezione*: 400 florins to Andrea de' Pazzi and Company, international merchants; 350 florins to Gabriello Panciatichi; and 300 florins to Matteo di Bartolo Boni, *setaiolo*.[19] On all of these loans,

15. ASF, Catasto, 72 (S. Croce, Leon Nero, 1427), fols. 41, 115*v*, 167*v* (tax declarations of three brothers).

16. Catasto, 66 (S. Spirito, Ferza, 1427), fols. 33–37 (Benedetto Gini), and Catasto, 31 (S. Croce, Bue, 1427), fols. 640–45 (Gini's partner, Luca di Matteo da Panzano). The third partner was Leonardo di Ridolfo de' Bardi. The capital is also given in Carlo Carnesecchi, "Un fiorentino del secolo XV e le sue ricordanze domestiche," *Archivio storico italiano*, Ser. 5, IV (1889), 153.

17. ASF, Catasto, 72 (S. Croce, Leon Nero, 1427), fol. 283, report of Bartolo di Segna and his son Lorenzo.

18. Estranei, 73, fols. 14, 27–30, 32–35. Most of the land purchased was south of Florence in the vicinity of Grassina, but some was northwest near Campi Bisenzio on the way to Prato. The house next to his residence cost 500 florins, the *fondaco* 750 florins, and the farms varied in price from 200 to 380 florins. Altogether, land purchased outside the city represented 2,208 florins.

19. Estranei, 73, fols. 2, 3. "Deposits at discretion" meant that the rate of interest would be determined by the borrower and that no interest might be paid if earnings were low or if there was a loss instead of a profit. Such loans were not regarded as usurious because of the element of risk, although some strict theologians condemned them.

or deposits, Banchi received 8 per cent annual interest. In 1425 and 1426 he had 700 florins with his bankers, Vanni di Niccolò di Ser Vanni and Company, to be kept on exchange and reexchange with Venice (*cambium ad Venetias*), a transaction frowned upon by the theologians as palliate usury.[20]

In 1428 Banchi decided to expand his business activities. As an independent merchant-entrepreneur, he continued the production and sale of silk cloth. In addition, he formed a partnership with Piero d'Andrea Petrini to carry on a retail shop dealing in silk goods.

The partnership began April 15, 1428, and was to be of three years' duration, according to the articles of association.[21] It was frequently renewed, so that it lasted almost twenty years—until the death of Petrini late in 1446. Andrea Banchi contributed 600 florins to the capital and Piero Petrini 200 florins. Piero, only twenty-four years old, was to devote his full time to running the shop. Andrea would direct policy but was not required to spend any time in the shop. Profits and losses were to be divided equally.

Probably because Andrea had found the shop he owned in Por S. Maria somewhat small for his stock of raw silks, goods in process, and finished fabrics, he decided to install Petrini in this shop and to rent a larger one for himself. The partnership was charged 45 florins annual rent for Banchi's shop, and Andrea leased another *bottega* in the same street from Domenico Pollini for 50 florins per year.[22]

The silk shop of the partnership opened for business on May 1, 1428, and prospered under young Petrini's management. Profits were divided at irregular intervals, but about every two or three years. As Table 2 shows, they steadily increased until 1442, and then they declined. Banchi did not withdraw any of his profits but plowed them back into the business, until the early 1440's. In 1439 the total amount invested in the shop was about 9,000 florins, a considerable sum.

Andrea di Guglielmo Pazzi was the twelfth richest man in Florence according to the catasto returns of 1427, and Gabriello di Messer Bartolomeo Panciatichi was the third wealthiest (Martines, *Social World*, p. 369). Matteo Boni had two partners and had been a silk merchant since the beginning of the century. He rented the shop next to Andrea Banchi's, which belonged to the heirs of Banchi's uncle Lodovico (ASF, Catasto, 79 [S. Giovanni, Drago, 1427], fols. 43–45).

20. Estranei, 73, fol. 2. On *cambium ad Venetias*, a form of dry exchange, see Raymond de Roover, "Cambium ad Venetias: Contribution to the History of Foreign Exchange," *Studi in onore di Armando Sapori* (Milan, 1957), pp. 631–48.

21. Estranei, 73, fol. 4. None of the partnership's account books are extant, but Banchi summarized the partnership agreement and recorded profits in his personal *libro segreto*.

22. Estranei, 73, fols. 4, 5; ASF, Catasto, 393 (S. Spirito, Scala, 1430), fol. 2v.

TABLE 2

ANDREA BANCHI'S SHARE OF THE PROFITS OF HIS PARTNERSHIP
WITH PIERO PETRINI

Period		Duration	Banchi's Share (one half)		
Beginning	Ending	(Months)	Florins	s.	d.
May 1, 1428	Oct. 31, 1429	18	260	9	3
Nov. 1, 1429	May 19, 1431	19	460	16	4
May 20, 1431	May 31, 1432	12	403	5	0
June 1, 1432	Oct. 31, 1434	29	1,806	16	0
Nov. 1, 1434	Dec. 31, 1436	26	3,253	6	11
Jan. 1, 1437	Dec. 31, 1438	24	3,020	15	1
		128	9,205	8	7
Jan. 1, 1439	Dec. 31, 1441	36	5,063	7	9
Jan. 1, 1442	Dec. 31, 1444	36	4,140	3	4
Jan. 1, 1445	Dec. 31, 1446	24	1,806	17	9
		224	20,215	17	5

SOURCE: Archivio dello Spedale degli Innocenti, Florence, Estranei No. 73, Libro segreto d'Andrea Banchi proprio, fols. 4, 9, 27.

After years of having conducted his silk manufacturing enterprise alone, Banchi took a partner in 1433, when he was sixty-one. The reason was probably that the management of a silk establishment was becoming too heavy a burden at his age; and he had been ill for several months. The partner was Bernardo dalla Palla, whose father, Marco di Bernardo, was a druggist (*speziale*). Bernardo had been in the employ of Banchi at least since 1425. When the partnership was formed, on August 15, 1433, Bernardo was almost thirty years of age. Unfortunately, he lived only six years longer, dying in September, 1439. After his partner's death, Banchi again carried on alone—with the help, that is, of faithful employees, two of whom he eventually admitted to partnership in 1454.

To the partnership with Bernardo dalla Palla, Banchi contributed 2,500 florins, and Bernardo only his services.[23] Whether the latter's share in the profits was less than half is not clear. In his libro segreto Andrea gives only the profits he himself received: from August 15, 1433, until September 15, 1435, 1,767 florins, and for the four years from September 15, 1435, until September 15, 1439, 2,564 florins—an average of 641 florins per year.[24] These profit figures are considerably lower than those

23. Estranei, 73, fol. 13.

24. *Ibid.* When the partnership with Bernardo dalla Palla began, in 1433, Banchi opened a new general ledger, "Libro rosso C," which is extant (Estranei, 83), and a *libro segreto* for this partnership in which full details regarding profits were entered. The latter book has not survived.

for the retail shop for the same years (Table 2). But whereas Banchi left his profits in the partnership with Petrini, he drew against the profits of the manufacturing firm for living expenses, taxes, and so on.

Piero Petrini, who managed the retail shop, died in December, 1446, but the silk shop had been too successful for Andrea Banchi to liquidate it. Instead, he formed a partnership with Piero's two brothers, Giovanni, age forty, and Zanobi Petrini, age thirty-two.[25] Andrea did not appear as a partner. In his place was his son Piero, who was twenty years old in 1447. The new Petrini partners may have been employed in the silk shop during their elder brother's lifetime.

We do not know how successful the new partnership was, because no account books for it are extant and there are no entries for its profits in Andrea Banchi's libro segreto. His son Piero probably began a private ledger in which such entries were made; unfortunately, however, Piero Banchi died in August, 1453, a great blow to his father,[26] and the partnership was dissolved. By 1454 Andrea Banchi had given up the shop he had been renting since 1428 and had moved back into his own shop. He was also using the nearby storeroom (*fondaco*) in Via Vacchereccia which he had purchased in 1440 for 750 florins.[27]

The Petrini brothers moved to Rome, where they opened a silk shop, and Andrea Banchi furnished them with some goods which they were to sell for him on a commission basis. Apparently, they could not get along without Banchi's constant advice. By April, 1455, the Petrini were doing so poorly in Rome that Banchi sent a trusted employee, Benvenuto di Francesco Nuti, to take possession of the goods belonging to Banchi, to try to sell at least some of them, and to collect as many receivables as possible. Nuti was to keep half of the profits from the outstanding accounts he collected.[28]

---

25. Estranei, 83, Libro rosso C, fols. 30–32; ASF, Catasto, 687 (S. Spirito, Scala, 1451), fol. 504 (Andrea Banchi's report).

26. Piero had married (September 10, 1452) Alessandra, daughter of Luigi di Messer Lorenzo Ridolfi, but the couple was childless. Andrea Banchi was so deeply affected by his son's death that in December, 1453, he made plans to leave the bulk of his fortune to the foundling hospital—and even to enter the institution and serve there for the remainder of his life (Archivio Spedale degli Innocenti, Ser. X, No. 1: Contratti dal 1435 al 1459, fols. 87–89).

27. Banchi's shop was on the east side of Via Por Santa Maria between Via Lambertesca and Via Vacchereccia, the third shop from the latter street. The fondaco, facing on Via Vacchereccia, and near the corner of Via Por S. Maria, extended behind Banchi's shop, so that it was possible to connect the two by a doorway.

28. Estranei, 83, Libro rosso C, fols. 166, 168, 169.

In 1454 Andrea Banchi formed his last partnership, which was carried on for five years after his death, in 1462, according to a provision in his testament. His partners were two employees whom he had trained and of whose ability he was reasonably certain. One was Bernardo di Dato di Bernardo Dati, who had worked first in the silk shop of Piero Petrini and Company, in which Banchi was a partner. Bernardo's father was a strap-maker (*correggiaio*), and from his catasto declarations we learn that Bernardo was born about 1412.[29] Thus in 1454, when he became a junior partner, he was already over forty years of age. The other partner, Bartolomeo d'Andrea di Domenico, a few years younger than Dati, had been employed by Banchi since 1433. From October, 1436, to October, 1437, his salary was 22 florins. The following year it was increased to 30, and eventually to 50 florins.[30]

The partnership was formed on May 15, 1454, to last three years, and it was renewed several times.[31] At first the capital was 5,600 florins; and Banchi's share was 4,800 florins in goods and cash. Each junior partner contributed 400 florins, which were advanced to them by Banchi and were to be repaid from their shares of the profits without interest charges.[32] A year later Banchi added another 200 florins in the name of Bernardo Dati, and Bartolomeo was able to contribute an additional 200 florins himself.[33] In 1455, then, the *corpo* or capital was 6,000 florins. In addition, Banchi had a *sopraccorpo* (deposit above the capital) which by May 15, 1457, amounted to 1,142 florins, on which he received 8 per cent interest per year in the *saldo*, or division of profits, of that date—204 florins were added to the principal.[34]

Andrea was to receive two-thirds of the profits and each of the others one-sixth. As appears in Table 3, profits amounted to about 2,591 florins in the six years from 1454 to 1460, an average of 436 florins per year or a return of less than 8 per cent, not a very satisfactory result.

During the first year of the partnership Bernardo Dati journeyed several times to Aquila where he succeeded in making good sales to

29. ASF, Catasto, 489 (S. Spirito, Ferza, 1433), fols. 177–78; 610 (Ferza, 1442), fol. 436 (reports of Dato di Bernardo Dati).

30. Estranei, 83, fols. 24–25.

31. To celebrate the formation of this new partnership in 1454, seventy barrels of wine from Banchi's vineyards were distributed free among the silk workers (*ai manifattori di bottega*). Estranei, 83, fol. 167.

32. Estranei, 77, Libro segreto segnato A d'Andrea Banchi, Bernardo Dati e Bartolomeo d'Andrea, compagni insieme all'arte della seta in Porta Santa Maria, fols. 1–7.

33. *Ibid.*, fols. 6, 7.

34. *Ibid.*, fol. 5.

mercers, sometimes bartering silk products for Abruzzi raw silk. Banchi decided it would be worthwhile to have someone stationed in Aquila. In August, 1455, an *accomanda* or *accomandita*, a partnership with limited liability, was formed by Andrea Banchi and Company with another employee of long standing, Benvenuto di Francesco Nuti, age thirty-three. Mention has already been made that in April, 1455, when Banchi terminated his relations with the Petrini brothers in Rome, Nuti had taken over the goods belonging to the Banchi firm. He had spent a few months in Rome the preceding year, on salary from the firm, to sell silks before the Petrini shop was opened. In two months he had sold silk cloth and

TABLE 3

PROFITS OF BANCHI'S PARTNERSHIP WITH BERNARDO DATI
AND BARTOLOMEO D'ANDREA

Period	Total f. s.d.	Banchi's Share (2/3) f. s. d.	Each Partner's Share (1/6) f. s. d.
May 15, 1454, to May 15, 1457 .	1373. 5.0	915.10.0	228.17.6
May 15, 1457, to May 18, 1460 .	1222.13.6	815. 2.4	203.15.7
	2595.18.6	1730.12.4	432.13.1

SOURCE: Archivio dello Spedale degli Innocenti, Estranei, 77, Libro segreto A of Andrea Banchi and Company, fols. 5, 6, 7, 21.

belts amounting to more than 400 florins.[35] Nuti had shown enough managerial and sales ability that the firm decided to entrust him with the opening of what was virtually a branch in Aquila.

The capital of the accomanda was to be 1,600 florins in cash and goods: 800 florins invested by the Banchi partnership and 800 by Andrea Banchi himself, with Nuti contributing only his services. The firm was to be called Benvenuto di Francesco Nuti and Company, and the accomanda was to last three years, until August 8, 1458. On that date it was renewed, and again in 1461.

The contract gave Nuti a free hand to deal in any goods that seemed profitable, but he could not give credit to a nobleman or ruler without

35. Estranei, 84, Libro rosso A di Andrea Banchi e compagni (1454–58), fol. 3; Estranei, 74, Giornale e Ricordanze A, fols. 2, 28. Nuti had been sent to Rome as early as 1450 to collect receivables on silks sold by Banchi's agent, Giusto di Vieri Guidi, who had just died. The procuration given to Benvenuto Nuti is dated October 29, 1450 (ASF, Notarile antecosimiano, S. 642, Ser Silvano Frosini, atti del 1450 al 1451, fols. 152v–53v).

good security—or any related loss would be charged to him personally. All expenses for rent and living were to be charged to the accomanda. Nuti could employ one shop boy (*fanciulletto*) of Aquila, but other employees, if needed, would be sent from Florence; thus Banchi's second grandson, Francesco Ginori, after a year's experience in his grandfather's shop, was sent to Aquila at the age of sixteen. Nuti could draw 40 florins per year for his needs (*per suoi bisogni*). He was not to take up any money by bills of exchange or at interest (*non possi torre danari a chosto o chanbio*) without special permission. Nor was he to lend money to anyone. All this has a familiar ring because of similar provisions in Medici articles of association.[36]

Of the profits or losses, Benvenuto would receive one-fourth. The remaining three-fourths was to be divided equally, half to Andrea Banchi personally and half to the Banchi partnership. When the accomanda was renewed in 1458 no change was made in the division of profits, but two years later, in September, 1460, Benvenuto's share was increased to one-third.[37]

One of Nuti's account books for this accomanda still exists. It is a book of sales and purchases for the entire period of the accomanda and it shows that Nuti sold most of the silk goods he received from the Banchi firm at different fairs: Castel di Sangro, Lanciano, and Sermona (modern Sulmona) in the Abruzzi, and Recanati in the Marches.[38] Besides ribbons and belts, the fairs were a good outlet for vestments and altar cloths. The Banchi firm had the vestments made in Florence from its silks by two vestment-makers, Cristofano and Tommaso d'Antonio.[39] Nuti used part of the proceeds of these sales to purchase raw silk from the Abruzzi and from Calabria.

36. A copy of the *accomanda* contract with Nuti is in Ricordanze C (Estranei, 76), fols. 270*v*–71. For Medici contracts, see Raymond de Roover, *The Rise and Decline of the Medici Bank, 1397–1494* (Cambridge, 1963), pp. 86–90.

37. A note stating the increase is added at the end of the copy of the contract (Estranei, 76, fol. 271).

38. Estranei, 645, *passim*. The title page has this description of the contents: "Questo libro si è di Benvenuto di Francesco Nuti e compagni d'Aquila, dove terrà il conto del taglio e vendite e compere. . . ."

39. A vestment-maker is called a *banderaio*, a word easily confused with the term for a banner-maker (*bandieraio*). Cristofano was apparently employed only in the summer of 1458 (Estranei, 83, Libro rosso C, fol. 183, and Estranei, 75, Ricordanze B, fol. 164), whereas Tommaso d'Antonio did work for Banchi over a period of thirty years. He was paid £2 *picc.* (see n. 44), for each cope or chasuble he cut and sewed (Estranei, 84, Libro rosso A, fol. 179; Estranei, 86, Libro bianco B, fol. 16).

Liturgical vestments yielded a handsome profit—12 to 20 per cent for silk and around 30 per cent for brocaded fabrics—but the sales were limited. On smaller articles the mark-up was lower; some even sold at a loss. A *saldo*, or profit-and-loss statement, was not drawn for three and a half years, not until December, 1458; total profits were not high, only 171 florins—an average of 49 florins per year, a rather poor showing. But in the next two years Nuti was more successful, so that by September, 1460, when the second saldo was prepared, the total net profits were 158 florins for 20½ months, or 105 florins a year. Banchi was sufficiently pleased with the returns to increase Nuti's share of the profits from one-fourth to one-third, as already mentioned. This encouragement resulted in a tremendous increase in the profits—or were times better and profitable sales easier? In any case, the third saldo, prepared 13 months and 20 days later (October 27, 1461), showed a total net profit of 543 florins 15s. a oro.[40]

After Banchi's death the accomanda with Benvenuto Nuti was slowly liquidated, and Nuti returned some of the goods he felt could not be sold. In June, 1463, an agent was sent from Florence to Aquila to make an inventory of the remainder of the stock belonging to the partnership and to sell as much of it as possible. The inventory is found in Nuti's book of sales and purchases; it shows there were four brocaded chasubles, two damask copes, two tunicles, one altar cloth, two brocaded crimson belts, and several remnants.[41] Three chasubles, a cope, and a belt were sold in this final liquidation. A few items were consigned to Lorenzo d'Agnolo Biliotti, another Florentine merchant in Aquila, to sell on commission,[42] and the others were sent back to Florence. Nuti then moved to Pesaro, where he acted as a commission agent for Florentine merchants who sent him goods to be taken to the different fairs.

When the final accounts were prepared, Nuti was unable to return all of the capital he had received, so that a loss of 272 florins 18s. 3d. had to be recorded—one-third of which was charged to Nuti, one-third to the heirs of Andrea Banchi, and one-third to the partnership, which was still carrying on.[43] But even with this final loss the accomanda for Aquila had been a profitable outlet for many of the products of the silk partnership.

40. All these profit figures are in the secret account book of the partnership (Estranei, 77), fol. 20. The account is entitled "Benvenuto di Francesco Nuti d'Aquila per l'accomanda."

41. Estranei, 645, fol. 155.

42. *Ibid.*, fol. 155*v*.

43. Estranei, 77, fol. 20.

MANUFACTURING PROCESS

Bookkeeping and General Organization

The private libro segreto of Andrea Banchi and the one for the last partnership (1454–1462) have permitted us to outline Banchi's business career, the partnerships he formed, and the profits he reaped. However, they do not enable us to enter his silk shop and storeroom to see what raw materials he purchased and from whom; to know how production was organized, how many workers were employed, and what they were paid; and to have an accurate idea of the silk fabrics he produced, how many, and how they were sold.

Some of this information can be gathered from the other Banchi account books in the Spedale degli Innocenti, although the sets are unfortunately incomplete. Three ledgers have been preserved: the Libro rosso segnato C, which covers the period 1437 to 1454, and two ledgers that belong to the last Banchi partnership and cover successively the entire period of the partnership, 1454 to 1467, the Libro rosso A and the Libro bianco B. The books for this last period are the more complete. Besides the two ledgers and the libro segreto of the partnership are three journals (*giornali e ricordanze*), two cash books (*entrata e uscita*), two *quaderni di cassa* (which are not just cash books but small ledgers that also contain petty merchandise expense accounts and accounts with bankers), one letter book (*Registro di lettere*, 1462–1465), and several auxiliary books. One of the auxiliary books is entitled Entrata di lavori e mercatanzie, in which is recorded all the finished silk cloth brought from the looms and the names of the purchasers, beginning in May, 1460. There is also a Book of Shipments (Mandate di mercatanzie, 1456–1457) and a precious Book of Weavers (Libro di tessitori B), which contains not only the accounts with weavers but also those with throwsters, dyers, and warpers for the years 1458–1462.

Unfortunately, three auxiliary books that contain the accounts of workers are lost: the Libro di maestre di seta cruda, with the accounts of women who worked on inferior silk from perforated cocoons and spun it into thread; the Libro di maestre di seta cotta, with the accounts of the women silk winders; and the Libro di maestre e manifattori di fette, with accounts for the men and women who wove ribbons and belts.

Because of the loss of these auxiliary books, it is impossible to give full information about wages and production costs. However, the *saldi* or general financial statements prepared in 1457 and 1460 give some of the data necessary for forming an idea of the number of persons employed.

Andrea Banchi did not use double entry bookkeeping. The chief difficulty seems to have been that the woolen and the silk manufacturers dealt in two different currencies: they bought raw materials and sold their finished products in gold florins, but they paid their workers in *lire di piccioli*, or silver currency,[44] and there was no fixed ratio between the two currencies. The ledgers and libri segreti are kept in bilateral form; that is, the debits and credits of each account are on facing pages. Usually the entries give a cross-reference to another page in the ledger—in the *quaderno di cassa* or in one of the auxiliary books. However, there are no accounts for operating results. To determine profits, Banchi and his partners had to go to the trouble of making a detailed inventory and then preparing a *saldo*, or general financial statement. Profits were not determined by balancing and closing the books but by the more laborious process of deducting liabilities and initial investment from assets (receivables, cash, and inventories of raw materials, goods in process, and finished products).

Mention of the special auxiliary account books, such as the Book of Weavers, can also be found in the Florentine treatise on the silk industry, Trattato dell'arte della seta.[45] It contains sample pages from an unnamed silk manufacturer's accounts of the year 1453.

The Florentine silk industry was not carried on in factories in the modern sense but was organized according to the putting-out system. The master manufacturer bought the raw materials, sold the finished product, and controlled all phases of the manufacturing process in between. He distributed the materials to be worked on by craftsmen or small masters in their own homes or in small establishments. These materials were returned to the manufacturer's shop after each successive operation. In order to control the quality of the work done and to prevent "cabbaging"

---

44. *Lire di piccioli* will henceforth be abbreviated £ picc.
45. See note 1. Henceforth cited as *Trattato della seta*.

or pilfering, all materials were inspected and weighed as they went out and came in.[46]

Warpers and weavers are good examples of craftsmen. Throwsters and dyers are examples of small masters who operated their own establishments, in which they probably employed one or more assistants.

The silk industry was highly specialized but it involved fewer steps than the woolen industry. The major steps in the silk industry were throwing, boiling, dyeing, warping, and weaving. There was no finishing process as in the woolen industry. After each step, except weaving, the silk was either wound or reeled.

Raw Materials: Silk and Metallic Threads

As raw material, Andrea Banchi used chiefly raw silk, besides metallic threads needed for brocades. What were the sources of his raw materials?

The Caspian Sea region, especially the southern and western shores, which had been the chief source of supply for silk to medieval Lucca, was still very important in the fifteenth century.[47] In some years the Banchi firm supplied more than one-third of its annual needs with *seta stravai*, *seta leggi*, and occasionally *seta talani*, all terms for silk from the Caspian Sea area.[48] These silks were of medium price: in quantities of 200 pounds or more the *leggi* was purchased for about 2 florins and 5s. per pound, the *stravai* and *talani* for 2 florins 10s. per pound. These were the prices for cash payment or credit up to four months. In barter transactions the

46. Most operations in silk manufacturing resulted in small losses of weight. Tables of allowable reductions in weight were issued by the Silk Guild and were used constantly by the manufacturers. Only a few examples of theft or loss of materials have been found in the Banchi account books. In August, 1454, Bruno di Piero and Company, dyers, were debited 2 florins 14s. for 10 ounces of *stravai* silk which was apparently stolen from the dyehouse (*che gli fu tolta di bottegha*), Estranei, 74, Ricordanze A, fol. 31. Late in 1456 the weaver Meo d'Antonio da Bogoli was charged for the loss 3 of ounces of beige weft threads for one damask cloth and for 3 ounces of black weft threads for another damask, a total value of one florin 15s. After the second theft he no longer wove for Banchi (Estranei, 84, Libro rosso A, fol. 137). Domenico di Michele was charged 3½ florins in 1460 for 12 ounces of vermilion weft threads which disappeared from his home while he was weaving a brocaded velvet (Estranei, 85, Libro tessitori B, fol. 117).

47. For the silk industry in Lucca, see my study, "Lucchese Silks," *Ciba Review*, No. 80 (June, 1950), pp. 2902–30.

48. *Stravai* silk came from Asterabad, at the southeastern corner of the Caspian Sea; *leggi* from Lahidjan, on the southwestern side; and *talani* from Talich, on the western shore (Wilhelm Heyd, *Histoire du commerce du Levant* [Paris, 1885, reprinted Leipzig, 1923], II, 671–72).

stravai prices were increased two to four soldi. Even immediately after
the capture of Constantinople by the Turks, the Caspian Sea silks still
reached Italy in abundant quantities. Between June, 1454, and June,
1455, the Banchi partnership purchased 1,034 pounds of Caspian Sea silk
at the regular prices,[49] and during that year the firm used some 3,000
pounds of raw silk.

Spain was the second important source for silk. This had not been true
in earlier centuries, and little Spanish silk reached Lucca before the
fifteenth century. The best quality came from Almería, but all silk from
the kingdom of Granada found a ready market in Italy. Spanish silk was
priced higher than most other silks: in 1438 Banchi paid 3 florins 6s. a oro
per pound for 190 pounds and 3 florins 10s. per pound for 20 pounds, in
cash sales.[50] In the 1450's the prices were 3 florins to 3 florins 3s. 6d. per
pound, cash, and 3 florins 6s. to 3 florins 9s. for terms of seven months
to one year. Spanish silk had a high luster; it was fine, sinewy, and strong,
and it could be used for all kinds of fabrics. The stravai silk was duller
and somewhat coarser, but also adaptable for all purposes,[51] and Banchi
used it primarily for warps of velvets and *zetani vellutati*. The leggi silk was
used for warp, weft, and pile of velvets, and for damask weft.

From Chios in the Aegean came a silk that resembled the Spanish in
color, elasticity, and weight, but it was apt to have knots or lumps.[52] In
August, 1454, 108 pounds were bought from a Genoese merchant, Maffeo
Leccavela, at 2 florins 2s. per pound, cash.[53] But Banchi did not purchase
much Chios silk.

By the fifteenth century sericulture in various parts of Italy was producing moderate quantities of silk. The highest-priced of all the silk

49. Estranei, 84, Libro rosso A, fols. 6, 15, 16, 27, 47, 56; Estranei, 74, Ricordanze A,
fols. 3, 14, 15, 28, 37, 71, 80. The Genoese continued to ship some raw silk from their
colonies of Kaffa and Tana—which were not seized by the Turks until 1475—but
apparently after the fall of Constantinople most Caspian Sea silk was brought by caravan
via Tabriz, Erzerum and Sivas to Brusa. From Brusa, some was taken to Pera, and a good
deal was carried to the Genoese island of Chios and then shipped to Italy (Jacques Heers,
Gênes au XVᵉ siècle; activité économique et problèmes sociaux [Paris, 1961], pp. 380, 388–89;
Philip P. Argenti, *The Occupation of Chios by the Genoese and their Administration of the Island,
1346–1566* [Cambridge, Eng., 1958], I, 427–28, 520).

50. Estranei, 83, Libro rosso C, fol. 35. Since all references to raw silk and metallic
threads purchased in the 1430's are to this ledger, fols. 7–99, I shall not give a specific
folio reference for each statement in the following paragraphs. Anyone who consults
Ledger C will easily find the entries for the purchases of raw materials.

51. *Trattato della seta*, p. 103.

52. *Ibid.*, p. 104.

53. Estranei, 74, Ricordanze A, fol. 32.

purchased by Banchi came from the Romagna, *seta di Modigliana*. In a list of prices for raw silk in the oft-mentioned Florentine Trattato della seta, Modigliana silk is highest in price and Spanish silk is second.[54] The Banchi account books confirm this listing. In 1437 Modigliana silk could be purchased for cash for 2 florins 12s. per pound. By the 1450's its price had increased. Although the firm succeeded in buying some Modigliana silk a few times for as low as 3 florins and 3 florins 2s. per pound, cash, the price was more often between 3 florins 8s. and 3 florins 12s., with terms of six to eight months for quantities of 100 pounds or more. It was used chiefly for warps of all fabrics and for velvet pile.

Silk from the Abruzzi and the Marches was used in fairly large quantities, that is, 300 to 500 pounds per year. The prices increased from 2 florins 3s. or 2 florins 6s. per pound in 1437 to 3 florins for *seta di Marca* and 3 florins 5s. for *seta d'Abruzzi* in the 1450's. These silks were used for warps of all fabrics, except satin and taffeta, and for velvet pile.

Silk from Calabria was the cheapest that Banchi purchased, and it is also at the bottom of the list in the Trattato. The firm paid from 1 florin 5s. per pound, cash, to 1 florin 12s., barter. It was used for the weft threads in velvet.

I have found one purchase of silk from Messina: 173 pounds at 2 florins per pound bartered for silk cloth in June, 1455.[55] This silk was good for the weft in satins.

Silk produced in the Val di Nievole, west of Pistoia, was marketed almost entirely in Lucca. The Banchi firm occasionally, but rarely, purchased very small amounts of Val di Nievole silk, never more than three pounds at a time. It was paid for in silver coin and the sellers were from the local region. The price in terms of florins was usually about $2\frac{1}{2}$ florins per pound. It was of good quality but apparently not easily obtainable in large quantities.

The Banchi firm purchased only small quantities of inferior grades of silk—from broken cocoons and outer layers of cocoons. These short lengths were spun, not thrown. The spun thread was called *filugello* and was used in weaving certain kinds of belts.

Most of the raw silk, both foreign and Italian, was purchased from Florentine international merchants. In the 1450's the firm of Francesco di Nerone Neroni and Company furnished large quantities of Spanish and

54. *Trattato della seta*, pp. 108–9.
55. Estranei, 84, Libro rosso A, fol. 77. References for raw silk purchased in the 1450's are from this ledger and from the two journals, Ricordanze A (1454–56) and B (1456–59), which correspond to this ledger.

Caspian Sea silk, often accepting part payment in goods. Piero d'Andrea de' Pazzi and Company and Luigi di Giovanni Tegghiacci and Company would also accept part payment in silk cloth, and sometimes the entire payment. Piero Partini and Company and Bernardo d'Uguccione Lippi and Company gave credit terms of three or four months but did not accept silk fabrics. Giovanni di Paolo Rucellai and Company, Andrea Banchi's bankers, gave credit terms up to one year for Spanish and Italian silk. The Rome branch of the Medici bank sold several lots of Spanish silk to Banchi and also provided generous credit terms of one year. Filippo di Leonardo Bartoli and Company supplied most of the silk from the Marches that Banchi purchased, with credit terms of ten months to one year. After the accomanda was formed in August, 1455, with Benvenuto Nuti, Abruzzi and Calabrian silk was sent to the firm from Aquila, where Nuti resided. The annual purchases of raw silk represented an outlay of close to 9,000 florins, a considerable sum in those days.

For brocaded silk cloths and for many of the belts, gold and silver metallic thread was used. It was sold wound on spools (*cannelli* or *fusa*), for which a tare was deducted from the gross weight. In 1437 and for several years thereafter, Banchi made most of his purchases of *oro fine filato* from Giovanni di Iacopo d'Ubertino degli Strozzi. He usually paid cash, and the price was always 14 florins 10s. per pound. In the 1450's Tommaso di Luigi Ridolfi and Company, goldbeaters (*battilori*), had become the chief furnisher. The price for fine gold thread remained constant until 1456, when it rose one florin *di suggello* per pound. The best silver thread (*ariento fine filato*) cost 14 florins per pound in the 1450's.

Ledger A and Journals A and B for the years 1454 to 1458 show that some purchases of fine gold and silver thread and a medium quality of gold thread (*oro mezzano*) were made from other firms of goldbeaters: from Bernardo Galilei and Mariotto di Salvestro Gondi and Company, with payment half in silk cloth and half in cash; from Giovanni d'Antonio di Iacopo and Company, with similar terms; from Giovanni d'Antonio di Salvestro and Company, some payments cash, some half cash and half cloth; and from Giuliano di Leonardo Gondi and Company, which accepted only cash but charged one florin less per pound for silver thread —and in 1456 only 15 florins per pound for *oro fine* when others were asking 15½ florins. Probably the main reason that most purchases were made from the Ridolfi Company was its more favorable terms: for years there was an agreement that payment for the metallic threads would be two-thirds in silk cloth and one-third in cash, within four months.[56]

56. Estranei, 84, Libro rosso A, fol. 13; Estranei, 74, Ricordanze A, fol. 208v.

Another reason was doubtless the fact that in 1452 Andrea's son, Piero, had married Alessandra, sister of Tommaso Ridolfi, *battiloro* (goldbeater).

The two ledgers for the period 1454 to 1462 show that between 65 and 75 pounds of fine gold thread were purchased annually at an outlay of about 1,000 florins. Less than half that amount of silver thread was purchased, about 30 pounds, which cost more than 400 florins. Very little *oro mezzano* was acquired annually—only a few pounds, for approximately 100 florins.

Throwing

The skeins of raw silk purchased by the Banchi firm were composed of strands formed by reeling long filaments together from several cocoons. The filament or thread spun by the silkworm to form his cocoon is so fine that the filaments of from four to eight cocoons are reeled together to form the strand which is called raw silk. The natural gum of the silk, plus a slight twist given the threads in the reeling process, hold the filaments together in the strand.

In the Banchi shop the first step in the manufacturing process was the sorting of the skeins of raw silk according to the thickness of the strands and inspecting them for knots or other defects. The skeins were then delivered to a woman winder (*maestra* or *incannatrice*) to be wound on spools or bobbins that would fit on the spindles of a throwing-mill. This winding had to be done skillfully and evenly.

The first major step was the throwing of the silk on a twisting- or throwing-mill (*torcitoio*) to form strong threads, even in thickness and elasticity throughout their length. Weft threads were twisted or thrown in only one direction, warp threads usually in two, that is, first in one direction and then in the opposite direction. The Lucchese had invented a rather elaborate throwing-mill with 200 or more spindles that could be run by water power. The Florentine throwsters of the fifteenth century used a smaller, man-operated throwing-mill with perhaps 100 or so spindles; and they were small masters who worked alone or with only one assistant.

In the 1450's the Banchi firm kept one throwster almost constantly employed, Bambo di Tommaso, *torcitore*, whose residence and workshop was near the loggia of the Neghittosa—at the corner of Via Calzaioli and Via delle Oche, a short walk from the Banchi shop. He was paid 4 soldi di piccioli for each pound of thread for velvet pile and 6 soldi for all other silk thrown. His average monthly earnings from work done for Banchi were only £25 picc.—or £300 annually, about 66 florins.[57] He probably worked for several other setaioli, otherwise his income would have been less than that of many silk weavers. Four to seven other throwsters were given work at irregular intervals during each year of the Banchi partnership.

Some threads were doubled and redoubled to obtain the thickness needed for heavy silks. Although some of the doubling was done by the Banchi shop boys (*garzoni di bottega*), the Libro di tessitori has accounts with three doublers (*addoppiatori*). They handled the most expensive silks: the Modigliana and the Spanish.

Degumming by Boiling

After throwing and doubling, the next major step was degumming by boiling in soapy water; but first the spools were sent to the maestre to unwind the thread from the spools and form it into skeins. The silk yarn from each spool was wound loosely around a revolving winder (*arcolaio*) and then slipped off the winder and tied with a little cord. Before boiling, the skeins were placed in bags. The boiling of the silk was necessary to remove the sericin, the natural gum, which had been useful up to this stage but which would now prevent the silk from taking an even dye. As the gum constitutes between 15 and 25 per cent of the weight of raw silk, the loss in weight through boiling is considerable.

In Lucca, boiling was done in the establishment of a boiler of silk (*cocitore*), not in a dyeing establishment, but in Florence the boiling was done by the silk dyers. This is made clear both by the sample accounts of a setaiolo in the Trattato della seta and by entries in the accounts of dyers in the Banchi records. The rate for boiling, according to both sources, was one soldo di piccioli per pound. The setaiolo supplied the soap. In 1437 Andrea Banchi purchased soap from a Salvestro di Latino, *saponaio*.[58] In the 1450's Salvestro's son, Giovanfrancesco, furnished soap to Banchi and to the unknown setaiolo whose accounts are used in the Trattato. After boiling, the skeins of silk were removed from the bags,

57. There are twenty-eight pages of accounts for the throwster, Bambo di Tommaso, in Estranei, 85, Libro tessitori B.

58. Between October 11, 1437, and April 15, 1439, Banchi purchased 1,614 pounds of *sapone da seta* at £13 picc. per hundred pounds (Estranei, 83, Libro rosso C, fol. 5).

rinsed in clear water, and hung up to dry. This process left the silk soft, lustrous, and pearly white. Silk that was to be used as white thread was now bleached in a closed chamber by being exposed to fumes of sulphurous acid.

Almost all silk was dyed in the thread; even monochrome fabrics were seldom dyed in the cloth. There was specialization among dyers, so that dyers of silk did not dye any wool; and dyeing prices varied considerably, according to the dyestuff used and the difficulty of the process.

The dyes constantly used for silks in fifteenth-century Florence were brazilwood, indigo, kermes, madder, orchil, and scarlet grain. The most expensive dyestuff was kermes, used for crimson, which cost about one florin per pound and was imported from the Levant. However, the dried bodies of the kermes insect that came from Spain, called *grana*—"grain" or "scarlet grain"—cost 2 soldi a oro less per pound. Both produced rich, lasting shades of red. Silk thread that was dyed crimson only once, to be used for damask and satin, cost the Banchi firm 34s. per pound; and twice-dyed crimson thread, usually used for velvets, cost 44s.

Forty soldi piccioli was the price for thread dyed alessandrino blue, using a combination of three dyes: orchil, indigo, and madder. To obtain this deep, rich shade of blue, the silk had to be dipped in the dyevat, dried, redipped, soaped and rinsed, and resoaped and rerinsed several times.[59] Thread dyed purple (*paonazzo*) with brazilwood was 35s. per pound. For vermilion, using brazilwood, the price was only 25s. per pound. Azure was 24s. per pound. Green was 20s. per pound of thread, and black was only 15s. The least expensive colors were beige and tawny, both 12s. per pound. These prices agree with those given in the Trattato della seta except that the Banchi firm paid 4 soldi more per pound for crimson thread.[60]

Andrea Banchi seems to have made regular use of three dyeing establishments in the 1430's and 1440's, all of them located along the Arno near the Ponte al Rubaconte (now the Ponte alle Grazie): Bruno di Piero and Company, Domenico di Tommaso and Company, and Vito d'Andrea di Vito and Company.[61] The last two firms were replaced in

59. *Trattato della seta*, Ch. XVII: "A tignere l'alessandrino," pp. 37–40.

60. *Ibid.*, pp. 78–79. The Banchi prices are taken from the dyers' accounts in Libro tessitori B.

61. All three dyeing firms have accounts in Ledger C (Estranei, 83) for 1437 and following years. Vito d'Andrea is already listed as a creditor in the financial statement attached to Andrea Banchi's return for the catasto of 1427 (ASF, Catasto, 64, fol. 19v). Vito and Bruno di Piero are creditors in similar statements attached to Banchi's returns of 1430 and 1433 (Catasto, 331, S. Spirito, Scala, fol. 64v; 429, fol. 30).

the period of the last Banchi partnership by Mariotto di Giovanni Ciriagi and Company and by Stagio d'Antonio Bandini. The Book of Weavers (1458–1462) shows that Bruno di Piero received much more work than the two other dyeing firms combined. All three were given the same kinds of silk to boil and to dye in the various colors from crimson to black and beige. It is interesting to note that one firm of dyers was used regularly for more than thirty years.

The gross annual earnings of Bruno di Piero and Company from the boiling and dyeing of thread done for the Banchi firm varied between £1,400 and £1,500 picc. (310 to 335 florins).[62] How many other customers the dyers had we do not know, but certainly each firm worked for a number of silk manufacturers. Besides such costly supplies as dyes and alum, dyers needed rather expensive equipment, mainly an array of dye vats and utensils. Because they invested capital and employed journeymen, their status was above that of any other group of silk workers.

Some of the most expensive dyestuffs, such as kermes, grain, and brazilwood, were often purchased by the Banchi firm directly from Florentine importers. Once it acquired 1,300 pounds of Spanish grain at 17s. 5d. per pound, whereas the usual price in small quantities was 18s. a oro per pound.[63] The journals and ledgers show that Banchi resold the dyestuffs to the dyers at cost and allowed them to pay in work done (a scontare a tingere). Probably the setaiolo was in a better bargaining position than the dyer in dealing with importers, but another reason for these purchases was that he wanted to make sure only dyes of the best quality were used and he therefore preferred to supply them himself.

Warping

After dyeing, the skeins were again sent to the maestre to be rewound, this time on spools that would fit into the warpboard of a warp-frame.

During the period of its last partnership the Banchi firm kept three warpers—two men and a woman—on the payroll at the same time. For years the warpers all lived within a two- or three-minute walk from the silk shop in Por S. Maria: Domenico di Niccolò above the Taverna del Buco in Vacchereccia, the short street between the Piazza della Signoria and Por S. Maria; Domenico di Giovanni near the Parte Guelfa, just beyond the street of silk shops; and Monna Tessa di Lorenzo at the Loggia

62. Estranei, 85, Libro tessitori B, fols. 2, 4v, 5, 10v, etc. There are more than twenty-five pages of accounts for this firm of dyers.
63. Estranei, 74, Ricordanze A, fol. 216.

de' Pulci in Via Lambertesca, parallel with Via Vacchereccia. The last-named ceased to work for the firm in 1460 and was replaced by Monna Alessandra, wife of the damask weaver Niccolò di Meo di Cino. She was not so conveniently located since her dwelling was at the Piazza degli Alberti in what is now the Via de' Benci. Nevertheless, a warp for which she received the threads in the morning was often returned the same day, as was the case with the other warpers. If not returned the same day, a warp was usually back in the shop the next day and in the hands of a weaver before nightfall. A few warps were kept for two or three days because of intervening Sundays or holy days.

The Banchi firm made no attempt to keep a warper so steadily employed that he need not work for another setaiolo; this would have required a much larger production schedule. Frequently, two or three warps were measured for Banchi within one week, then there might be an interval of a week or ten days without any work from the firm. Material for the two warps needed for a piece of velvet would be delivered at the same time, and occasionally material for two unrelated cloths. There was no specialization as to kind of warp: all warpers prepared warps for different kinds of fabrics. The piece rate for warps varied from 3 to 6 denari piccioli per *braccio*: taffeta, 3d.; satin and voided satin velvet, 4d.; damask, 5d.; brocades and the double warps for plain velvet, 6d.[64] As taffeta warps were very long, and could be prepared in a day, the total pay received for a taffeta warp was often greater than the pay for a much shorter warp at a higher rate per braccio. The average remuneration per warp was a little over £1 picc.

The potential earnings of a warper, if he received a warp or two almost daily from one or another of several *setaioli*, might be between £20 and £30 picc. per month, or £240 and £360 (53 to 80 florins) a year. The latter figure is probably too high because of the many holidays prescribed by the guild statutes.

Weaving

The Banchi firm employed men and women weavers and produced every kind of silk cloth that was being woven in Florence, from plain taffeta to complicated pile on pile velvets, voided satin velvets, and rich brocades.[65]

64. These rates are taken from the warpers' accounts in Libro tessitori B.

65. Pile on pile velvets were produced in two or more heights of pile (*in due peli, in tre peli*). In fifteenth-century Florence, *alto (e) basso* was apparently used only for a patterned velvet in three heights of pile. The voided satin velvet (*zetani vellutato*, plur. *zetani vellutati*)

The weavers were highly specialized. This specialization was due chiefly to the fact that greater skill and efficiency could be achieved if the weaver worked on only one kind of loom and one kind of cloth. There was a special type of draw-loom for almost every variety of figured cloth. A weaver, once he was used to operating a certain type of loom, could not shift easily to another type without a loss of speed and efficiency. Some of the more elaborate looms could be operated only with the aid of a draw-boy perched on top of the loom to pull the cords that controlled the pattern.

Unlike the other silk workers, weavers could work for only one manufacturer at a time. They were free, however, to change employment provided they were not in debt to an entrepreneur. Consequently they are the only group on whose total annual earnings we can give fairly accurate information.

Earnings varied greatly, according to the kind of fabric and according to the skill and speed of individual weavers. The taffeta weavers received only 5 or 6 soldi piccioli per braccio.[66] A weaver of brocades earned as high as £8 picc. per braccio. However, it took much longer and required more skill to weave a braccio of brocade than a braccio of taffeta. For example, Domenico di Michele, who wove velvets in three heights of pile brocaded with gold, took six months to weave about 50 braccia. A piece of taffeta of the same length did not require more than a month. Nevertheless, taffeta weavers earned much less than highly skilled weavers of brocade or figured velvet. A widow, Monna Antonia, for instance, earned about £145 picc. or approximately 32 florins in one year, producing close to 500 braccia of taffeta at the rate of 6s. picc. per braccio.[67] On the other hand, Domenico di Michele earned £740, or close to 165 florins, between December 10, 1459, and November 26, 1460. During this period he produced only two pieces of brocaded pile on pile velvet that measured $92\frac{1}{2}$ braccia in all.[68] His output, consequently, was about one-fifth that of

---

had a foundation fabric of satin on which velvet pile intermittently appeared above the surface to form a pattern. Both kinds of velvet were sometimes brocaded. Renaissance painters delighted in reproducing the richness of texture and beauty of design in pile on pile and voided velvets.

66. The standard Florentine measure of length for cloth was the *braccio* (pl. *braccia*), corresponding to 58.4 centimeters or 0.6383 of a yard (close to 23 inches), or about one-half of the old English ell. "Brace" was used as the English translation in past centuries, but it will probably be less confusing to use the Italian term in roman type, since it is found in large English dictionaries.

67. Estranei, 85, Libro tessitori B, fols. 112*v*, 123*v*, 130*v*, 140*v*, 156*v*.

68. *Ibid.*, fols. 117, 138.

Monna Antonia, yet his annual earnings were much higher because his rate of pay was sixteen times that of a taffeta weaver. The reason for this wide difference was undoubtedly that his work involved great technical ability and that qualified weavers of brocaded velvets were scarce and therefore well paid.

Taffeta weavers were usually women. Monna Antonia worked fast and steadily and earned more than others in the same category. Another widow, Monna Mea, earned only £56, about 12½ florins, in five months.[69] A man, perhaps a beginner, wove more slowly than either of these women. He received only 5s. 4d. per braccio and his earnings totaled only £103 13s. picc. (23 florins) in 1459–1460 during the first year of his employment by the Banchi firm.[70] Perhaps his performance was below par. After an interval during which he worked for others, he was rehired in the spring of 1462 at the piece rate of 6 soldi per braccio.

After the weavers of taffeta, those who wove satin—likewise mainly women—were the next-lowest-paid group. The rate varied from 8 to 9 soldi piccioli per braccio, instead of 5 to 6 soldi, but it took nearly twice as long to produce 50 braccia of satin, with the result that total earnings were about the same in both categories. A man named Simone di Bartolo, the only weaver employed by the Banchi firm to make double satin (*zetani raso doppio*), rated 11 soldi per braccio. As it usually took him two months to weave 50 braccia, his yearly earnings amounted to £165 picc. (37 florins), hence he did not do much better than Monna Antonia.[71]

As Table 4 shows, there was a wide range in rates of pay and annual earnings, depending upon skill and output. In general, the weavers of plain or monochrome silks were paid less than those who specialized in polychrome or figured fabrics. Weavers of monochrome flowered damask occupied a medium position. Their output averaged around 300 braccia a year and their earnings around £340 picc. (75 florins), or twice as much as the earnings of taffeta and satin weavers.

One can hardly say that silk weavers were exploited—surely not a man like Domenico di Michele whose earnings one year reached the respectable figure of 170 florins, as much as, or perhaps more than, the salary of branch managers of the Medici bank. But Domenico di Michele was an exception and his superior skill enabled him to make demands without

69. *Ibid.*, fols. 204, 208, 215v.

70. *Ibid.*, fols. 79, 86, 104v, 117v (Battista d'Andrea).

71. *Ibid.*, fols. 90, 100, 144, 169. It is not clear what was meant by "double satin." It was not double in width, and as it had only one warp it was probably not double faced. In any case, it was thicker and heavier than the satins woven by women.

TABLE 4

EARNINGS OF WEAVERS EMPLOYED BY THE BANCHI FIRM

Kind of Cloth	Piece Rate per Braccio in Soldi di Piccioli			Time Required to Weave 50 Braccia	Annual Earnings	
	Guild Statute of 1429	Trattato della seta c. 1453	Paid by A. Banchi 1458–62		Lire di Piccioli	Florins
Taffeta	8	6	5–6	4–5 weeks	125–145	28–32*
Satin	...	9	8–9	6–10 weeks	120–135	26–30
Double satin	14	...	11	2 months	165	37
Damask	25	23	22–23	2 months	330–340	73–75
Brocaded damask	...	...	43	3–4 months	325–430	72–95†
Velvet with linen warp	14	12	13	9–10 weeks	156–170	35–38
Plain silk velvet	25	22	22–25	10–14 weeks	200–250	44–55‡
Pile on pile velvets	30	...	32–36	5 months	192–216	42–48
Voided satin velvet (zetani vellutato)	36	30	30–40	3–4 months	300–400	67–89
Zetani vellutato in two heights of pile	...	...	40	5–6 months	200–292	44–64
Polychrome zetani vellutato	42	...	44	18–19 weeks	400	89
Polychrome brocaded zetani vellutato	...	...	100	23–26 weeks	500–560	111–124
Brocaded velvet in three heights of pile	...	...	160	about 6 months	740–770	165–171§
Orphreys	35	38	32	5 months	190	42

* For comparative purposes, shop boys annually earned from 6 to 15 florins with the Banchi firm and from 10 to 18 florins with the Medici bank; more experienced young clerks went up to 30 florins with Banchi and up to 50 florins with the Medici.
† Older and experienced clerks with the Medici bank received up to 80 florins per year.
‡ The older, very capable Banchi employees did not earn more than 50 florins.
§ A salaried branch manager of the Medici bank received 150 florins per year.
SOURCES: Statuti dell'Arte di Por Santa Maria, p. 98; Trattato della seta, pp. 490–91; Libro di tessitori B of Andrea Banchi and Company.

having to worry much about rivals. Even damask weavers were rather
well off, and their earnings also compare favorably with those of the more
experienced clerks of the Medici bank. Only satin and taffeta weavers
were poorly paid; their wages were on a level with the wages paid for
similar work in the woolen industry.

Andrea Banchi certainly paid competitive wages. For example, he
produced very little velvet with a linen warp (*velluto in accia*), the output of
only one weaver, and Niccolò d'Andrea Ginevri, who wove it for him
from 1437 to 1459, did not receive more than 13s. per braccio.[72] This was
above the standard rate of 12s. picc. in the Trattato della seta.[73] The
minimum rate Banchi paid weavers of plain all-silk velvet, according to
his account books, was 22s. per braccio, which corresponds to the rate in
the Trattato. However, Banchi gradually increased velvet weavers to 25s.,
the rate he paid to those who had given him satisfactory service for a
period of years. Thus Spazziano di Giovanni, who had been weaving
plain velvet for Banchi before 1454, received 24s. in 1458 and 25s. by the
end of 1459. Spazziano's annual earnings ranged from £182 picc. (40½
florins) in 1458–1459 to £250 (55½ florins) in 1461.[74] However, he lost
considerable time in 1458 because of illness.

There is one puzzling exception to Banchi's paying the standard
wages. Weavers of orphreys (*brusti*) earned 38s. per braccio according to
the Trattato and 35s. per braccio according to the guild statute of 1429,
but Agnolo di Luca, who wove all the orphreys for the Banchi firm, was
paid only 32s. per braccio. As he could produce only ten braccia of
figured orphreys in a month, his annual earnings were around £190 picc.,
or about 42 florins.[75]

Table 4 shows not only that there were great wage differentials
among the silk weavers, according to the required degrees of dexterity, but
also that during the period from 1429 to 1458–1462 piece rates remained
much the same for the more skilled groups, whose bargaining position was
apparently more favorable. However, the rates paid to the weavers of
plain silks went down instead of up, presumably because of greater
competition for jobs. For taffeta weavers the drop was greatest: from 8
soldi to 6 soldi per braccio, a reduction of 25 per cent. The downward

72. *Ibid.*, fol. 89v.
73. *Trattato della seta*, p. 98.
74. Estranei, 85, Libro tessitori B, fols. 60, 80, 97v, 115v (November, 1458 to November,
1459), 153v, 164v, 177, 182v, 193 (1461). Spazziano also owned a second loom on which
his wife wove satin for Banchi at 8s. per braccio.
75. Estranei, 85, fols. 56, 69v, 87.

trend may explain why the minimum rates enacted by the guild in 1429 were repealed nine years later.

As a result of declining wage rates there may well have been a slow but steady deterioration of living standards in the less skilled categories of weavers. Moreover, wages were fixed and paid in constantly depreciating silver currency: between 1430 and 1460 the rate of the *fiorino di suggello* rose from £4 to £4 10s. di piccioli.[76] In the absence of statistical data on the cost of living, it would be rash to state categorically that the standard of living went up or down; it is likely, however, that conditions did not improve for the working classes: the renaissance, in general, was not a period of great prosperity and expansion.

The Banchi account books disclose that some of the silk weavers owned looms that were operated by relatives or assistants, and such weavers may be considered as small masters who acted as subcontractors since they paid their assistants less than the rate received from Banchi. It is true, of course, that this practice may be justified on the grounds that the master weaver, in addition to providing a loom, assumed all responsibility toward the Banchi firm for finishing the job on time and for maintaining quality.

Sometimes the master weaver received a better rate of pay for the work he did himself than for that done by his journeyman. For example, Bartolomeo di Papi, a weaver of velvet who in 1460 owned two looms, was paid 24s. for cloth he wove himself and only 22s. for the cloth his assistant wove. In other instances there was no wage differential and the piece rate was identical for master and journeyman, as in the case of Domenico di Salvestro and his helper, Francesco di Santi, weavers of *zetani vellutati* (voided satin velvets): both earned 40s. per braccio in 1460. As they were rapid workers, each turned out four to four and one-half cloths per year. In 1459 their joint earnings amounted to £722 picc. (160 florins) and in 1460 climbed to £808 (179 florins). In 1461 their joint earnings reached a maximum, £835 picc. (185 florins).[77]

It happened occasionally that a master weaver owned as many as three looms. Such was the case with Lorenzo d'Antonio di Cristofano, who had a second loom operated by his son Iacopo and a third loom operated by a journeyman named Salvadore (not related to the family).

76. Raymond de Roover, *The Medici Bank* (New York, 1948), p. 61, "Rate of the Gold Florin in Lire and Soldi Piccioli from 1415 to 1515" (chart).

77. There are thirty-one pages of accounts for Domenico di Salvestro in Libro tessitori B. In 1458 Domenico received 36s. per braccio for himself and his assistant (fols. 54*v*, 70*v*, 71*v*, 81*v*); in 1459 he received first 38s., and later 39s. for both (fols. 88, 93*v*, 98*v*, 103).

One of the three looms was equipped for weaving velvets in two heights of pile and the other two were equipped for weaving voided satin velvets. But annual combined earnings were not as high as might be expected; they did not exceed £720 picc., or 160 florins. (A younger son of Lorenzo's, Andrea, was employed as an errand and shop boy by the Banchi firm from 1455 onward.)

Since many of the silk weavers were highly skilled their condition was probably much better than that of the weavers of woolen cloth. Moreover, the greater their skill the greater their independence. Although the silk guild, the Arte di Por S. Maria, was controlled by the employers, the revised guild statute of 1429 enjoined the manufacturers to treat their weavers as masters (*maestri*) and not as journeymen (*lavoranti*), even if the looms belonged to the employer—which was not usually the case, according to the Banchi records. The statute, furthermore, forbade employers to pay less than the statutory wage under the penalty of a fine of one lira *picc.* per braccio, to be collected from both employer and weaver.[78] To be sure, this legislation was not inspired by welfare considerations but rather by the fear that skilled weavers might emigrate and transfer the industry to rival towns, as had happened in Lucca while it was under Pisan rule (1342–1369).

Undoubtedly, most of the silk weavers, like weavers in the woolen industry, worked hard to earn only a rather poor living. They suffered from cold and dampness, from drafts in winter and great heat in summer; yet in order to eke out their living they sat at their looms from morning to night, day after day, month after month. Up and down went the heddles, while the shuttle was thrown relentlessly back and forth. The work was tedious but not as monotonous as most factory jobs today.

However much one may sympathize with the workers, one must not overlook the problems of the employer. Then, as now, he had to meet his payroll and to find a market for his product. The setaiolo did not have a large investment in equipment but he needed capital to buy raw materials and to pay wages, until, several months later, he recovered his outlay in the sale of his product.

His chief preoccupation was maintaining quality, which required constant vigilance. An employer could not afford to tolerate "cabbaging" or to have expensive materials spoiled by slipshod or careless work. Quality was affected by every step in the production process, but corrections could usually be made prior to weaving. The weavers were the most

78. *Statuti dell'Arte di Por S. Maria*, pp. 487–88.

important workers in the textile industry. Since silks, unlike woolen cloth, required no finishing, the silk weavers' mistakes could not easily be concealed or remedied.

From the Banchi records one gathers the impression that conscientious, meticulous weavers were not overly numerous in fifteenth-century Florence. In order to keep his best workers Banchi raised their wages rather regularly and kept them steadily employed. The next warp was often delivered while the preceding one was still on the loom and not quite finished—perhaps to prevent the weaver from going to a competitor or to induce him to hurry.

Banchi was quite successful in retaining his good weavers. During the four years covered by the Book of Weavers, fourteen weavers were regularly employed throughout this period and seventeen during most of it—but four weavers wove three or four cloths in succession and then stopped working for Banchi, perhaps because they were tempted away by competitors. Seventeen weavers were given only one cloth to weave and were never employed again, presumably because they were too slow or because their work was unsatisfactory. A few accepted a warp and the weft threads, then returned this material after a week or a month, untouched. One woman, a satin weaver who had been doing well for some time, ended by returning two braccia of woven cloth and the rest of the warp. Perhaps illness prevented her from finishing the job.

Some weavers had to be prodded to finish their work within the expected time by the threat of a reduction in their rate of pay. Thus a Piero d'Antonio, who worked for the Banchi firm after 1456, by 1459 became either lazy or infirm because his work slowed down considerably. On May 20, 1460, he received the materials for a plain velvet cloth with the understanding that the work must be completed by the end of July, if he was well (sano), and that his rate of pay would be reduced from 22s. to 16s. 6d. if the job was not finished on schedule. He did not complete the cloth until October 15, two and a half months late; nevertheless, he was paid at the rate of 22s. per braccio, presumably because his work had been delayed by illness.[79] The Banchi firm, however, was unwilling to risk further delays and ceased to employ his services.[80]

79. Estranei, 85, Libro tessitori B, fol. 133. The agreement is written on this page, which also contains the account of materials issued to Piero d'Antonio for a green velvet and the record of the return of the finished cloth and payment for the weaving.

80. Another instance of the use of a threat of reduction in pay is that of the velvet weaver, Battista di Ambrogio, who received a warp (July 13, 1461) on condition that he would work steadily and not "befool" the firm (e non ci dileggiare), as he had done before, by taking four to six months. If the finished cloth was not delivered within three months

Because silk cloths took months to weave, weavers received advances of 2, 3, or 4 lire, paid weekly or fortnightly, and sometimes every ten days. Replacements of parts of their looms, such as heddles (*licci*) and reeds (*pettine*), were often paid for by the partnership and debited to their accounts.[81] The firm paid the weavers' bills with hosiers, mercers, and retail sellers of linen and woolen cloth. Usually the amounts were small enough to be charged against one cloth without interfering with the weekly advances or causing the weaver to become heavily indebted to the Banchi firm. Small indebtedness frequently occurred at the end of a cloth account, but it would be canceled by the next or the following account. The Banchi firm seems to have followed a definite policy of not permitting its weavers and other workers to become seriously indebted to the firm, which protected both worker and employer.

If a merchant allowed a weaver to become indebted to him for a considerable sum, perhaps to provide a trousseau for a daughter, a form of what today is called attachment of wages would be agreed upon between the merchant and the Banchi firm. For example, on June 10, 1461, the partnership promised the wool merchant, Agnolo di Leonardo, that it would pay a debt of 11 florins for the weaver, Simone di Giovanni, on a monthly basis of one florin each month, beginning July 1, and debit Simone accordingly.[82]

When a weaver purchased a new loom, payment would be made by the firm on an installment basis. For example, in June, 1456, Meo d'Antonio, a weaver of damasks, sold a damask loom to Antonio di Bardo Bagnesi for 36 florins. A down payment of 7 florins 7s. a oro was made by the firm and charged to the account of a black damask Bagnesi was weaving for them. The balance was to be paid over an eighteen-month period and one-fourth of the total charged to each of the next four damasks Bagnesi wove for the firm on the new loom.[83]

---

his pay would be reduced from 22s. to 14s. per braccio (Estranei, 76, Ricordanze C, fol. 276*v*). This threat had the desired effect: 48 braccia of solid black velvet were returned by October 10 (Libro tessitori B, fol. 186*v*).

81. A pair of new heddles with linen cords varied in price from £3 6s. picc. for a velvet loom to £10 for a damask loom (Estranei, 84, Libro rosso A, fol. 82, an account of Domenico di Nofri fa licci). A new reed cost from £3 to £5 for a velvet loom, and from £3 10s. to £4 10s. picc. for a damask loom (*ibid.*, fols. 55, 81, 143, an account of Andrea d'Antonio del Redito, comber; and fol. 199, an account of Lorenzo di Tommaso, comber).

82. Estranei, 76, Ricordanze C, fol. 276.

83. Estranei, 84, Libro rosso A, fol. 137; Estranei, 75, Ricordanze B, fol. 18*v*. The deduction of 7 florins per damask was too high, so the Banchi firm spread the deductions

The firm did not make any payments in truck, in goods produced by the partnership. This practice was forbidden by the guild regulations since the weavers had no use for silk and would sell it at reduced prices, thus spoiling the market. The Banchi firm occasionally acquired woolen cloth through barter transactions and sold some of it to weavers and other workers at prices certainly no higher than they paid when they purchased directly from drapers. The guild statutes prohibited the use of cloth as part payment for work done, but apparently if a worker paid cash for a small amount of cloth an employer could sell it to him.

Earlier, in the 1430's, Andrea Banchi had begun to purchase large quantities of wine and olive oil at very favorable prices. Some he used in his own household and the rest he offered to workers at cost, which meant a saving to them—unless the quality was so much better than they would normally purchase that the price would still have been too high. They were apparently under no compulsion to buy anything from him. By the 1450's Banchi still offered wine, from his own farms and from other vineyards, but no oil. Only a few of the weavers purchased barrels of wine from him. In selling oil or wine to workers, Banchi was not violating the general rule of the Silk Guild that no payment was to be made in kind; the first provision of the amendments of 1420 stated that a setaiolo could sell food or provisions to workers provided the amounts were not more than their families could use and did not exceed a fourth of their wages.[84]

Weaving, as has been noted, was probably the most important stage in the entire manufacturing process, from raw silk to finished product. Table 5 gives a rough idea of the cost of weaving as a percentage of the total value of finished cloth of different kinds. This total value is not exactly a cost figure but it is based on an inventory valuation which was probably conservative and was certainly below the market price. As the table shows, there is a wide range, from 6.3 per cent to 26 per cent of estimated value. In general, the cost of weaving is proportionately higher for brocaded and figured silks than for plain weaves. Crimson colored silks dyed with kermes, the most expensive dyestuff, were worth more than

---

over a much longer period, but the seller of the loom was fully paid at the end of eighteen months because the firm advanced the difference between the amount withheld from Antonio's earnings and the amount due the seller.

84. *Statuti dell'Arte di Por S. Maria*, p. 459. To have sold wine in an amount smaller than a cask or barrel would have violated the rights of the vintners (*vinattieri*), the retail sellers of wine. The Banchi firm usually purchased wine in the country and added cartage and excise, which was rather high, to the price charged the silk workers.

TABLE 5

WEAVING AS A PROPORTION OF INVENTORY VALUE

Kind of Cloth	Cost of Weaving per Braccio Soldi Piccioli	Inventory Value of Finished Cloth per Braccio (Florins and soldi a oro)	Percentage of Inventory Value
Gold brocaded alto basso velvet	160	8	22.2
Crimson brocaded damask .	43	$5\frac{1}{2}$	8.7
Blue brocaded damask .	43	$2\frac{1}{2}$	19.1
Polychrome voided velvet (picciolato) . . .	44	$2\frac{1}{8}$	21.8
Crimson zetani vellutati .	40	$2\frac{1}{2}$	17.7
Other zetani vellutati .	40	2	22.2
Same	35	$1\frac{1}{2}$	26.0
Velluti spianato ricco dyed with kermes . . .	25	$2\frac{1}{2}$	11.1
Plain velvets . . .	22	1 3s.	21.5
		$1\frac{1}{2}$	16.3
Figured damask . .	22	$1\frac{1}{8}$	21.7
Crimson damask . .	22	$2\frac{1}{8}$	11.5
Velluto in accia (linen warp)	13	$\frac{2}{3}$	21.6
Double satin . . .	11	1 14s.	7.2
Single satin . . .	8	1	8.7
Taffeta dyed with kermes .	6	1 1s.	6.3
Other taffeta . . .	5s. 4d.	15s.	7.5

SOURCE: Saldi of 1457 and 1460, Libro segreto A of Andrea Banchi e compagni, fols. 7–18, 21–30.

the same fabrics in other colors, so that the cost of weaving was relatively lower when kermes was used.

A difficulty arises from the fact that satin and taffeta were sold by the pound rather than by the braccio. There were between $7\frac{1}{2}$ and 8 braccia of taffeta to the Florentine pound, about 5 braccia of single satin, and only $2\frac{1}{4}$ to $2\frac{1}{2}$ braccia of double satin. Thus double satin valued in the inventory at $4\frac{1}{4}$ florins per pound would be worth about 1 florin 14s. a oro per braccio. Taffeta dyed with kermes is listed at $8\frac{1}{2}$ florins per pound in the inventory, which corresponds to 1 florin 1s. per braccio. Other taffetas, including changeable, are inventoried at $5\frac{1}{4}$ florins per pound, which comes to 15s. a oro per braccio.

Another group of workers employed by Andrea Banchi and his partners were the *maestre* and *maestri di fette*, the men and women who wove ribbons, belts, girdles, and sashes on narrow ribbon looms. In the saldo of May, 1457, six women and ten men had work in progress or were creditors for work just completed.[85] Some were using pile threads, probably to weave velvet bands, and some had been issued gold or silver metallic thread as well as silk. *Filugello*, that is, thread spun from inferior silk, was apparently used for the warp of belts. Mention has already been made of the purchase of perforated cocoons, which came chiefly from the Abruzzi and Calabria; the Banchi firm used four women to prepare such silk for spinning and two spinners.[86]

Andrea Banchi used two designers of cartoons for silks: Giovanni d'Antonio and his son Baldassarre di Giovanni, *che dipigne l'opere*. They prepared designs for voided satin velvets (*zetani vellutati*), for brocaded pile on pile velvets (*velluto alto e basso in 3 alti di pelo*), and for brocaded polychrome damask. The prices of the cartoons varied from £4 for the simpler designs to £15 and £16 picc. for the most elaborate.[87]

We have already mentioned the vestment maker, Tommaso d'Antonio, the worker who was employed by Banchi throughout most of his business career. For more than forty years Tommaso d'Antonio, *banderaio*, prepared fine altar frontals and cut and sewed copes, chasubles, and dalmatics for the leading Florentine silk merchants.[88]

Issuance of Materials

Where did the workers live? As already mentioned, the dyers employed by the Banchi partnership were located near the present Ponte alle Grazie. The throwsters were on the right bank but scattered from Via Vacchereccia and Via Porta Rossa (in the immediate vicinity of the silk shops) to Via San Gallo, a good distance away and toward the outskirts of town. The warpers lived close by, a convenience since they usually received thread in the morning and returned the warp the same day. Most of the weavers employed by Banchi resided in the Oltrarno, the term used for the quarter of the city on the left bank of the Arno. Only a few

85. Estranei, 77, Libro segreto A, fols. 13–14, 16.

86. *Ibid.*, fols. 13, 16.

87. Estranei, 84, Libro rosso A, fols. 58, 145, 146, 169; Estranei, 85, Libro tessitori B, fol. 122*v*.

88. In 1421 Tommaso d'Antonio prepared vestments for the firm of Bartolomeo and Giuliano di Vieri Guidi and Francesco di Niccolò Buti (Archivio dello Spedale degli Innocenti, Estranei, 190, fol. 16*v*). He was working for the Banchi firm as late as the early 1460's (Estranei, 86, Libro bianco B, fol. 16). Also see note 39.

lived on the right bank, chiefly near the church of Ognisanti. Across the Arno the silk weavers were clustered in three areas: San Pier Gattolino, on the edge of town near the present Porta Romana; Piazza di San Felice, near the Pitti palace; and Camaldoli, formerly a small monastery beyond the Carmine church (which contains Massaccio's famous frescoes).[89]

Since most of the work was done in the home and not in a central workshop it was a problem to get the materials to the artisans to be processed. The setaioli apparently dealt directly with their workers and made little use of industrial factors, or subcontractors, as was the custom in the woolen industry. Shop boys apparently delivered most of the threads to the winders, whose services were needed between all stages of the production process. They were scattered all along the right bank. Dyers often sent employees to call for the skeins to be dyed and to return them upon completion of the job. Warpers, as already mentioned, came in person to pick up the warp yarn and they returned the prepared warp by nightfall or the next morning. Weavers also usually called in person for new warps, and received selvage thread at the same time. The weft thread and velvet pile, however, were frequently brought to the weavers by the shop boys.

One of the Banchi partners, Bernardo Dati, who wrote most of the entries in the Book of Weavers, was apparently in charge of the fondaco and the issue of materials. His duties also involved paying the weekly advances to weavers, inspecting the work on the looms, keeping check on delays of whatever cause, and prodding slow workers.

Workers' Contributions to the Guild

The Silk Guild of Florence was controlled by the master manufacturers. The silk workers were *sottoposti* (underlings), under the guild's jurisdiction; they could not participate in the election of guild consuls and they were strictly prohibited from forming their own organization. Nevertheless, the sottoposti were expected to contribute to the guild's expenses. The dyers, having a somewhat higher status than the others, paid their share directly to the guild treasurer. The contributions of the weavers, the throwsters, and the warpers, however, were collected by the setaioli in the form of a withholding tax of 4 denari di piccioli per lira, or $1\frac{2}{3}$ per cent of wages.

89. The location of a worker is given at the top of each page of his account in the Libro di tessitori and the entries mention the person who called for or delivered materials.

As the extant Libro di tessitori of the Banchi firm reveals, this deduction was made without fail.

In 1446 the weavers and the throwsters, by a vote of 344 to 9, approved an additional deduction (*ritenzione*) of 2d. per lire for the weavers and 1d. per lire for the throwsters for creating a fund to aid sick, indigent, or imprisoned members of these two groups, to contribute toward childbirth expenses of poor members and toward dowries for their daughters, and to help the Spedale degli Innocenti, which was also supported by the guild as a group. The setaioli were to distribute the proceeds of this new tax every four months: two-thirds to the welfare fund for weavers and throwsters and one-third to the foundling hospital. The fund was to be administered by the treasurer of the hospital, who would make payments from it as directed by the representatives of the weavers and throwsters.[90]

In accordance with the provisions, the Banchi firm withheld 4d. per lira from weavers, warpers, and throwsters, and an additional 2d. from the weavers and 1d. from the throwsters. On several pages of the Book of Weavers the amounts withheld are carefully itemized and the total is posted to the accounts of the Silk Guild and the foundling hospital.[91] Every year a guild official (*proveditore*) inspected the books of the setaioli to see that the withholdings were duly made and duly paid.[92]

Size of the Banchi Firm

Today the size of a textile mill is gauged by either the number of spindles or the number of looms in operation, but for Andrea di Francesco Banchi's firm we have information on only the number of looms. The annual production of full-length cloths varied between 130 and 140. To attain this output about thirty looms were kept busy. As Table 6 shows, the partners had twenty-nine looms working for them on June 14, 1460. Checklists for May 6, 1457, January 1, 1459, March 25, 1459, and March 10, 1460, show the same number—or one more. The data also reveal that Banchi specialized in the production of luxury fabrics: brocades, figured velvets, plain velvets, and damasks. Only one or two taffeta weavers and not more than one satin weaver were in his employ on these various dates. Most of his weavers earned more than 20 soldi or one lira

90. *Statuti dell'Arte di Por S. Maria*, pp. 565–69.
91. Estranei, 85, Libro tessitori B, fols. 95, 207, 241.
92. *Statuti dell'Arte di Por S. Maria*, pp. 568–69.

picc. per braccio, but only two of them, Domenico di Michele and Buono di Geri—weaving brocaded damask or velvet—earned more than 40 soldi per braccio.

Throwing was already a mechanized process in the silk industry. Although mechanization had not progressed as far in Florence as in Lucca, the few throwsters that Banchi employed must have operated a considerable number of spindles; unfortunately, however, no figures are available.

In any case, measured by medieval standards the Banchi firm was a large enterprise and probably gave employment to about one hundred persons, perhaps even more. In May, 1460, the staff in the shop numbered seven (besides the partners): a bookkeeper, a cashier, a clerk, and four shop boys. Outside the bottega Banchi employed five throwsters, three dyers, three warpers, four maestre and two spinners of inferior silks, about thirty winders and as many weavers, ten weavers of belts and ribbons, one designer of cartoons, and one vestment-maker—nearly one hundred persons.[93] It is difficult to be more precise, but it can be pointed out that this count is not complete since it omits the journeymen of the throwsters and the dyers engaged by the firm.

Marketing

The Florentine silk industry was dependent upon exports, but some of its products were marketed locally. As was previously mentioned, the Banchi firm sold part of its fabrics in its own retail shop. The shop was an important outlet in the 1430's and 1440's when Piero Petrini was in charge, as the profits shown in Table 2 indicate, but it never absorbed Banchi's entire production. Some silks were sold by Banchi to merchants engaged in the import-export business, and the extant records for 1454 and later years show that about a third of the firm's output was bought by such merchants, partly in exchange for raw silk. Banchi also tried to sell his products abroad by sending them on consignment to commission agents. Furthermore, as we have seen, through the accomanda with Bernardo Nuti the firm was fairly successful in finding a profitable market at the fairs of the Abruzzi.

93. *Saldo* of May 18, 1460 (Estranei, 77, Libro segreto A, fols. 21–30). The figures based on the *saldo* of May, 1457, are the same except that there were eight employees in the shop (instead of seven), eight throwsters, and sixteen weavers of *fette* (instead of only ten), giving a total of 105 persons employed (*ibid.*, fols. 7–18).

TABLE 6

Looms in Use June 14, 1460

No.	Name of Weaver	Kind of Cloth	Length in Braccia	Piece Rate per Braccio Piccioli Soldi	Warp Received 1459	Cloth Returned 1460
1.	Zanobi di Francesco	blue zetani vellutato	55	35	Nov. 28	July 7*
2.	Domenico di Michele	brocaded alto basso velvet	48	160	Dec. 10 (1460)	June 20
3.	Buono di Geri	brocaded white damask	62	43	Jan. 4	July 19
4.	Lorenzo d'Antonio di Cristofano	black zetani vellutato, 2 peli	42	40	Jan. 30	June 21
5.	Gregorio di Francesco	black velvet	45	22	Feb. 28	June 20
6.	Giovanni di Michele	black damask	38	22	Mar. 4	June 17
7.	Alessandro d'Ivo	rich crimson velvet	46	23	Mar. 6	June 18
8.	Bencivenni di Neri	blue zetani vellutato	52	35	Mar. 11	July 7
9.	Spaziano di Giovanni	rich blue velvet	53	25	Mar. 11	July 19
10.	Matteo di Marco	black zetani vellutato	47	33	Mar. 18	July 22
11.	Marco di Domenico	blue zetani vellutato	46	30	Mar. 22	July 10

12. Niccolò di Bartolo Talani . . .	green damask	75	23	Apr. 8	July 22
13. Lorenzo d'Antonio (2d loom) .	crimson zetani vellutato	46	38	Apr. 10	July 2
14. Wife of Spaziano di Giovanni .	black satin	46	8	Apr. 24	July 19
15. Domenico di Salvestro . . .	green zetani vellutato	45	40	Apr. 30	July 17
16. Piero d'Antonio	green velvet	46	22	May 2	Oct. 10
17. Fino di Papi	black damask	52	22	May 6	July 1
18. Nofri di Francesco . . .	blue zetani vellutato	44	40	May 6	Aug. 4
19. Alamanno di Lazzero . . .	black zetani vellutato	45	30	May 9	Aug. 8
20. Bartolomeo di Papi . . .	blue velvet	50	22	May 9	Aug. 30
21. Domenico di Salvestro (2d loom).	purple zetani vellutato	41	40	May 20	July 28
22. Antonio di Bernardo . . .	black velvet in 2 peli	44	36	May 20	Dec. 1
23. Lorenzo d'Ant. (3d loom), son Iacopo .	crimson zetani vellutato	48	36	May 24	Sept. 4
24. Antonio di Conte	black velvet	49	22	June 5	Oct. 24
25. Bartolomeo di Papi (2d loom) .	rich black velvet	48	22	June 6	Nov. 26
26. Piero di Papi	purple damask	56	23	June 10	Aug. 9
27. Battista di Ambrogio . . .	rich black velvet	47	22	June 10	Oct. 10
28. Monna Antonia. . . .	crimson taffeta	76	6	June 10	July 31
29. Piero di Tommaso . . .	black damask	55	22	June 13	Sept. 23

* This weaver was ill a long time, which explains why he was slow in returning the cloth.
SOURCE: Archivio dello Spedale degli Innocenti, Estranei, 85, Libro di tessitori B of Andrea Banchi and Company.

Before Nuti opened the branch in Aquila the Banchi firm had been represented in Rimini by Simone di Niccolò della Tosa, who regularly attended the fairs of Lanciano, Pesaro, and Recanati to sell silk cloth, vestments, orphreys, belts, and ribbons. According to a contract renewed in October, 1454, he was to receive a commission of $2\frac{1}{2}$ per cent on all the goods sold at the fairs, plus his expenses for "going, staying, and returning." On goods sold in Rimini, however, he received no commission but was entitled to all the profits above the price at which the goods were invoiced to him by the Banchi firm.[94] Therefore this price must have included a mark-up on cost.

Elsewhere Banchi had had disappointing experiences; he had run into the usual troubles with unreliable agents over whom he had no control or with customers who were slow in paying. Brocades and brocaded velvets were the most difficult to sell. They were so expensive that the demand for them was very small, practically confined to the Church and to princely courts, partly because of their high cost and partly because of the restrictions of sumptuary laws. In Florence itself the market was very small because the Medici, Cosimo the Elder and later even Lorenzo the Magnificent, affected republican simplicity in dress, although some of the women wore brocaded sleeves or bodices and occasionally entire gowns of brocades for weddings and other very festive occasions.

Banchi was unsuccessful in selling silks at a profit in Milan and Naples. In Milan, Venetian silks were preferred. Florentine silks were prized in Naples but the Strozzi of Florence were entrenched as the chief furnishers of both woolen and silk cloths at the court of Alfonso I (1442–1458).[95] In 1455 Banchi sent rich gold and silver crimson brocades to Antonio di Romolo Cecchi in the expectation of selling them to the Aragonese court. However, Antonio apparently did not have the right connections in those circles; he took the silks to the wardrobe officials at the Castello Nuovo, the king's residence, and to Castel Capuano, the residence of Alfonso's illegitimate son Ferrante and his wife Isabella, and to Torre del Greco, the home of Madonna Lucrezia d'Alagno, the royal favorite, but he met with little success. Nobody was interested in the silver brocade. After much effort the gold brocade was finally sold to the king's *vicedomo* at an apparent gross profit, but after deduction of the carriage charges, brokerage, and other expenses there was a net loss of six florins on the price at which

94. Estranei, 74, Ricordanze A, fol. 209v. Between fols. 3 and 64 this journal contains copies of numerous invoices of goods sent to Simone della Tosa in 1454. His ledger account is in Libro rosso A (Estranei, 84), fols. 6, 31, 37.

95. Lina Montalto, *La corte di Alfonso I di Aragona; vesti e gali* (Naples, 1922), pp. 105–18.

Banchi had valued the brocade when he sent it.[96] As this price doubtless included a mark-up over actual cost, the loss, if any, may have been slight.

Andrea Banchi was more successful in Mantua, at least for a decade. Since 1431 his customer there was Giovanni di Burato and Company, *ritagliatori* (cloth retailers), probably furnishers to the Gonzaga court. However, in 1438 a sale was made directly to Paula Malatesta of Rimini, marchesa of Mantua (d. 1449), and another to Lodovico Gonzaga, the son and heir of the reigning marchese and Paula. The marchesa purchased 43 braccia of alexandrine blue velvet, brocaded with gold stars, for the sum of 200 florins, and she paid very promptly.[97] Messere Lodovico, who purchased plain crimson velvet, was less prompt, but he paid eventually.[98] The Mantua firm purchased a good quantity of zetani vellutati, both monochrome and in two colors; for example, one cloth with a design in black pile on a purple satin ground and another with a design in crimson pile standing out on a white satin ground. Plain velvet was also purchased, especially crimson, as well as some damask, satin, and taffeta.[99] But purchases from Mantua had ceased by 1440; the reason is not clear.

One would expect Rome to be a good market for silks because of a presumably large demand for them at the papal court, and although Banchi sent silk cloths to Rome throughout his business career he had difficulty finding agents who could sell them profitably. We have seen that he was dissatisfied with Giovanni and Zanobi Petrini's attempts. But Benvenuto Nuti apparently did fairly well during the months he was in Rome selling for the Banchi partnership.

After Benvenuto was sent to Aquila in August, 1455, the Banchi firm began dealing with Iacopo Bischeri and Brothers. Several small chests of silks were sent to them before the end of 1455. The first, sent in August, contained blue, white, and crimson velvets, red and black damask, crimson satin, red and white taffeta, and green voided satin velvet (zetani vellutato). The second chest, sent in October, contained only purple velvet, blue voided satin velvet, and crimson brocade. The third chest, in November, contained black velvet, blue and red taffeta, and one white damask brocaded with gold.[100] The Bischeri did rather well for

96. Estranei, 83, Libro rosso C, fols. 164, 189. For Lucrezia d'Alagno, see Montalto, *op. cit.*, pp. 43, 84–85.

97. Estranei, 83, Libro rosso C, fol. 29.

98. *Ibid.*, fol. 39.

99. *Ibid.*, fols. 13, 34, 47, 53, 59, 77.

100. Estranei, 84, Libro rosso A, fol. 88; Estranei, 74, Ricordanze A, fols. 151, 167, 176. In August, Benvenuto Nuti had turned over to the Bischeri several orphreys and 28 braccia of crimson alto basso velvet which they sold (Estranei, 83, Libro rosso C, fol. 172).

more than a year, making small profits on taffeta and net profits of 10 to 12 florins on pieces of velvet and brocades.[101] But by 1457 there were net losses on the sales, so Banchi tried another agent, Stefano di Guelfo, who did not do as well as the Bischeri were doing even at the end.[102] Both of these agents had charged 2 per cent commission; then in August, 1458, silks were turned over to a new agent, Francesco di Bruno Mazzei, whose charge was 3 per cent. Probably the Banchi partners hoped that by paying a higher commission they would again have profits instead of losses.

Mazzei served his principal, the Banchi firm, longer than his predecessors, from August, 1458, until December, 1460. He seemed to be doing fairly well in getting good prices but he sold very little, and in the end there was a small loss.[103]

The Banchi firm had Mazzei turn over 753 florins' worth of goods to a new agent, Matteo Baroncelli e Guglielmo Rucellai and Company. This firm was still serving as agent at the time of Banchi's death in October, 1462, and when the account with them was closed later in 1462 the same story was repeated. After the commissions and all expenses were deducted the firm suffered its highest loss of all.[104] Sales had been greater in volume than under Mazzei or Stefano, but not as high as the sales of the Bischeri, who had served about four months longer. Table 7 summarizes the sales and losses of the four agents in Rome.

Despite apparent losses, Rome must have been somewhat profitable to the Banchi firm because goods sent there on consignment, it seems, were always marked up from 1 to 5 soldi a oro per braccio. Therefore even in the years when the books recorded a small loss there must have been a concealed profit. Banchi, a shrewd businessman, would not have continued to send silks to Rome if this outlet had been persistently unsatisfactory. The recorded losses most probably indicate that results fell short of his expectations. Sales in Rome were usually for cash, and sometimes for credit, but never in barter for other commodities since the papal court was a consumer of luxury articles and had nothing to offer in exchange.

Around 1435 Andrea Banchi decided to find out how his silks would sell at the Geneva fairs and he sent a second cousin there, Priorozzo di Giovanni di Lodovico Banchi (born c. 1402). Since the cousin had business ability, the experiment turned out so well that Andrea decided

101. Estranei, 84, Libro rosso A, fols. 88, 125, 201, 206.
102. *Ibid.*, fols. 208, 239, 240.
103. *Ibid.*, fols. 233, 249, 260; Estranei, 86, Libro bianco B, fols. 43, 142.
104. Estranei, 86, Libro bianco B, fols. 139, 194, 278.

TABLE 7

SALES MADE BY BANCHI AGENTS IN ROME

Period	Length of Period	Agent	Sales f. s. d.	Net Losses f. s. d.	Per Cent of Loss
Aug. 1455 to Oct. 1457 .	2 years 2 months	Bischeri Brothers	1,759 9 8	83 18 11	4.8
Oct. 20, 1457 to July 19, 1458 .	9 months	Stefano di Guelfo	743 11 2	23 3 2	3.1
Aug. 1458 to Dec. 1460 .	2 years 4 months	Francesco Mazzei	368 2 6	20 6 7	5.5
Jan. 1461 to Oct. 1462 .	1 year 10 months	Matteo Baroncelli e Guglielmo Rucellai	1,479 0 6	163 10 1	11.1

SOURCE: Archivio dello Spedale degli Innocenti, Estranei, 84, 86, Libro rosso A and Libro bianco B of Andrea Banchi and Company.

to station him in Geneva as a permanent representative, and Priorozzo moved to Geneva in October, 1437. He was to receive a salary of 60 florins per year in addition to having all his living expenses paid by the firm.[105]

In the first half of the fifteenth century, Geneva had perhaps the best-attended fairs in Europe. The city was not only a market for all kinds of commodities but also an international clearing center where all important Italian banking houses, including the Medici, maintained branch offices.[106] The city was favorably located at the crossing of an east-west route from southern Germany to Spain and a north-south route from Italy to Flanders—through Burgundy and Lorraine, away from the theatre of the Hundred Years War. In Geneva, Florentine silks had to compete with the products of Venice, Genoa, Bologna, and Lucca on the basis of price and quality, but there was not the discrimination that was likely to exist at courts which bought only from their favorite suppliers.

From Florence, Priorozzo Banchi received every kind of velvet—from monochromes of various colors to rich polychromes, in two or three heights of pile, and priced from $1\frac{1}{2}$ to 4 or 5 florins per braccio.[107] The most sumptuous velvet—judging from the price of 20 florins per braccio—was a crimson *alto basso* in three heights of pile, brocaded and looped with fine gold.[108] Besides velvets, which predominated, damask and satin were also sent to Geneva in considerable quantities, but relatively little taffeta, perhaps because of the popularity of Bologna taffeta at the fairs. Some of the Banchi taffeta was changeable, and this was priced at 7 florins per pound.[109]

The shipments of silk, sent to Priorozzo by pack train with a common carrier (*vetturale*), usually had a value of 700 to 950 florins, but the value of two shipments was more than 1,600 florins—one sent on October 10, 1437, and the other on December 23, 1439.[110] The shipments were

105. Estranei, 83, Libro rosso C, fols. 24, 25. Living expenses for Priorozzo from October 12, 1437, until May 29, 1439 (one year, seven and a half months) amounted to 61 florins 19s. 4d. (*ibid.*, fol. 73).

106. For Geneva and its fairs, see the excellent volume by Jean-François Bergier, *Genève et l'économie européenne de la Renaissance* (Paris, 1963), which supersedes the old work of Frédéric Borel, *Les foires de Genève au XVe siècle* (Geneva, 1892).

107. Estranei, 83, Libro rosso C, fols. 24, 33, 42, 57, 68.

108. *Ibid.*, fol. 88. This very expensive brocaded velvet was in the shipment of December, 1439. Priorozzo was unable to sell any of the $39\frac{1}{2}$ braccia; the piece was later sent from Geneva to Barcelona (see below, n. 123).

109. Estranei, 83, Libro rosso C, fol. 24.

110. *Ibid.*, fols. 24, 88, for the two most valuable shipments.

spaced according to the dates of the Geneva fairs. Each year silks were sent around October 10 for the fair of All Saints; the next shipment was usually in December, before the snow completely blocked the Alpine passes, for the Epiphany fair in January. The third large shipment was for the fair of Easter or of Quasimodo, and it left Florence early in the spring but after the passes were clear. There were usually one or two shipments in mid-summer, scheduled to arrive for the fair of Saint Peter in Chains (August 1).

Most of the silks were sold by Priorozzo for cash or on credit payable one or two fairs later. He occasionally bartered silks: twice for fustians from Constance and twice for dyestuff, scarlet grain from Valencia.

The Geneva fairs usually had an unfavorable monetary balance with Italy in general and with Florence in particular, which could be settled only by shipping specie. This fact, although already known from the Medici records, finds confirmation in the Banchi accounts.[111] Priorozzo Banchi made only a third of his remittances by bill of exchange and the balance in specie, using the services of common carriers and of Florentine merchants who were returning home. Andrea's partner, Bernardo dalla Palla, made a trip to Geneva in the summer of 1438 and brought back 182 florins in Venetian and papal ducats.[112] The day after Bernardo's return, September 24, 1438, a common carrier delivered another batch of ducats, along with a few Turkish gold coins, that amounted to 160 florins.[113]

In these shipments papal ducats seemed to predominate, perhaps reaching Geneva by way of the Council of Basel but more likely by way of a circuit through Hungary where the papacy was paying subsidies to stem the Turkish peril. (The Turkish coins make this hypothesis even more plausible.) The sums that had been entrusted to carriers (in sealed bags) were seldom more than 350 florins, but a few remittances were of 400 florins, and one, in September, 1440, was for 530 ducats.[114] The remittances sent after each fair would be distributed among three or four carriers to reduce the risk of loss by robbery or accident.

What was not sent in specie was remitted by bill of exchange, usually indirectly through drafts on Venice or Rome, which underlines the fact that there were no regular connections between Florence and the fairs of

111. R. de Roover, *Rise and Decline of the Medici Bank*, pp. 123, 279–80, 284–85.

112. Estranei, 83, Libro rosso C, fol. 42.

113. *Ibid.*, fol. 42.

114. *Ibid.*, fol. 97 (for 530 ducats). Other large specie shipments were received on September 10, 1439 (483 papal ducats, fol. 75) and on March 11, 1440 (425 papal ducats, fol. 88).

Geneva. In other words, it was not always easy to buy direct drafts on Florence at the Geneva fairs. Some of the bills of exchange were purchased from the Geneva branch of the Medici bank, Giovanni d'Amerigo Benci and Company. Others were issued by the Borromei. The bills were drawn on several Florentine banking houses of good repute: Adoardo Giachinotti and Company, Bernardo da Uzzano and Company, Mariotto Lippi and Company, Giovanni Portinari and Company, and Bartolo Corsi and Company.[115] All of the bills were paid at maturity.

Priorozzo remained in Geneva until September or early October of 1444, when he returned to Florence to marry and settle down.[116] Since June, 1441, he had been on commission instead of salary. Geneva was such a satisfactory outlet that after Priorozzo's return Andrea sent his silks to a Florentine merchant, Bartolomeo Scali, to sell at the Geneva fairs on a commission basis.[117] Shipments to Geneva ceased after 1456, perhaps because the Banchi firm did not find a reliable agent to succeed Scali.[118]

Geneva was the only city outside Italy where Banchi was successful in selling silks profitably over a number of years, but Barcelona had seemed promising for a time. Florentine silks had been selling rather well there since the late fourteenth century,[119] and Andrea Banchi twice sent silks to Barcelona between 1440 and 1443. In July, 1440, Niccolò Banchi, brother of Priorozzo in Geneva, took two pieces of damask to Catalonia. One was crimson, $46\frac{1}{2}$ braccia long, appraised at $3\frac{1}{4}$ florins per braccio, and the other green, 61 braccia long, worth $1\frac{1}{2}$ florins per braccio. Niccolò also took an expensive piece of crimson velvet in three heights of pile, brocaded with fine gold thread and with loops of gold appearing on the surface (*broccato d'oro fine e ricciuto*); it was only $35\frac{1}{2}$ braccia long but it was valued at 20 florins per braccio.[120]

115. *Ibid.*, fols. 24, 48, 58, 73, 81, 97.

116. Estranei, 73, Libro segreto d'Andrea Banchi proprio, fol. 29.

117. The first shipment of silks to Bartolomeo di Luigi Scali was sent on October 17, 1444 (Estranei, 83, Libro rosso C, fol. 121).

118. There is one small exception. In March, 1458, the Banchi firm purchased a fardel of Spanish raw silk from the Geneva branch of the Medici company for 564 florins and sent three velvets, valued at 221 florins, in part payment. The balance was paid in cash to the Medici bank in Florence to be credited to the account of the Geneva branch (Estranei, 84, Libro rosso A, fol. 215).

119. Valencia was also an important outlet for Florentine silks (*Il Libro segreto di Gregorio Dati*, pp. 18, 54, 105). Silk merchants' catasto returns of 1427 and 1433 frequently mention representatives in Barcelona or Valencia. In his merchant manual, completed about 1440, Giovanni da Uzzano states that Barcelona is a good market for Florentine silks (Pagnini, *Della Decima*, IV, 163).

120. Estranei, 73, Libro segreto d'Andrea Banchi proprio, fol. 18.

From Barcelona, Niccolò Banchi carried the silks to the fairs of Castile, but he was unable to sell them. His expenses of £63 9s. 9d., Barcelonese currency, were paid by Piero di Niccolò Piaciti, a Florentine merchant residing in Barcelona, with whom the cloths were left when Niccolò Banchi returned to Italy.[121] Piaciti eventually succeeded in selling all three, but it took a great deal of sales effort. First he sold the green damask, which brought—commission and other charges deducted—a net return of 94 florins, very little above the value of 91 florins 10s. The crimson damask and the crimson brocaded velvet were both sold on March 1, 1442, on credit terms of eight months. Total net proceeds were apparently £640 6s. 8d., Barcelonese currency, or about 854 florins, which corresponded to their appraised value.[122]

Since these results were rather encouraging, Banchi had his cousin Priorozzo, in Geneva, send Piaciti another luxurious brocaded pile on pile crimson velvet. It was 39½ braccia in length and was appraised at 20 florins per braccio, or 790 florins in all. Piaciti received this cloth in January, 1443, and sold it on April 27 at 70 florins per *canna* of Barcelona on credit terms of nine months.[123]

The settlement with Piaciti, however, gave rise to difficulties. At various dates he remitted 1,235 florins 15s. in several bills of exchange, then stopped making further payments.[124] In 1445 Andrea Banchi succeeded in getting Piero's mother, Monna Piera, widow of Niccolò Piaciti, to promise to pay 300 florins on the balance still owed by her son, and in the summer of that year he accepted a farm from her in final settlement of her son's account.[125] In the end, the Barcelona venture resulted in a loss instead of a profit. Piero Piaciti joined the banking firm of Raimondo Mannelli and Company; it failed in 1451, deeply in debt to several branches of the Medici bank.

The Banchi firm also made an attempt to sell brocades, velvets, and damask in Paris and Bruges, but again it met with failure. On September 26, 1461, a contract resembling the medieval *commenda* was made with Niccolò d'Andrea de' Greci, who was to receive one-fourth of the net profits on the silk he sold. In addition to 612 florins' worth of damask and velvets, he took with him four pieces of brocade, three gold and one silver,

121. *Ibid.*, fols. 18, 21.
122. *Ibid.*, fol. 18.
123. This brocaded velvet had been sent to Geneva in a shipment of December, 1439 (see above, n. 108).
124. Estranei, 73, Libro segreto, fol. 18.
125. *Ibid.*, fols. 18, 32.

valued at 803 florins. He could sell for cash or on credit or barter. However, he was to be wary in giving credit, especially with nobles or princes (*signori*), from whom he was to obtain surety.[126]

This was shortly after the accession of Louis XI to the French throne, and probably the Banchi partners and Niccolò de' Greci hoped to sell the rich fabrics at the French court. They were taken to Tours, where Louis XI was residing. But Niccolò met with no success, for this monarch, from what we know of his character, was miserly and not given to ostentation. Because he was simple in his attire he had no use for brocades, and his courtiers evidently did not dare outshine their king. From Tours, Niccolò took the silks to Rouen, but he had no luck there either. Next he journeyed to Bruges, where he met with partial success; he was able to sell the velvets and the damask to four mercers, but only at a loss. After the deduction of all expenses from Florence to Bruges, the net proceeds on silk worth 612 florins were only 477 florins.[127] This was a substantial loss, even if the figures given in the contract somewhat overvalued the silks.

The four pieces of brocade found no market and were left on consignment with the Bruges branch of Antonio da Rabatta and Bernardo Cambi and Company, of Florence. In 1463 two velvets brocaded with gold were bartered for English cloth at the Antwerp Easter fair, but at a loss.[128] Even as late as the 1460's Bruges was not a good outlet for Florentine silks since the market was tightly controlled by the Lucchese. It was not until 1468 that Tommaso Portinari, the Medici representative in Bruges, finally succeeded in obtaining a substantial order for Florentine silks from the Burgundian court on the occasion of the marriage of Charles the Bold and Margaret of York.[129]

Another area in which the Banchi firm sought an outlet for its fabrics was "Romania," by which the Italians meant what is now Greece and the European part of Turkey. It is fairly well known that after the Turkish

126. The contract with Niccolò de' Greci is copied in Ricordanze C (Estranei, 76), fol. 277; the invoice is on fol. 168*v*.

127. *Ibid.*, fol. 262*v*, has the detailed account of sales and expenses; Estranei, 86, Libro bianco B, fols. 184, 185.

128. Estranei, 76, Ricordanze C, fols. 307, 313; Estranei, 86, Libro bianco B, fol. 277. The two brocaded velvets were valued at 652½ florins. After the 16 English cloths were sold, the loss on the barter transaction was entered as 245½ florins in Libro bianco B (fol. 307).

129. Brussels, Archives générales du Royaume, Chambre des comptes, No. 1923: Premier compte de Guilbert de Ruple, argentier de monseigneur le duc de Bourgogne, etc., fols. 352–61.

conquest of Constantinople the Florentines quickly resumed their export of woolen cloth to that city,[130] but it is less known that Constantinople was also a market for Florentine silks.

The Banchi firm began relations with "Romania" by entrusting 54 woolen cloths to Piero di Niccolò di Piero Popoleschi who was to sell them in Constantinople and elsewhere in Turkey and then purchase raw silk from the Caspian Sea region with the proceeds. In addition, Popoleschi received 200 ducats in coin.

Popoleschi's contract with Banchi and his partners also took the form of the old medieval *commenda*: one-fourth of the net profits of the whole venture to the traveling partner and three-fourths to the investing partners. Losses were to be borne entirely by the investing partners, as was customary. If necessary, Popoleschi was free to journey to Adrianople or to Brusa on horseback or to go by galley into the Black Sea. He was to return with the Florentine galleys but he could send some of his purchases via the French galleys or via Genoese or Anconan nefs (*per galee franciose o navi genovesi o d'Ancona*). On his return home he was to furnish a detailed report of sales, purchases, and expenses.[131]

Piero Popoleschi sailed from Pisa on a Florentine state galley at the beginning of August, 1459. He sold most of his cloth in Pera and Adrianople and bartered the rest for silk.[132] With the ducats he had brought from Italy and the receipts from the sales he purchased raw silk in Brusa and Gallipoli—and one female Tartar slave for Andrea Banchi's household.[133]

He returned almost a year later with the slave and with 594 pounds

130. Heyd, *Histoire du commerce du Levant*, II, 337–41; Pagnini, *Della Decima*, II, 64, 73, 104, 255–56, 303, 306–7; Gertrude R. B. Richards, *Florentine Merchants in the Age of the Medici* (Cambridge, 1932), pp. 9, 45–46, 50–51. Also see Giuseppe Vedovato, *L'ordinamento capitolare in Oriente nei privilegi toscani dei secoli XII–XV* (Florence, 1946), pp. 158–60; Gino Masi (ed.), *Statuti delle colonie fiorentine all'estero, secoli XV–XVI* (Milan, 1941), pp. 53, 65.

131. The *commenda* contract, dated July 31, 1459, is copied in Ricordanze B (Estranei, 75), fol. 280. Two of Piero's brothers acted as guarantors for the execution of the contract.

132. Estranei, 86, Libro bianco B, fols. 66, 115.

133. *Ibid.*, fols. 116, 125. The slave cost 90 florins; expenses, including some clothes for her, were another 5 florins (*ibid.*, fols. 115, 125). This was the second female slave Banchi had acquired, but the first was no longer with him. In October, 1438, Andrea had obtained her by barter, giving a piece of purple damask priced at 67½ florins to her master, Bartolomeo Boezi (Estranei, 83, Libro rosso C, fol. 51). The second slave stole money from Andrea's heirs in April, 1464, but the theft (20 large florins and 160 lire di piccioli) was discovered and the money was returned (Spedale degli Innocenti, Ser. CXX, No. 5, Libro giallo C, fol. 190).

(net weight in Florence) of seta stravai, valued at 1,409 florins. The net profit of the venture was only 155 florins 11s. 1d., of which Popoleschi received 38 florins 18s.[134]

A new commenda contract was entered into by the Banchi firm on August 11, 1460, this time with Niccolò di Niccolò Dietifeci, a Florentine residing in Pera who had a partner named Bastiano da Foligno. Dietifeci was about to return to Constantinople on a Florentine galley. He was given fifteen woolen cloths, valued at 452 florins, and a chest containing eleven silk cloths to the value of 765 florins. From the proceeds, raw silk was to be purchased and shipped to Florence. As his traveling and living expenses were not chargeable against the goods, Dietifeci was to receive one-third of the profits instead of the usual one-fourth, and, as customary, he would not share in any losses.[135]

The wool and silk cloths were sold and bartered for raw silk (stravai and leggi); the net profit was 243 florins, of which the Banchi firm received 162 florins.[136] Further shipments, of silk fabrics only, were sent to Dietifeci. A shipment on April, 1461, on a nef from Ancona, was valued at 786 florins; another, on Florentine galleys in August, 1461, was worth 1,409 florins. Net profit on these two shipments was 762 florins,[137] and would have been more than 800 florins if the Banchi partners had not felt it necessary to insure the Ancona shipment for 400 Venetian ducats at 8 per cent premium.

The Florentine state galleys made only one trip a year to Constantinople, usually sailing in August from Porto Pisano. Goods sent in any other month had to be shipped by ordinary nefs, Genoese carracks, or Venetian state galleys. Ancona was a popular port with Florentine merchants for shipping goods to Romania and the Levant because its freight rates were quite low, lower than the rates from Porto Pisano or Venice on the galleys.

The first two shipments of silks had the same number of cloths, almost the same value, and nearly the same weight, but one was shipped via Porto Pisano and the other via Ancona. Because of the similarities between these two shipments it is possible to make a cost comparison. Table 8 shows that total charges were higher via Ancona than via Porto Pisano because it was the practice to insure goods shipped by ordinary nef, whereas the state galleys, traveling in consort, were considered so safe that

134. Estranei, 86, Libro bianco B, fols. 115, 116.
135. The contract with Dietifeci is copied in Ricordanze C (Estranei, 76), fol. 274v.
136. Estranei, 86, Libro bianco B, fols. 120, 150; Estranei, 76, Ricordanze C, fol. 195.
137. Estranei, 86, Libro bianco B, fols. 120, 180.

some merchants did not take out insurance.[138] But carrying charges to Ancona were also higher because the goods had to be sent across the Apennines by pack animal.[139] On the other hand, freight charges were less than one-third of those on the state galleys between Porto Pisano and Constantinople. Although it cost Banchi more to ship via Ancona than via Porto Pisano, the difference between the two routes was not considerable, a little less than 3 per cent on valuable shipments like silks.

TABLE 8

COMPARATIVE CHARGES ON TWO SHIPMENTS OF 11 SILK CLOTHS FROM FLORENCE TO CONSTANTINOPLE VIA PORTO PISANO AND VIA ANCONA*

Items	Via Porto Pisano (Value: 765f. 1s. 9d.)		Via Ancona (Value: 785f. 18s. 6d.)	
	Charges f. s. d.	Per Cent of Value	Charges f. s. d.	Per Cent of Value
Packing and roping . . .	1 16 8	0.2	2 16 0	0.4
Florentine gabella	14 3 7	1.9	14 7 4	1.8
Carrying charges to the coast . .	1 4 0	0.1	7 16 0	1.0
Local charges in seaport . .	4 4 9	0.6	10 8 0	1.3
Freight charges on sea trip .	41 0 0	5.4	12 0 0	1.5
Marine insurance	none	0.0	39 1 10	5.0
Total	62 9 0	8.2	86 9 2	11.0

* Both shipments had approximately the same value and approximately the same weight, 97 pounds and 95½ pounds, respectively, so the figures are comparable.
SOURCE: Estranei, 76, Ricordanze C of Andrea Banchi and Company, fols. 73r, 126v, 195r–v.

The three lots of silks sent to Constantinople in 1460 and 1461 totaled 36 cloths, chiefly damasks in a variety of colors and designs, including two brocaded with gold. There were also ten velvets in the total, of which four pile on pile velvets were especially rich and costly because they were heavily brocaded with gold, and some zetani vellutati with the large floral motif and the serpentine stem so often reproduced by renaissance painters.[140]

138. For some instances of insuring goods shipped on the galleys, see my article, "Early Examples of Marine Insurance," *Journal of Economic History*, V (1945), 190–93.

139. The eleven silk cloths sent to Porto Pisano for shipment were transported by cart, so that only one chest was used for packing them, but the same number of cloths sent to Ancona were placed in two small chests because they had to be carried by a pack animal.

140. Estranei, 76, Ricordanze C, fols. 73, 126v, 164.

Who were the customers in Constantinople for these expensive silk-stuffs? One was the ambassador from the Greek empire of Trebizond, who made large purchases in October and November, 1460, not long before the Turks put an end to the tiny empire and its embassies. A Persian, and several Greeks, Turks, and Jews were other purchasers. An Italian physician resident in Pera, and Iacopo Tedaldi—the Florentine who left us such a vivid description of the siege and fall of Constantinople—were also customers.[141] All of the brocaded velvets and some of the damasks were bartered for raw silk from the partners Bartolomeo Zorzi and Girolamo Michiel, who were important Venetian merchants as well as the farmers of the Phocean alum mines.[142]

Pleased with the results obtained by Niccolò Dietifeci and his partner, the Banchi firm sent another chest of silks in April, 1462;[143] and the following August a large shipment of woolen cloth and silks was sent on the annual voyage of the Florentine galleys. There were 107 cloths packed in twenty-one bales, and 20 pieces of silk in three chests. Andrea Banchi's eldest grandson, Giuliano Ginori, age twenty, accompanied this shipment to Pera where he was to get experience in selling the woolen cloths under Dietifeci's guidance. The silks were to be consigned to Niccolò immediately, and Giuliano was to leave the unsold cloths in Constantinople, with Niccolò, when he returned to Florence with the galleys. He would bring back raw silk and dyestuffs.[144]

Giuliano Ginori reached Constantinople in mid-October, 1462, about the time that his grandfather died in Florence. More than half of the woolen cloths were sold before the departure of the three Florentine galleys on their return voyage. On board, bearing the merchant mark of Banchi, were several bales of the expensive red dye, kermes, which Dietifeci had

141. *Ibid.*, fols. 195–96. For Tedaldi, see Heyd, *Histoire du commerce du Levant*, II, 304 n. 3, 306 n. 4, 308; and Steven Runciman, *The Fall of Constantinople, 1453* (Cambridge, Eng., 1965), 141, 196, 239, who misspells Iacopo Tedaldi's name as Jacobo Tetaldi. The Tedaldi family was prominent in fifteenth-century Florence.

142. Estranei, 76, Ricordanze C, fols. 195–96; Heyd, *op. cit.*, II, 328.

143. Estranei, 86, Libro bianco B, fol. 210. Dietifeci was in Florence in the spring of 1462 and accompanied the chest of silks on a galley of the Grand Master of Rhodes (Ricordanze C, fol. 278v).

144. Estranei, 86, Libro bianco B, fol. 210; Estranei, 76, Ricordanze C, fols. 233v, 239v, 246. Seventy-six of the woolen cloths belonged to Andrea Banchi alone (Estranei, 83, Libro rosso C, fol. 215). The instructions given to Giuliano Ginori by the partner Bernardo Dati are copied in the only extant letter book (Estranei, 78, Registro di lettere segnato C di Andrea Banchi e compagni e poi della Commesseria di Andrea Banchi, 1462–65, fols. 128v–129).

acquired by bartering most of the silks in the April shipment and some of the woolen cloth brought by Ginori. There were also four fardels of raw silk, received in exchange for woolen cloth, and even a few sables, obtained by barter for a piece of silk.[145] Left with Dietifeci were over 2,000 florins' worth of silks and woolens.

The rest of the story is the sad, familiar tale of difficulties with an agent. From late 1462 onward, Dietifeci was slow in selling and even slower in remitting. In 1463, when he finally remitted by bills of exchange drawn on Venice, his drafts were protested and dishonored. By the time the protested bills were returned to Constantinople, the Venetian drawers and their sureties had fled because of the outbreak of war between Venice and Sultan Mehmet II.[146] Attempts to recover the amounts of the bills dragged on for about two years. In 1464 Dietifeci wrote that silk cloth was not selling: there were quantities of Florentine silks in Pera and no demand.[147] Finally in April, 1465, a procuration was given to Cosino di Leonardo Molletti, who was journeying to Pera, to collect as much cash as possible from Dietifeci and take from him the few unsold cloths which belonged to the Banchi firm. Molletti sent back 300 Venetian ducats and returned some woolen cloth.[148]

The disappointments of Andrea Banchi and his partners in trying to sell their goods in foreign markets illustrate the fact that silk manufacturers were not well-placed to secure distribution for their products abroad unless they had permanent and reliable representatives. Quality was not enough to find buyers; one must also know the clientele, its tastes, and its habits. Then, even with a good representative, political events could quickly change a profitable outlet to a poor market.

145. Estranei, 86, Libro bianco B, fols. 297, 298; Estranei, 76, Ricordanze C, fols. 296v–297.

146. Estranei, 78, Registro di lettere C, fol. 130 (letter from Dietifeci, dated January 9, 1464, and received March 19). The reply, dated March 28, is copied in Ricordanze C, fol. 283. I have not found precise information about the amounts of the bills of exchange. It is probable that they totaled more than 1,000 ducats. One cannot blame the Venetians for fleeing; to remain meant imprisonment and death.

147. Letter of January 9, 1464 (Registro di lettere C, fol. 130).

148. The commission given Molletti is copied in Registro di lettere segnato C (Estranei, 78), fols. 130–31. Dietifeci was notified by a letter dated April 28, 1465 (*ibid.*, fol. 131). The 300 ducats were carried to Florence by Nofri di Bernardo Serristori, delivered to the treasurer of the foundling hospital, and 370 florins *di suggello*, the value of the ducats, were credited to the account of the Commesseria di Andrea Banchi in ledger C of the Spedale degli Innocenti (Ser. CXI, No. 5, Libro giallo C, fol. 101). Niccolò Dietifeci died of the plague in Pera in 1469 (Pagnini, *Della Decima*, II, 263).

Banchi as a Person and as an Entrepreneur

What kind of man does Andrea Banchi seem to have been? Account books are not very good sources for revealing a person's character or personality, and Andrea's private libro segreto is not as much a personal diary as his coeval's, the setaiolo Goro (Gregorio) Dati. Nevertheless, from the libro segreto, from the other account books, from Banchi's catasto reports and from his testament, we get revealing glimpses here and there of the human being.

Banchi was not another Francesco di Marco Datini, a poor boy who by dint of energy, ability, and luck accumulated a fortune.[149] Andrea had undoubtedly inherited some property from his father: the shop in Via Por S. Maria, probably the house in Via de' Bardi, and perhaps some farmland.

As already mentioned, Andrea Banchi's taxable wealth in 1427, when the catasto was introduced, was 7,441 florins, on which he was assessed 37½ florins. This figure put him in the higher brackets but not at the top. In his own gonfalon, or district, twelve other taxpayers had larger assessments.[150] By 1457, a few years before his death, Banchi was among the ten highest taxpayers in the entire city and second-highest in the Scala gonfalon, exceeded only by Castello di Piero Quaratesi.[151]

When Banchi made his will, March 14, 1460, he estimated his fortune at 18,000 florins, not including his house in Via de' Bardi nor his villa at Montaguto Pegolotti ("La Rocca") nor the farm of Casa Vecchia (the dwellings and the land were to go to his wife). Nor did the figure include the building in Via Por S. Maria in which the silk shop was located, the fondaco in Via Vacchereccia, or the house in Via S. Niccolò that was occupied by his daughter Caterina Ginori and her family (these were to go to Caterina). The 18,000 florins included only the money invested in the silk shop, shares in the Monte Comune, and the value of several farms. One-third was bequeathed to his descendants: his daughter

149. Iris Origo, *The Merchant of Prato: Francesco di Marco Datini, 1335–1410* (New York, 1957); Federigo Melis, *Aspetti della vita economica medievale: Studi nell'Archivio Datini di Prato* (Siena, 1962), Vol. I.

150. Biblioteca Nazionale, Florence, MSS Magl. XIII.72.2, fol. 34v.

151. R. de Roover, *Rise and Decline of the Medici Bank*, Table 5, p. 31. By 1457 Andrea Banchi was the wealthiest *setaiolo*. Next came Zanobi and Guglielmo di ser Martino Martini, with taxable wealth of 6,900 florins and a tax of 34 florins 14s.; then Piero di Giovanni d'Andrea Minerbetti, 6,600 and 33 florins; Bartolomeo di Lorenzo Lenzi, 5,900 florins and 29 florins 14s.; Lodovico and Leonardo di Leonardo Boni, 4,200 florins and 21 florins 3s. Other *setaioli* were taxed less than 20 florins.

Caterina and his grandchild Alessandra, the only child of his deceased daughter Bice; and two-thirds were bequeathed to the Spedale degli Innocenti, which was named universal heir with the responsibility of paying all the legacies. The funeral expenses and some other debts were to be deducted from the third that had been left to his descendants. Part of the inheritance of Caterina and Alessandra was land in the Val di Pesa and two farms at San Martino a Strada, near Grassina, a village in Val d'Ema. This part was valued at 2,000 florins; the remaining 4,000 florins would eventually come from the silk partnership.[152]

In the course of thirty years, between 1427 and 1457, Andrea's fortune trebled. Although Banchi disapproved of lavish display and did everything in moderation, he probably lived according to his station. He maintained both a town house and a country place.[153] He built the latter residence, and spent considerable sums on the oratorio in the church of Santa Maria at Montaguto and on the chapel in San Niccolò in Florence where he is buried. For the main hall of his villa he ordered (from the Jesuats) two windows with his coat of arms at a cost of £34 3s. picc.—not a tremendous sum, but this expense satisfied his vanity.[154] His armorial bearings (azure, a cross moline or) were also prominently displayed in another colored-glass window in the oratorio of the church at Montaguto.[155]

In the years when his cousin Priorozzo was in Geneva as his factor, Banchi ordered some Flemish tapestries for his home. He occasionally purchased jewelry for himself, his wife, and his daughters, but not very much nor very expensive.

Banchi was apparently a good husband to a wife thirty years younger, and a devoted father and grandfather. The loss of his only son, Piero, at

152. Archivio Spedale degli Innocenti, Testamenta et Donationes ab Anno 1411 usque ad Annum 1576, fols. 145–65. These pages contain a copy of the testament of Andrea Banchi, drawn up in his residence by a notary on March 14, 1460, in the presence of seven witnesses, and the codicils added October 7 and 9, 1462, a few days before Banchi's death on October 12.

153. A small account book is extant that contains an incomplete record of expenses for the building of the castlelike villa at Montaguto (Estranei, 72, Ricordo di danari spesi nel Castello di Monte Aguto e ne' lavoratori, d'Andrea Banchi e di Piero Banchi suo figliolo). Work was begun in 1448, and by 1452 some 1,500 florins had been spent on construction and the interior (fols. 1, 11, 16, 20). Part of the festivities for Piero's wedding, on September 10, 1452, were probably held at "La Rocca" because in the preceding weeks rooms were painted and tables and benches were ordered (fol. 20).

154. Estranei, 83, Libro rosso C, fol. 180. The Jesuats (Ingesuati) were an Italian religious order founded in 1363 and suppressed in 1668.

155. Estranei, 83, fol. 180.

the age of twenty-six and childless, was naturally a great blow to Andrea, and his second son had died in infancy. His older daughter, Bice, married Ser Mariotto di ser Giovanni Bencini, apparently a notary; she too died young, leaving a girl, Alessandra. Andrea's younger daughter, married to Domenico Ginori, had eight children, six boys and two girls.[156]

The fact that Andrea Banchi lived long enough to see three of his grandsons working for him was probably some consolation for the death of Piero. Giuliano di Domenico Ginori (born 1442), his eldest grandson, worked in the silk shop from January, 1455, until the summer of 1462, the year he was sent to Pera with cloth. Francesco (born 1444), the second grandson, began to work in the shop in 1459; in 1460 he was sent to Aquila to assist Benvenuto Nuti, Banchi's partner in the accomanda for the Abruzzi. Lorenzo (born 1446), the third grandson, began working in the silk shop in January, 1462. The fourth grandson, Giovanni, was twelve at the time of his grandfather's death; the other two were much younger.

Andrea left all his books and those of his son to Giovanni Ginori. They were mainly in the vernacular, and some were *libri d'opere gentili*. But it is unlikely that Banchi had much of a library; he did not belong to the circle of the humanists. His business left him little time to read.

His two Ginori granddaughters had dowries from him in the Monte delle Fanciulle for 1,000 florins each. Banchi was always generous with his son-in-law, Domenico di Giuliano di Francesco Ginori (1409–1487), whose lack of business ability must have been somewhat disappointing. Son of a successful retail cloth merchant and brother of Gino and Antonio, who prospered as merchants, Domenico entered a dyeing partnership for wool, which failed in the mid-1440's. In the 1450's he had money invested in two firms of hosiers. He also owned a number of farms but they did not yield much income. His tax assessment for the catasto of 1457 was only 12 soldi a oro.[157] A codicil to the testament, dated October 7, 1462, released Domenico from repayment of the 250 florins which he had borrowed from his father-in-law in small amounts.

Banchi left gifts in goods or money to his three eldest grandsons, and they were to inherit the shop in Via Por S. Maria after their mother's death. But their name was Ginori, not Banchi. After the death of his wife, Monna Dianora, the house in the Via de' Bardi and the villa at Montaguto, adorned with the feudal symbols of the Banchi family,

156. ASF, Catasto, 824 (S. Giovanni, Leon d'Oro, 1457), fol. 50, where Domenico Ginori lists his children.
157. *Ibid.*, fols. 44v–51v.

were to go not to his descendants but to collaterals bearing the family name.

Even in communal Florence, the feudal cult of the name and family was not entirely dead. The dowry system favored sons over daughters and the prestige of a family depended not only on wealth but also on the number of male representatives. Banchi's behavior conformed to this traditional pattern, inherited from the pre-communal age, and which has not entirely disappeared even today.

Apparently Andrea Banchi's family allegiance overrode his shrewd business sense. Impoverished members of the Banchi family or those temporarily in financial difficulties usually turned to him for loans and were not disappointed. His testament released all relatives from unpaid loans and gave 2,000 florins of Monte Comune shares to five male Banchi relatives.

As was customary, Banchi also remembered the servants who had been in his household for many years; they received small legacies. What is more significant, he did not overlook his partners, and in codicils added five days before his death he bequeathed 300 florins to Bernardo Dati and 200 florins to Bartolomeo. It was for their sake that Banchi stipulated that the partnership was to continue for five years after his death under the name "Commesseria d'Andrea di Francesco Banchi di Firenze."

Banchi, in accordance with custom, left the arrangements for the funeral to his executors, but he gave specific instructions in his will about elaborate anniversary services in the chapel of the foundling hospital for the repose of his soul and the soul of his son Piero—with twenty priests in attendance and twenty-five pounds of wax. This is not necessarily a sign of piety; the number of candles and priests at a requiem or memorial mass is more the mark of social rank and family standing than of concern for the dead man's soul. The executors evidently felt the social position of the deceased required an impressive display. They spent more than 800 florins on the funeral, which took place in San Niccolò on October 15, three days after Andrea's death.[158]

In his testament, again according to custom, Banchi ordered restitution for any usurious interest which he might have received under the color

158. Estranei, 86, Libro bianco B, fol. 240; Estranei, 76, Ricordanze C, fols. 254*v*, 255, 259*v*. Cloth of silver to cover the coffin; banners and hatchments in the Banchi armorial colors (blue and yellow); church hangings of vermilion silk; over 250 pounds of torches and almost 500 pounds of wax candles; mourning costumes for the servants and the members of the family; capons, meats, Trebbiano wine, spiced breads, savories, and tarts for the funeral repast; 68 florins to the priests of Sán Niccolò for vigils, masses, obsequies: all this and more to lay to rest a man of moderation.

of deposit or exchange. However, no specific instructions were given and it is doubtful that any claimants presented themselves and that any restitution was made by the executors of the will. Although Banchi had no compunction about placing money on deposit *a discrezione* and investing in interest-bearing shares of the public debt, he obviously, and perhaps sincerely, did not regard himself as a usurer. Such practices were considered usurious by the more rigorous theologians, but practical businessmen like Banchi held more lenient views. Whatever theologians wrote or preached on the matter, there was no usury—in the opinion of businessmen —except in barefaced loans at interest, especially if fully secured.

One gets the impression that Andrea showed concern not only for the employees in his shop but also for his silk workers, at least for those who were in his service a long time. Nothing suggests exploitation: he paid the prevailing rates and his profits were not excessive. His account books indicate that the turnover among his workers was low, which means they preferred to work for him rather than for his competitors. Banchi paid his workers promptly, never withholding their wages. The withholding of wages was severely condemned by Sant'Antonino, archbishop of Florence, but it was unfortunately rather common since it was repeatedly forbidden by the guild statutes.

The fact that Andrea Banchi offered oil and wine to his workers at low prices was to their advantage rather than the opposite, and there is no evidence that they were overcharged or compelled to buy unneeded commodities. Perhaps one may conclude that Banchi, while he was not a philanthropist, showed more concern for the welfare of his workers than was usual among Florentine employers.

Banchi was not a political man and did not seek public office. However, he usually assumed the burden when his name was drawn by lot from the *borse* or purses. In his youth he served as treasurer of Arezzo to finish the term of office of his cousin Mariotto di Lodovico, who died in Arezzo in 1398.[159] In 1425 he was on a commission to revise the statutes of the Mercanzia tribunal, the commercial court.[160] He was a prior four times: in 1417, 1423, 1432, and 1445.[161] In 1447, however, when he was named captain-governor of Volterra, he refused to accept the post because his business affairs required his presence in Florence.[162] As one of the major setaioli of Florence, Andrea was an active member of the silk guild,

159. ASF, Registro delle Provvisioni, 87, fol. 110*v*.
160. ASF, Tribunale di Mercanzia, 5, fol. 60*v*.
161. ASF, MSS Mariani, Priorista fiorentino, Vol. II, fol. 405.
162. ASF, Provvisioni, Protocolli, 17, fols. 11, 113.

and between 1414 and 1451 he served ten times as consul and one year as treasurer of the foundling hospital.[163]

Andrea Banchi had the very human failing of disliking to pay taxes. He had no scruples about cheating the officials of the catasto and understating his income. Like modern income taxes, the catasto was based on individual returns filed by the taxpayer according to a prescribed form. For the first catasto, in 1427, Banchi and the other Florentine businessmen made fairly accurate reports. But soon he and others learned how to evade part of the tax. By 1430 Banchi had managed to reduce his tax burden and befuddle the examiners who came to inspect his books.

One way in which Banchi deceived the tax officials was by reporting the annual rent he received from Piero Petrini and Company for his shop in the Via Por S. Maria as 32 florins instead of 45, the actual figure. Then, since the examiners questioned his report, he had a notary draw up a fictitious lease for the lower figure.[164] Furthermore, in his 1430 return he claimed to have suffered losses when in reality he had made a profit. The tax commissioners, very dubious about the loss, checked his books but came away no wiser. Although the accounts were confused, they decided to accept Banchi's statement because "they could not spare the time needed to clear up the matter." [165]

Banchi later discovered better ways of concealing his assets and reducing his profits. After juggling the figures, he claimed in his return for 1457 (January, 1458) that the capital of his silk shop was only 2,800 florins, of which 2,400 florins were supplied by himself and 200 florins by each of his partners. In reality, the total was 6,000 florins: 4,800 florins invested by Banchi and 1,200 florins by the two junior partners. To eliminate the capital of the accomanda, Benvenuto Nuti, the partner in Aquila, was credited in the general ledger for shipping raw silk and silk thread in the amount of 1,644 florins 12s. 4d., when in fact no shipments were made.

163. ASF, Arte della Seta, 4, Libro di tutti quelli che sono stati Consoli dell'Arte di Por Santa Maria dall'anno 1393 in qua, fols. 9*v*, 10, 11, 12, 14*r–v*, 15*v*, 17, 22*v*, 25*v*. Banchi was treasurer (*camarlingo*) of the hospital for one year, beginning May 1, 1428 (Spedale degli Innocenti, Ser. CXX, No. 1, Libro debitori e creditori, 1421–35, fols. 166, 184).

164. Estranei, 73, Libro segreto d'Andrea Banchi proprio, fol. 5. Here, in his secret ledger, Banchi states that he is doing this "per fugire di non avere a paghare tanto chatasto di detta botegha."

165. The tax officials wrote this comment on Banchi's *portata*: "Abiamo veduto il suo bilancio e i suoi libri e non ci pare questa ragione bene chiara. Mettiamolla chome ci è dato per non aver tempo a poterllo chiarire, chè ci da di danno in uno anno f. 352." ASF, Catasto, 393, Campione del 1430 (S. Spirito, Scala), fol. 3.

Bernardo Dati, the partner who kept the libro segreto of the firm, states sardonically that Banchi tampered with the records "for love of the catasto" (*per amore del catasto*).[166]

Knowing Banchi's reputation, the tax commissioners of 1458 were as skeptical of the eighty-six-year-old setaiolo's report as their predecessors. They refused to accept his figures at face value. After much discussion they reached a compromise on an investment of 3,400 florins, which we know was still too low, and this compromise was notarized.[167]

The tottering old man—he claimed a tax reduction because he needed a servant who walked behind him to give him support—probably chuckled over the fact that he had again outwitted the tax officials, even though they assessed him 54 florins 4s. 8d., or 5 per cent, on his taxable wealth of 10,845 florins 8s. 11d.[168]

Banchi was not alone in evading taxes; the Medici, although they were the virtual rulers of Florence, did the same.[169] So many frauds were perpetrated, especially on business investments which were uncontrollable, that the catasto was abolished in 1495 and replaced by the *decima*, a tax which fell only on real estate and which remained in force until the French conquest of Tuscany at the time of Napoleon I.

Banchi was not an innovating entrepreneur. His success in business was probably due more to conservative policies, hard work, and caution than to daring, novelty, and experimentation. Although he experimented in seeking outlets abroad, these attempts—except in Geneva and Aquila, and for a short time in Constantinople—were not crowned with success. The difficulty was in securing trustworthy agents, since slow communications deprived the principal of a means of control and forced him to rely on the honesty and integrity of his representative.

The records show that Banchi specialized in the manufacture of luxury fabrics—brocades, figured velvets, and damasks—and produced relatively few of the less expensive satins and taffetas. This was perhaps a mistake from a pecuniary point of view because such high-priced articles had a small market and were therefore hard to sell. It is not surprising that the turnover of Banchi's stock was slow, a problem that was often aggravated by the necessity of granting generous credit terms to customers.

166. Estranei, 77, Libro segreto A, fols. 5, 20. Banchi still reported too low a figure for rent: 50 florins for the shop and fondaco instead of the 90 florins actually paid each year by the partnership (fol. 5).

167. ASF, Catasto, 785 (S. Spirito, Scala, 1457), fol. 607v.

168. The *portata* and *bilancio* cover fols. 600–7v.

169. R. de Roover, *Rise and Decline of the Medici Bank*, pp. 73–74.

Andrea Banchi apparently prided himself on producing the high-quality products which had established the reputation of the Florentine silk industry. Indeed, although they lack the variety and freshness of Lucchese medieval silks, the few fragments of Florentine brocades and patterned velvets that have escaped destruction are prized museum pieces today.

Two general financial statements (saldi) of Andrea Banchi's last partnership have survived.[170] They should not be called balance sheets because profits were determined by taking a physical inventory of goods in stock, and adding receivables, then deducting from this total the liabilities and the initial investment. This procedure is correct, of course, but it clearly indicates that the Banchi firm did not keep its books in double entry.

Banchi's two financial statements reveal that assets were composed of finished fabrics, raw materials, half-finished products in the hands of weavers and other workers, supplies of various sorts, wages paid in advance, goods consigned to agents, and other receivables. Tools and equipment are not recorded, which proves that the amount invested in them was negligible. Liabilities were made up of unpaid wages, sundry accounts payable, and money placed on deposit a discrezione by Banchi himself as *sopraccorpo*, that is, in addition to his share in the capital.

The earlier statement, of May 6, 1457, reveals that an inventory had not been taken since the formation of the partnership three years earlier and that assets amounted to 14,823 florins and liabilities to 7,332 florins. The partners' equity was therefore 7,491 florins, of which 6,118 represented initial investment and 1,373 represented accrued profits over a period of three years, or a return of about 7.3 per cent a year.

The second statement, drawn up three years later, on May 18, 1460, lists total assets of 16,597 florins and total liabilities of 6,195 florins. The net worth was therefore 10,402 florins, including an initial investment of 9,179 florins and accumulated profits for three years of 1,223 florins. This corresponds to a return of about 4.4 per cent, a less favorable result than that of the three previous years. In an age when the commercial rate of interest often reached 14 per cent and rarely dropped below 12 per cent, and when banks paid 8 per cent on time deposits a discrezione, a return of 7 per cent on a business venture was not spectacular and 4 per cent was decidedly poor.

From 1460 to Banchi's death in October, 1462, and afterwards, the

170. Both are in Estranei, 77, Libro segreto A d'Andrea Banchi e compagni, fols. 7v–18v, 21v–30.

silk firm was apparently even less prosperous. Banchi, approaching the age of ninety, was far past his prime, and his junior partners may not have had his earlier initiative and ability. One sign of growing difficulties is that the partners accepted a number of deposits in amounts varying from 100 to 600 florins on which they paid 8 per cent interest (discrezione).[171] Even more disquieting, early in 1462 the partners began to raise money by means of dry exchange with the Geneva fairs. On the first of these exchange transactions the loss was nearly 7.5 per cent in six and a half months, almost 14 per cent a year—a figure which greatly exceeded the return on industrial investments.[172] This onerous form of borrowing must have cut profits drastically.

Confirmation of this may be found in the fact that the liquidation of the Banchi firm five years after Andrea's death, in accordance with a provision of his testament, had unfortunate results for the partners and Banchi's heirs, whom the Spedale degli Innocenti held responsible for the losses. One of the partners, Bartolomeo d'Andrea, after deducting losses and withdrawals from his share of the capital, was left with a debit of 280 florins. The hospital allowed him to pay off 120 florins in 1468, and the balance in eight years, at the rate of 20 florins a year. Because Bernardo Dati, the other partner, had just died, his heirs were called upon to make good his losses and to acknowledge a debt of 700 florins. They agreed to pay 100 florins in 1468 and the balance in twelve years at the rate of 50 florins per year.[173]

Poor management by Banchi's partners, however, is only a partial explanation for the losses. General business conditions were unfavorable. The year 1460 saw the beginning of a long depression which shook the foundations of the Florentine economy and which lasted until the end of

171. Four of the deposits were by women and may have been accepted partly to give the women the feeling of a safe investment. The widowed mother of the partner, Bartolomeo d'Andrea di Domenico, deposited 110 florins, and her daughter deposited 280 florins (Estranei, 86, Libro bianco B, fol. 254). Monna Piera, wife of Ser Ruggieri and herself a winder of silk thread, and her son Niccolò, a Banchi employee, had 400 florins with the firm from October, 1461 (ibid., fols. 207, 338). Monna Alessandra, mother of Niccolò d'Antonio di Benozzo, who began working for the firm in November, 1460, lent 400 florins (ibid., fol. 166). The men who lent the firm money were outsiders. Interest of 8 per cent was paid annually on all the deposits even if the firm was losing money.

172. Estranei, 86, Libro bianco B, fol. 204, account of Rede d'Antonio della Casa e Simone Guadagni e compagni di Ginevra.

173. Spedale degli Innocenti, Ser. CXX, No. 6, Libro azzurro D, 1467–72, fols. 51, 76, 77.

the century. The depression was widespread, extending from England and the Low Countries to the Mediterranean, but it ended sooner in some areas than in others. One of its most tragic manifestations was the slow and then precipitous decline of the Medici bank, which began even before the death of Cosimo in August, 1464. Numerous firms of silk merchants failed during this period—five of them in the month of November, 1464.[174] Several international merchants declared bankruptcy in 1464 and 1465 and others were saved only by the prompt action of the Medici in their behalf.[175]

The more one studies Benedetto Dei's list of the wealthiest citizens in Florence in 1472 the more one realizes that most of the sizable fortunes had been made before 1450.[176] The Banchi firm is another illustration of this general trend. It prospered for half a century and then fell into an abrupt decline which it would perhaps be wrong to attribute exclusively to Andrea Banchi's old age and to the ineptitude of his junior partners.

174. Alamanno Rinuccini, in the continuation of his father's chronicle, mentions the failure of these setaioli: Matteo di Giorgio del Maestro Cristofano Giorgi, Giovanni and Angelo d'Antonio Baldesi, Bernardo di Mariotto Banchi and Brothers, Priorozzo di Giovanni Banchi (who had been Andrea Banchi's factor in Geneva), and Piero di Bartolomeo Partini and Brothers. *Ricordi storici di Filippo di Cino Rinuccini dal 1282 al 1460 colla continuazione di Alamanno e Neri suoi figli fino al 1506*, ed. G. degli Aiazzi (Florence, 1840), p. 94.

175. R. de Roover, *Rise and Decline of the Medici Bank*, pp. 359–60.

176. ASF, MSS, 119, Cronaca di Benedetto Dei, fol. 34: "E magiori ricchi di Firenze dell'anno 1472." A large fortune made after 1450 was that of Filippo di Matteo Strozzi (1428–91), but most of his wealth was gained while he was in exile in Naples.

THE ECONOMIC PREDICAMENT
OF RENAISSANCE CARDINALS

D. S. Chambers

University of St. Andrews

Ce n'est pas assez d'avoir de grandes qualités,
il en faut avoir l'économie.
—La Rochefoucauld, *Maximes*, CLIX

THE ECONOMIC PREDICAMENT OF RENAISSANCE CARDINALS[1]

The luxury and extravagance of the papal court during the so-called High Renaissance period, or roughly the half-century up to about 1530,[2] has long been popularized by historians of the Reformation. The well-known image of renaissance Rome can arouse indignation very easily, but it can also obscure an understanding of the attitudes and difficulties of those held responsible for the tone of the curia. In this context, the resident cardinals were nearly as important as the pope himself. Each virtually a prince within his own court as well as a member of the papal court, they were the pope's electors and principal counsellors; they stood at the apex of the great pyramid of papal officialdom, courted by ambassadors, proctors, job-seekers, litigants, artists, writers, relatives, and flatterers. It is curious that no thorough analysis has been attempted of the cardinals and their affairs in this crucial period in the history of the Church. Although they were satirized by contemporaries and have been deplored by generations of historians, they had special problems of their own, and certain things are worth saying on their behalf.

The heyday of the cardinals' more extreme claims to a share in papal authority, even to convoke councils or to depose popes, had passed by the middle of the fifteenth century. There was a dual reaction to monarchy. In fashionable theory there was the reaction, for example, of Nicholas Cusanus and Torquemada. And there was a reaction in practice: the calling of a

1. I am especially grateful to Professor Lionel Butler for his help and encouragement, to Professor E. F. Jacob for his valued suggestions and criticism, and to A. V. Antonovics for some of the information I have used in this article.

2. The most useful lists of cardinals and the most basic information about them are in C. Eubel, *Hierarchia Catholica Medii Aevi* (Münster, 1901–10), II and III. J. Arle's *Beiträge zur Geschichte des Kardinalkollegiums* (Bonn, 1914) unfortunately ends in 1484, although the author had intended to continue it to the Council of Trent. L. von Pastor's *History of the Popes*, ed. F. I. Antrobus, London, 1894 (IV, 408–15; V, 361–62, 369–70), digresses about the college of this period with disapproval. The sybaritic ostentation of many cardinals is emphasized by E. Rodocanachi, *La première renaissance, Rome au temps de Jules II et de Léon X* (Paris, 1912), Ch. II, "Luxe et richesses des cardinaux"; but this is a work to be used with caution as it is so uncritical of sources. A more balanced view was sketched in a paper read to the Académie française by Duchesne, reported in a short article, "La ricchezza dei cardinali nel Rinascimento," *Nuova Antologia*, 5th ser., cli (1911), 748–49. Jacob Burckhardt, with characteristic vision, referred to "the secret misery of the prelates, who, notwithstanding heavy debts, were forced to live in a style befitting their rank." *The Civilization of the Renaissance in Italy* (trans. Middlemore, Greenwich, Conn., 1944), p. 113.

council by anyone except the pope was pronounced anathema by the bull *Execrabilis* (1460); and attempts to control a new pope by means of public and (after 1458) secret capitulations or promises signed in the conclave were always overruled.[3]

Popes also tended to make the college larger; hence its will became more diffuse. Pope Sixtus IV (1471–1484) created thirty-four cardinals; Popes Alexander VI (1492–1503) and Leo X (1513–1521) each created forty-three. Between December, 1471 (Sixtus' first creation) and May, 1527 (the sack of Rome)[4] there were one hundred and eighty-three cardinals, of whom twenty-three were survivors from creations before 1471. Of these, only about twenty, little more than a tenth, can be classified as permanently nonresident; the vast majority spent an appreciable part of their careers as curia cardinals. The death rate, of course, was high, so this figure does not give a fair idea of how many cardinals were resident in or based on the curia at any particular time. However, twenty-five or thirty would be a reasonable average estimate, though this number might have swollen to at least forty after a large creation, as in 1517.

But even if the cardinals' constitutional pretensions were in decline and their numbers inflated, the prestige, power, and dignity of the red hat were still tremendous. The old analogy of the college with the senate of the Roman emperors, which may have derived from the forged Donation of Constantine or from a statement of St. Jerome,[5] received a new luster from the craze of fifteenth-century scholars for antiquity.[6]

There can be little doubt that most cardinals sincerely believed it was their duty to follow a princely way of life; moreover, many of them came from princely families, or had close connections with the secular powers. In a hierarchical age, they were very conscious of the dignity of their station. This awareness has already been pointed out in connection with

3. W. Ullmann, "The Legality of the Papal Electoral Pacts," *Ephemerides Iuris Canonici*, XII (1956), 246–78, points out that they transgressed Gregory X's bull *Ubi Periculum* in any case. Also see J. Lulvès, "Päpstliche Wahlkapitulationen," *Quellen und Forschungen aus italienischen Archiven*, XII (1909), and nn. 71–75 below.

4. This study is more concerned with the early sixteenth-century cardinals, but the limitations of date have not been rigidly observed: 1534, the year of Clement VII's death and Henry VIII's breach with the papacy, is in some respects a better terminal date than 1527.

5. J. B. Sägmüller, *Die Tätigkeit und Stellung der Kardinale bis Bonifaz VIII* (Freiburg im B., 1896), pp. 160–66, 239.

6. See Flavio Biondo, *Romae Instauratae*, III, 271, quoted in Garin, *Il Rinascimento Italiano* (Milan, 1949), p. 93; or in Pius II, *Commentaries*, tr. F. A. Gragg, Smith College Studies in History, XXII, XXV, XXXV, XLIII (Northampton, 1936–57), *passim*. See von Pastor's *History of the Popes*, V, 143, 370, and J. Burckhardt, *op. cit.*, p. 150.

the cardinals of the Avignon period,[7] but perhaps it applies even more to the cardinals of the restored papacy after the Council of Constance. The rejection of the Franciscan ideal, the quasi-official policy since the time of Pope John XXII, was further stressed with the revival in Florence of Aristotle's moral arguments in favor of affluence. Lapo da Castiglionchio the Younger, a secretary of Pope Eugenius IV and protégé of Cardinal Giordano Orsini, wrote a dialogue which argued that the pope and cardinals were obliged to be rich: in Apostolic times the Church had taken up the cause of poverty to make converts, but now it was necessary to gain men's eyes by splendor and munificence.[8] Paolo Cortese's *De Cardinalatu* (1510) had much the same message. *De Cardinalatu* is virtually an anthology of data from contemporary life and from literary sources that was concerned to present the moral, economic, and administrative attributes of the "perfect cardinal" in the same manner as other literary paragons of the day: the "perfect merchant" of Benedetto Cortugli or the "perfect courtier" of Baldassare Castiglione.

Cortese, who wrote his book at Cardinal Ascanio Sforza's suggestion,[9] assumed that the cardinals were the reincarnation of Roman patricians. Using rather far-fetched parallels for togas, lictors, quaestors, and other ancient things, Cortese even asserted that cardinals should preferably be rich and noble by birth since men greatly admire these qualities.[10] This snobbish preference was echoed in Castiglione's dialogues on the courtier, where a cardinal, Ippolito d'Este, is given as an example of the perfect courtly type.[11] According to Cortese, cardinals should display liberality and magnificence and be munificent with alms;[12] they should live in splendidly decorated palaces.

This last requirement had been increasingly fulfilled since the middle

7. G. Mollat, *The Popes at Avignon* (translated from the 9th French edn.; Edinburgh, 1963), pp. 307–8; W. Ullmann, *The Origins of the Great Schism* (London, 1948), pp. 161–62.

8. H. Baron, "Franciscan Poverty and Civic Wealth in Humanistic Thought," *Speculum*, XIII (1938), esp. pp. 29–30. The tract has been edited by R. Scholz, "Eine humanistische Schilderung der Kurie aus dem Jahre 1438," *Quellen und Forschungen aus italienischen Archiven*, XVI (1913–14).

9. P. Paschini's "Une famiglia di curiali nella Roma del Quattrocento; i Cortesi," *Rivista di Storia della Chiesa in Italia*, XI (1957), provides information about the genesis of *De Cardinalatu*, but unfortunately without much reference to sources.

10. P. Cortese, *De Cardinalatu* (1510), pp. xlvi, cxxvii (erratic page numeration).

11. B. Castiglione, *Il Libro del Cortegiano*, ed. V. Cian (4th. edn. Florence, 1947), pp. 40–41. See Cardinal Pompeo Colonna's alleged objection to his colleagues as "huomini nuovi e pieno d'ogni vitio" in Paolo Giovio's *Vita di Pompeo Colonna*, tr. L. Domenichi (Venice, 1557), p. 148.

12. *De Cardinalatu*, pp. lii ff., cii–iii.

of the fifteenth century, when a sort of building boom in palaces for curia cardinals had developed.[13] Some cardinals had rooms in the papal palace, and so enjoyed the special access to the pope of the "palatine cardinals,"[14] but this did not preclude having a palace of their own[15]— which obviously was the most substantial way of expressing their dignity. In Pietro Barbo's palace (now the Palazzo Venezia) or in Riario's (now the Cancellaria), the building might be even grander than Nicholas V's reconstructed Vatican Palace. It is therefore not surprising that Barbo chose to stay in his own palace, and further enlarge it, when he became Pope Paul II in 1464 (it passed afterwards to his nephew, Cardinal Marco Barbo).

13. T. Magnuson, *Studies in Roman Quattrocento Architecture* (Uppsala, 1958), pp. 227 ff.

14. Such an inner court of the cardinals is quite often distinguished in contemporary sources. The Venetian orators recorded, after calling on the pope on December 10, 1510: "trovassemo oltre i cardinali palatini . . . el Rmo. San Zorzi" (R. Cessi, *Dispacci degli ambasciatori veneziani alla corte di Roma presso Giulio II* [Venice, 1932], p. 193). The papal master of ceremonies allowed them precedence in processions; see J. Burchard, *Liber Notarum*, ed. E. Celani, *Rerum Italicarum Scriptores*, XXXIII, ii (Città di Castello, 1906), II, 437. Paolo Cortese also refers to them: "Hi senatores . . . qui in pontificio famalatu vivunt" (*De Cardinalatu*, p. cxxviii), and notes as such Julius II's newly created cardinals of December, 1505, viz., Santori, Gabrielli, and del Carretto. These cardinals are also mentioned by Paris de Grassis: "omnes in palatio papae habitantes," in O. Raynaldus, *Annales Ecclesiastici* (Lucca, 1754), XI, 470. A hint of their special influence was given in a letter of the Mantuan orator Ludovico di Camposampiero on March 20, 1508: "uno cardinale palatino che ama molto el nostro Cardinale Ferrarese," he wrote, had interceded for a bishopric for Cardinal Sigismondo Gonzaga (Archivio di Stato, Mantua, Gonzaga, Busta 858).

15. Paris de Grassis' diary recorded, August 21, 1506, that when Cardinal Sangiorgio was appointed a legate: "non fuit a cardinalibus collegialiter associatus ad eius domum nec ad cameram quam in palatio habitabat" (L. Frati, *Le due spedizioni militari di Giulio II* [Bologna, 1886], p. 21). In December, 1520, de Grassis noted that Cardinal Passerini, as legate to the March, was accompanied to his room, not his palace (diary in British Museum, Additional MS 8443, fol. 201). On July 9, 1521, the English ambassador John Clerk wrote to Wolsey that as Cardinal Rafaelle Riario was dead, Cardinal Giulio de' Medici had possession of "his fayr howse [in] Rome, whiche is a marvellose goodly palayce for any prynce to dwell yn"; on the other hand, he wrote in the following December: "The Cardinal de'Medici hath a logyng within the popis palais and so hath dyverse other cardinals" (British Museum, Cotton MS, Vitellius B, IV, fols. 133, 238; abstracts are in *Letters and Papers, Foreign and Domestic* [ed. J. S. Brewer, referred to below as *LP*], III, 1402, 1895). But on June 11, 1523, Clerk wrote to Wolsey about the Cardinal "Campegius qui solus ex omnibus cardinalibus habitat in Palatio" (*State Papers, Henry VIII*, VI, 122; abstract in *LP*, III, 3093), despite the fact that Campeggio had been granted Cardinal Castellesi's former palace to live in. It would appear from this that Pope Hadrian VI had turned Leo X's palatine cardinals out of their rooms. If de' Medici and Campeggio were lucky enough to have a choice of palaces, there were some palatine cardinals, nevertheless, who had no homes of their own, such as Leo X's favorite, Cardinal Dovizi (G. L. Moncallero, *Il Cardinale Bernardo Dovizi* [Florence, 1953], pp. 499–500).

Enormous households were necessary in such palaces. Cortese suggested about sixty *familiares* and eighty lesser attendants,[16] but in real life the average may well have been even higher. A document drawn up in December, 1509, shows an average of one hundred and fifty-four *familiares* for twenty-six cardinals' households,[17] and the *Descriptio Urbis* of 1526 yields a similar average for twenty-four households[18]—although average figures do not of course reveal the significant differences between the largest and smallest establishments.[19]

Cortese made the resemblance between cardinals and lay princes even closer when he went on to suggest that they should ride and hunt,[20] but it should be borne in mind—even if cardinals have been much criticized for these pastimes—that they were approved by respectable opinion: by Guarino of Verona, the famous humanist teacher, and—on medical grounds—by Leo X's doctor.[21] Cardinal Castellesi (created in 1503) wrote a poem on the salutary effects and the delights of hunting;[22] Lorenzo de' Medici, in a famous letter of advice to his son Giovanni (later Pope Leo X, who had been created a cardinal at the age of thirteen), insisted that he should take plenty of exercise and keep a well-appointed stable.[23] Lorenzo advised his son to be moderate in his pomp, and his letter was full of moral precepts, but he did not suggest what most would call an austere or inexpensive style of life. Cortese, similarly, made some acknowledgment of the ascetic ideal by stressing the virtues of moderation and continence, but this was not to diminish the cardinal's princely station; it was perhaps equivalent to the advice Petrarch gave Cardinal Talleyrand in 1351: to despise riches while living in the midst of them.[24]

A high style of living was definitely recognized as the condition of being

16. *De Cardinalatu*, pp. lvi–vii.

17. "Numeri familiarum Reverendissimorum dominorum Cardinalium et vegetarum vini quod quilibet dominus debet habere gratis, videlicet de Gabella a Gabellariis Dohanae Ripae" (Vatican Archives, Acta Consistorialia, Miscellanea III, fol. 28).

18. D. Gnoli, "Un censimento di Roma sotto Clemente VII," *Archivio della Reale Società Romana di Storia Patria*, XVII (1898), 375–520.

19. In 1526 they varied from Cardinal Scaramuccia Trivulzio's household of four hundred and fifty-six to Cardinal Salviati's sixteen.

20. *De Cardinalatu*, pp. lxiii–vi.

21. G. Calamari, *Il confidente di Pio II, Iacopo Ammanati* (Rome-Milan, 1932), II, 360; E. Rodocanachi, *Le Pontificat de Léon X* (Paris, 1931), p. 175.

22. "Ad Ascanium cardinalem S. Viti Vicecancellarium Venatio" (Venice, 1505). See P. Paschini, "Adriano Castellesi," *Tre illustri prelati del rinascimento* (Rome, 1957), pp. 108–14.

23. A. Fabronio, *Laurentii Medicei Magnifici vita* (Pisa, 1784), II, 308–12. Much of the letter is translated in von Pastor, *History of the Popes*, V, 358–61.

24. Baron, *op. cit.*, pp. 9–10.

a cardinal, and not even the decrees that urged reform altogether denied this. In 1514 the Fifth Lateran Council asserted that cardinals should continue to keep open house to scholars, men of good character, and nobles in reduced circumstances.[25] "The dignity of their station" was the common defence for the cardinals' possession of wealth. It was quoted in bulls that permitted them to hold pluralities "to assist them to bear the burden of expense which their office imposed on them."[26] As Cortese declared, "the senators are occupied with the cares of administering the republic,"[27] and the cardinals themselves resolved in the first conclave of 1503 that "having to perform higher duties so ought they to enjoy greater privileges than the other servants of Christ."[28]

A large income might then be justified as a right. Cortese suggested the figure of 12,000 ducats a year;[29] but even reform commissions held out for very substantial sums: 6,000 ducats, the figure originally suggested by Martin V,[30] was recommended in 1493 and 1523.[31] A reform minute of Cardinal Costa in 1497 suggested between 3,000 and 4,000 ducats,[32] and Cardinal de Vio (Cajetan) in 1522 proposed 4,000 with allowance for extra income from private sources.[33] These, moreover, were minimum figures. Erasmus may have been ironical when in 1535 he wrote that no one with an income of less than 3,000 a year could become a cardinal,[34] but certainly the nature of things made it difficult to make ends meet on less.

The facts about the cardinals' resources for this magnificent style of living are hard to discover; much research must still be done even though

25. O. Raynaldus, *Annales Ecclesiastici*, XII (Lucca, 1755), 68.

26. E.g., Cardinal Gabrielli in September, 1507: "Ut statum tuum iuxta cardinalatus dignitatis sublimitatem decentius tenere" (Vatican Archives, Reg. Vat. 922, fol. 217v).

27. *De Cardinalatu*, p. xlvii.

28. *Calendar of State Papers, etc., Spain*, ed. G. A. Bergenroth (referred to below as *Span. Cal.*) I, 371 (Ch. I).

29. *De Cardinalatu*, p. xlvii; mentioned by H. Jedin, "Analekten zur Reformtätigkeit der Papste Julius II und Pauls IV," *Römische Quartalschrift*, XLIII (1935), 153. Cortese arrived at his figure by dividing a (presumably) fictitious corporate income of 490,000 ducats among forty fictitious cardinals.

30. B. Hübler, *Die Constanzer Reformation* (Leipzig, 1887), p. 153.

31. Vatican Archives, Arm. XI, Vol. 88, fol. 6; M. Sanuto, *Diarii* (Venice, 1879–1903), XXXIII, 440.

32. L. Celier, "Alexandre VI et la Réforme," *Mélanges d'archéologie et d'histoire de l'École française de Rome* (1907), p. 87.

33. *Concilium Tridentinum* (Freiburg im B., 1930), XII, 33.

34. J. Huizinga, *Erasmus of Rotterdam* (London, 1952), p. 253.

precise findings are impossible. However, from the material that is available certain conjectures can be made—and at least one valid generalization: there was a great inequality in the distribution of cardinals' wealth, and this went beyond the minimal resources provided by the corporate income of the college.

The corporate income had been regularized in 1289 by the bull of Pope Nicholas IV, *Coelestis Altitudo*, which decreed that half of certain items of papal revenue were to be divided among cardinals resident in Rome. A special accounting office, a chamber of the college, was set up for the cardinals to receive and distribute the funds, with one of the cardinals annually appointed as chamberlain.[35] Unfortunately, however, the records of *solutiones* or payments to the chamber of the college are missing for the period 1479–1534, and those of the earlier period of the restored papal monarchy have not yet been thoroughly analysed,[36] so it is not possible to be definitive about the size of the corporate income that was shared in our period.

The items of revenue to which the cardinals were entitled, according to the bull of 1289, included—among other things—a half-share of the "census." This census had four distinct parts, of which the revenues of the papal state were a major item: rent from lands, hearth tax, tolls, customs, profits from jurisdiction, etc. However, a recent work has stated "that for some considerable time before Martin V's pontificate the popes had ceased sharing these temporal monies with the cardinals." Reform commissions of the cardinals which sat in 1423 and 1429 (or 1430) demanded a resumption: "whether the college succeeded at any time in the fifteenth century in recovering this lost ground is again far from clear," but it seems probable they had "lost this battle" by the end of the century.[37] Whether there was an attempt to re-open the battle under Pope

35. J. P. Kirsch, *Die Finanzverwaltung des Kardinalkollegiums im XIII und XIV Jahrhundert* (Münster, 1895); P. M. Baumgarten, *Untersuchungen und Urkunden über die Camera Collegii Cardinalium für die Zeit von 1295 bis 1437* (Leipzig, 1898); and P. D. Partner, *The Papal State under Martin V* (London, 1958), p. 138. Statutes relating to the chamber of the college, drawn up in 1466, 1498 and 1514, are printed in Baumgarten, *op. cit.*, pp. xl–xcv, and in Eubel, *Hierarchia Catholica*, II, 65–68; III, 98.

36. W. E. Lunt, *Financial Relations of the Papacy with England, 1327–1534* (Cambridge, 1962), Appendix II, p. 722. A. V. Antonovics is preparing an Oxford *D. Phil.* thesis concerned with the chamber of the college in the fifteenth century and has sent me some of his findings (mentioned below).

37. Partner, *The Papal State under Martin V*, pp. 139–40. Antonovics, however, has found a reference to the cardinals' sharing in receipts from one *dogana* of the Patrimony (Vatican Archives, Obligationes et Solutiones, Vol. 65, fol. 134v), which he thinks may be an important lead.

Julius II and his successors, who were greatly concerned with consolidating the papal state in Italy, has yet to be shown, but we would surely have heard about it if an attempt had ended in a victory for the cardinals.

The other three items of the census were miscellaneous tributes and taxes raised from lands under secular lordship, which special papal collectors were supposed to gather. These were payments received from certain "exempt" religious houses which came directly under papal jurisdiction instead of under local bishops and temporal lords, tribute from the rulers of certain lands over which the papacy claimed a nominal lordship, and Peter's Pence—paid by certain countries, including Poland and England, and in some cases raised by a levy on each household or on each person. Except for the second item, the papal collectors were still receiving these monies during our period; but whether the cardinals shared in them is another matter; the probability is that they did not.[38]

Another item of shared revenue, according to the bull of 1289, was the tax on visitations *ad limina apostolorum* which all bishops were obliged to make either in person or by proxy at stated intervals, according to the distance of their sees from Rome. It is possible that the cardinals still received their share of these payments during our period, but this has yet to be proved. In any case, it would not amount to a very large annual sum when divided among them.

The main item of corporate income, however, and one which was certainly still shared, was from the *servitia* or common-services tax, which was one-third of the annual value of major benefices bestowed by papal provision. The cardinals themselves played an important part in the procedure of papal provisions. One cardinal (the cardinal *relator* or *ponens*) was responsible for giving an account of the candidate for provision in the presence of the pope and cardinals assembled in consistory.[39] Exact figures have yet to be collected from the registers of *obligationes et solutiones*

38. Lunt, *op. cit.*, pp. 1–73, and *idem, Papal Revenues in the Middle Ages* (New York, 1934), I, 61–71, 91–93. He shows that as early as 1314 Clement V was inquiring whether he was obliged to share Peter's Pence with the cardinals (*op. cit.*, p. 166). English tribute was not paid after 1333 (Lunt, *Financial Relations*, pp. 67–73).

39. On the common services (*servitia communia*) and the procedure for consistorial provisions, see A. Clergeac, *La Curie et les Bénéficiers Consistoriaux* (Paris, 1911); A. I. Cameron (Annie Dunlop), *The Apostolic Camera and Scottish Benefices, 1418–88* (St. Andrews University Publications No. xxxv, 1934), pp. xiii–lvi, *passim*; W. E. Lunt, *Papal Revenues* I, 81–91, and *Financial Relations of the Papacy with England, 1327–1534*, pp. 169 ff. The five "petty services" (*servitia minuta*) were each reckoned as one fourteenth of the cardinals' total share of the common services. The fifth "petty service" went to the cardinals' *familiares*, but otherwise the cardinals' only benefit from them was the Apostolic Chamberlain's three-quarter share of the first "petty service" and the Vice-Chancellor's one eighth of the second.

in the Vatican archives, but as a source of income it was certainly insufficient for a cardinal's living expenses. It was also highly variable; the total changed each year, depending on the number and value of the particular bishoprics which came up for the papal provision. It also varied according to the number of cardinals present in consistory. And shares fell, of course, after new cardinals had been created, which was one of the reasons why the cardinals so strenuously opposed new creations.

Light is thrown upon the average figure a cardinal might expect from some account sheets of Cardinal Niccolò Fieschi, which show the sums he received from 1504 to 1520.[40] The distributions were supposed to be made every two months in the cardinal chamberlain's house, according to the statutes of the chamber, but in Fieschi's accounts they are slightly less frequent. It is very unlikely that Fieschi was present at every consistory, but his attendance as a curia cardinal was probably as frequent as the others. On this assumption, then, we can reckon that a cardinal would have averaged 900 ducats a year from the common services.[41] But an average figure hides the extraordinary fluctuations. In 1517, for instance, Fieschi received 1,489 ducats but only 407 the following year. This reflects the creation by Leo X of thirty-one new cardinals, of whom all but five or six took up residence. This sudden drop is also reflected in some accounts of Cardinal Giulio de' Medici for 1521/22, when his average was quoted as about 700 ducats a year.[42]

40. Vatican Archives, Fondo Sacro Collegio dei Cardinali, Lib. Cedularum et Rotulorum, I (unfoliated). The collocation of this document would suggest that it was the official record of the whole college, but in fact it consists of just Fieschi's receipts, as the headings of the *cedulae* make clear: "Facta fuit generalis divisio pecuniarum communum et minutorum servitium . . . . de quibus Rmus d. Cardinalis de Flisco capit ut sequitur." See the table in Appendix I, below.

41. The total in 1499 of "23,000 ducatos per expeditiones" received by the chamber of the college (Eubel, *Hierarchia Catholica*, II, 62) would work out to much the same per head. Lunt estimates that, from English provisions alone, the annual revenue from the *servitia* from 1501 to 1533 was 8,231 ducats, half of which would have gone to the cardinals (*Financial Relations*, p. 305). Clearly, much more arithmetic must be done. Antonovics has analyzed the only surviving register of general divisions of *servitia* among the cardinals from the latter half of the fifteenth century (Vatican Archives, Obligationes et Solutiones, Vol. 80, covering the years 1460–70), and from this he has worked out the annual average receipts of the college as 21,716 florins, varying from 9,836 in 1462 (two divisions) to 31,702 in 1466 (six divisions). He estimates that in 1463—a rather lucrative year for receipts—at least twelve cardinals, individually, received more than 1,200 florins (rather higher than Fieschi's totals except in 1505, 1508 and 1517), although Cardinal Rolin ("Eduensis") received only six florins for the entire year, presumably because he was absent. Papal "florins" and "ducats" were synonymous.

42. "La distributione del capello per li tempi passati e redutto di 700 ducati in l'anno in circha" (Archivio di Stato, Florence, Carte Strozziane, Ser. 1, X, fol. 299).

Apart from the corporate funds, there was one other source of income in Rome which all the cardinals enjoyed, but this income was unequal and we are quite uncertain of its amount. This was the revenue of each cardinal's "title" church: the suburbicarian bishoprics for the seven cardinal-bishops and the Roman churches for the rest. Cardinals were sometimes allowed to hold an additional title in commendam, which suggests that the revenues were very uneven, but that there were revenues is definitely stated in various bulls of provision.[43]

The six bishoprics probably had an additional source of income and perquisites from their estates. The senior cardinal-bishop, with the title of Ostia—Cardinal Riario—received 330 ducats a year from leasing out fishing rights and 100 pounds of sturgeon, according to a record of 1520.[44] The bishopric of Porto evidently included a fixed place of residence, for when Alexander VI made it over to Cardinal Michiel in 1492, he also transferred all the furnishings and cellar well-stocked with wine.[45] There is also evidence that in 1510 the church of Santa Sabina was worth 1,000 ducats a year,[46] and that Santa Maria in Via Lata was attractive enough to buy a Genoese vote (Cardinal Campofregoso's) for Alexander VI in the 1492 conclave.[47]

Of particular interest is some information about Wolsey's titulary church of Santa Cecilia. On September 8, 1522, soon after arriving in Rome, the English ambassador Thomas Hannibal wrote to Wolsey:

> "I am enformyde by my Lord Campegius your Grace hath wronge in your title of Sancta Cecilia by the provest that is there. He taketh apon him to ressave that proffette that of olde tyme the Cardinalys of that title hadde. It is not of smale valow."[48] And again on September 12:

43. E.g., the bull providing Cardinal Fieschi S. Prisca in October, 1506, permitted him to retain S. Lucia in Septemsolii: "de dicte ecclesiae S. Luciae fructibus redditibus et proventibus disponere et ordinare" (Vatican Archives, Reg. Vat. 926, fol. 51). Cardinal Bainbridge, appointed to S. Prassede in December, 1511, was given possession of the church "et locorum illi subiectorum ... et de illorum fructibus redditibus et proventibus disponere et ordinare" (ibid., 960, fol. 151).

44. See E. Rodocanachi, La première Renaissance, p. 11 and Appendix II (p. 384) for the notarial document in Archivio di Stato, Rome, Not. Capitolini Atti Originali 279, No. 1, p. 31.

45. Diario della Città di Roma di Stefano Infessura, ed. O. Tommassini, Fonti per la Storia d'Italia (Rome, 1890), V, 281.

46. Sanuto, Diarii, X, 114.   47. As above, n. 45.

48. British Museum, Cotton MS, Vitellius B, V, fols. 111v–112r; omitted in abstract in LP, III, 2521. See D. S. Chambers, "Cardinal Wolsey and the Papal Tiara," Bulletin of the Institute of Historical Research, XXXVIII (1965), 20–21.

"Sens ye wer cardinal ye lost much in your title . . . not little money."[49] Wolsey was curiously indifferent about the matter; and Hannibal wrote in vain on January 13, 1523: "I hadde never answer of your grace . . . it wer necessary to send a proxy and a commission for your ryght in the said title . . . I have commensyde an action agenst certen romayn in rota."[50]

But the case proves that titularies should not be overlooked in an assessment of cardinals' incomes.[51]

All other sources of income for the curia were not only variable in yield, their acquisition depended upon luck, graft, or favor. There were only a few important offices at the head of the Roman bureaucracy which cardinals held, but these appointments were usually for life. The vice-chancellor, head of the papal chancery and "dexter oculus" of the pope and his deputy for many routine functions, was the most important of these officers, and he received a handsome salary of 6,000 ducats a year.[52] The penitentiary, head of another great office, concerned with the expedition of papal letters relating to matters of conscience, also received 6,000 ducats.[53] The chamberlain, head of the papal chamber—which was both the chief financial department and an alternative route for the expedition of certain kinds of papal letters—was almost as preeminent as the vice-chancellor, and his emoluments were perhaps even greater.[54] Life-appointments meant that very few cardinals could hope to enjoy these offices, and it is not surprising that conclave capitulations (in 1513, for

49. British Museum, Cotton MS, Vitellius B, V, fol. 113 (*LP*, III, 2539).

50. *Ibid.*, fol. 146*v* (*LP*, III, 2771).

51. Pierre Dubois, in the early fourteenth century, asserted: "paucos quasi nullos habent redditus suis titulis appropriatos" (G. Barraclough, *Papal Provisions*, p. 74); but this clearly cannot be taken as the last word.

52. Cardinal Giulio de' Medici's accounts for 1521–22 include the entry "Cancelleria di Roma facendo el solito d[ucati] 6000" (above, n. 42, *loc. cit.*). It should be noted, however, that in 1505 Baldassare Castiglione had written to his mother telling her that the office yielded 12,000 ducats (P. Serassi, *Lettere del Conte Baldesar Castiglione* [Padua, 1769], I, 22). On the attributes of the vice-chancellorship, see W. von Hofmann, *Forschungen zur Geschichte der Kurialen Behörden* (Rome, 1914), I, pp. 18 ff.; a list of vice-chancellors is in *ibid.*, II, 69–71.

53. Cardinal Campeggio wrote on October 10, 1520, that the office was worth 6,000 ducats (abstract, *LP*, III, 1016). Lists of the cardinal penitentiaries are given by von Hofmann, *op. cit.*, II, 97–98; also by E. Göller, *Die päpstliche Pönitentiarie* (Rome, 1907–11), I, 85 ff. (where the fullest account of the office is also to be found).

54. A. Gottlob, *Aus der Camera Apostolica* (Innsbruck, 1889), describes the office; a list of chamberlains is in von Hofmann, *op. cit.*, II, 87–88.

instance) [55] demanded that they should change hands, or rotate, every three years. To cite only two cases of long tenure: Cardinal Rodrigo Borgia was vice-chancellor from 1457 to 1492, for thirty-five years, and Cardinal Raffaelle Riario was chamberlain almost as long, from 1483 to 1517.

There were relatively few attractive appointments beneath these three major offices. There was the office of prefect of the *segnatura*, the tribunal wherein the referendaries presented supplications to receive the pope's *fiat*. Cardinal Campeggio described the office in a letter to Wolsey of October 20, 1520, as "the hinge of the whole court," but he complained that it did not carry any emoluments. [56] Cardinals appointed to legations in the papal state or abroad received a salary, but this cannot be counted a financial privilege since during their absence from the curia they forfeited their rights to any share in the corporate income. [57] There were desirable perquisites in the form of castellanships and other titular appointments in the papal state, but a frequent complaint of reform minutes and conclave capitulations was that they were unfairly distributed among the cardinals. [58]

Other cash perquisites existed in the form of free-will gifts from the pope, such as legacies after death or the largesse distributed among supporters after elections, but gifts from the pope or from patrons and clients were necessarily unequal in value and distribution. One of the most interesting perquisites which developed in our period was the *propina* or tip paid to the cardinal who related a candidate for provision in con-

---

55. There is a copy of public capitulations from the papers of an unknown conclavist, edited by C. A. von Höfler, in his "Zur Kritik und Quellenkunde der ersten Regierungs-jahre K. Karls V", *Denkschriften der Kaiserlichen Akademie der Wissenschaften*, Phil-Hist. Kl., XXVIII (Vienna, 1878), 221.

56. Abstract, *LP*, III, 1016 (original in Public Records Office, SP 1/21, fol. 101); also see below, n. 102. In the secret conclave capitulations of 1522 an attempt was made to establish a tax of 3 per cent on all annates paid into the papal chamber, as a salary "cardinali qui pro tempore signaturae justiciae praeerit" (von Höfler, *op. cit.*, p. 235). On the *segnatura*, see von Hofmann, *op. cit.*, I, 7–8; B. Katterbach, *Referendarii utriusque Signaturae*, Studi e Testi, 55 (Vatican, 1931), pp. xi–iv. Campeggio's own treatise on the Office is in *Concilium Tridentinum* (Freiburg im B., 1930), XII.

57. E.g., Cardinal Marco Vigerio was paid 200 ducats a month while on legation in the Patrimony; bull of 1513–14, in Hergenröther, *Regesta Leonis X* (Freiburg im B., 1884), p. 470.

58. "Videmus quod multe terre et arces sunt in manibus cardinalium. Hec est una pessima res, in primis quod unus habeat terras et alius non," complained an anonymous reform tract in 1497 (L. Celier, *op. cit.*, *Mélanges d'archéologie et d'histoire* [1907], p. 107).

sistory.[59] The function of *ponens* or *relator* became almost a monopoly in the hands of a few cardinals due to the institution of "cardinal protectors" for each secular power by the end of the fifteenth century.

The monopoly was not rigid, of course, and a protector might often be absent from the curia, but from 1492 to 1503 Cardinal Piccolomini, as protector of England, related thirty-five English and Irish benefices whereas other cardinals undertook only five[60] (a memorable instance being Cardinal Cesare Borgia's relation of John Blythe to Salisbury).[61] The system provokes some criticism. Charles V's ambassador, Mai, wrote in May of 1529:

> His imperial Majesty has here three protectors: Campeggio for Germany, Colonna for Castile, and Caesarino for Aragon. This is an innovation, for in olden times the imperial ambassadors by paying a gratuity now to this cardinal, now to the other, induced them to propose candidates for the vacant churches. Nowadays the whole of your Majesty's Kingdom is in the hands of three cardinals who, considering their protectorate as part and portion of their patrimony, are not the least grateful for their fees.[62]

In theory, the fee or *propina* paid for relations had been a voluntary present (literally, the cardinal was to be stood a drink), but in time this had turned into a matter of bargaining for a sum of money by the proctors.[63] By about 1530 a fixed charge had been introduced: 15 per cent of the annual taxable value of the benefice, if this was over $33\frac{1}{3}$ ducats, and a further 5 per cent for the cardinal's chamberlains. This is established in

59. Cameron, *The Apostolic Camera*, p. xxi. The Acta Consistorialia which survive for the years 1489 to 1504 and 1517 to 1533 generally name the cardinal relators. Transcripts in the Public Records Office are useful for English entries.

60. J. Wodka, "Zur Geschichte der nationalen Protektorate der Kardinäle an der römischen Kurie," *Publikationen des Oesterreichischen Historisches Instituts in Rom*, IV (1938), i, 42, and *passim*. On cardinals as "protectors," also see D. S. Chambers, *Cardinal Bainbridge in the Court of Rome* (Oxford, 1965), especially pp. 2–5. For new evidence on "cardinal promoters" (as distinct from "protectors") see A. A. Strnad, "Aus der Frühzeit des nationalen Protektorates der Kardinäle," *Zeitschrift der Savigny-Stiftung für Rechtsgeschichte* kan. abt. 1 (1964), 264–71.

61. Vatican Archives, Acta Consistorialia, Camerarii I, fol. 58.

62. *Span. Cal.*, IV, 3.

63. Some surviving proctors' accounts show how the *propina* could vary. See M. Mayr-Adlwang, "Ueber Expensenrechnungen für päpstliche Provisionsbullen des 15 Jahrhunderts," *Mitteilungen des Oesterreichischen Instituts für Geschichtsforschung*, XVII (1896), 105–9, and von Hofmann, *op. cit.*, II, 218–19.

a letter dated October 26, 1531, from the Mantuan orator in Rome, Fabrizio Peregrino,[64] who reported an interesting debate on the subject, which was probably provoked by the outrageous fees demanded for providing Lee to York and Gardiner to Winchester.[65]

One can sympathize all the more with Henry VIII's act restraining annates in the face of this new extortion. For one of the last English provisions, that of Cranmer to Canterbury, which was hurried through to suit the king's purpose in February, 1533, Cardinal Campeggio claimed no less than 1,500 ducats just for his *propina*—according to a letter Haukins wrote to Henry VIII.[66] This confirms Fabrizio Peregrino's report that huge sums were being made by the protectors, up to 5,000 ducats a year. On the other hand, the cardinals who were not recognized protectors opposed the system; and if it solved the financial problem for a few cardinals, it was yet another case of inequality for most of them. Most of the cardinals wanted a return to unfixed fees which could be divided like their shares of the common services at regular intervals.

Apart from these curial sources, then, cardinals' incomes depended upon their unequal revenues from benefices, or on pensions upon benefices which they had been able to pick up from external patrons, or upon private means. Benefices were of course a very important source, and some cardinals were pluralists on the grand scale, but proof of possession was not always proof of actual income. Private means were the most desirable of all, and cardinals like Melchior von Meckau, with his silver mines,[67] or Alessandro Farnese, with his family estates near Rome,[68] were probably the richest. Farnese and another Roman noble, Cardinal Cesarini, had

64. Archivio di Stato, Mantua, Gonzaga, Busta 880; see Appendix II, below. A. Clergeac, *La Curie et les Bénéficiers Consistoriaux*, pp. 189–92, only proves that the date was after 1505 and before 1555. W. E. Lunt, *Financial Relations of the Papacy with England, 1327–1534*, p. 258, states that it was "probably after 1532 but possibly shortly before"; he does not, however, cite the evidence.

65. A letter of October 29 mentions the "XX per cento che togliono i cardinali della Chiesa Eboracensis e l'altra essa in Engelterra" (Archivio di Stato, Mantua, Gonzaga, Busta 880).

66. "aboute a thousand and 5 hundred ducates, wonli for proponing the vacation in Consistori" (*State Papers* [1849], VII, 425).

67. A. Schulte, *Die Fugger in Rom* (Leipzig, 1904), I, 45–46; G. von Polnitz, "Jacob Fugger und der Streit mit Melchior von Brixen," *Quellen und Forschungen aus italienischen Archiven*, XXX (1940).

68. Clerk wrote on January 4, 1522, that Farnese "hath patrimony to the valew of VI or VII mil doketts and besides hath II or III bishopryches" (British Museum, Cotton MS, Vitellius B, V, fol. 5; abstract in *LP*, III [1932]).

two of the largest households in 1526.[69] A recent study has shown that cardinals who owned land further profited from the rise in agricultural prices later in the sixteenth century, when the rich cardinals grew richer and the poor cardinals poorer.[70]

Since the corporate income of the college seems to have diminished, and since in any case it always fluctuated, as did the other sources, it is not surprising that some of the cardinals voiced their complaints. The secret or private capitulations which were drawn up in conclave after conclave, as well as the public clauses, included provisions to bind the new pope to allow the cardinals more money, to appoint specified cardinals to specified offices, and not to increase the membership of the college.

From the 1458 conclave onward, the cardinals demanded a grant from the papal chamber to supplement their incomes according to a means test,[71] but the most surprising thing about this claim is its modesty: only 100 ducats a year for cardinals with an income below 4,000 ducats. This claim was raised, in 1503, to 200 ducats a month for cardinals with less than 6,000.[72] In 1513 a precedent for such a subsidy was quoted from the time of Boniface VIII,[73] and the need to preserve the dignity and honor of the cardinals was emphasized because their expenses had greatly increased.[74] In 1521, instead of a moderate subsidy awarded by a means test, it was proposed that poor cardinals should be subsidized with up to 6,000 ducats of income from the earliest-vacated benefices.[75] However, it

69. In 1526 his household contained three hundred and sixty-six persons; Cesarini had 275. No other cardinal, except Scaramuccia Trivulzio, had more than two hundred. D. Gnoli, "Un censimento di Roma," *Archivio delle Reale Società Romana di Storia Patria*, XVII (1898), 275–520, esp. pp. 454, 471, 481.

70. J. Delumeau, *Vie économique et sociale de Rome dans la seconde moitié du XVIe siècle* (Paris, 1957), I, 450.

71. Raynaldus, *Annales Ecclesiastici*, X, 159. See the similar capitulations in 1484 in Burchard's *Liber Notarum*, ed. E. Celani, *Rerum Italicarum Scriptores*, XXXII, ii (Città di Castello, 1906, etc.), I, 30–31.

72. *Span. Cal.*, I, 371 (Ch. I).

73. "Prima, li cardinali poveri, visto la bolla *de symonia* fece Julio, si penso un bel trato e trovo una antiqua constitutione di Bonifazio octavo, qual volea che ogni cardinal, che non havesse ducati 4000 de intrada a l'anno, el papa li desse ducati 200 al mexe per uno fin arivasse a la suma" (Sanuto, *Diarii*, XVI, 29).

74. Sanuto, *Diarii*, XVI, 86. C. A. von Höfler prints another copy in *op. cit.* (above, n. 55), p. 229: "item quia impensae R[everendissimorum] D[ominorum] Cardinalium plurimum auctae sunt . . ."

75. von Höfler, *op. cit.*, p. 235.

does not seem that any of these suggestions was ever put into effect, unless one counts the subsidy allegedly paid to Cardinals Sanseverino and Carvajal upon their restitution in 1513 after the "schism" of Pisa.[76]

Although the cardinals had a good statutory claim upon the papal chamber, it must be remembered that the papal chamber had a hard task balancing its income with its expenditure. Various possibilities were considered for providing new funds. In 1497 it was suggested that incomes could be found for the cardinals by a 5 per cent levy on cathedrals that had an annual income of more than 2,000 ducats;[77] in 1523 Cardinal De Vio, general of the Dominicans, proposed a tax on all of the ecclesiastical resources of every kingdom, though he recognized that this would be strongly resisted by cardinals already beneficed abroad.[78] Paolo Cortese was enthusiastic for a levy on the monasteries, and quoted a curiously unorthodox remark of the chamberlain, Rafaelle Riario, that they were like the Dead Sea, neither useful to the Christian commonwealth nor sustaining life.[79] A similar levy was proposed in the 1521 conclave's secret capitulations, but it was admitted that the papal chamber could not afford to pay 200 ducats a month to indigent cardinals. Instead, 24,000 ducats raised from monastic revenues might be shared among the "cardinales pauperes," defined—as in the 1497 scheme—as those with less than 5,000 ducats a year.[80]

It is difficult, of course, to do much more than surmise about the level of the cardinals' incomes. For instance, the crusade tax assessment of 1511 which we find in the diary of the papal master of ceremonies, John Burchard,[81] might seem providential evidence, but there is no clue as to how it was drawn up, and it probably takes no account of private income —let alone capital assets of property and valuables. Nevertheless, it is interesting that from a total of forty-one cardinals only seven are cited as having an income beyond Cortese's decent maximum of 12,000 ducats; many were undoubtedly of only mediocre or even of meager means.

76. "se li da ducati 6000 per uno a lanno per il Papa fin arano ducati 8000 de intrada per uno" (Sanuto, *Diarii*, XVII, 433).

77. Celier, *op. cit.* (above, n. 31), p. 114; reference from Biblioteca Vaticana, MS Vat. Lat. 3883, fol. 142.

78. *Concilium Tridentinum*, XII, 34.

79. *De Cardinalatu*, p. xlvii.

80. von Höfler, *op. cit.*, p. 229.

81. *Liber Notarum*, ed. E. Celani, II, 226–27; discussed by von Pastor, *op. cit.*, VI, 91–92.

Indeed, it is very probable that most cardinals' careers were based on a vast and precarious structure of credit, on loans from bankers and merchants in Rome. For instance, when Cardinal Peraud died, in 1505, he was deeply in debt to the Fuggers.[82] Cardinal Sanseverino took loans from the Grimaldi; and Cardinal Innocenzo Cibo borrowed from the Pallavicini.[83] In the court of Rome, as elsewhere, prestige depended on expenditure,[84] and credit could be raised on status and expectations.[85] There was little point in saving.

The evidence shows that some cardinals ran into serious difficulty. Cardinal Sigismondo Gonzaga wrote to his brother, the marchese of Mantua, about their poverty in October, 1508,[86] and he was also described as poor by a Mantuan ambassador.[87] In September, 1509, a Venetian dispatch records that some cardinals refused to accompany the pope on a progress through the Patrimony because of the expense this would involve.[88] Burchard's successor as papal master of ceremonies, Paris de Grassis, noted in his diary in 1511 that Cardinal Gabrielli had a very humble funeral for want of money.[89] In 1513 he noted that after the death of Cardinal Argentino no furniture was found in his house,[90] and in 1516

82. "et par che'l Focheri sia grosso suo creditor" (Sanuto, *Diarii*, VI, 222).

83. von Polnitz, *op. cit.* (above, n. 67), p. 240.

84. For instance, a Venetian commented about Vice-Chancellor Cardinal Sisto della Rovere, who died in 1517: "al Cardinal Vincula di nazion zenoese e sta trovato ducati 5000 in contadi, e prima ne dete 3000 al Papa, di richissimo che era, ma la sua entrata spendeva, come dicono quelli sanno" (Sanuto, *Diarii*, XXIV, 58). Also see some suggestive evidence I have cited in *Cardinal Bainbridge in the Court of Rome*, pp. 128–30.

85. The Medici bank, in Martin V's time, had allowed its manager in Rome to lend up to 300 florins to a cardinal when he received his red hat, but instructions were sent to discourage borrowing by a cardinal who had run up a large debt. See R. de Roover, *The Rise and Decline of the Medici Bank* (Cambridge, 1963), p. 204.

86. Archivio di Stato, Mantua, Gonzaga, Busta 858 (Roma, Lettere del Cardinal Gonzaga): "Havemo molti cardinali poveri." When new cardinals were proposed next month, he wrote "non se ne dovria far per honor de la chiesa perche assai vi ne sono de poveri."

87. *Ibid.* Ludovico di Campo Sampiero wrote on March 20, 1508, that the pope wished to give the bishopric of Como to the cardinal "qual è poverissimo." The Marchese's brother-in-law, Cardinal Ippolito d'Este, also seems to have had difficulties. Isabella d'Este complained that she had been lending him jewels and money which he was unable to pay back. See her letter of August 10, 1512 to the Mantuan ambassador in Rome, Folenghino, in A. Luzio, "Isabella d'Este di fronte a Giulio II," *Archivio Storico Lombardo* XXXIX, fasc. xxxv (1912), 107.

88. Sanuto, *Diarii*, IX, 181.

89. British Museum, Additional MS 8442, fols. 143–44.

90. *Ibid.*, fol. 126r.

that Cardinal Sanseverino had left debts of 27,000 .ducats—having indulged in too much "liberalitas" and habitually running up large debts.[91]

Cardinal Fieschi was discounted as a candidate for pope in the 1513 conclave because he did not have much money;[92] when he died, in 1524, most of his more valuable goods appeared to be in pawn (including some candlesticks, a silver water jug, and a large cross).[93] Cardinal Isvalies was criticized for wearing artificial jewelry, and his supposed or alleged treasure could not be found in the castle of Imola after his death in 1511.[94] Even the magnificent Cardinal Luigi d'Aragon was said to be in need in Julius II's pontificate;[95] and Bernardo Dovizi, cardinal of Bibbiena and associate of the famous court circle of Urbino, who became Leo X's secretary, in 1520 left debts of 7,000 ducats, which included some loans from bankers.[96]

Two illustrious vice-chancellors, the Cardinals Galeotto della Rovere and Giulio de' Medici, ran up enormous debts. The former, who died in 1508, was said to have owed more than 90,000 ducats, and his collection of antiquities had to be sold for a partial repayment.[97] The latter, who was Leo X's cousin and afterwards Pope Clement VII, was in acute difficulty, according to his accounts of 1521/22. This document reveals that offices and benefices yielded him 19,790 ducats, but there were 19,384 ducats on the debit side, and beyond this a list of creditors in Rome and Florence to whom he owed 17,559 ducats, and there was also a note for more than 5,000 ducats' worth of silver and jewels in pawn.[98] The same predicament was expressed by Cardinal Silvio Passerini, another prominent member of Leo X's court circle, in a letter of February 2, 1521, to the duke of

91. *Ibid.*, fol. 190v. The figure is quoted as 25,000 ducats in Sanuto, *Diarii*, XXII, 432.

92. Sanuto, *Diarii*, XVI, 16.

93. E. Rodocanachi, *La première Renaissance*, Appendix XVIII, pp. 395–97; from Archivio di Stato, Rome, Atti Apocello, A. C. Prot. 411, fols. 233–34.

94. G. L. Moncallero, *Epistolario di Bernardo Dovizi* (Florence, 1957), I, p. 306.

95. Isabella d'Este wrote on April 25, 1511, about his preferment to a Spanish bishopric: "Lei havera le intrate che scio ne ha bene bisogno." Archivio di Stato, Mantua, Gonzaga, Busta 2996, Bk. 29, fol. 27.

96. G. L. Moncallero, *Il Cardinale Bernardo Dovizi* (Florence, 1953), pp. 498–500.

97. J. Cartwright, *The Perfect Courtier* (London, 1928), I, p. 248.

98. Archivio di Stato, Florence, Carte Strozziane, Ser. 1, X, fol. 299. Expenses included 14,400 ducats as "spese del vitto e di cavalcatura o salario dofiziali." The rest were "spese extraordinarie" and pensions.

Albany, regent for James V of Scotland. He declared he could not meet
the duke's request to resign Whithorn priory since he was in need of
money. To keep up a cardinal's dignity cost more than his income yielded,
he wrote, and his expenses were steadily increasing.[99]

One of the consequences of this economic struggle was that cardinals
were especially anxious to act as the friends and agents of secular powers
in order to obtain pensions and benefices. Cardinal Campeggio, for
instance, frequently wrote to inform Wolsey of his difficulties. In December, 1520, he complained he could not keep up his household,[100] and the
following year that he still received only 1,000 ducats a year as a cardinal
(almost certainly an underestimate, but his income probably was relatively
small).[101] Thomas Hannibal took up his case in 1523, writing to Wolsey:

> The Cardinall Campegius is a feithfull servant of the kyngs highnes
> and a sure friende of your grace. I pray God send him some promocion
> for the good man hath nothing of the pope but the signature of justice
> and a pension of 500 ducats, thies be very small things to fynde such a
> man.[102]

Cardinal Scaramuccia Trivulzio wrote a similar hard-luck story to the
French court.[103]

It may well be that after the creation of so many new cardinals in
1517,[104] and after the loss of the loans that many had made to Leo X[105] to
pay for his war of aggression against the duke of Urbino, the outlook had
become more severe around 1520. A Venetian observer commented in
1519 that the cardinals' households were less ostentatious than formerly.[106]

99. D. Hay, *Letters of James V* (Edinburgh, 1954), p. 84.

100. Abstract, *LP*, III, 1094.

101. *Ibid.*, 1222. Emperor Maximilian had provided him to the bishopric of Feltre,
worth 800 ducats, and had also given him a pension on that of Bressanone (Eubel,
Hierarchia, III, 211 n.). The Campeggi were, so far as is known, a prosperous Bolognese
family; the cardinal had been a successful lawyer.

102. British Museum, Cotton MS, Vitellius B, V, fol. 188; abstract in *LP*, III, 2891.

103. In 1526 he wrote to Montmorency: "sono vivuto in cinque anni in tanta extre-
mita et poverta, con tanti altri infortunii et calamita, ch'io non so come sia vivo, et pur
tutto ho tollerato voluntera per servitio del Re, con speranza che in una hora il Re
restoreria tutti li danni." (G. Molini, *Documenti di Storia Italiana* [Florence, 1836], I,
202-3.) On the other hand, if there is no mistake in the figures, he was living far beyond
his means that same year, with four hundred and fifty-six persons in his household—far
more than any other cardinal had. See above, n. 68.

104. "per esser tanti molti hanno bisogno del viver" (Sanuto, *Diarii*, XXIV, 449).

105. von Pastor, *op. cit.*, VIII, 101.

106. Sanuto, *Diarii*, XXVII, 73.

In March, 1523, the English ambassador, John Clerk, with some exaggeration described the pope as poor and the cardinals as mendicants.[107]

It is important to recognize that this was already the trend before 1527, but of course the sack of Rome impeded the cardinals' recovery; many must have lost their property and their reserves of cash and valuables, and consequently their credit with the bankers. The poverty was reported to Wolsey in the winter of 1528/29, when he was trying to obtain reductions for provision bulls.[108] Extraordinary demands were being made on the cardinals: contributions for the redemption of Civitavecchia and Ostia early in 1529,[109] for subsidies to the Swiss cantons,[110] and for the expense of repairing war damage. For example, Cardinal Gaddi wrote to the emperor in November, 1528, asking for a rich benefice to make good his losses as all his money was being spent on repairs.[111] In the spring of 1531 the Mantuan, Fabrizio Peregrino, reported that many cardinals were leaving Rome because they could not afford to live there.[112] Gregorio Casale, acting both as an English and French agent, painted a picture even more dismal; the cardinals, he wrote to Grammont, were so poor they were dying of hunger.[113] If this was an exaggeration, Casale made the important point that the cardinals were turning more and more to external patrons for their maintenance, and particularly to the emperor, who had more to offer than the pope.

Curia cardinals had of course been doing this for several centuries; by serving or obliging the ruling lay powers as special diplomatic agents and proctors they could increase their prestige and their incomes (the additional role some of them played as cardinal protectors has already been mentioned).[114] Such practices were not altogether approved by the

107. "papa pauper est Cardinales autem mendici the povertie is the cause that he may not shewe nor execute his mynde." British Museum, Cotton MS, Vitellius B, V, fol. 190; abstract in *LP*, III, 2891.

108. E.g., Giovanni Casale's letter of December 17, 1528 (*LP*, IV, 5038), or Vannes' in January, 1529 (*LP*, IV, 5235, 5344).

109. *Span. Cal.*, IV, 635.

110. Letter of Fabrizio Peregrino to the marchese of Mantua, October 21, 1521 (Archivio di Stato, Mantua, Gonzaga, Busta 880).

111. *Span. Cal.*, III, 577.

112. "Molti cardinali partino di Roma per non posser comportare la spexa a rispetto della grandissima carestia" (Peregrino, May 3, 1531, *loc. cit.*).

113. The proposal for new cardinals, he wrote on March 7, had been received "con grande dispiacere di questi altri Reverendissimi quali sono tanti poveri che si muoiono di fame et per il che sono necessitati ad andare a merce de gli altri principi idest dell Imperatore quale ha piu da dare in un mese che non ha il papa in un anno" (Molini, *Documenti di Storia Italiana*, I, 362).

114. Above, n. 60.

moralists—even Paolo Cortese warned against partisanship[115]—but the interesting thing is that not even the most principled cardinals could afford to renounce such arrangements when faced with the problem of maintaining their living standards.

Cardinal Oliviero Caraffa, when he was sitting on Alexander VI's reform commission of 1497, criticized the *propina* received by cardinals for relating candidates for consistorial provisions. He proposed that it should revert to the form of an offering of food and drink—not more than a cardinal could consume within a few days—and that no cardinals with benefices worth more than 1,000 ducats in any country should relate for its provisions.[116] Yet Caraffa was both archbishop of Naples and cardinal protector of the Aragonese kingdom of the Two Sicilies,[117] and as such an assiduous Neapolitan agent and relator. The Franciscan cardinal, Numai, who was noted for his piety and rectitude, in his own interests maintained a close correspondence with the French court. He was persuaded, but only after great effort, to resign a church in Provence worth 4,000 ducats a year. He had complained that the resignation would make him very poor,[118] and shortly afterwards he wrote to Montmorency most obsequiously, promising his services in return for preferment.[119] The austere general of the Dominican order, Cardinal Egidio of Viterbo, having received the red hat in 1517, commended himself to the marchese of Mantua in self-deprecating phrases,[120] and shortly afterwards openly declared that he looked on the marchese as the patron who had his interests most at heart.[121] In October, 1520, he even asked for permission

115. *De Cardinalatu*, p. cxc.

116. Wodka, *op. cit.* (above, n. 60), pp. 6, 34.   117. *Ibid.*, p. 15.

118. "Benche mi sia stato assai incommodo per ritrovarmi molto povero si per far cosa grata ad loro maesta de le quale so et semper sero devotissimo . . . multo voluntieri ho resignato dicta chiesa" (Bibliothèque Nationale, Paris, Fonds Français, MS 6635, fol. 25).

119. "Se voglia degnare di essere mio bono procuratore appresso il Re Christianissimo e Madama, ch'io sia provisto in quelli regni di qualche cosa ch'io possa vivere. . . . Questo non tacero, che ogni beneficio che quelle collocara in me lo collocora in un suo amantissimo et affectionissimo et un bon servitore de la Maesta del Re et de Madama" (Molini, *Documenti*, I, 72–73).

120. ". . . a me pare che quella sia signore di tal sorte che non ha bisogno di protectione: Et quando pur quella simil chosa richerchasse, o di alcun o favore servir si volessi: sono di grandi signori in questa corte: che secondo el mio iudicio non solo volentieri la servirebbano: ma ascriverabbano a lor beneficio singularissimo: poter farli chosa grata: et io . . . sebene da un canto, le forze, lingegno, et lauctorita manchassi: da l'altro supplirebbe la volunta, la diligentia et fede. . . ." Letter of September 11, 1517, in Archivio di Stato, Mantua, Gonzaga, Busta 863, "Cardinali."

121. ". . . fra gli altri signori et patroni mei Vestra Excellentia principalmente mostra di haver a cuore l'honor et dignita mia. . . ." Letter of January 24, 1518, *loc. cit.*

to transport grain from his abbey in Ferrara through Mantuan territory without paying dues.[122]

Cardinals of the most exemplary devotional life—tract writers like Adriano Castellesi, whose *De Vera Philosophia* condemned all but piety, and which was dedicated to his secular patron, Henry VII[123]—could also be notorious pluralists and political retainees. Cardinal Campeggio wrote a report for Adrian VI that deplored the system of papal provisions which deferred to the secular power,[124] yet he tirelessly sought secular patronage.

One wonders whether a dividing line was drawn between corruption and the common practices of an imperfect world, practices which most supposed would last out their time? Was the criterion perhaps the performance of just and necessary services in good conscience, for which the laborer was worthy of his hire—in distinction from manipulating the machine and silencing consciences to assist sinister ends?

This attitude is suggested in a letter of Cardinal Castellesi to Henry VII (December, 1503) that thanks him for providing the means to live affluently.[125] It also appears in the approaches made to the distinguished lawyer, Cardinal Pietro Accolti, to defend Henry VIII's matrimonial matter (December, 1531). Benet, the ambassador, was to make "the fair offer of a princely reward . . . not to corrupt him, whose integrity his Grace knoweth well, but only to animate and encourage him to empech such enjury and wrong as is enterprised against his Highness." [126] Accolti hesitated; he said it "would savour of corruption," but eventually he accepted a promise of preferments "to the yearly value of six or seven thousand crowns, and also a bishopric in England, which should be vacant next." He demanded as a pledge

> . . . some jewel of great estimation *in deposito* till the rest of the p[romise be] performed, and this the old man desired [not so] much to win this revenue as providing of his own living, for he [knoweth] well that whensoever the Imperials [shall] perceive that he shall be in opinion agayn[st them?] . . . the Emperor will imagine . . . not only to displease him, but also i[njure] him; which they may do lightly, considering his revenue lieth either with[in] his lands or his vassals. . . .[127]

122. *Ibid.*

123. B. Gebhardt, *Adrian von Corneto* (Breslau, 1886), II, 56.

124. "De Depravatu Ecclesiae," in *Concilium Tridentinum*, XII, esp. pp. 10, 20.

125. "Ago gratias Deo et vestrae majestati qui dant mihi affluenter unde bene vivere et sine corruptela degere valeam." N. Pocock, *Records of the Reformation* (Oxford, 1870), II, 590.

126. *Ibid.*, pp. 144–45.   127. *Ibid.*, pp. 213–14.

The imperial orator, Cifuentes, told his master in March, 1534, that the cardinals did not request a reward for doing justice but for other reasons, and because it was the custom.[128]

Anyone with experience of the papal curia, with its tradition of splendid living, its enormous bureaucracy, and its long involvement with temporal government and secular politics, must have found it difficult to maintain a radical point of view. Criticism might well have been regarded as impious, individual arrogance, and Giovanni Guidiccioni's advice to his nephew, Bartolomeo, that he should not believe he was called to renew the world—because the latter had been offered the office of datary—was perhaps typical.[129] To upset the historical establishment, with its vast accretion of offices and complicated practices, might have brought still greater disaster to an already-distracted world and to the arduous affairs of the universal Church. Even those who believed the millennium was at hand probably expected it to come mainly by transcendental means.

Curia cardinals may have varied in private attitudes and scruples, but it is probable that in haggling for fair salaries and by ingratiating secular patrons for material rewards so that they could live up to a high style of conspicuous consumption and munificence they felt they were neither endangering their own salvation nor the good of Christendom in an imperfect world: that these actions accorded well with the part they had to play as "senators of the Church."

128. Abstract, *LP*, VII, 369.
129. L. Celier, "Les Dataires du XVe Siècle", *Bibliothèque des Écoles françaises d'Athènes et de Rome*, CIII (Paris, 1910), 115–16.

Appendix i

This distribution of common-service money to Cardinal Fieschi from 1504 to 1520 is based on accounts and figures in Archivio Vaticano, Fondo Sacri Collegio dei Cardinali, Libri Cedularum et Rotulorum, I.

							Florins (Ducats)	Soldi	Denari
1504	.	.	Apr.	June	Oct.	Dec.	698	10	17
1505	.	.	Mar.	June	Oct.		1,341	106	20
1506	.	.	Apr.	June	Dec.		946	45	24
1507	.	.	Apr.	June	Oct.	Dec.	851	85	27
1508	.	.	June	Oct.	Dec.		1,208	170	17
1509	.	.	Apr.	June	Dec.		929	92	25
1510	.	.	Mar.	June	Oct.	Dec.	762	116	27
1511	.	.	Oct.	Dec.			659	82	6
1512	.	.	Apr.	Oct.	Dec.		956	49	25
1513	.	.	June	Sept.	Oct.		587	100	15
1514	.	.	Mar.	May	Aug.	Dec.	1,111	75	28
1515	.	.	Apr.	June	Oct.		1,166	51	11
1516	.	.	Jan.	June	Oct.	Dec.	1,064	62	13
1517	.	.	Feb.	Apr.	July	Dec.	1,489	89	261
1518	.	.	June	Nov.	Dec.		407	25	1
1519	.	.	Apr.	Dec.			426	23	20
1520	.	.	Apr.				626	123	25

Appendix ii

Extract from a letter of Fabrizio Peregrino, Mantuan ambassador in Rome, to the marchese of Mantua, October 26, 1531 (Archivio di Stato, Mantua, Gonzaga, Busta 880).

... Dippoi in detto Consistorio fu ragionato come e Principi se ricchiamano delle estorsione che dicano da un tempo in qua sogliono fare i cardinali nelle relatione de vescovati quando li propongano in consistoro, che dove gia altre volte solevano togliere un certo donativo all arbitero di colui per le qual la Chiesa ere proposta. Cosa di pocho pretio come sarebbe stato une coppa o tazza dargento una pezze di Ciambellotto o un cavallo et simile frascerie che hora lhanno ridotta a volere XV per cento et V per i Camerieri participanti che sono XXti per cento et une chiesa grossa importa gran somme per la relatione dessa. ... Vogliono che la cosa si riduca al consueto anticho et che l'XV per cento si metta da canto et si toglia quello puocho o assai chel promosso al vescovato di sua volunta et non forzato, vorra dare; et non sie in robba, ma in tanti denari, che poi di partiscano in capo de l'anno o due o tre volte lanno come se fanno le distributione del capel o fra tutti i cardinali. . . .

Et perche li Rev mi Cardinali che hanno le protettione de Principi se hanno usurpato inconsuetudine de proponer tutte le Chiese, cioe vescovati et Monasteri che vaccano sottol dominio del Principe, del qual habbino la protettione, cosa della qual ne guadagnano chi tre, chi quatro, et chi cinque milla ducati ognanno, se e ordinato che se vogliono haver protettione de principi lhabbino delle facende loro insieme con lambassadori di quelli, o esse in luogho de lAmbassatore in caso che in corte non vi sia, ma non per tutte le proposition de vescovati quale ordinano che vaddino di grado in grado per torno de Cardinali, incomminciando dal primo Vescovo Cardinale per insino alultimo diacono accio che ognuno senta e partecipi di questi emolumenti ugualmente si come e di ragione e honesta.